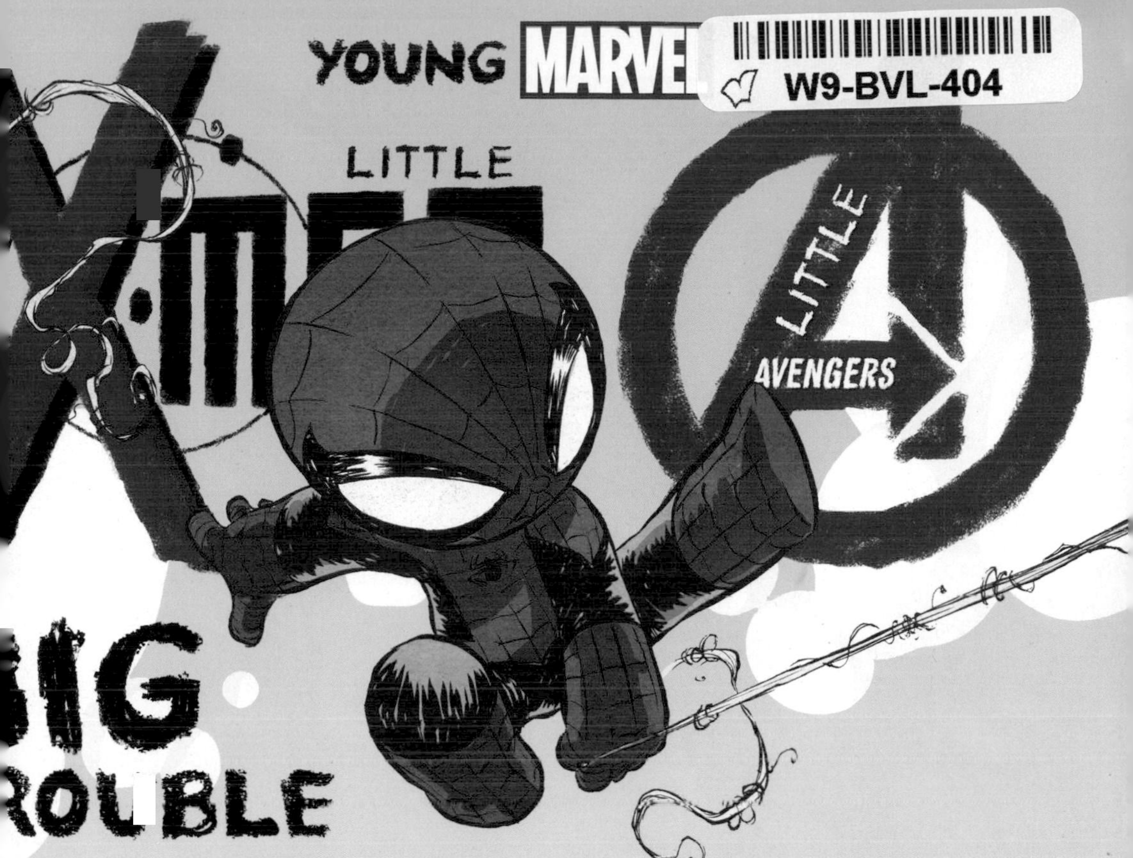
YOUNG MARVEL
W9-BVL-404
LITTLE
LITTLE
AVENGERS
IG
OUBLE

WRITERS:
Skottie Young, Dan Slott, Ruben Diaz & Chris Claremont with Juvaun J. Kirby

PENCILERS:
Gurihiru, Mark Buckingham, Juvaun J. Kirby & Tom Raney with Mike Wieringo

INKERS:
iru, Mark Buckingham, arsons, Caleb Salstrom & anna with Mike Wieringo, Koblish, Rich Perrotta, Vines, Vince Russell, Scott ams & Rodney Ramos

COLORISTS:
Gurihiru, Juvaun J. Kirby, Gina Going, and Paul Mounts & Bongotone Studio with Chuck Maiden, Jessica Ruffner, Matt Hicks, Gregg Schigiel, Tom Smith & Paul Tutrone

LETTERERS:
Arnie Sawyer, Virtual Calligraphy's Clayton Cowles & Rus Wooton, and Richard Starkings & Comicraft's Dave Lanphear & Albert Deschesne

ASSISTANT EDITORS: Lysa Kraiger & Sean Ryan
ASSOCIATE EDITOR: Nick Lowe
EDITORS: Tom Brennan, Matthew Morra, Matt Idelson, Jason Liebig & Mike Marts
INI MARVELS" STRIPS BY Steve "Ribs" Weissman COVER ARTIST: Skottie Young

AVENGERS AND X-MEN CREATED BY STAN LEE & JACK KIRBY

COLLECTION EDITOR: Mark D. Beazley ASSOCIATE MANAGING EDITOR: Alex Starbuck
EDITOR, SPECIAL PROJECTS: Jennifer Grünwald SENIOR EDITOR, SPECIAL PROJECTS: Jeff Youngquist
RESEARCH & LAYOUT: Jeph York PRODUCTION: ColorTek & Ryan Devall
BOOK DESIGNER: Rodolfo Muraguchi SVP OF PRINT & DIGITAL PUBLISHING SALES: David Gabriel

EDITOR IN CHIEF: Axel Alonso CHIEF CREATIVE OFFICER: Joe Quesada
PUBLISHER: Dan Buckley EXECUTIVE PRODUCER: Alan Fine

L: LITTLE X-MEN, LITTLE AVENGERS, BIG TROUBLE. Contains material originally published in magazine form as A-BABIES VS. X-BABIES #1, WOLVERINE #102.5, PINT-SIZED X-BABIES: MURDERAMA, RN, UNCANNY X-MEN #461 and MARVEL VISION #25-30. Second printing 2015. ISBN# 978-0-7851-8498-0. Published by MARVEL WORLDWIDE, INC., a subsidiary of MARVEL ENTERTAINMENT, PUBLICATION: 135 West 50th Street, New York, NY 10020. Copyright © 2013 MARVEL No similarity between any of the names, characters, persons, and/or institutions in this magazine with those dead person or institution is intended, and any such similarity which may exist is purely coincidental. **Printed in Canada**. ALAN FINE, President, Marvel Entertainment; DAN BUCKLEY, President, nd Brand Management; JOE QUESADA, Chief Creative Officer; TOM BREVOORT, SVP of Publishing; DAVID BOGART, SVP of Operations & Procurement, Publishing; C.B. CEBULSKI, VP of International Brand Management; DAVID GABRIEL, SVP Print, Sales & Marketing; JIM O'KEEFE, VP of Operations & Logistics; DAN CARR, Executive Director of Publishing Technology; SUSAN CRESPI, Editorial Operations MORALES, Publishing Operations Manager; STAN LEE, Chairman Emeritus. For information regarding advertising in Marvel Comics or on Marvel.com, please contact Jonathan Rheingold, VP of Custom Sales, at jrheingold@marvel.com. For Marvel subscription inquiries, please call 800-217-9158. **Manufactured between 6/10/2015 and 7/13/2015 by SOLISCO PRINTERS, SCOTT, QC, CANADA.**

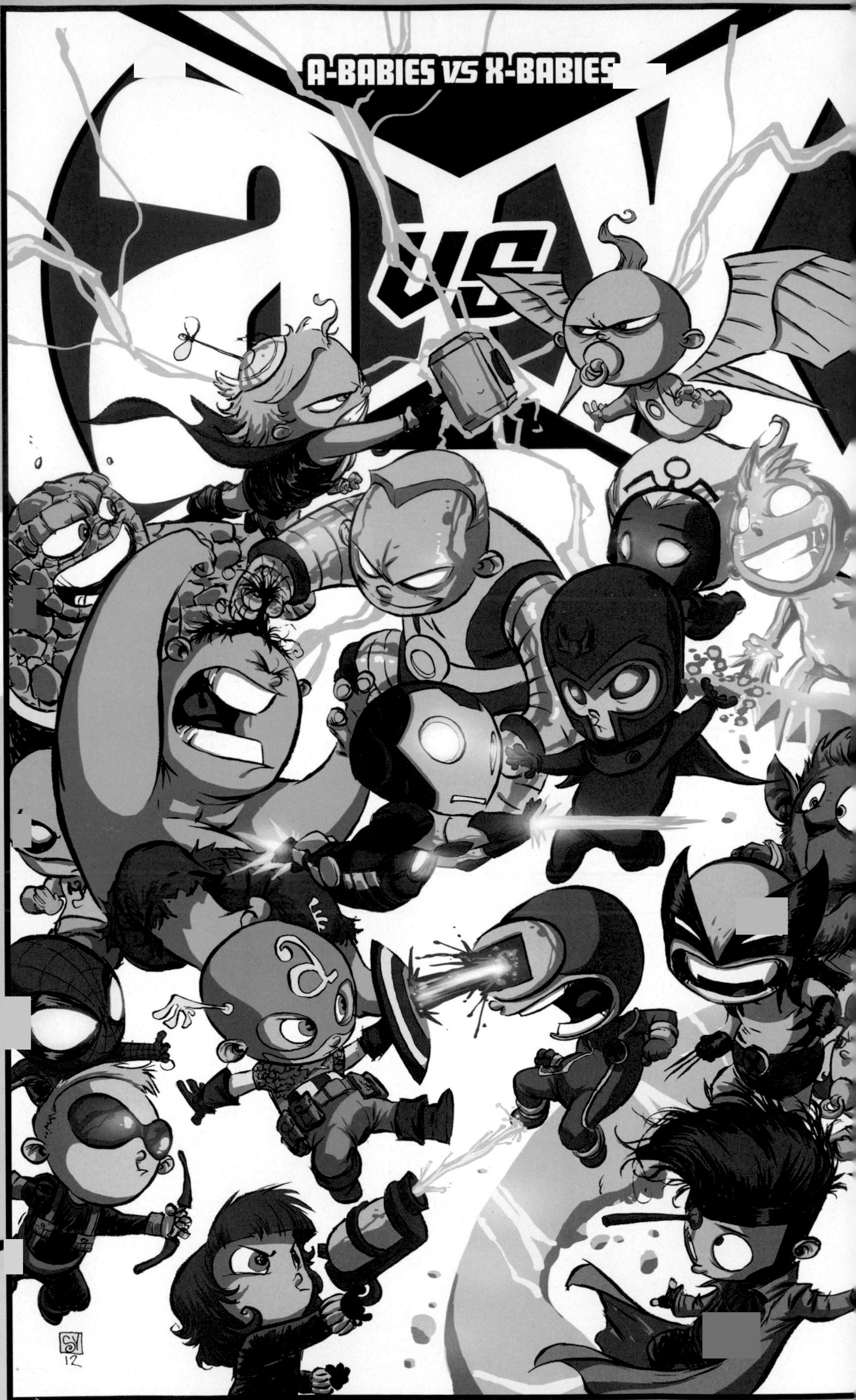
A-BABIES VS X-BABIES
A VS X

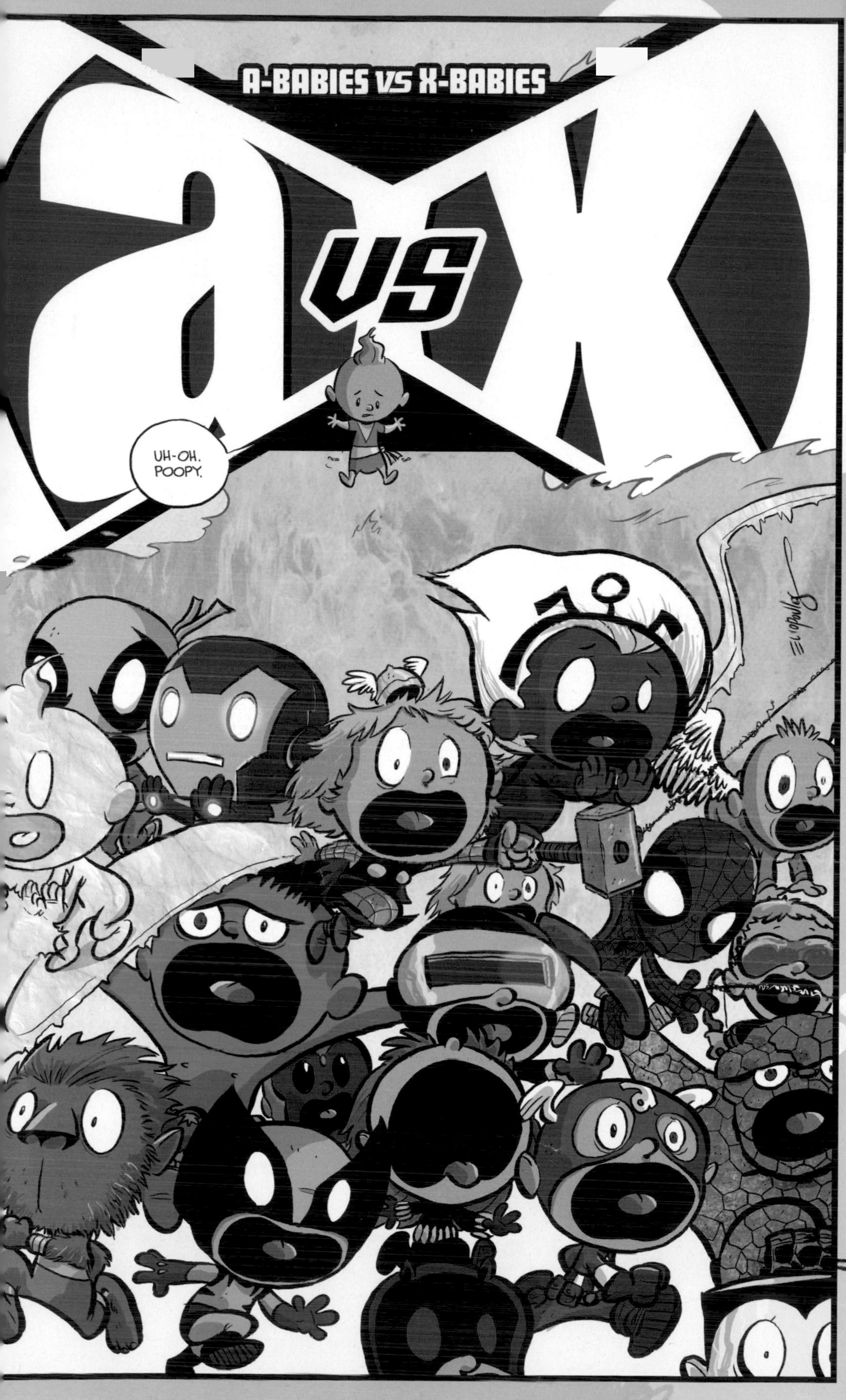
A-BABIES VS X-BABIES
A VS X
UH-OH. POOPY.

VARIANT COVER BY CHRIS ELIOPOULOS

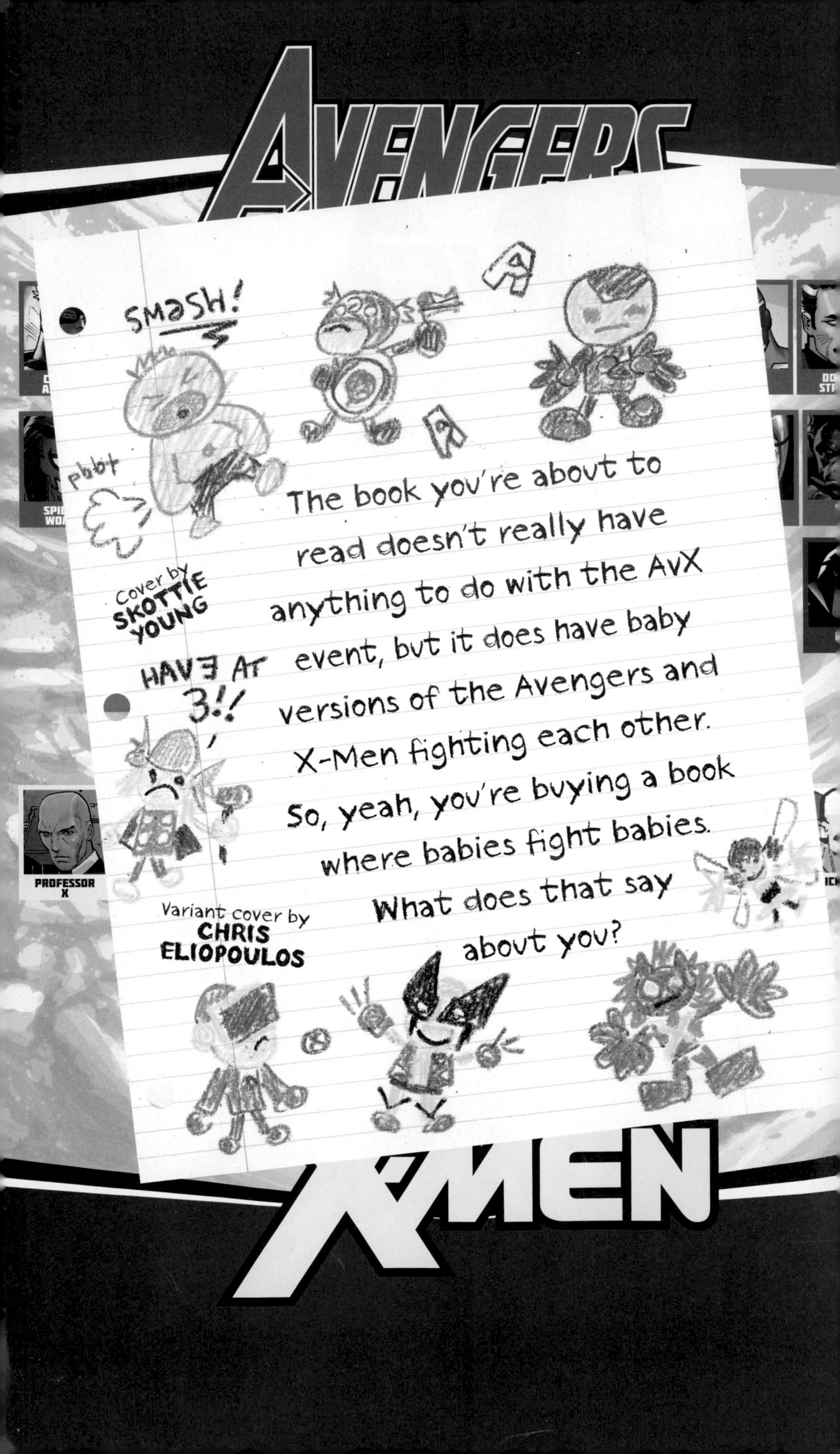
AVENGERS
SMASH!
pbbt
The book you're about to read doesn't really have anything to do with the AvX event, but it does have baby versions of the Avengers and X-Men fighting each other. So, yeah, you're buying a book where babies fight babies. What does that say about you?
Cover by SKOTTIE YOUNG
HAVƎ AT 3!!
Variant cover by CHRIS ELIOPOULOS
PROFESSOR X
X-MEN

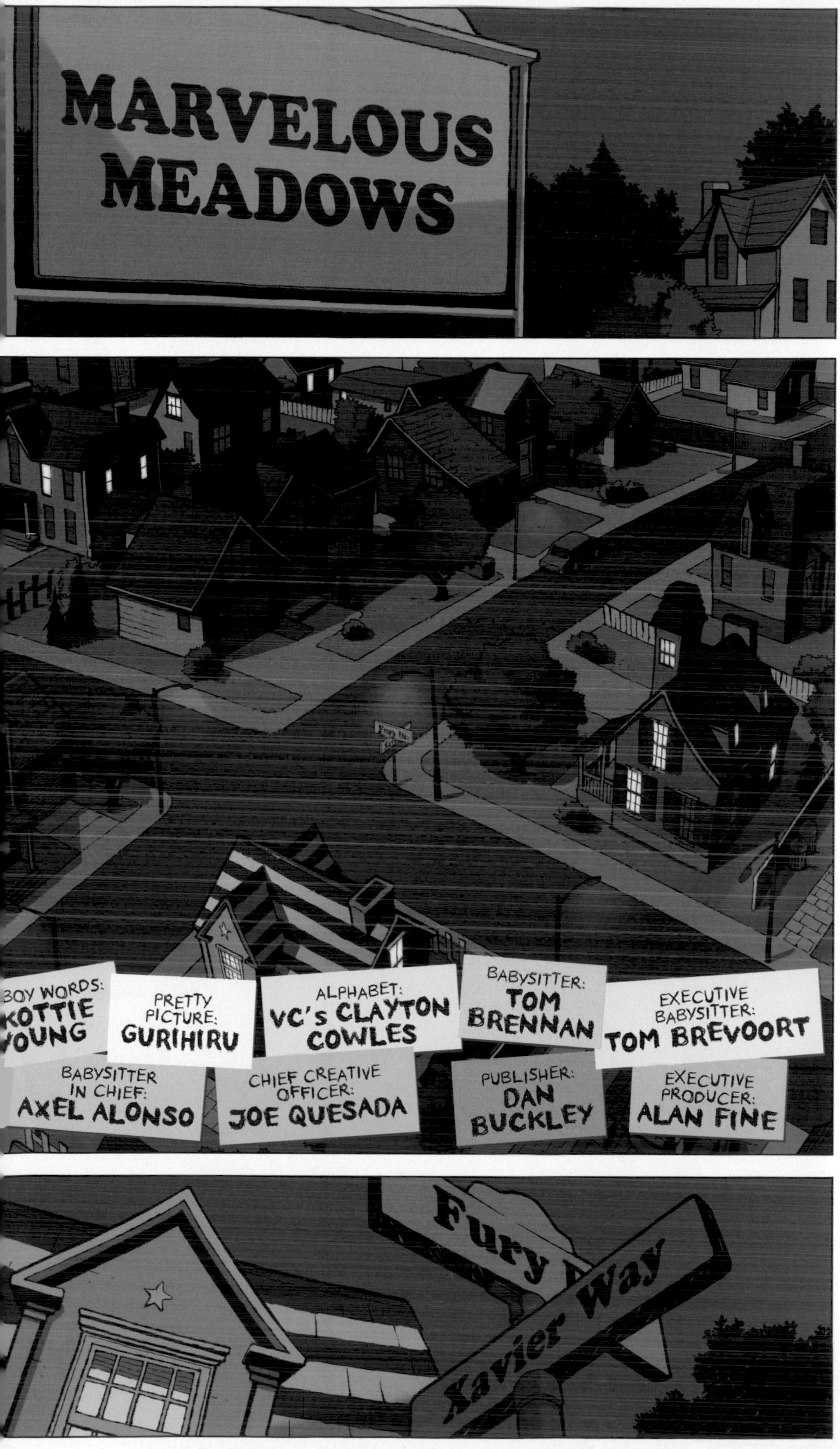
MARVELOUS MEADOWS
BOY WORDS: KOTTIE YOUNG
PRETTY PICTURE: GURIHIRU
ALPHABET: VC's CLAYTON COWLES
BABYSITTER: TOM BRENNAN
EXECUTIVE BABYSITTER: TOM BREVOORT
BABYSITTER IN CHIEF: AXEL ALONSO
CHIEF CREATIVE OFFICER: JOE QUESADA
PUBLISHER: DAN BUCKLEY
EXECUTIVE PRODUCER: ALAN FINE
Fury
Xavier Way

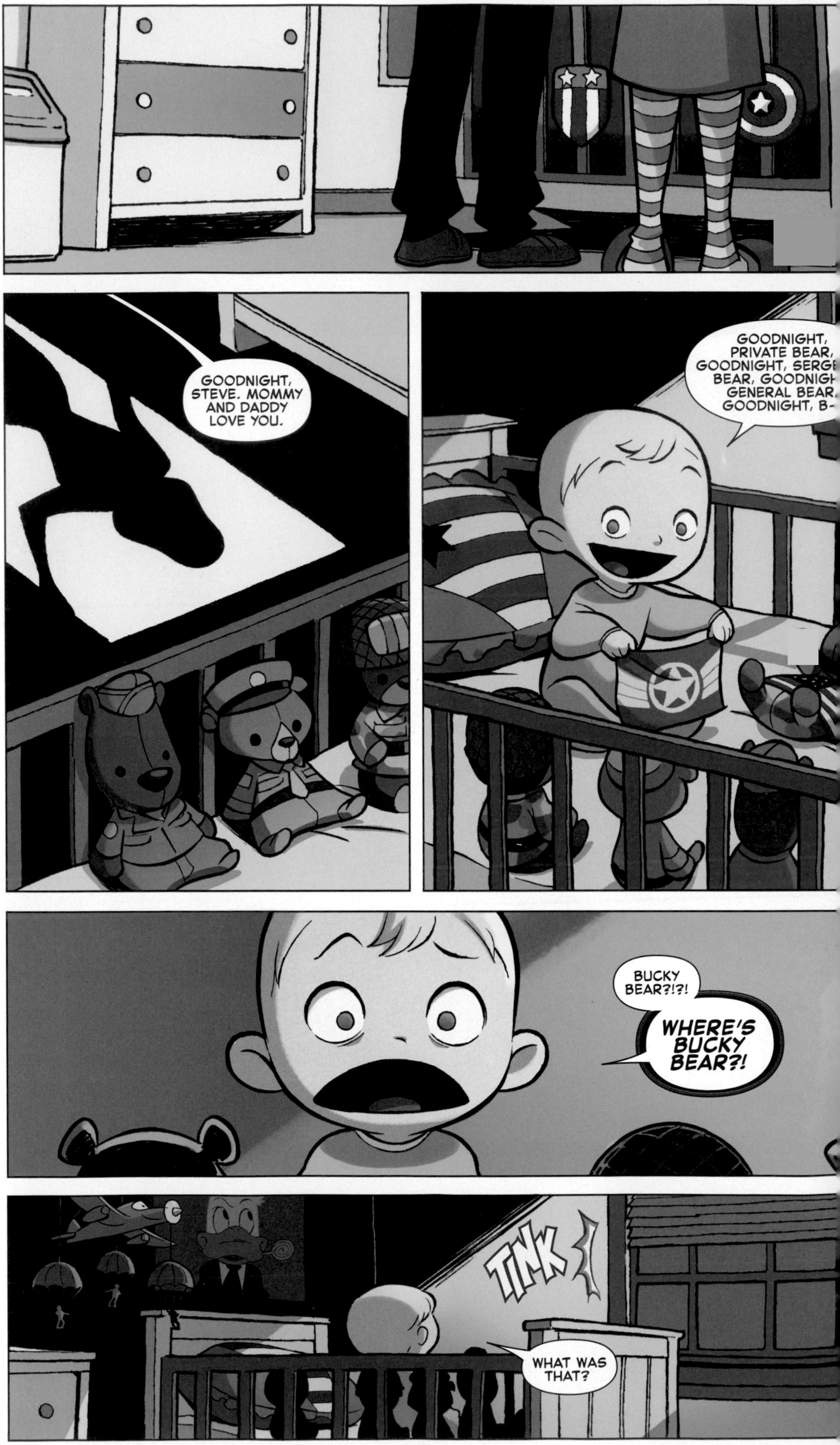
GOODNIGHT, STEVE. MOMMY AND DADDY LOVE YOU.
GOODNIGHT, PRIVATE BEAR, GOODNIGHT, SERGE BEAR, GOODNIGH GENERAL BEAR, GOODNIGHT, B-
BUCKY BEAR?!?!
WHERE'S BUCKY BEAR?!
TINK
WHAT WAS THAT?

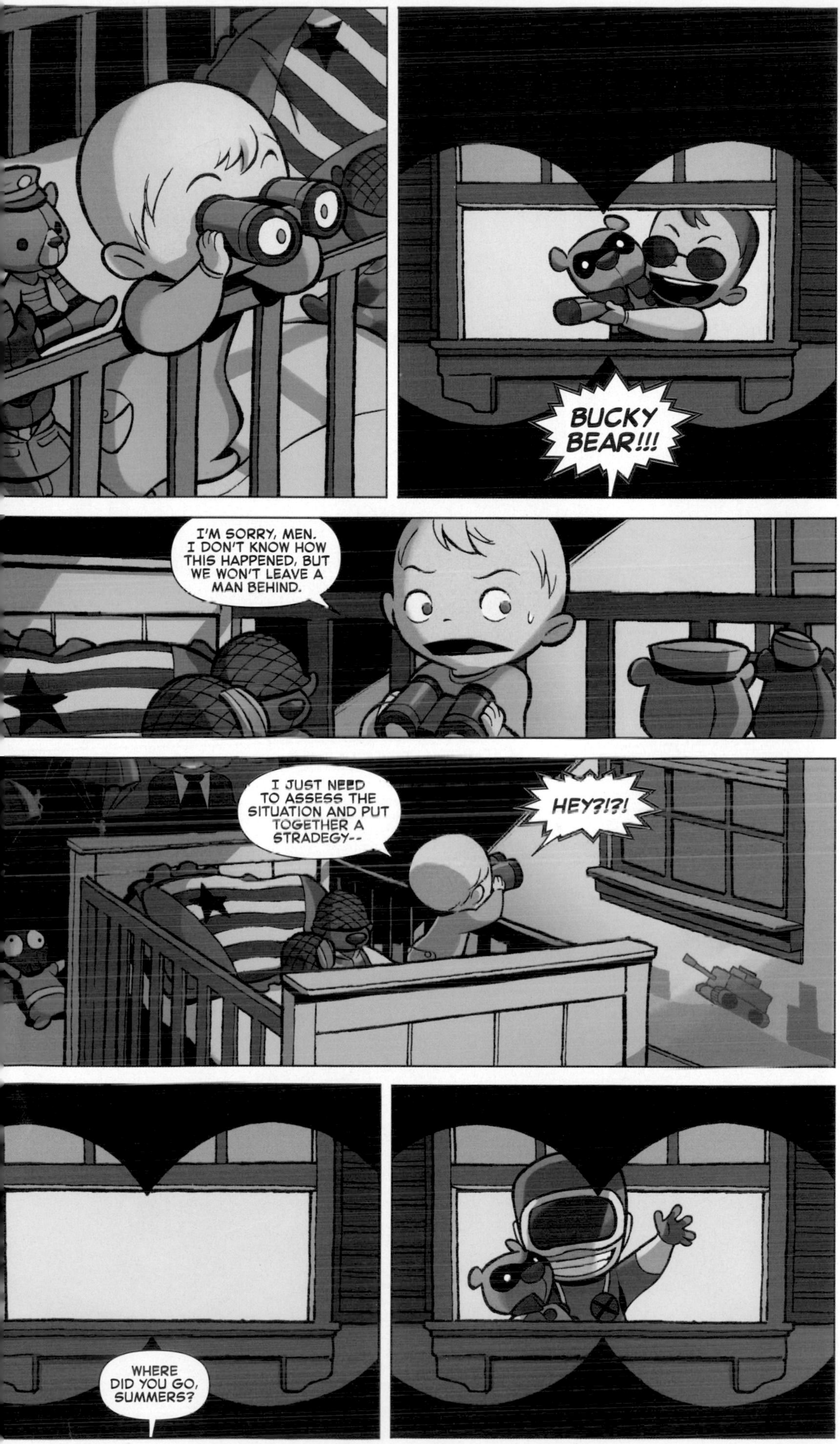
BUCKY BEAR!!!
I'M SORRY, MEN. I DON'T KNOW HOW THIS HAPPENED, BUT WE WON'T LEAVE A MAN BEHIND.
I JUST NEED TO ASSESS THE SITUATION AND PUT TOGETHER A STRADEGY--
HEY?!?!
WHERE DID YOU GO, SUMMERS?

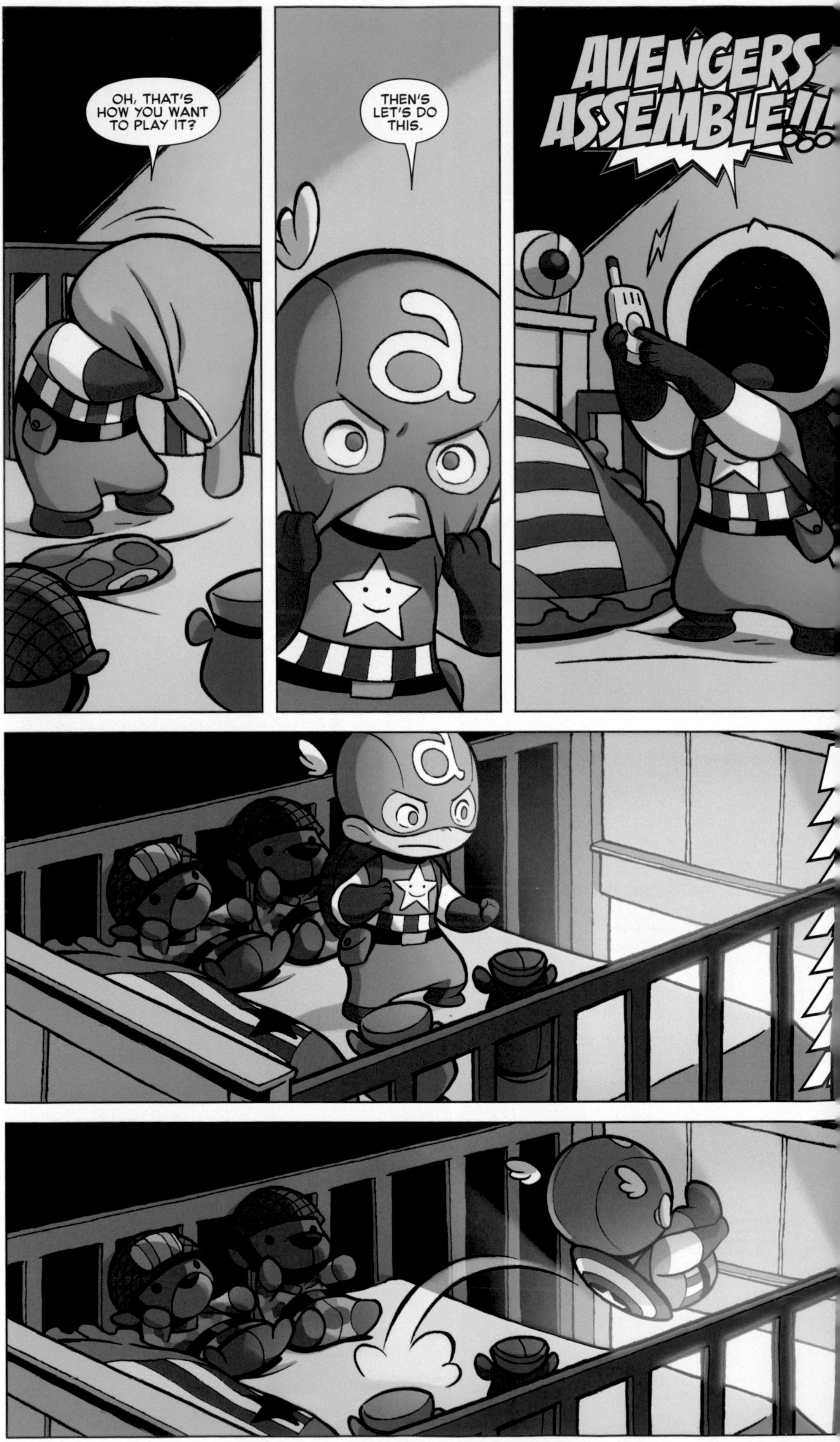
OH, THAT'S HOW YOU WANT TO PLAY IT?
THEN'S LET'S DO THIS.
AVENGERS ASSEMBLE!!

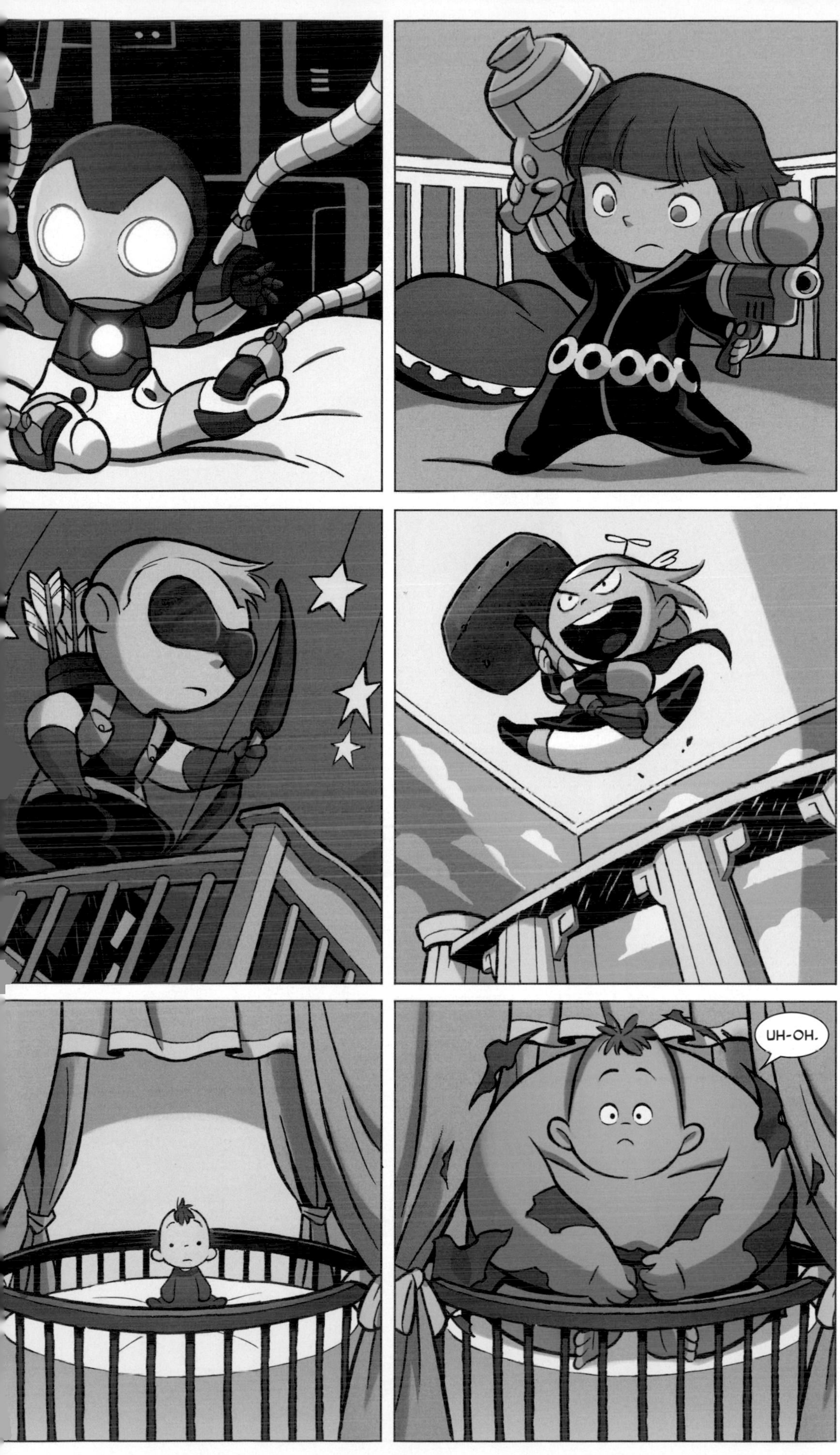
UH-OH.

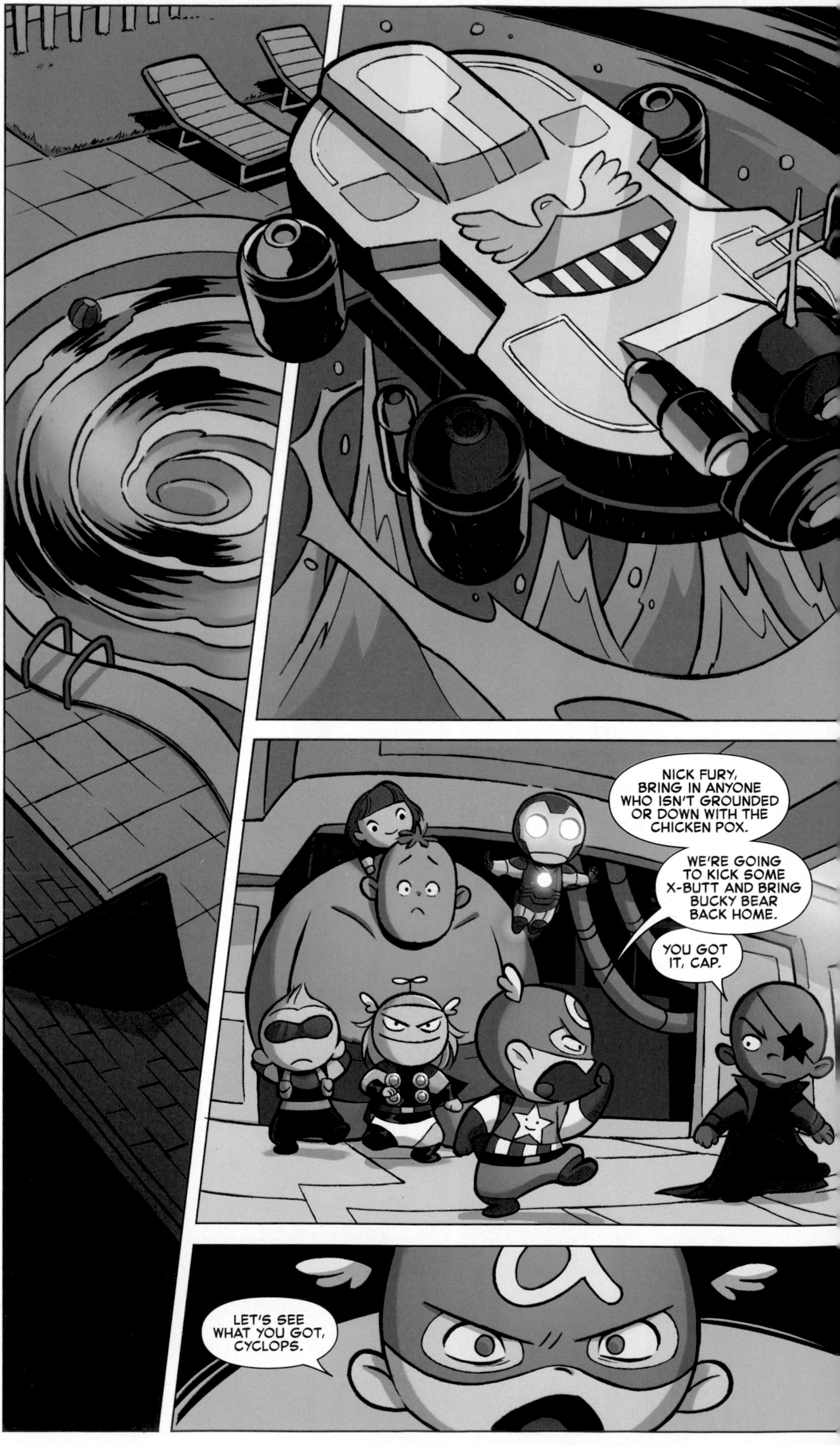
NICK FURY, BRING IN ANYONE WHO ISN'T GROUNDED OR DOWN WITH THE CHICKEN POX.
WE'RE GOING TO KICK SOME X-BUTT AND BRING BUCKY BEAR BACK HOME.
YOU GOT IT, CAP.
LET'S SEE WHAT YOU GOT, CYCLOPS.

X-MEN, IT'S TIME TO COME OUT HERE AND FIGHT WITH THE AVENGERS AND STUFF!!!

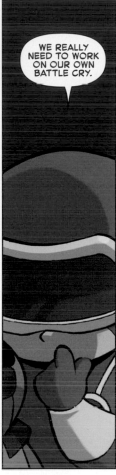

WE REALLY NEED TO WORK ON OUR OWN BATTLE CRY.

I THINK I HEAR THE ICE CREAM TRUCK!

ICE CREAM?

WHERE?

I WANT TUTTI FRUITY!

MY BUTT'S ITCHY.

HI, GUYS!

WHAT TIME IS IT?

LET'S HAVE SOME FUN.

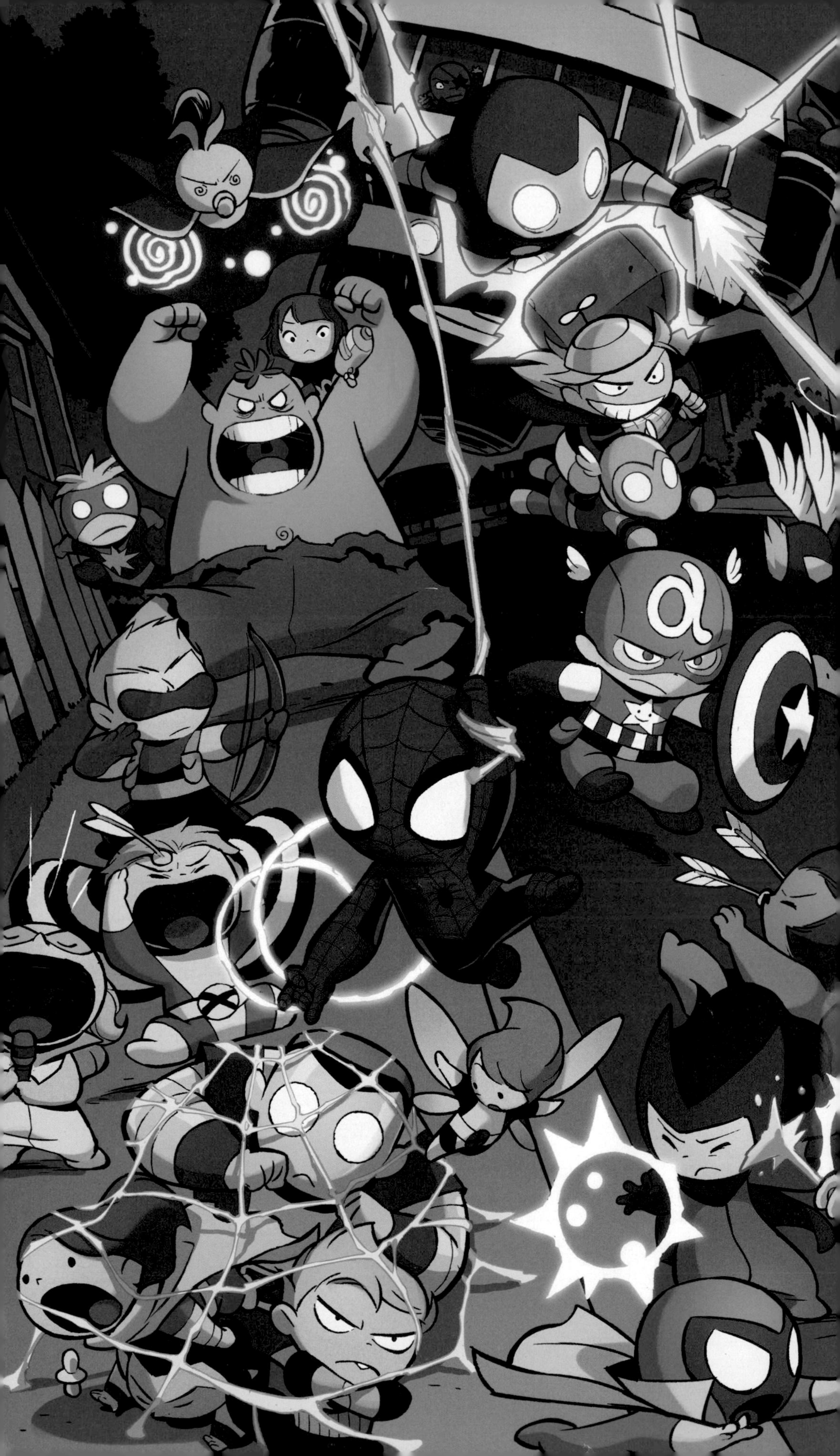

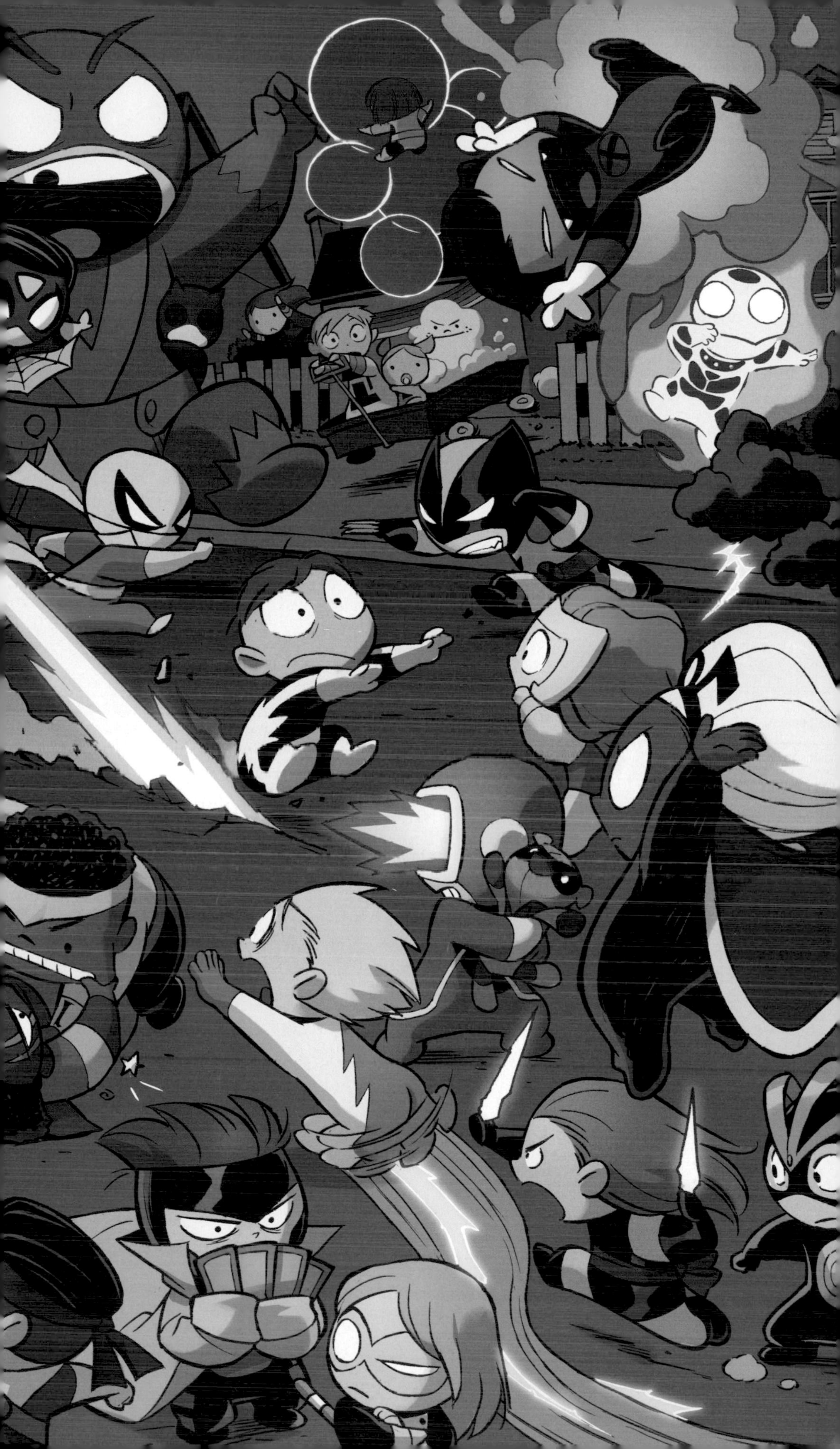

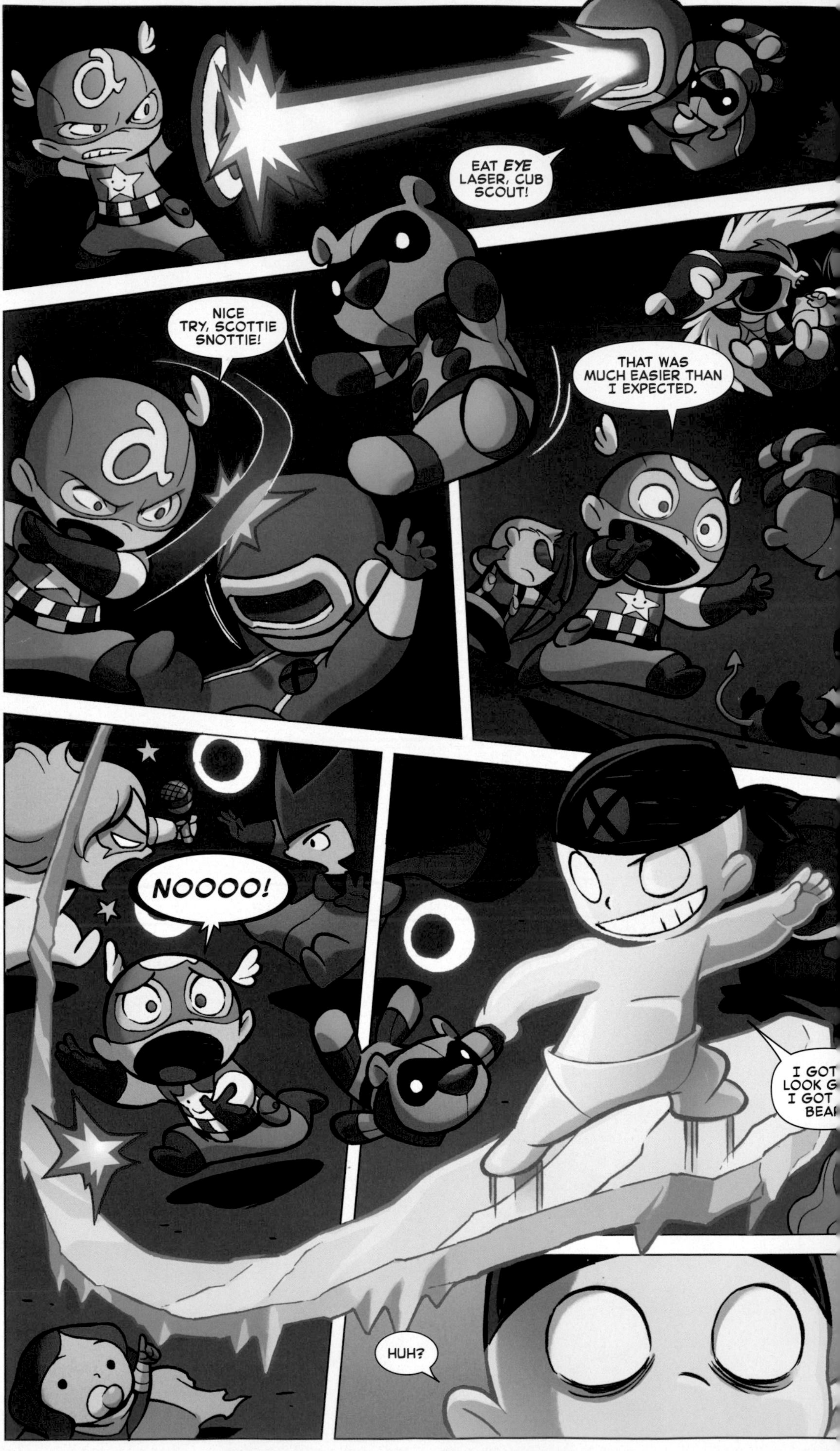
EAT EYE LASER, CUB SCOUT!
NICE TRY, SCOTTIE SNOTTIE!
THAT WAS MUCH EASIER THAN I EXPECTED.
NOOOO!
HUH?

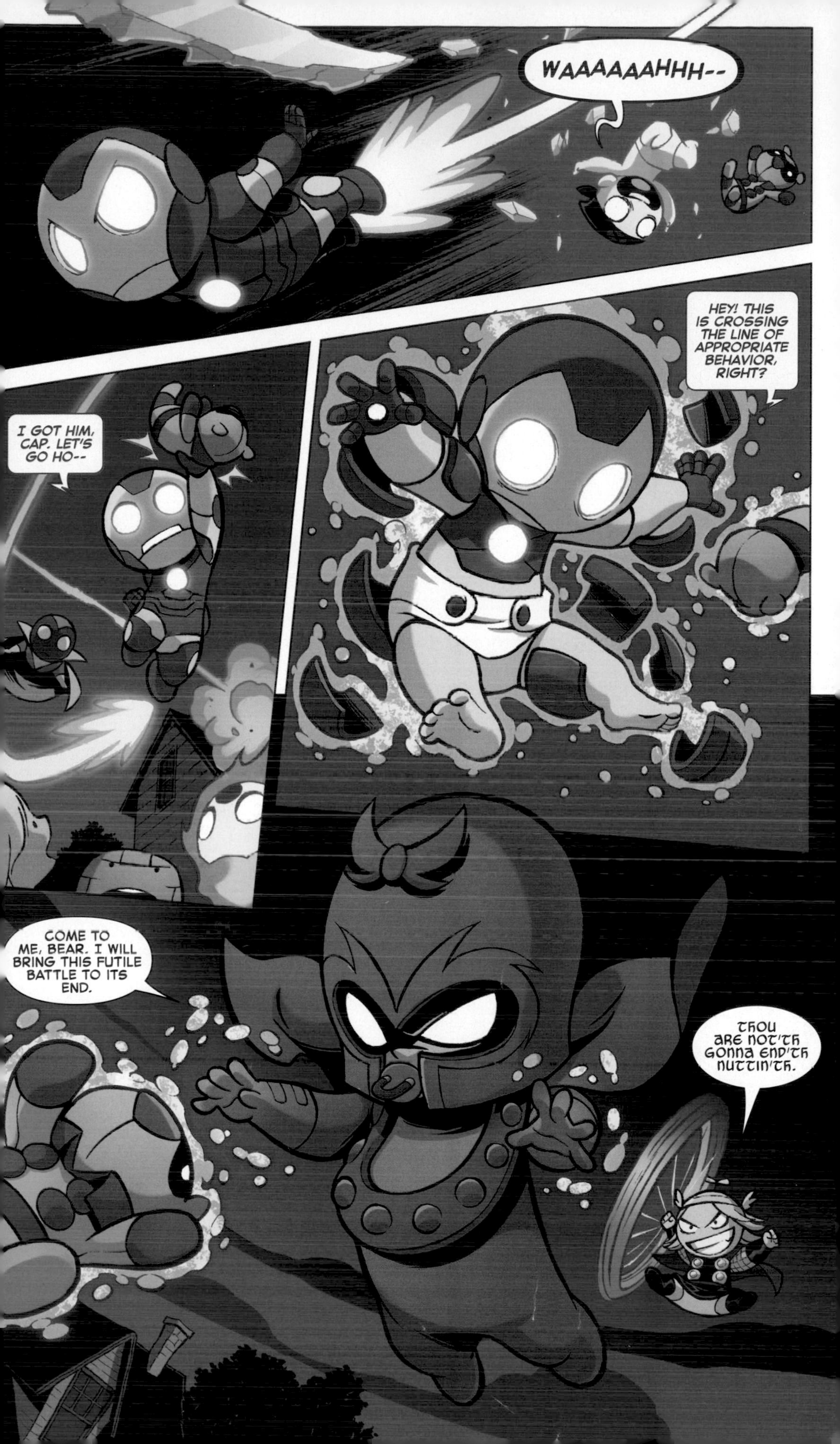
WAAAAAAHHH--
I GOT HIM, CAP. LET'S GO HO--
HEY! THIS IS CROSSING THE LINE OF APPROPRIATE BEHAVIOR, RIGHT?
COME TO ME, BEAR. I WILL BRING THIS FUTILE BATTLE TO ITS END.
THOU ARE NOT'TH GONNA END'TH NUTTIN'TH.

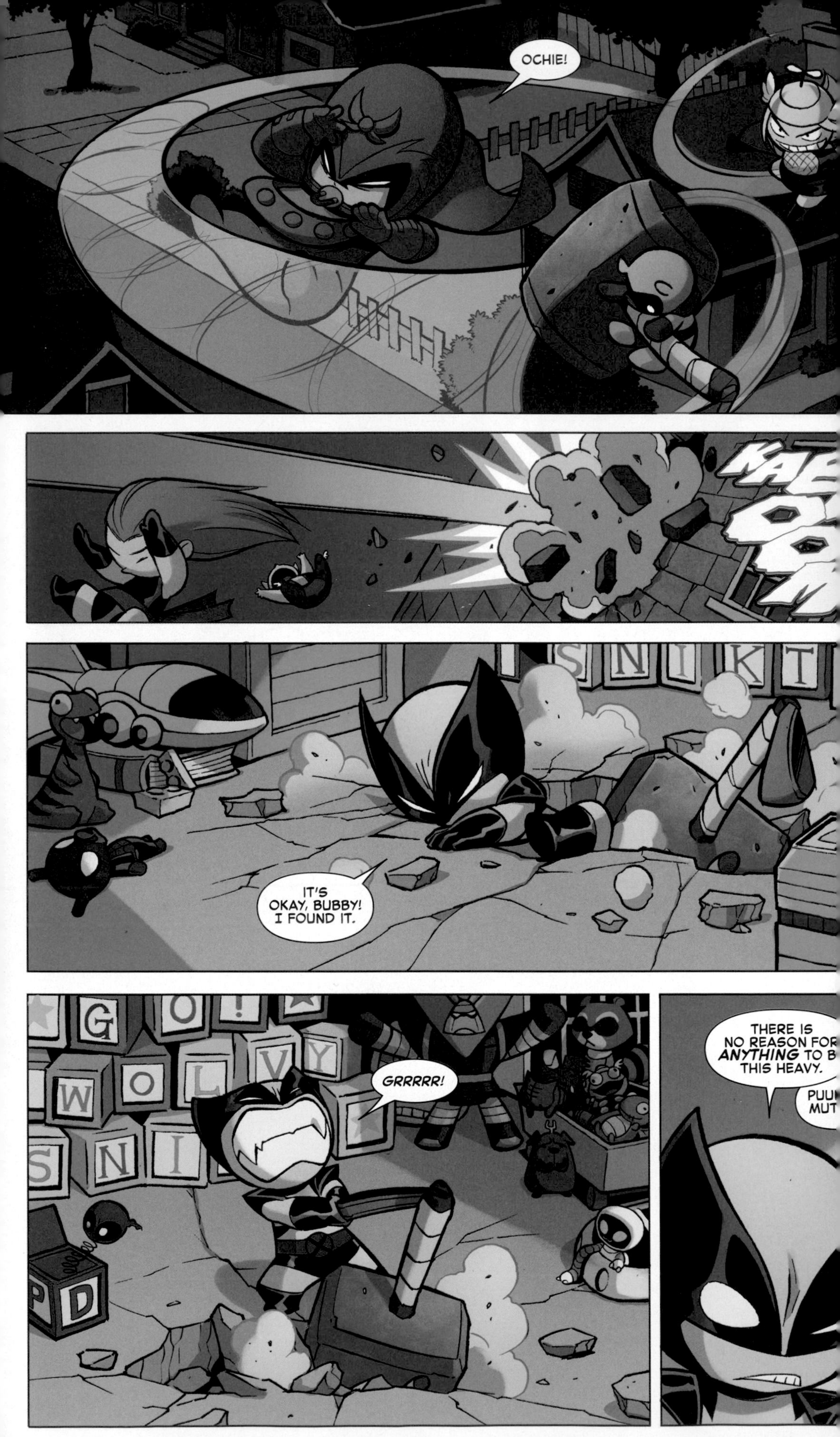
OCHIE!
SNIKT
IT'S OKAY, BUBBY! I FOUND IT.
GO!
WOLVY
SNI
PD
GRRRRR!
THERE IS NO REASON FOR *ANYTHING* TO B
THIS HEAVY.

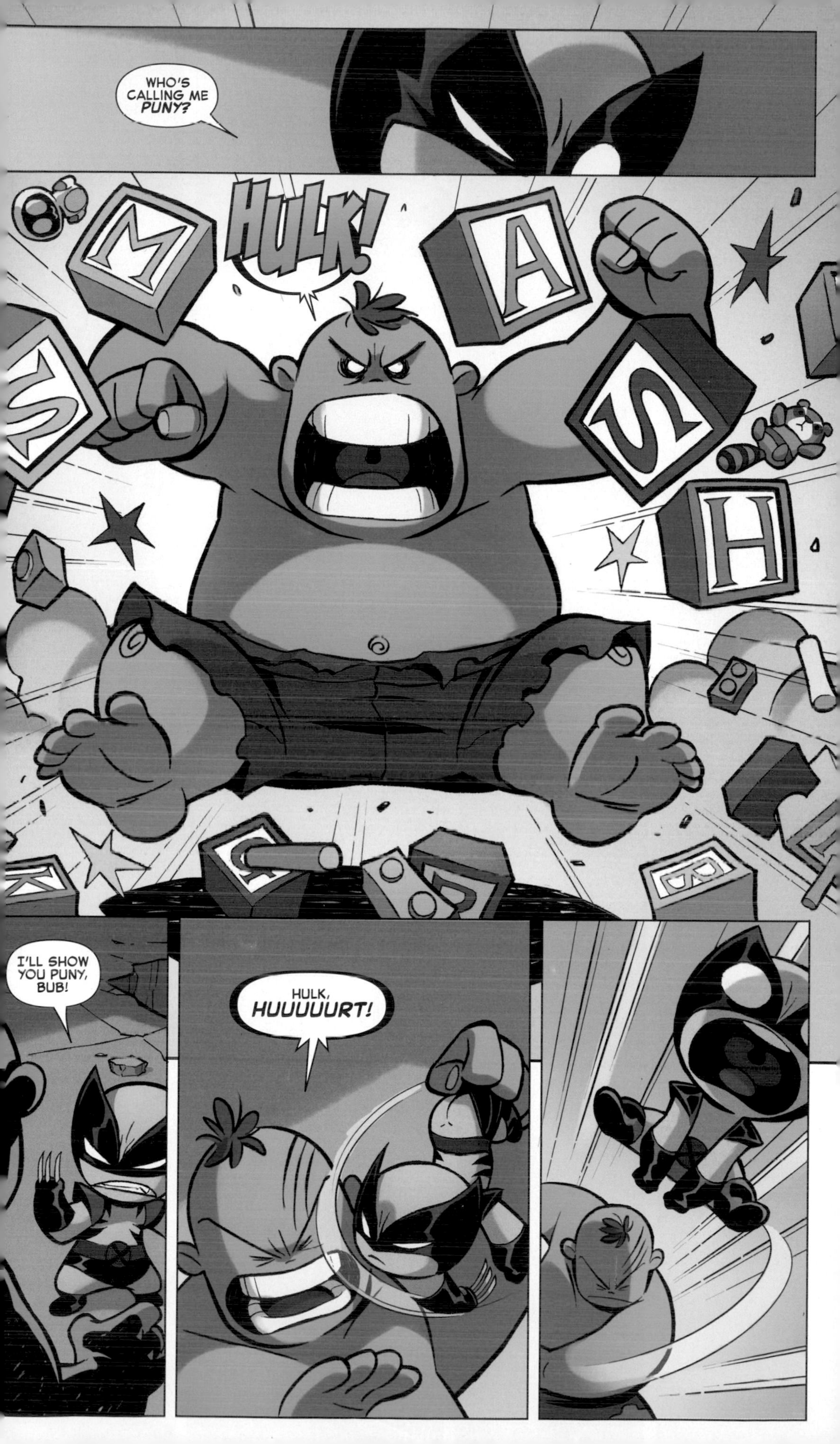
WHO'S CALLING ME PUNY?
HULK!
M
A
S
H
I'LL SHOW YOU PUNY, BUB!
HULK, HUUUUURT!

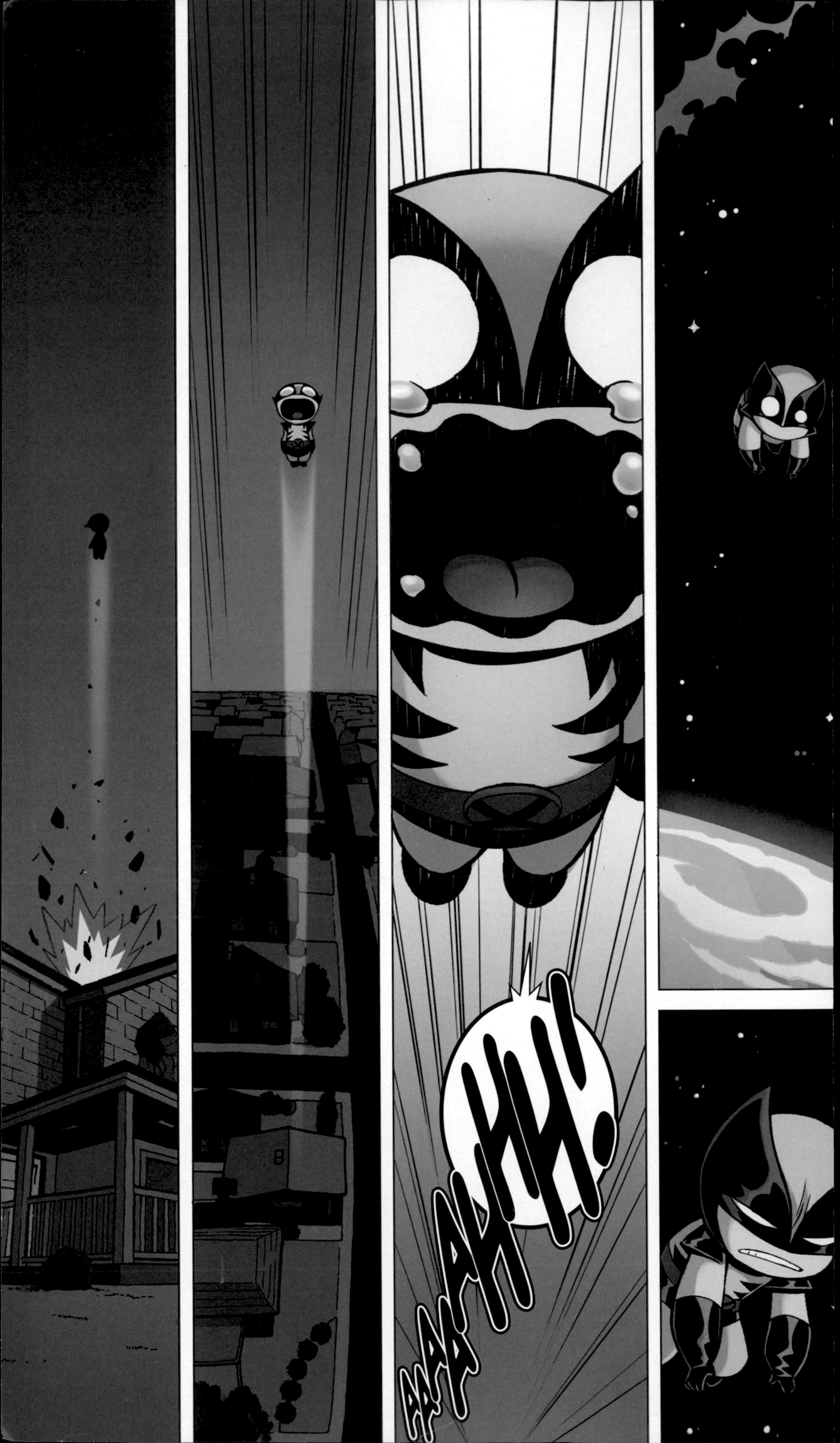
AAAAHHH!

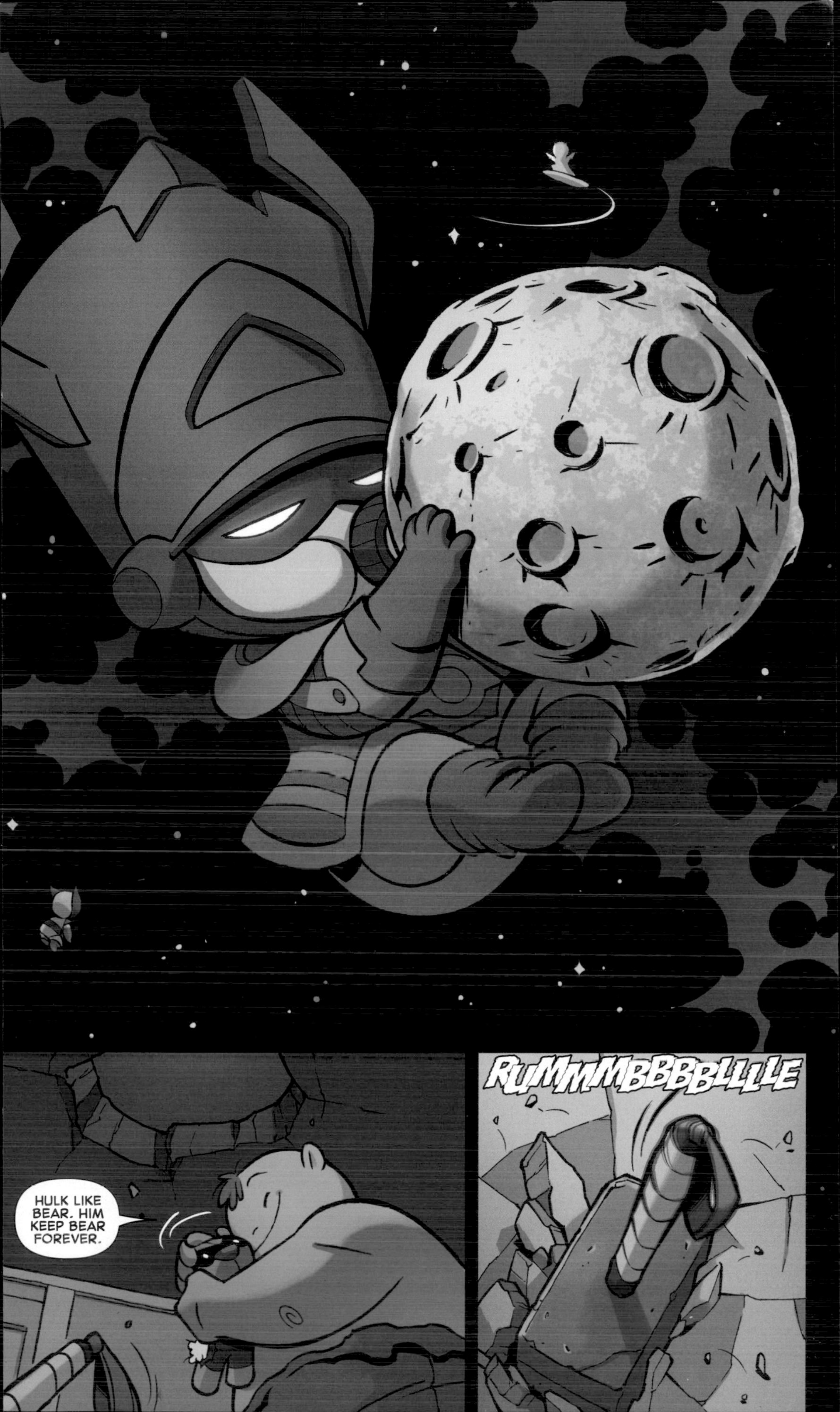
HULK LIKE BEAR. HIM KEEP BEAR FOREVER.
RUMMMMBBBBLLLLE

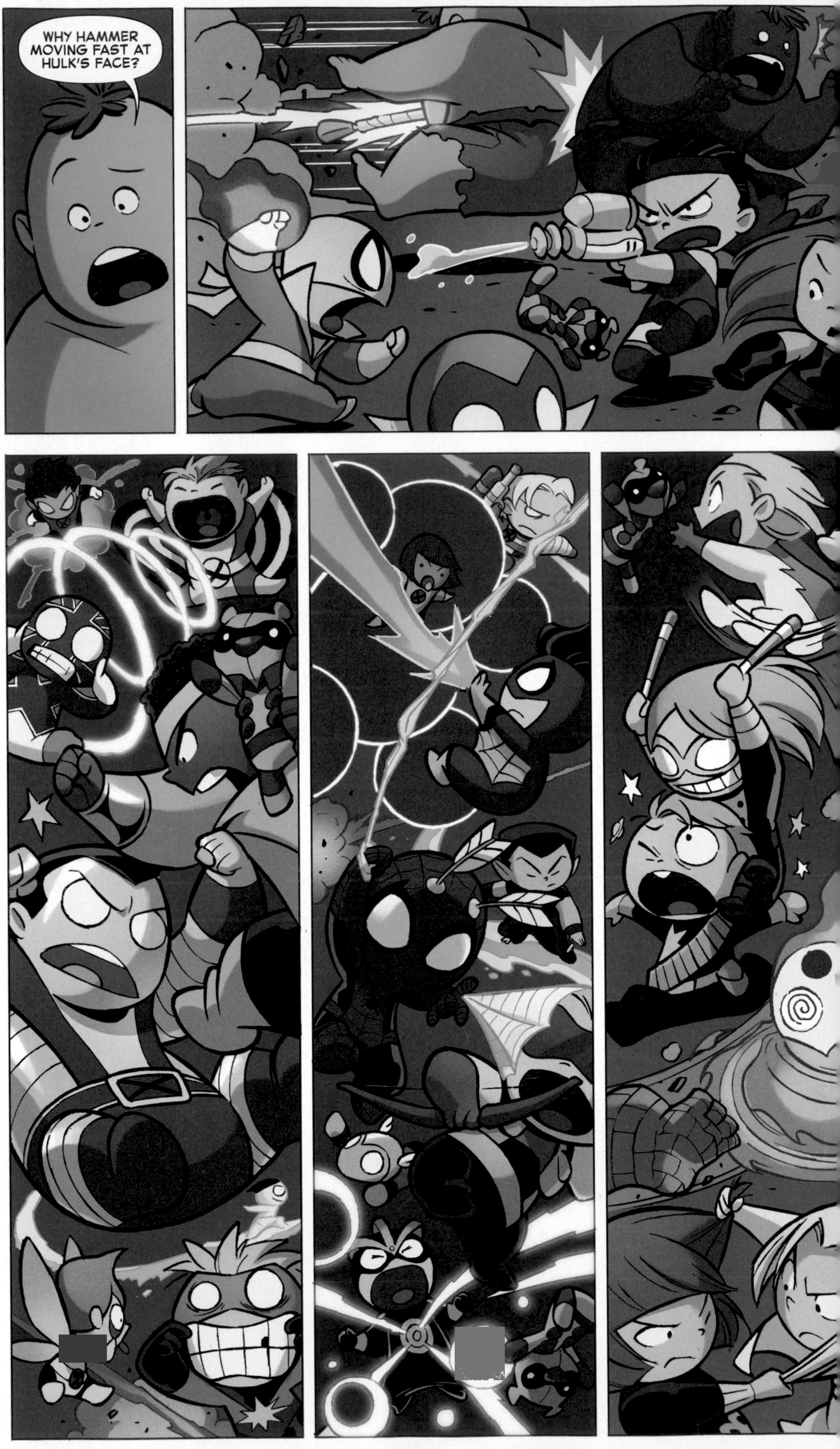
WHY HAMMER MOVING FAST AT HULK'S FACE?

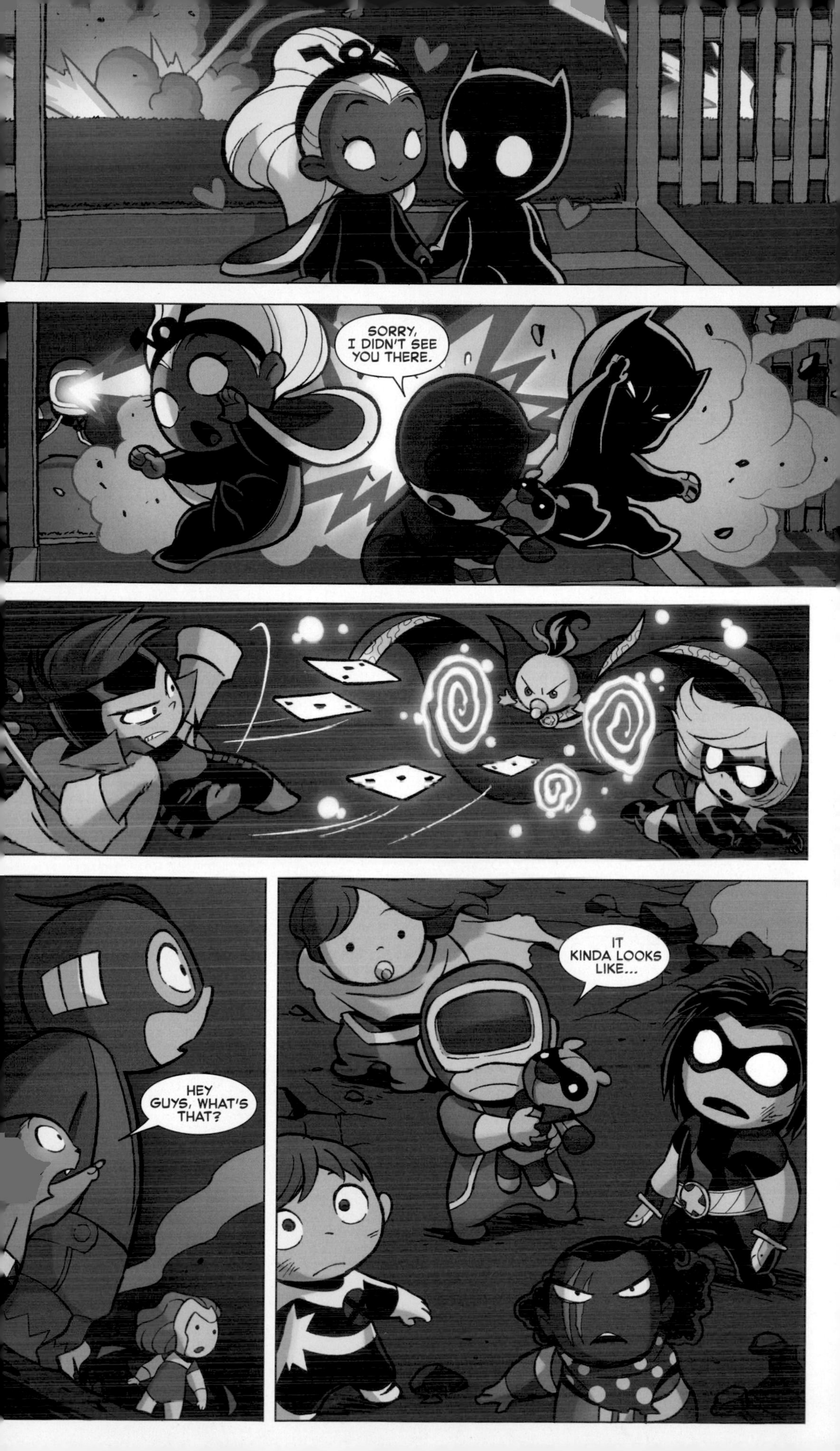
SORRY, I DIDN'T SEE YOU THERE.
HEY GUYS, WHAT'S THAT?
IT KINDA LOOKS LIKE...

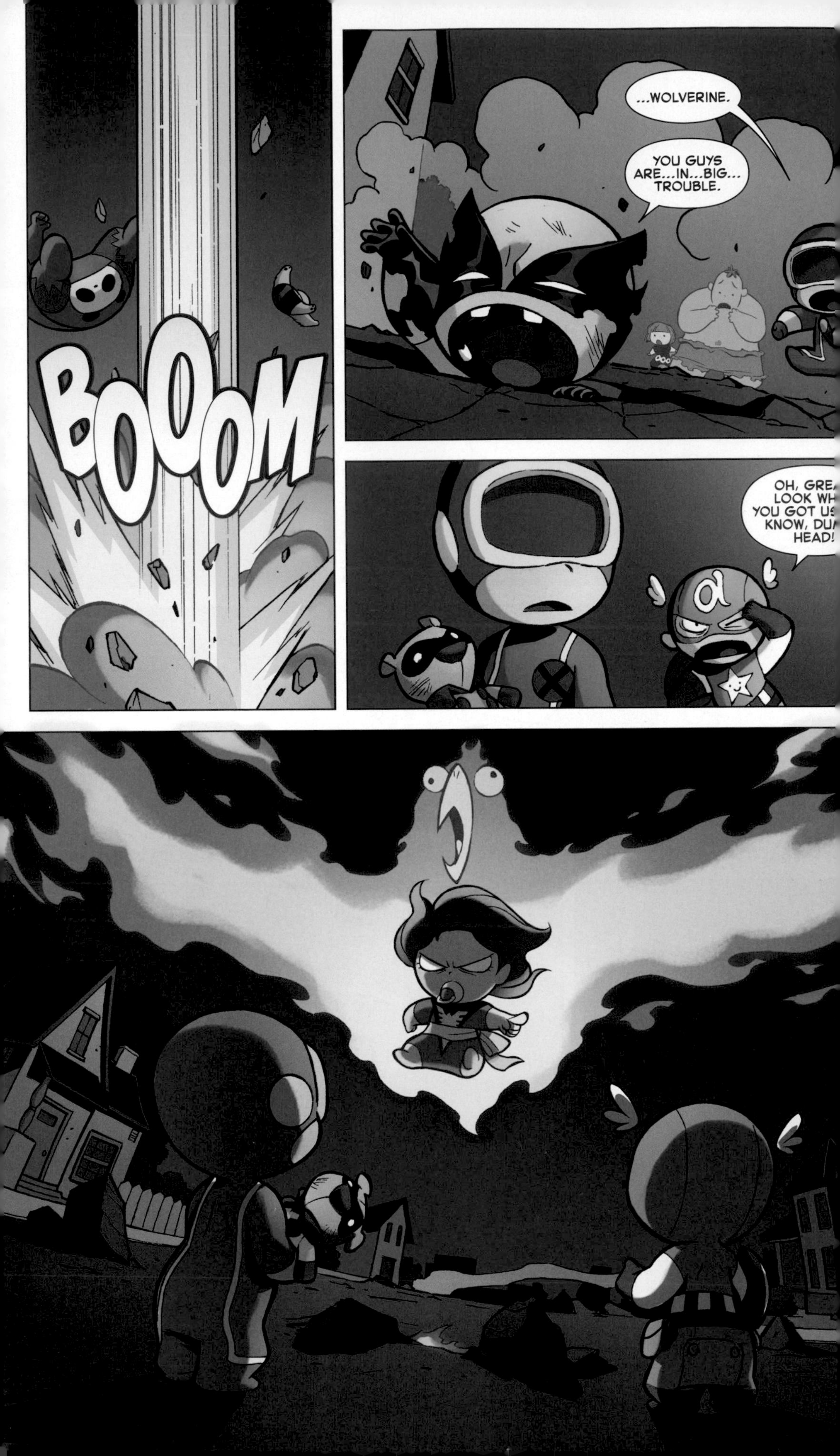
BOOOM
...WOLVERINE.
YOU GUYS ARE...IN...BIG... TROUBLE.
OH, GREA LOOK WH YOU GOT US KNOW, DU HEAD!

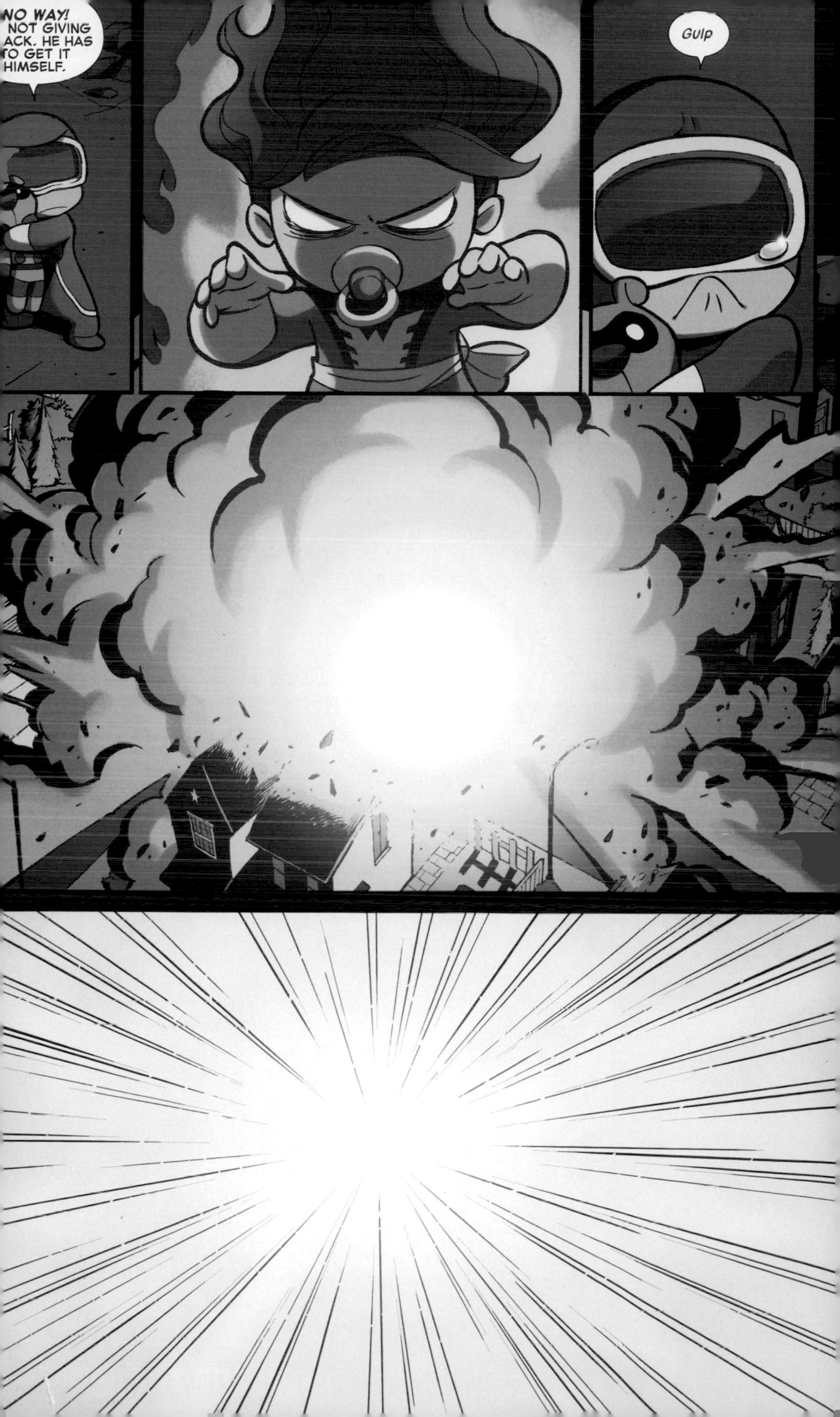
NO WAY! NOT GIVING ACK. HE HAS TO GET IT HIMSELF.
Gulp

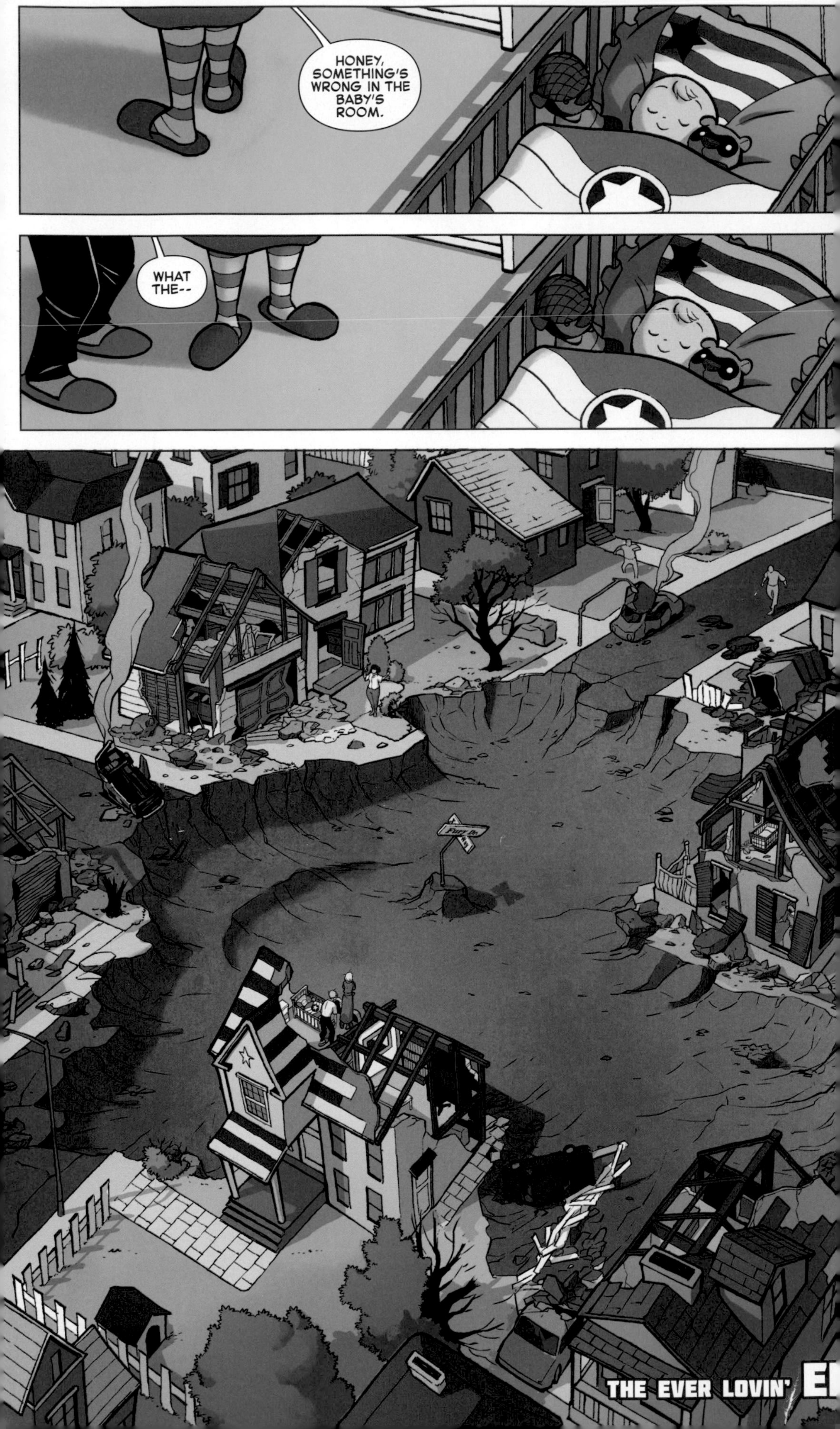
HONEY, SOMETHING'S WRONG IN THE BABY'S ROOM.
WHAT THE--
THE EVER LOVIN'

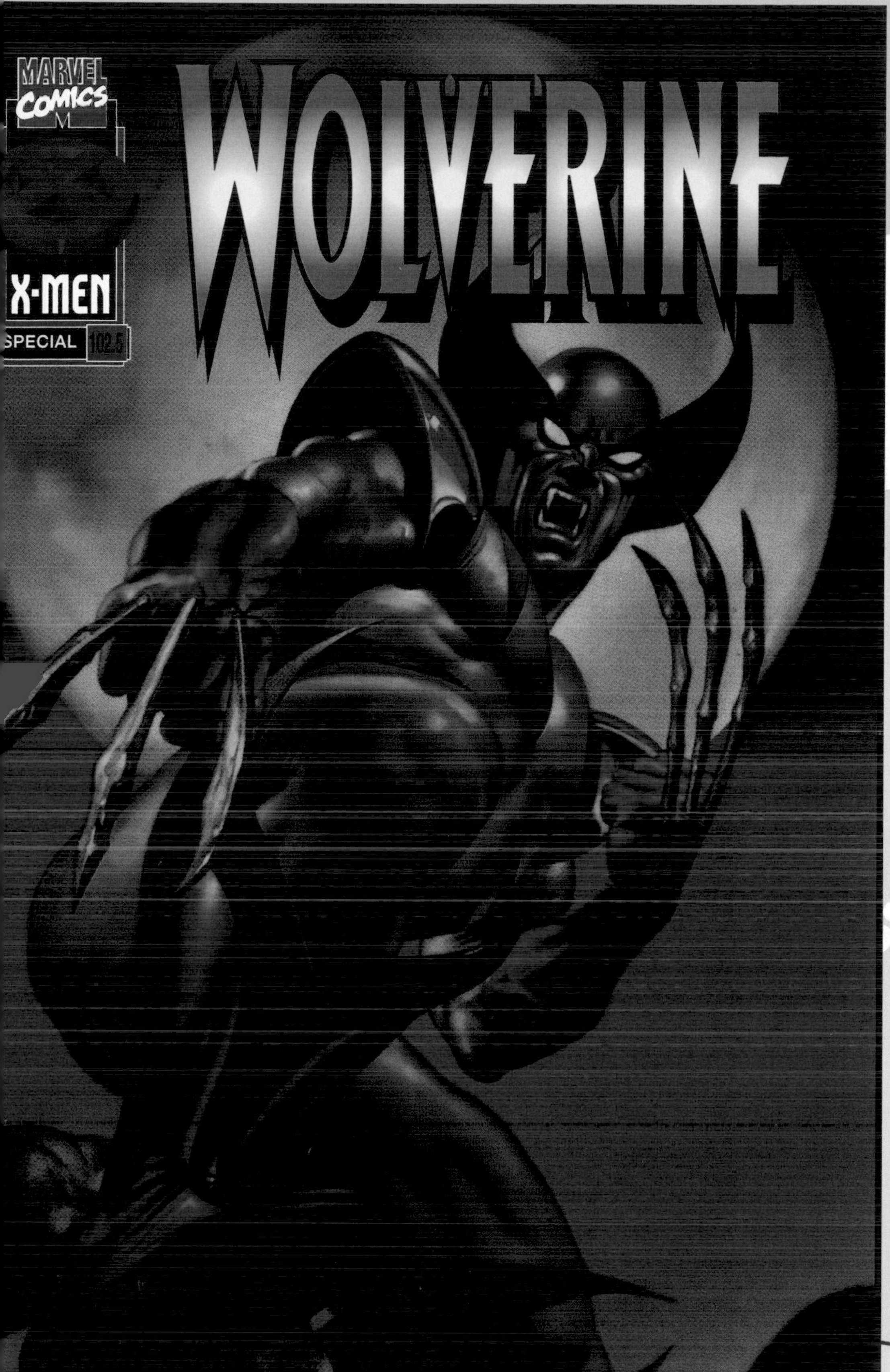
MARVEL COMICS
WOLVERINE
X-MEN
SPECIAL
102.5

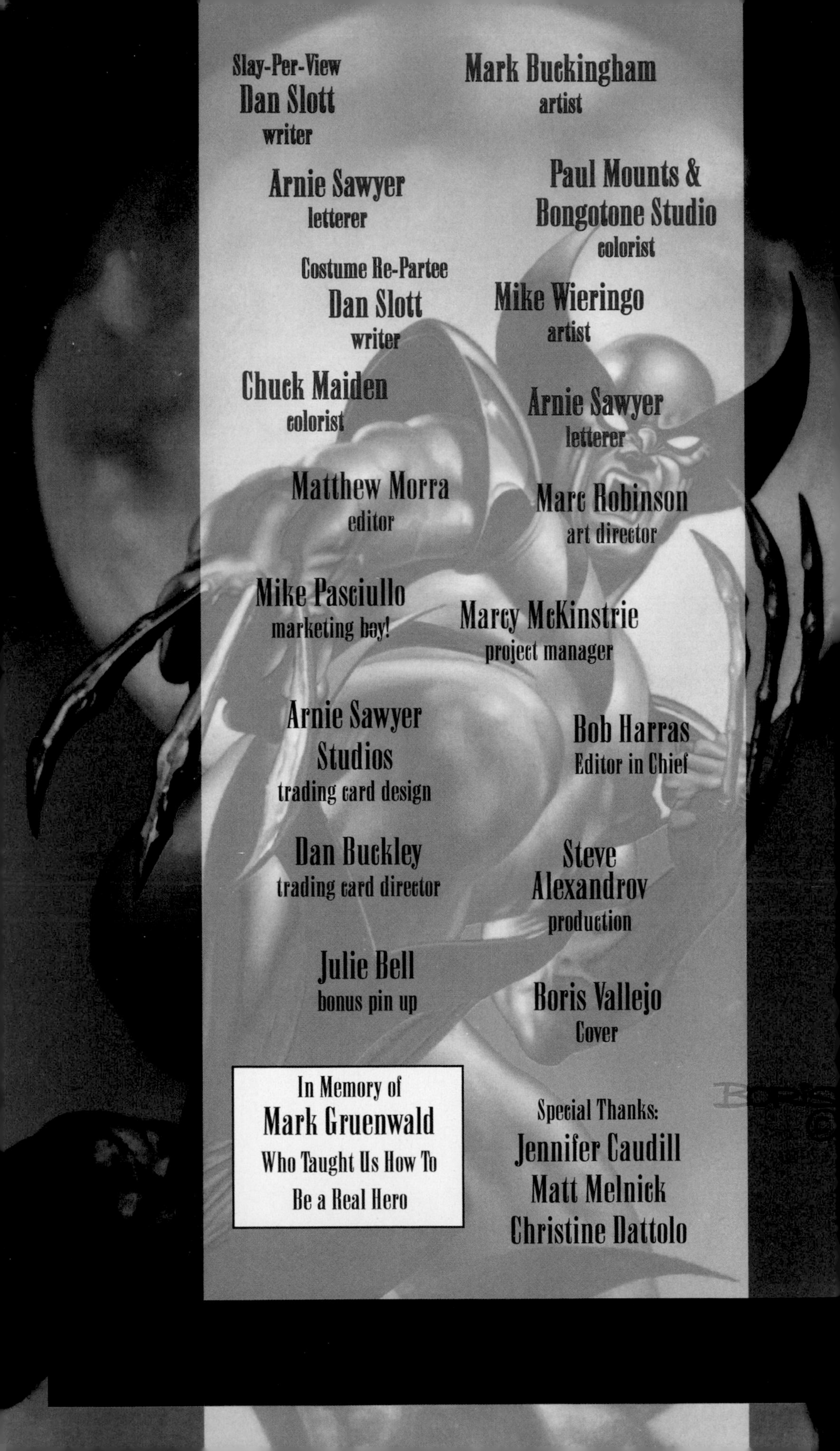

Slay-Per-View

Dan Slott
writer

Mark Buckingham
artist

Arnie Sawyer
letterer

Paul Mounts & Bongotone Studio
colorist

Costume Re-Partee

Dan Slott
writer

Mike Wieringo
artist

Chuck Maiden
colorist

Arnie Sawyer
letterer

Matthew Morra
editor

Marc Robinson
art director

Mike Pasciullo
marketing boy!

Marcy McKinstrie
project manager

Arnie Sawyer Studios
trading card design

Bob Harras
Editor in Chief

Dan Buckley
trading card director

Steve Alexandrov
production

Julie Bell
bonus pin up

Boris Vallejo
Cover

In Memory of
Mark Gruenwald
Who Taught Us How To
Be a Real Hero

Special Thanks:
Jennifer Caudill
Matt Melnick
Christine Dattolo

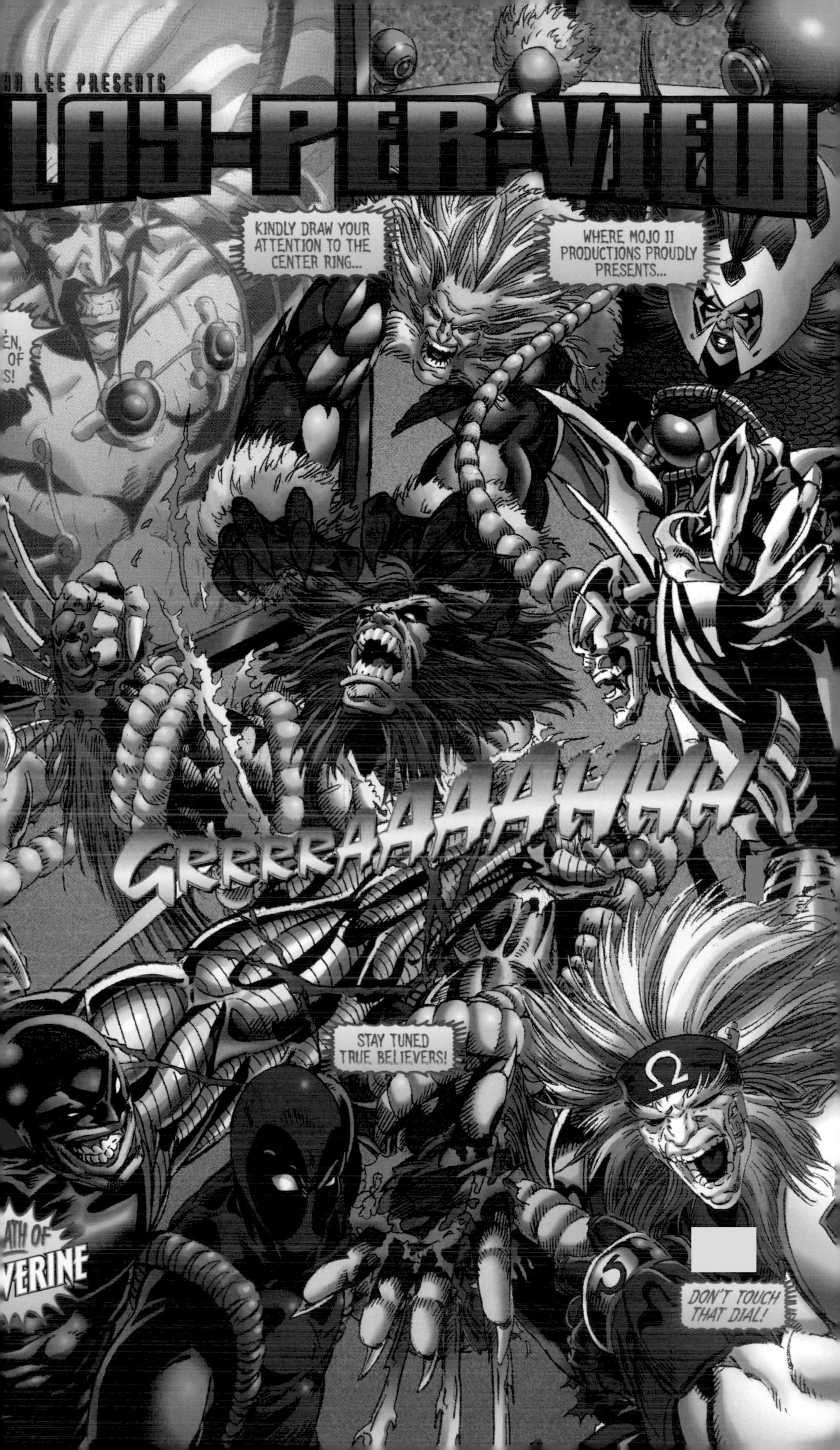

AN LEE PRESENTS
LAY-PER-VIEW
KINDLY DRAW YOUR ATTENTION TO THE CENTER RING...
WHERE MOJO II PRODUCTIONS PROUDLY PRESENTS...
GRRRRAAAAAHHH
STAY TUNED TRUE BELIEVERS!
DON'T TOUCH THAT DIAL!

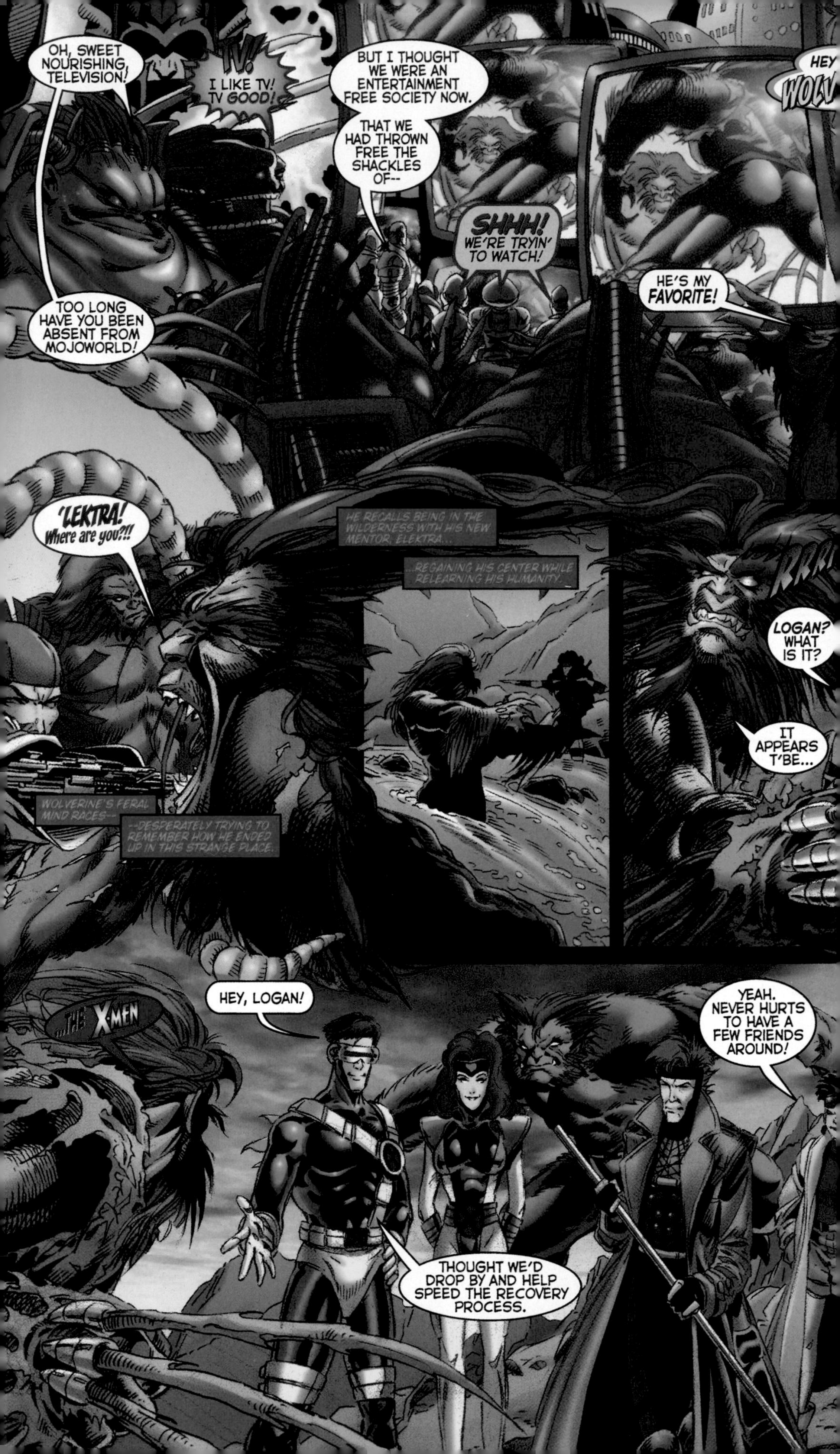

OH, SWEET NOURISHING TELEVISION!
TOO LONG HAVE YOU BEEN ABSENT FROM MOJOWORLD!
TV! I LIKE TV! TV GOOD!
BUT I THOUGHT WE WERE AN ENTERTAINMENT FREE SOCIETY NOW.
THAT WE HAD THROWN FREE THE SHACKLES OF--
SHHH! WE'RE TRYIN' TO WATCH!
HEY
HE'S MY FAVORITE!
'LEKTRA! Where are you?!!
WOLVERINE'S FERAL MIND RACES--
--DESPERATELY TRYING TO REMEMBER HOW HE ENDED UP IN THIS STRANGE PLACE.
HE RECALLS BEING IN THE WILDERNESS WITH HIS NEW MENTOR, ELEKTRA...
...REGAINING HIS CENTER WHILE RELEARNING HIS HUMANITY.
LOGAN? WHAT IS IT?
IT APPEARS T'BE...
...THE X-MEN
HEY, LOGAN!
THOUGHT WE'D DROP BY AND HELP SPEED THE RECOVERY PROCESS.
YEAH. NEVER HURTS TO HAVE A FEW FRIENDS AROUND!

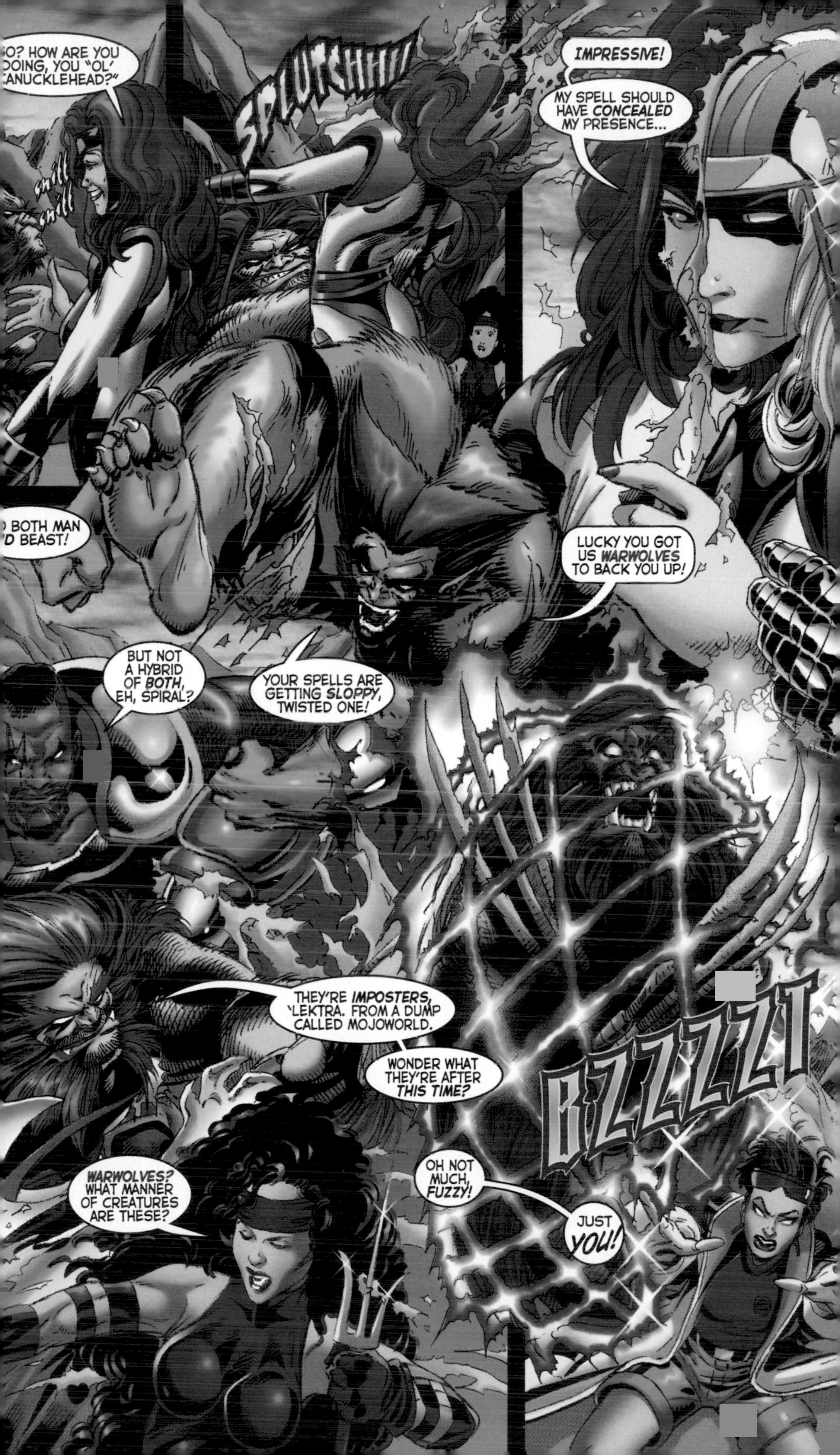

O? HOW ARE YOU DOING, YOU "OL' CANUCKLEHEAD?"
snill snill
SPLUTCHHH!
IMPRESSIVE!
MY SPELL SHOULD HAVE CONCEALED MY PRESENCE...
BOTH MAN BEAST!
LUCKY YOU GOT US WARWOLVES TO BACK YOU UP!
BUT NOT A HYBRID OF BOTH, EH, SPIRAL?
YOUR SPELLS ARE GETTING SLOPPY, TWISTED ONE!
THEY'RE IMPOSTERS, 'LEKTRA. FROM A DUMP CALLED MOJOWORLD.
WONDER WHAT THEY'RE AFTER THIS TIME?
BZZZZT
WARWOLVES? WHAT MANNER OF CREATURES ARE THESE?
OH NOT MUCH, FUZZY!
JUST YOU!

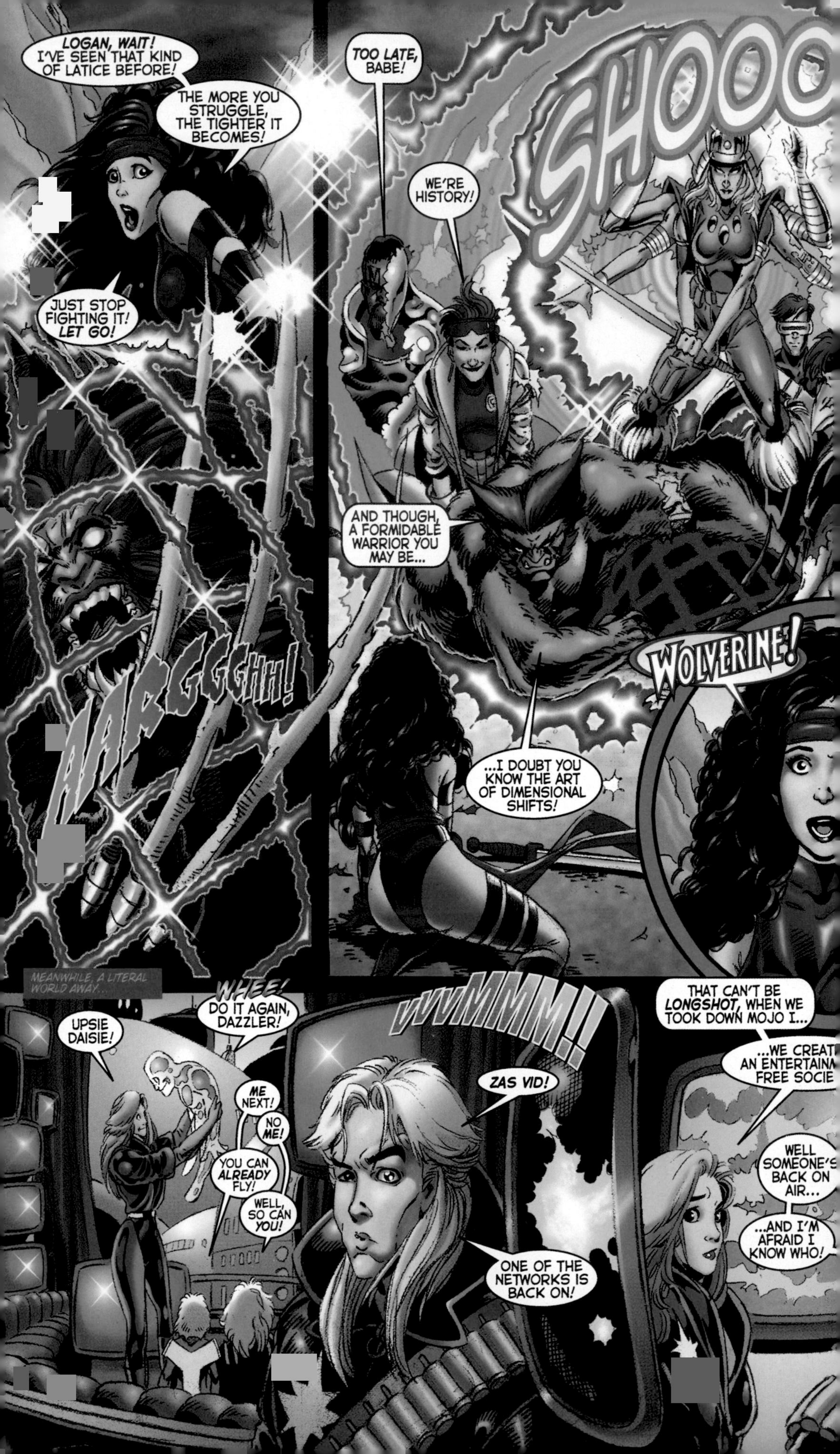

LOGAN, WAIT! I'VE SEEN THAT KIND OF LATICE BEFORE!
THE MORE YOU STRUGGLE, THE TIGHTER IT BECOMES!
JUST STOP FIGHTING IT! LET GO!
AARGGGHH!
TOO LATE, BABE!
WE'RE HISTORY!
SHOOO
AND THOUGH, A FORMIDABLE WARRIOR YOU MAY BE...
...I DOUBT YOU KNOW THE ART OF DIMENSIONAL SHIFTS!
WOLVERINE!
MEANWHILE, A LITERAL WORLD AWAY...
UPSIE DAISIE!
WHEE! DO IT AGAIN, DAZZLER!
ME NEXT!
NO ME!
YOU CAN ALREADY FLY!
WELL, SO CAN YOU!
VVVMMMM!!
ZAS VID!
ONE OF THE NETWORKS IS BACK ON!
THAT CAN'T BE LONGSHOT, WHEN WE TOOK DOWN MOJO I...
...WE CREAT AN ENTERTAINA FREE SOCIE
WELL SOMEONE'S BACK ON AIR...
...AND I'M AFRAID I KNOW WHO!

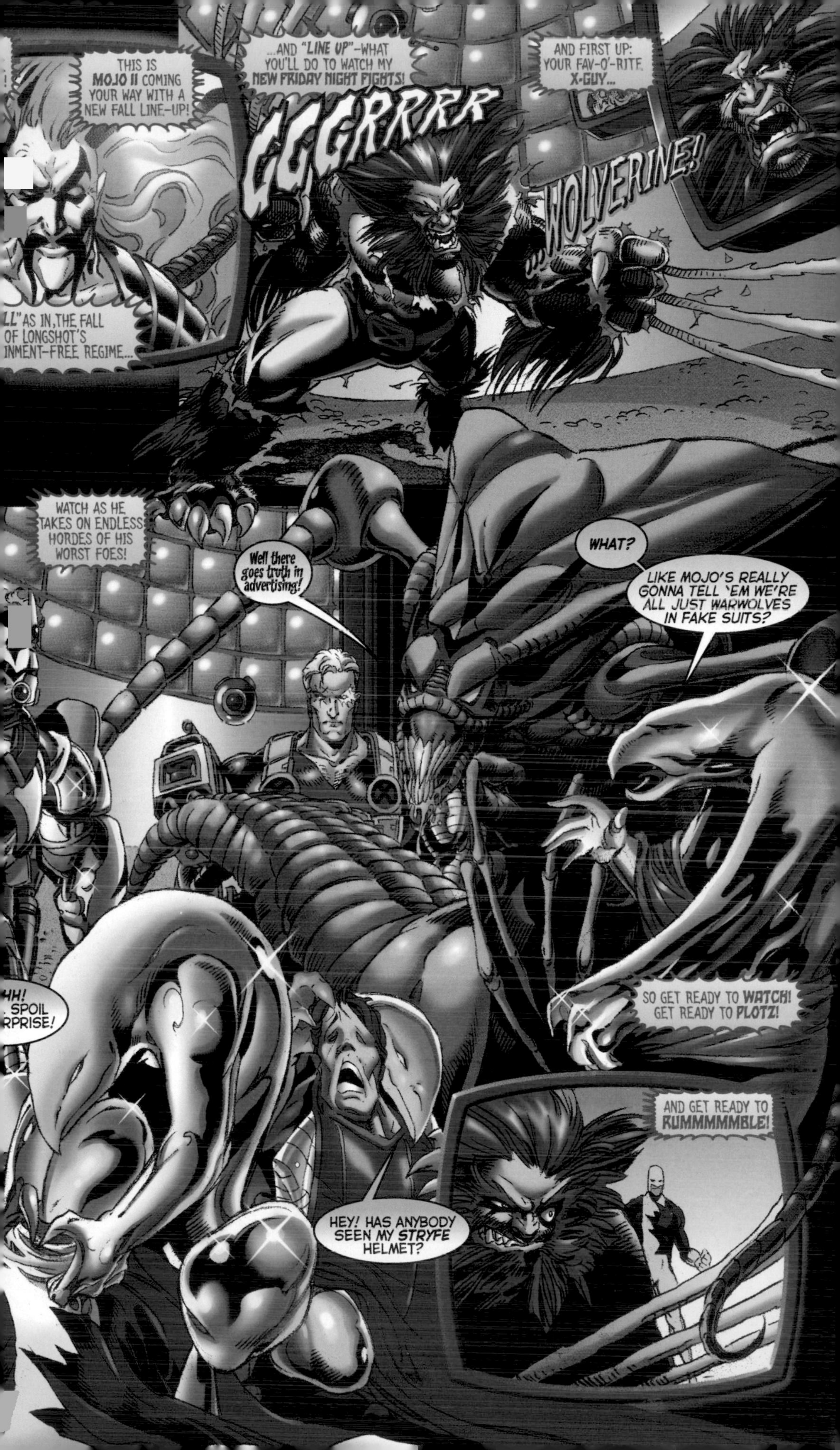
THIS IS MOJO II COMING YOUR WAY WITH A NEW FALL LINE-UP!
...AND "LINE UP"--WHAT YOU'LL DO TO WATCH MY NEW FRIDAY NIGHT FIGHTS!
AND FIRST UP: YOUR FAV-O'-RITE X-GUY...
GGGRRRR
...WOLVERINE!
LL" AS IN, THE FALL OF LONGSHOT'S INMENT-FREE REGIME...
WATCH AS HE TAKES ON ENDLESS HORDES OF HIS WORST FOES!
Well there goes truth in advertising!
WHAT?
LIKE MOJO'S REALLY GONNA TELL 'EM WE'RE ALL JUST WARWOLVES IN FAKE SUITS?
HH! SPOIL RPRISE!
SO GET READY TO WATCH! GET READY TO PLOTZ!
AND GET READY TO RUMMMMMBLE!
HEY! HAS ANYBODY SEEN MY STRYFE HELMET?

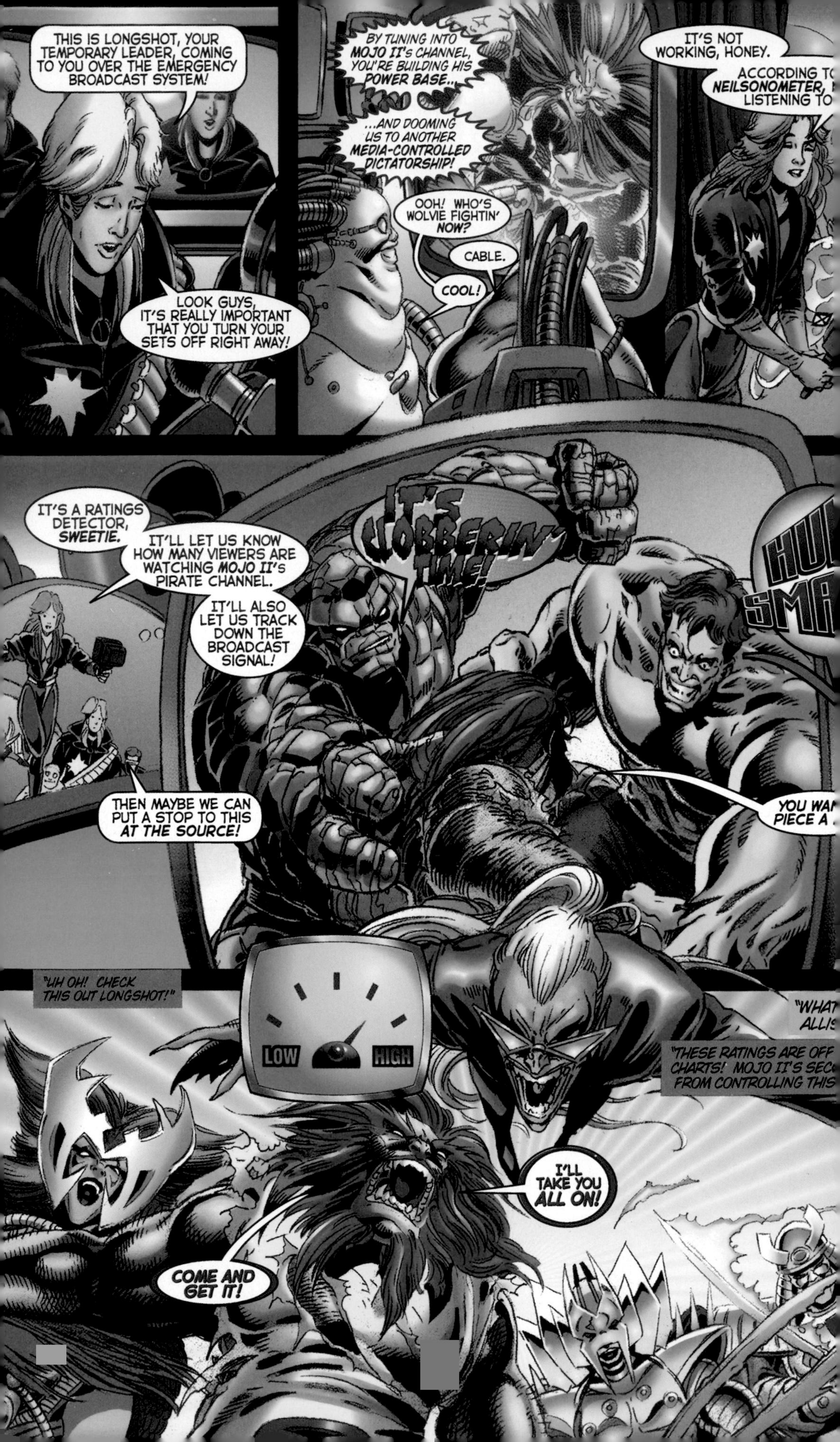
THIS IS LONGSHOT, YOUR TEMPORARY LEADER, COMING TO YOU OVER THE EMERGENCY BROADCAST SYSTEM!
LOOK GUYS, IT'S REALLY IMPORTANT THAT YOU TURN YOUR SETS OFF RIGHT AWAY!
BY TUNING INTO MOJO II's CHANNEL, YOU'RE BUILDING HIS POWER BASE...
...AND DOOMING US TO ANOTHER MEDIA-CONTROLLED DICTATORSHIP!
OOH! WHO'S WOLVIE FIGHTIN' NOW?
CABLE.
COOL!
IT'S NOT WORKING, HONEY.
ACCORDING T
NEILSONOMETER,
LISTENING TO
IT'S A RATINGS DETECTOR, SWEETIE.
IT'LL LET US KNOW HOW MANY VIEWERS ARE WATCHING MOJO II's PIRATE CHANNEL.
IT'LL ALSO LET US TRACK DOWN THE BROADCAST SIGNAL!
THEN MAYBE WE CAN PUT A STOP TO THIS AT THE SOURCE!
IT'S CLOBBERIN' TIME!
HU SMA
YOU WA PIECE A
"UH OH! CHECK THIS OUT LONGSHOT!"
LOW
HIGH
"WHAT ALLIS
"THESE RATINGS ARE OFF CHARTS! MOJO II'S SEC FROM CONTROLLING THIS
I'LL TAKE YOU ALL ON!
COME AND GET IT!

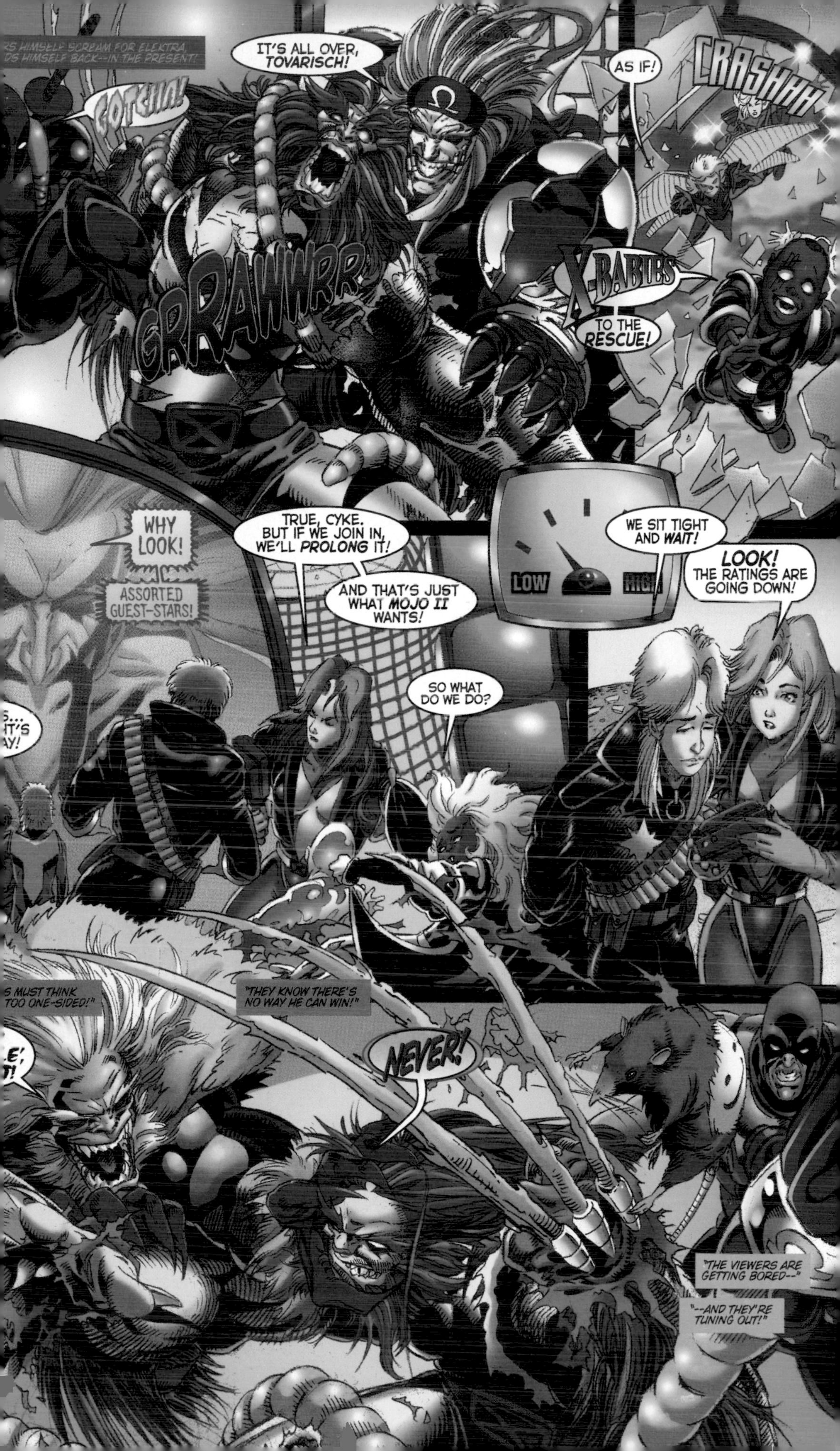
HIMSELF SCREAM FOR ELEKTRA,
HIMSELF BACK--IN THE PRESENT!
GOTCHA!
IT'S ALL OVER, TOVARISCH!
GRRAWWRR
AS IF!
CRASHHH
X-BABIES TO THE RESCUE!
WHY LOOK!
ASSORTED GUEST-STARS!
TRUE, CYKE. BUT IF WE JOIN IN, WE'LL PROLONG IT!
AND THAT'S JUST WHAT MOJO II WANTS!
LOW
WE SIT TIGHT AND WAIT!
LOOK! THE RATINGS ARE GOING DOWN!
SO WHAT DO WE DO?
TOO ONE-SIDED!"
"THEY KNOW THERE'S NO WAY HE CAN WIN!"
NEVER!
"THE VIEWERS ARE GETTING BORED--"
"--AND THEY'RE TUNING OUT!"

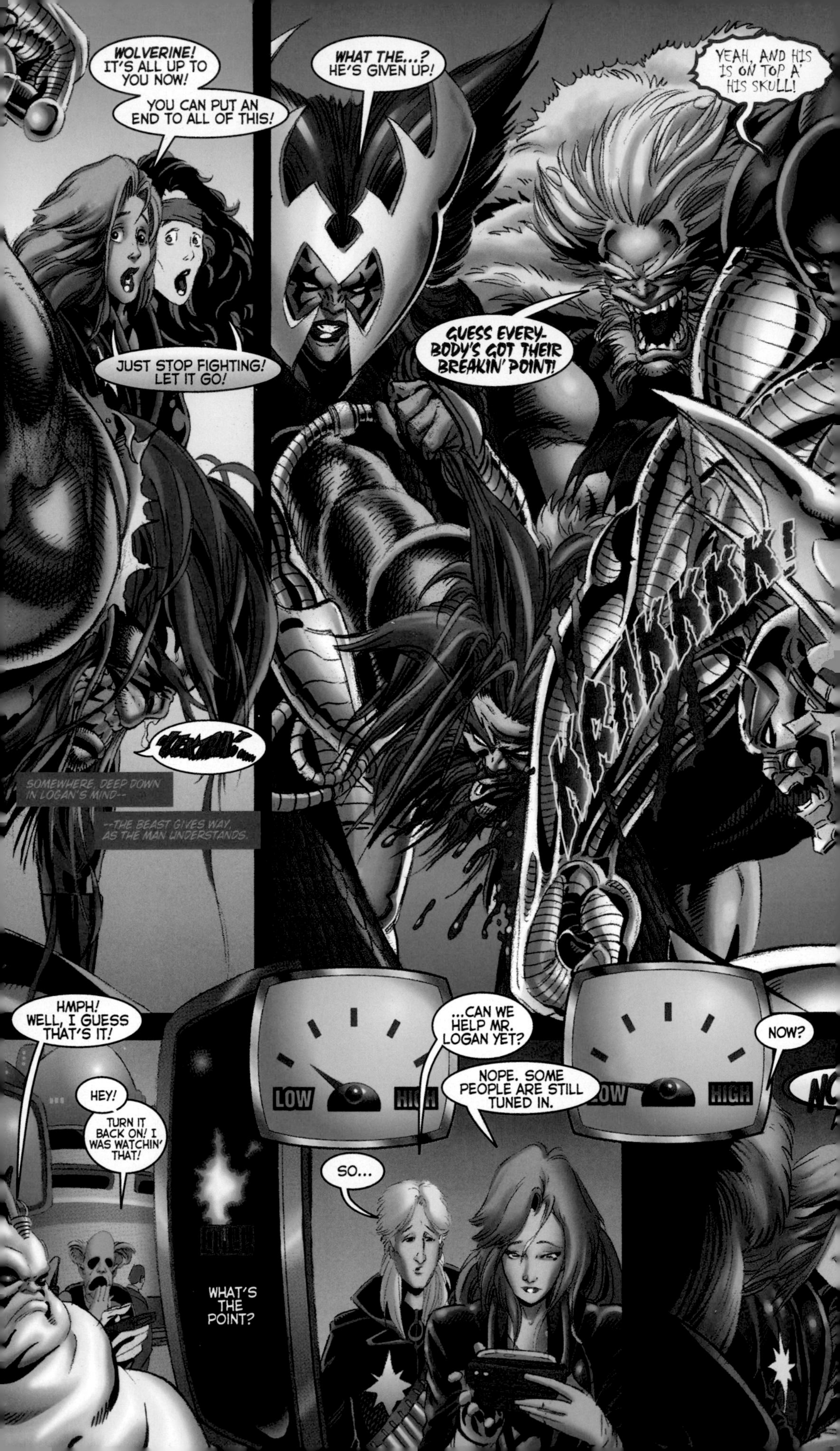
WOLVERINE! IT'S ALL UP TO YOU NOW!
YOU CAN PUT AN END TO ALL OF THIS!
JUST STOP FIGHTING! LET IT GO!
SOMEWHERE, DEEP DOWN IN LOGAN'S MIND--
--THE BEAST GIVES WAY, AS THE MAN UNDERSTANDS.
WHAT THE...? HE'S GIVEN UP!
YEAH, AND HIS IS ON TOP A' HIS SKULL!
GUESS EVERY-BODY'S GOT THEIR BREAKIN' POINT!
HMPH! WELL, I GUESS THAT'S IT!
HEY!
TURN IT BACK ON! I WAS WATCHIN' THAT!
WHAT'S THE POINT?
LOW
HIGH
...CAN WE HELP MR. LOGAN YET?
NOPE. SOME PEOPLE ARE STILL TUNED IN.
SO...
HIGH
NOW?

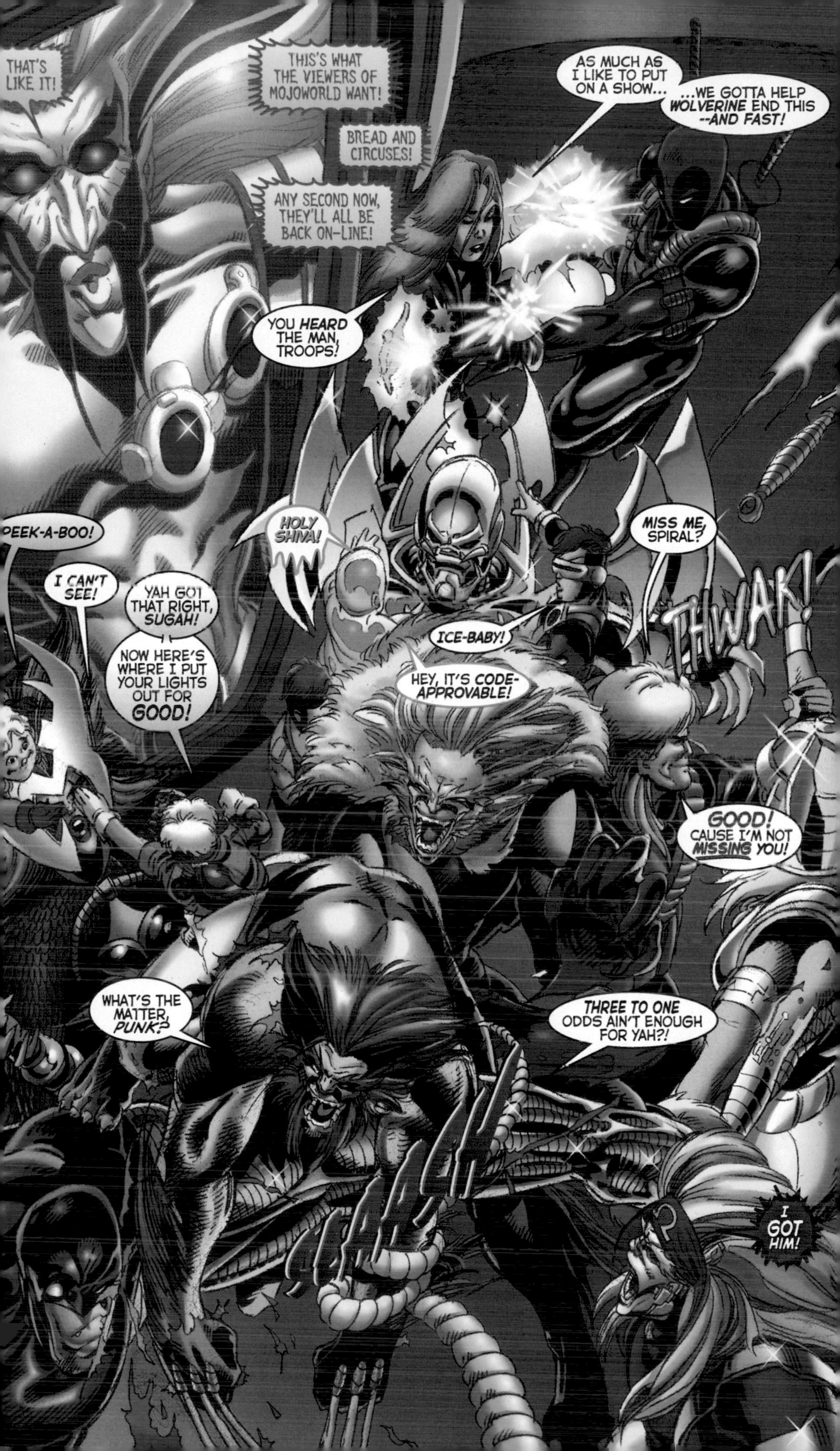

THAT'S LIKE IT!
THIS'S WHAT THE VIEWERS OF MOJOWORLD WANT!
BREAD AND CIRCUSES!
ANY SECOND NOW, THEY'LL ALL BE BACK ON-LINE!
AS MUCH AS I LIKE TO PUT ON A SHOW...
...WE GOTTA HELP WOLVERINE END THIS --AND FAST!
YOU HEARD THE MAN, TROOPS!
PEEK-A-BOO!
I CAN'T SEE!
YAH GOT THAT RIGHT, SUGAH!
NOW HERE'S WHERE I PUT YOUR LIGHTS OUT FOR GOOD!
HOLY SHIVA!
ICE-BABY!
HEY, IT'S CODE-APPROVABLE!
MISS ME, SPIRAL?
THWAK!
GOOD! CAUSE I'M NOT MISSING YOU!
WHAT'S THE MATTER, PUNK?
THREE TO ONE ODDS AIN'T ENOUGH FOR YAH?!
I GOT HIM!

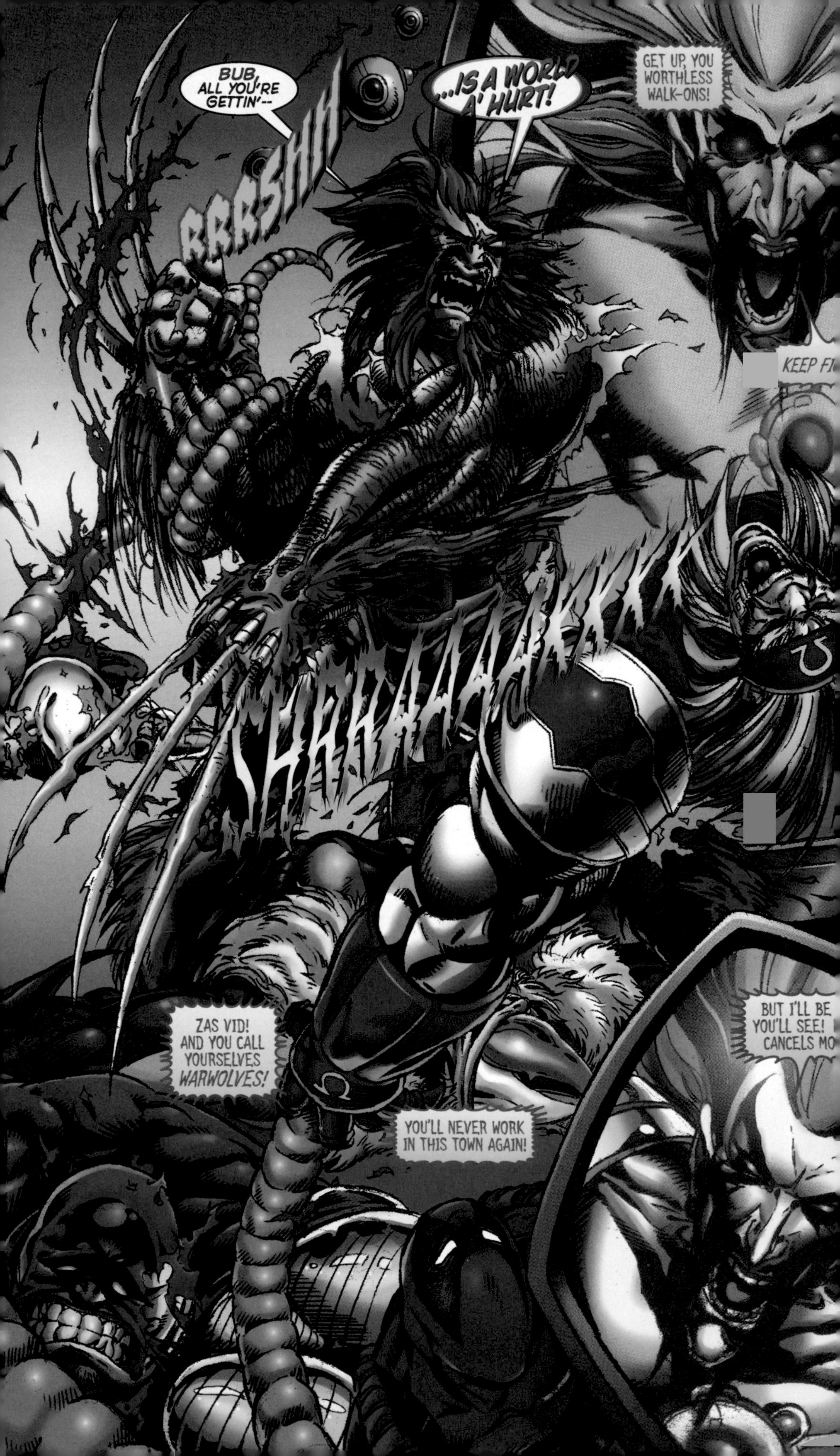
BUB, ALL YOU'RE GETTIN'--
...IS A WORLD A' HURT!
GET UP, YOU WORTHLESS WALK-ONS!
KEEP FI
ZAS VID! AND YOU CALL YOURSELVES WARWOLVES!
YOU'LL NEVER WORK IN THIS TOWN AGAIN!
BUT I'LL BE
YOU'LL SEE!
CANCELS MO

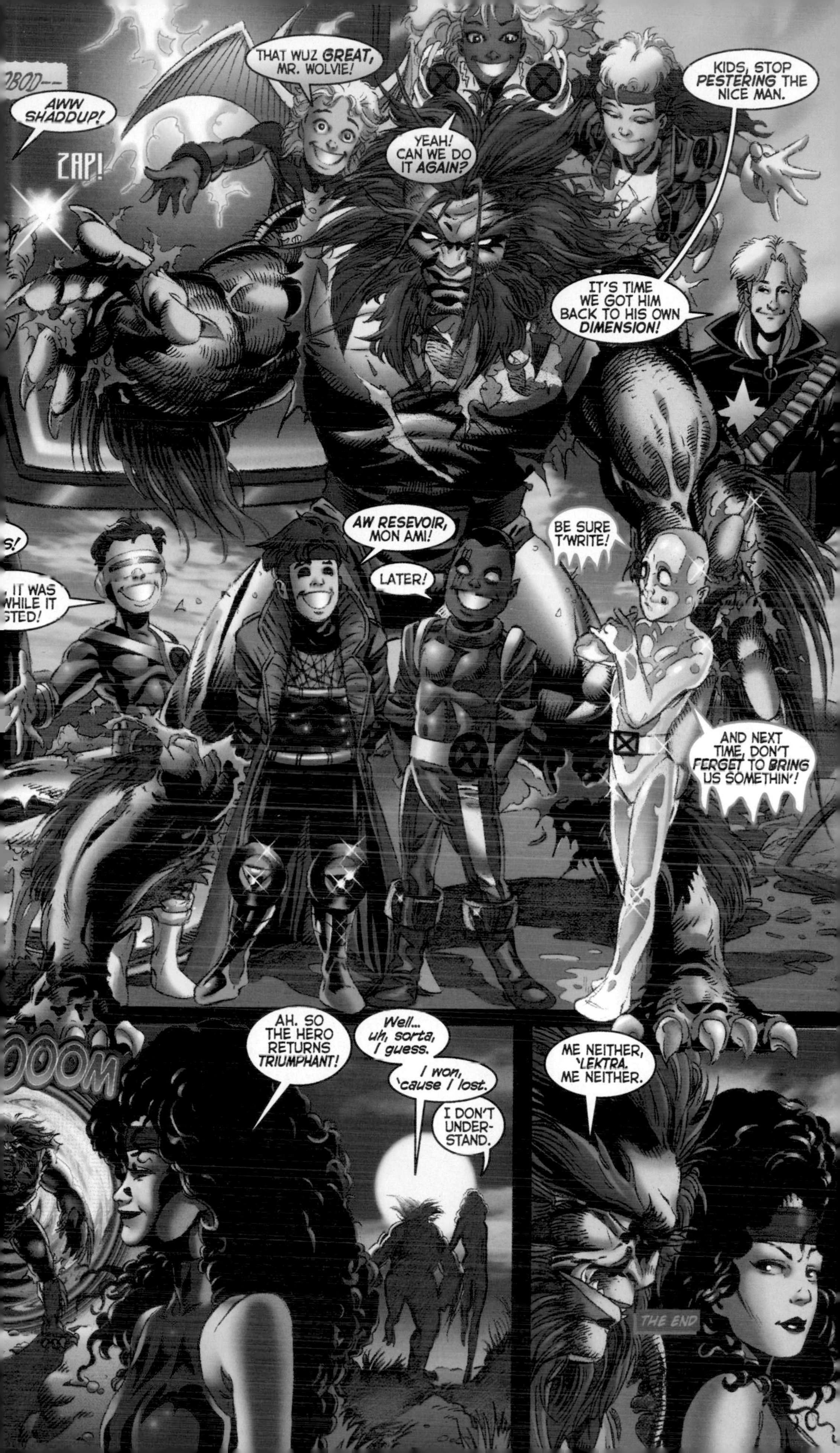
AWW SHADDUP!
ZAP!
THAT WUZ *GREAT*, MR. WOLVIE!
YEAH! CAN WE DO IT *AGAIN?*
KIDS, STOP *PESTERING* THE NICE MAN.
IT'S TIME WE GOT HIM BACK TO HIS OWN *DIMENSION!*
AW RESEVOIR, MON AMI!
LATER!
BE SURE T'WRITE!
AND NEXT TIME, DON'T *FERGET* TO *BRING* US SOMETHIN'!
AH. SO THE HERO RETURNS *TRIUMPHANT!*
Well... uh, sorta, I guess.
I won, 'cause I lost.
I DON'T UNDER-STAND.
ME NEITHER, 'LEKTRA. ME NEITHER.
THE END

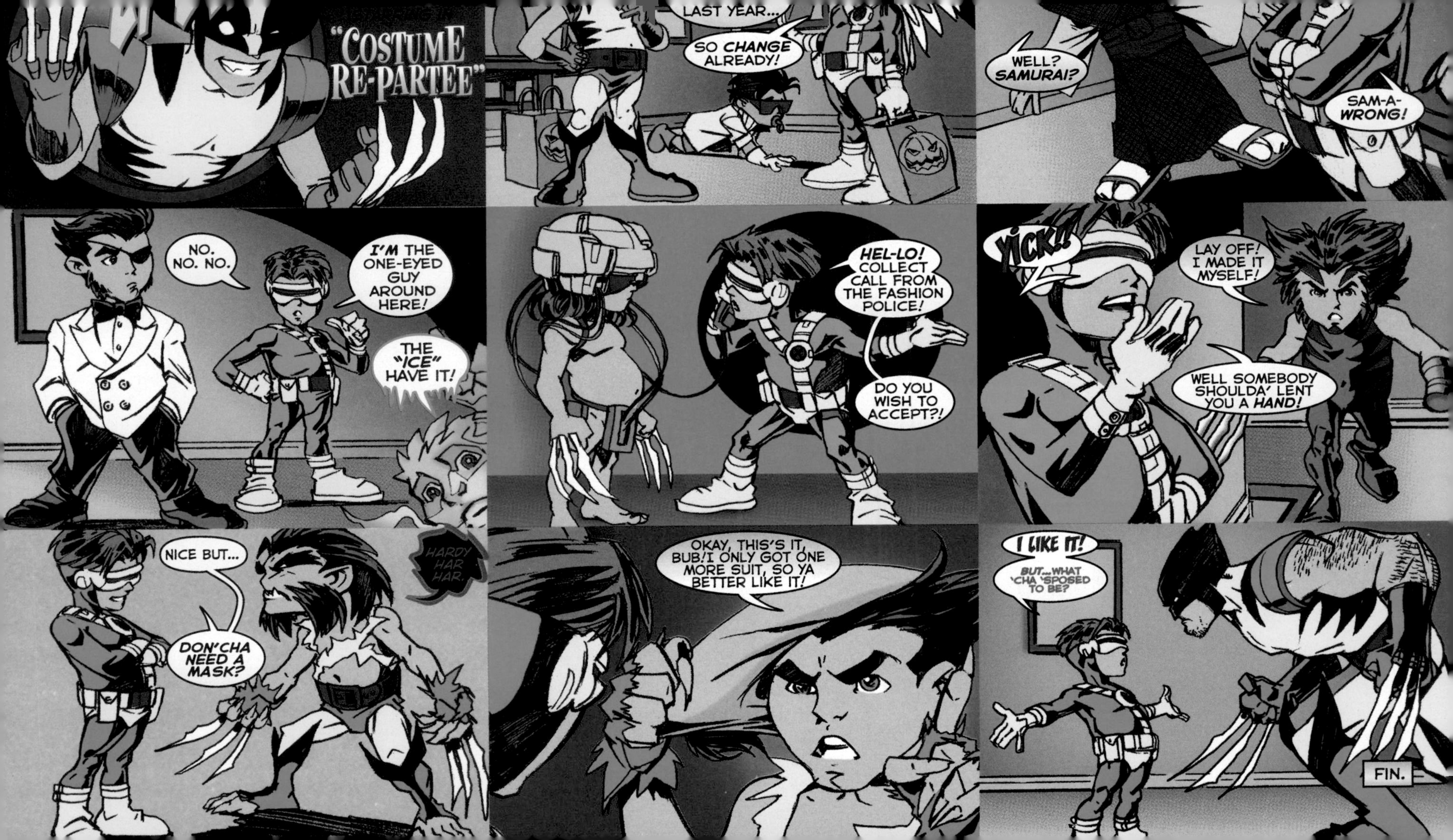
"COSTUME RE-PARTEE"
LAST YEAR...
SO CHANGE ALREADY!
WELL? SAMURAI?
SAM-A-WRONG!
NO. NO. NO.
I'M THE ONE-EYED GUY AROUND HERE!
THE "ICE" HAVE IT!
HEL-LO! COLLECT CALL FROM THE FASHION POLICE!
DO YOU WISH TO ACCEPT?!
YICK!!
LAY OFF! I MADE IT MYSELF!
WELL SOMEBODY SHOULDA' LENT YOU A HAND!
NICE BUT...
DON'CHA NEED A MASK?
HARDY HAR HAR.
OKAY, THIS'S IT, BUB! I ONLY GOT ONE MORE SUIT, SO YA BETTER LIKE IT!
I LIKE IT!
BUT...WHAT 'CHA 'SPOSED TO BE?
FIN.

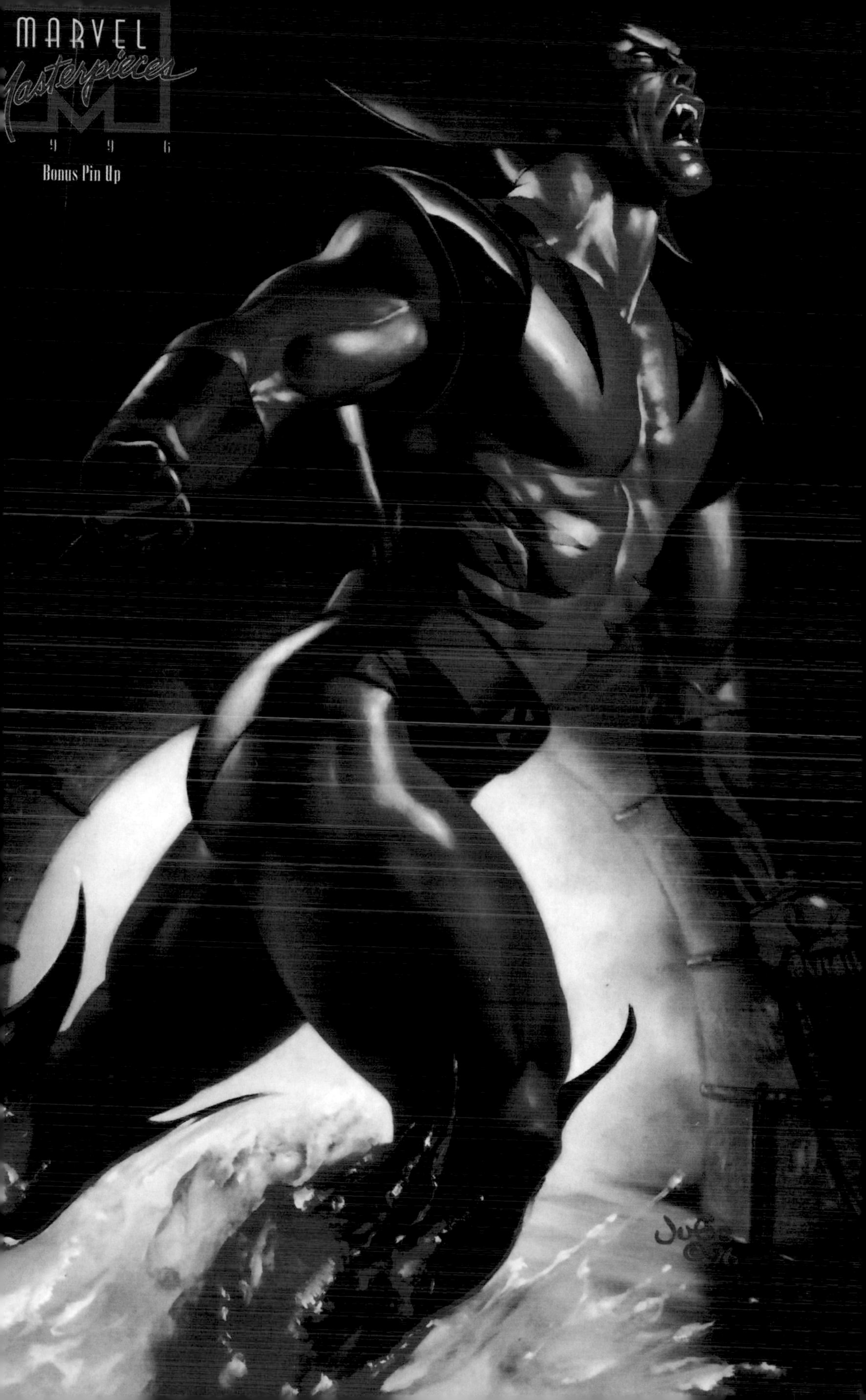
MARVEL
Masterpieces
9 9 6
Bonus Pin Up

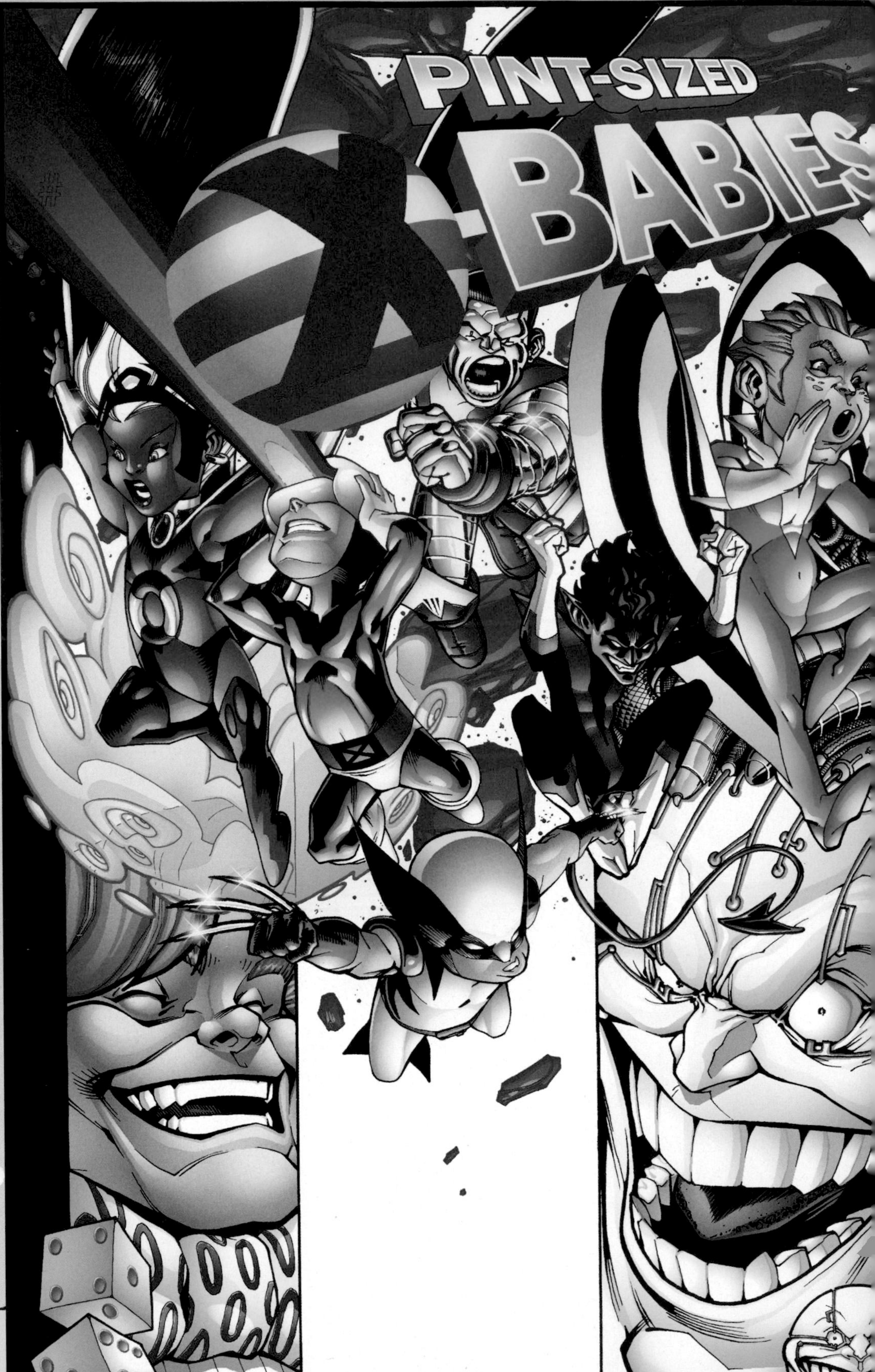
PINT-SIZED
X-BABIES

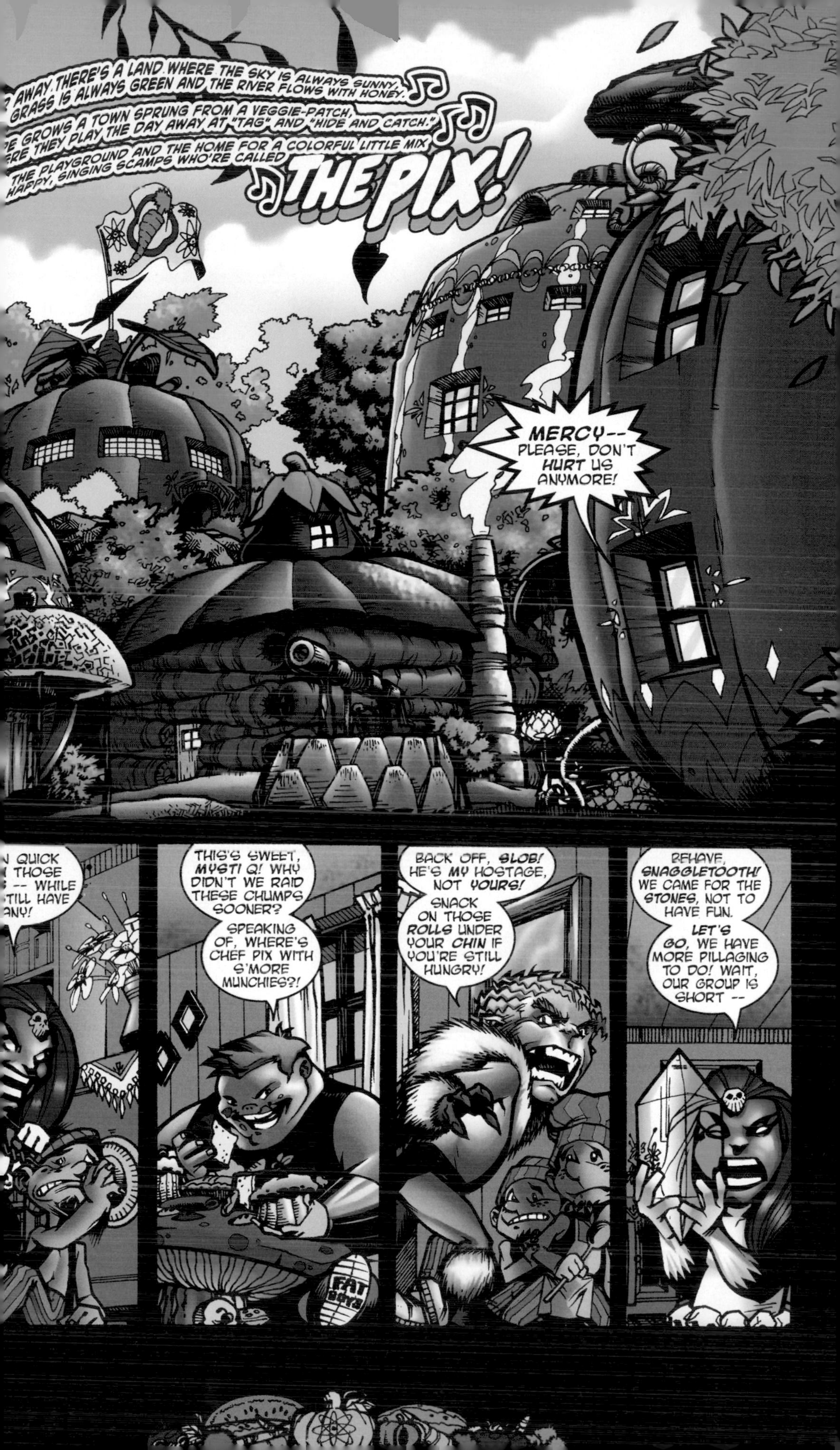

AWAY. THERE'S A LAND WHERE THE SKY IS ALWAYS SUNNY,
GRASS IS ALWAYS GREEN AND THE RIVER FLOWS WITH HONEY.
E GROWS A TOWN SPRUNG FROM A VEGGIE-PATCH,
ERE THEY PLAY THE DAY AWAY AT "TAG" AND "HIDE AND CATCH."
THE PLAYGROUND AND THE HOME FOR A COLORFUL LITTLE MIX
HAPPY, SINGING SCAMPS WHO'RE CALLED
THE PIX!
MERCY-- PLEASE, DON'T HURT US ANYMORE!
N QUICK THOSE -- WHILE STILL HAVE ANY!
THIS'S SWEET, MYSTI Q! WHY DIDN'T WE RAID THESE CHUMPS SOONER?
SPEAKING OF, WHERE'S CHEF PIX WITH S'MORE MUNCHIES?!
FAT BOYS
BACK OFF, SLOB! HE'S MY HOSTAGE, NOT YOURS!
SNACK ON THOSE ROLLS UNDER YOUR CHIN IF YOU'RE STILL HUNGRY!
BEHAVE, SNAGGLETOOTH! WE CAME FOR THE STONES, NOT TO HAVE FUN.
LET'S GO, WE HAVE MORE PILLAGING TO DO! WAIT, OUR GROUP IS SHORT --

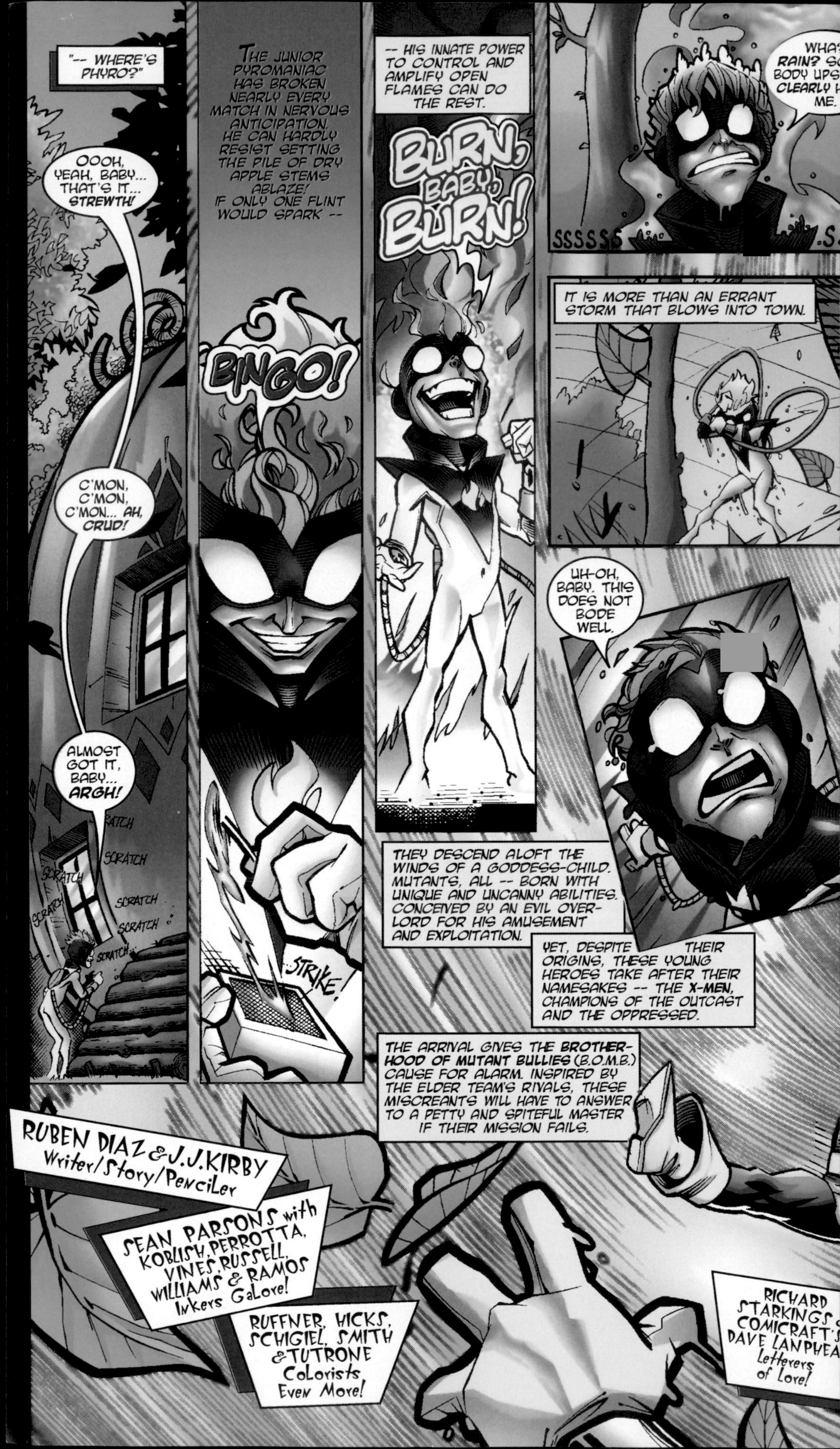
"-- WHERE'S PHYRO?"
OOOH, YEAH, BABY... THAT'S IT... STREWTH!
C'MON, C'MON, C'MON... AH, CRUD!
ALMOST GOT IT, BABY... ARGH!
SCRATCH
SCRATCH
SCRATCH
SCRATCH
SCRATCH
SCRATCH
SCRATCH
THE JUNIOR PYROMANIAC HAS BROKEN NEARLY EVERY MATCH IN NERVOUS ANTICIPATION. HE CAN HARDLY RESIST SETTING THE PILE OF DRY APPLE STEMS ABLAZE! IF ONLY ONE FLINT WOULD SPARK --
BINGO!
STRIKE!
-- HIS INNATE POWER TO CONTROL AND AMPLIFY OPEN FLAMES CAN DO THE REST.
BURN, BABY, BURN!
SSSSSS
IT IS MORE THAN AN ERRANT STORM THAT BLOWS INTO TOWN.
UH-OH, BABY. THIS DOES NOT BODE WELL.
THEY DESCEND ALOFT THE WINDS OF A GODDESS-CHILD. MUTANTS, ALL -- BORN WITH UNIQUE AND UNCANNY ABILITIES. CONCEIVED BY AN EVIL OVER-LORD FOR HIS AMUSEMENT AND EXPLOITATION.
YET, DESPITE THEIR ORIGINS, THESE YOUNG HEROES TAKE AFTER THEIR NAMESAKES -- THE X-MEN, CHAMPIONS OF THE OUTCAST AND THE OPPRESSED.
THE ARRIVAL GIVES THE BROTHER-HOOD OF MUTANT BULLIES (B.O.M.B.) CAUSE FOR ALARM. INSPIRED BY THE ELDER TEAM'S RIVALS, THESE MISCREANTS WILL HAVE TO ANSWER TO A PETTY AND SPITEFUL MASTER IF THEIR MISSION FAILS.
RUBEN DIAZ & J.J. KIRBY Writer/Story/Penciler
SEAN PARSONS with KOBLISH, PERROTTA, VINES, RUSSELL, WILLIAMS & RAMOS Inkers GaLore!
RUFFNER, HICKS, SCHIGIEL, SMITH & TUTRONE Colorists Even More!
RICHARD STARKINGS COMICRAFT'S DAVE LANPHEA Letterers of Lore!

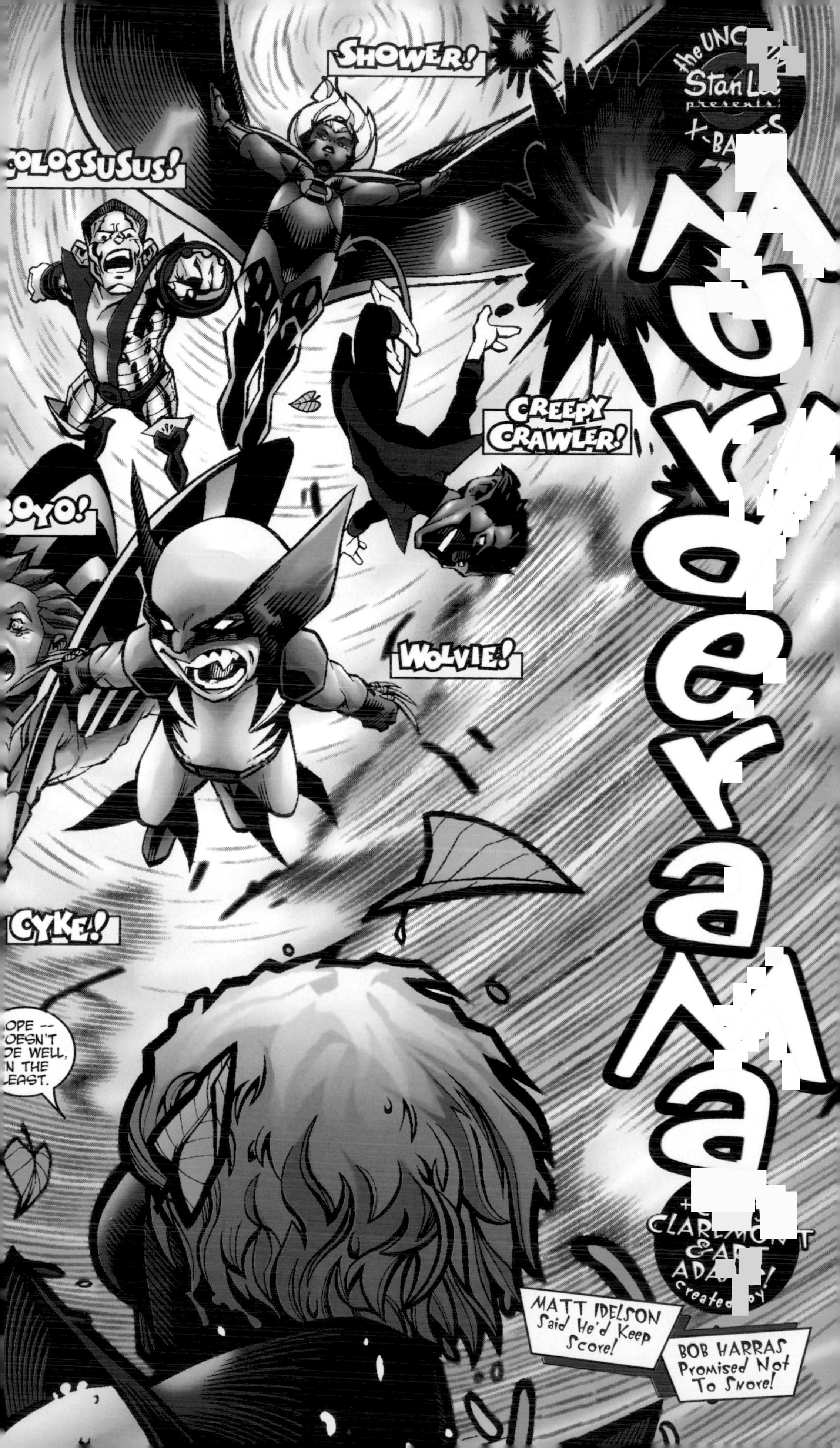

SHOWER!
CREEPY CRAWLER!
WOLVIE!
CYKE!
MATT IDELSON Said He'd Keep Score!
BOB HARRAS Promised Not To Snore!

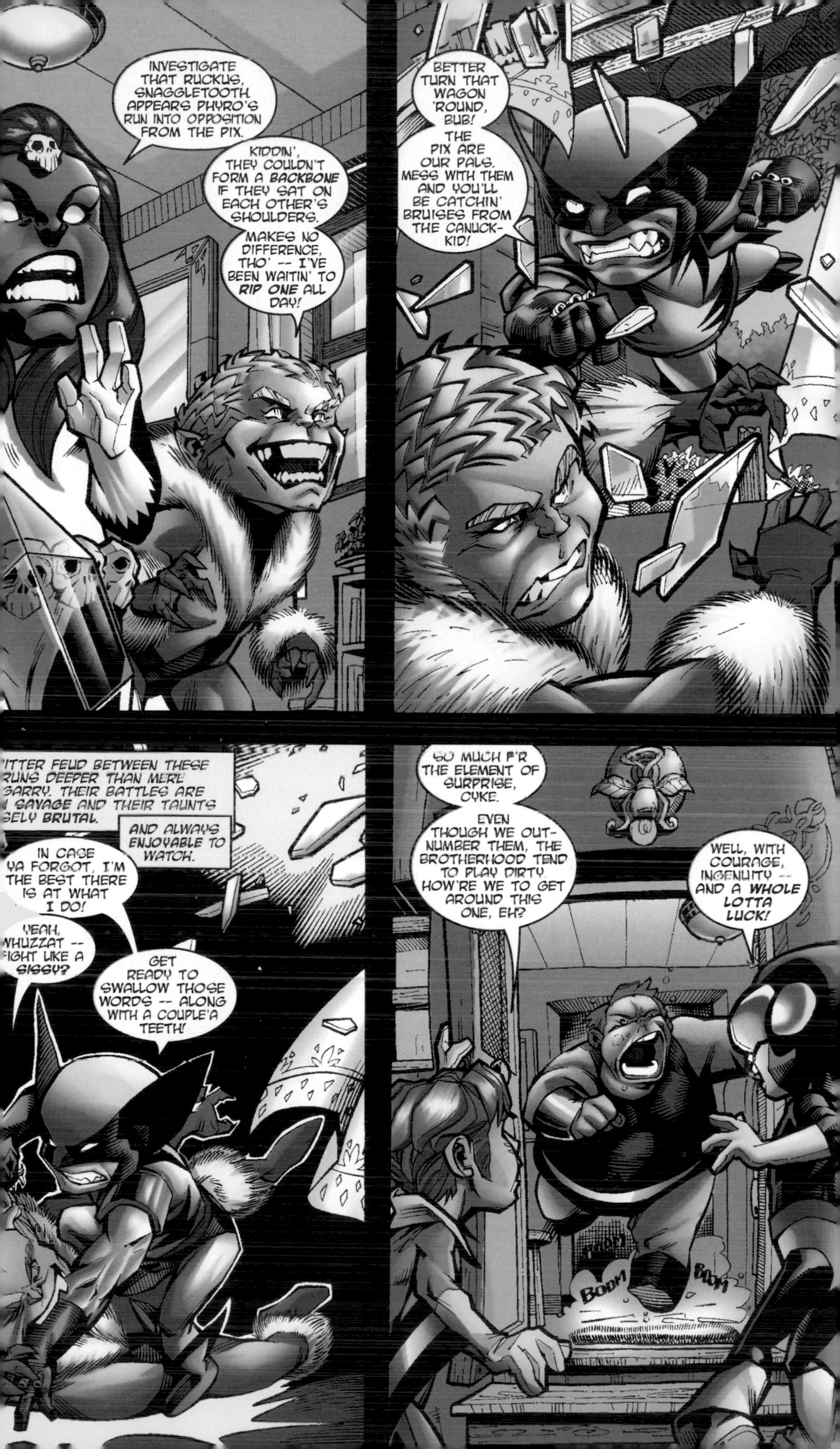

INVESTIGATE THAT RUCKUS, SNAGGLETOOTH. APPEARS PHYRO'S RUN INTO OPPOSITION FROM THE PIX.
KIDDIN', THEY COULDN'T FORM A **BACKBONE** IF THEY SAT ON EACH OTHER'S SHOULDERS.
MAKES NO DIFFERENCE, THO' -- I'VE BEEN WAITIN' TO **RIP ONE** ALL DAY!
BETTER TURN THAT WAGON 'ROUND, BUB!
THE PIX ARE OUR PALS. MESS WITH THEM AND YOU'LL BE CATCHIN' BRUISES FROM THE CANUCK-KID!
ITTER FEUD BETWEEN THESE RUNS DEEPER THAN MERE GARRY. THEIR BATTLES ARE SAVAGE AND THEIR TAUNTS SELY **BRUTAL.**
AND ALWAYS ENJOYABLE TO WATCH.
IN CASE YA FORGOT, I'M THE BEST THERE IS AT WHAT I DO!
YEAH, WHUZZAT -- FIGHT LIKE A **SISSY?**
GET READY TO SWALLOW THOSE WORDS -- ALONG WITH A COUPLE'A TEETH!
SO MUCH F'R THE ELEMENT OF SURPRISE, CYKE.
EVEN THOUGH WE OUT-NUMBER THEM, THE BROTHERHOOD TEND TO PLAY DIRTY. HOW'RE WE TO GET AROUND THIS ONE, EH?
WELL, WITH COURAGE, INGENUITY -- AND A **WHOLE LOTTA LUCK!**
BOOM
BOOM

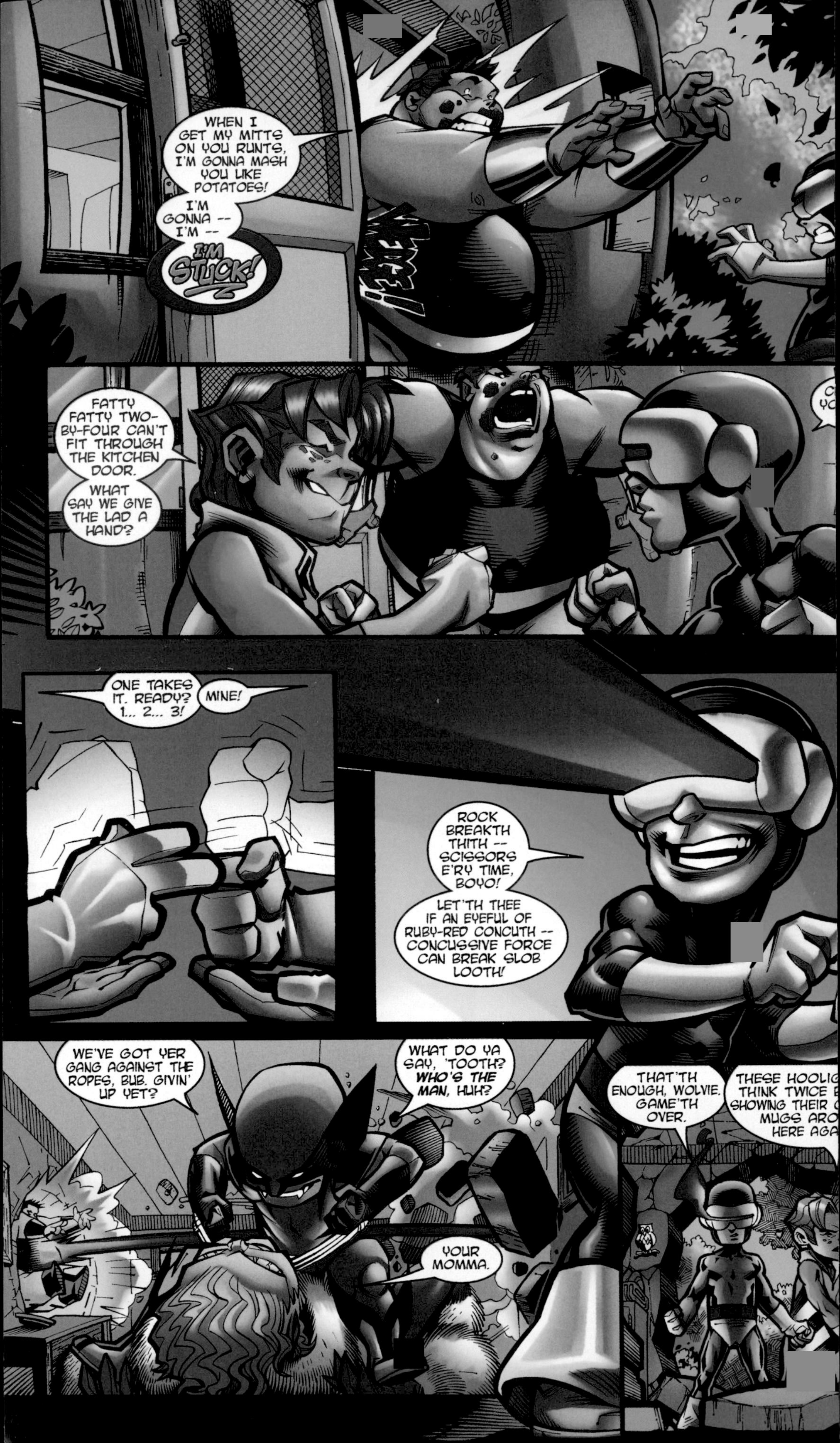
WHEN I GET MY MITTS ON YOU RUNTS, I'M GONNA MASH YOU LIKE POTATOES!
I'M GONNA -- I'M --
I'M STUCK!
FATTY FATTY TWO-BY-FOUR CAN'T FIT THROUGH THE KITCHEN DOOR.
WHAT SAY WE GIVE THE LAD A HAND?
ONE TAKES IT. READY? 1... 2... 3!
MINE!
ROCK BREAKTH THITH -- SCISSORS E'RY TIME, BOYO!
LET'TH THEE IF AN EYEFUL OF RUBY-RED CONCUTH -- CONCUSSIVE FORCE CAN BREAK SLOB LOOTH!
WE'VE GOT YER GANG AGAINST THE ROPES, BUB. GIVIN' UP YET?
WHAT DO YA SAY, 'TOOTH? *WHO'S THE MAN*, HUH?
YOUR MOMMA.
THAT'TH ENOUGH, WOLVIE. GAME'TH OVER.

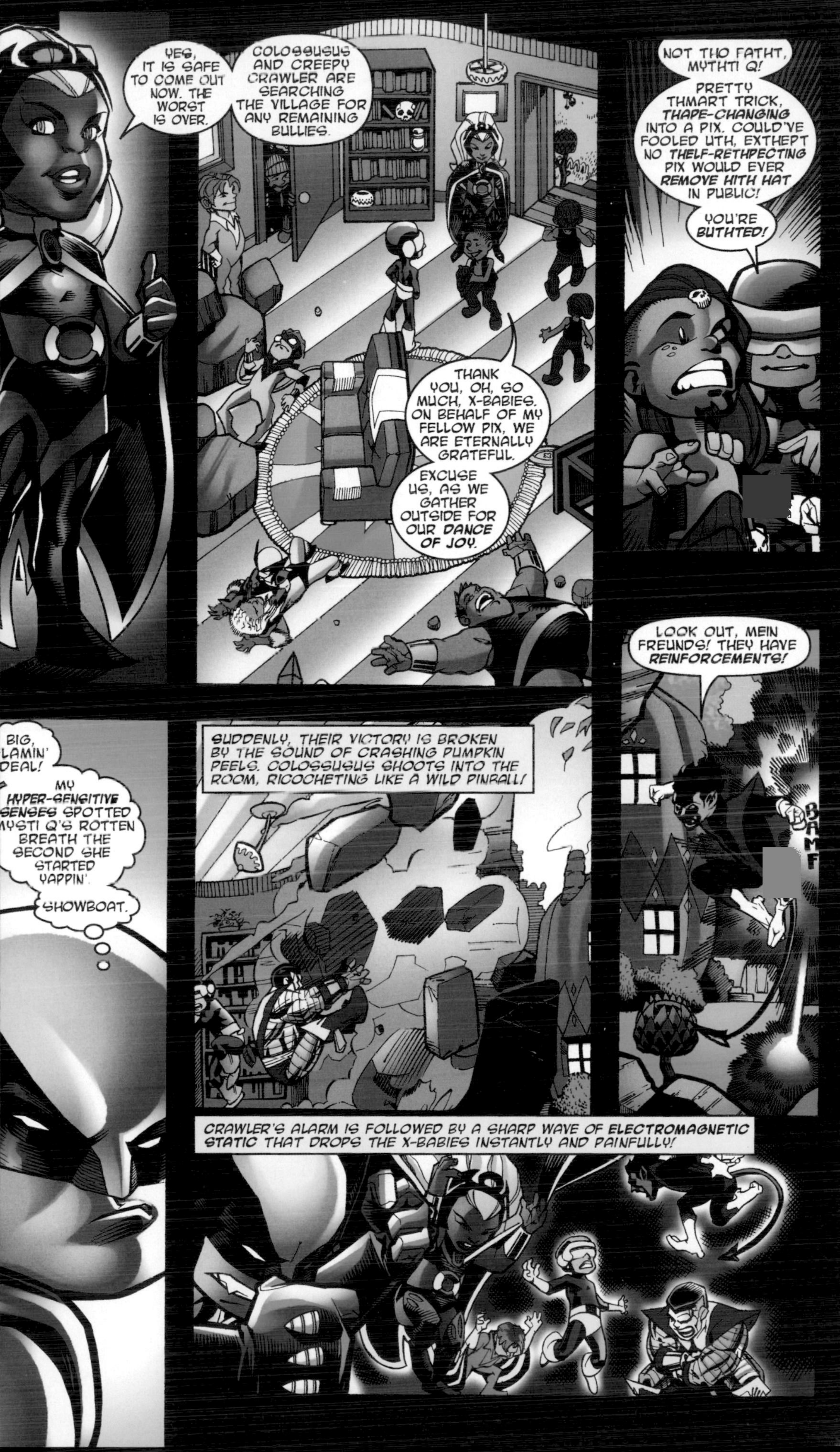

YES, IT IS SAFE TO COME OUT NOW. THE WORST IS OVER.
COLOSSUSUS AND CREEPY CRAWLER ARE SEARCHING THE VILLAGE FOR ANY REMAINING BULLIES.
THANK YOU, OH, SO MUCH, X-BABIES. ON BEHALF OF MY FELLOW PIX, WE ARE ETERNALLY GRATEFUL.
EXCUSE US, AS WE GATHER OUTSIDE FOR OUR DANCE OF JOY.
NOT THO FATHT, MYTHTI Q!
PRETTY THMART TRICK, THAPE-CHANGING INTO A PIX. COULD'VE FOOLED UTH, EXTHEPT NO THELF-RETHPECTING PIX WOULD EVER REMOVE HITH HAT IN PUBLIC!
YOU'RE BUTHTED!
BIG, LAMIN' DEAL!
MY HYPER-SENSITIVE SENSES SPOTTED MYSTI Q'S ROTTEN BREATH THE SECOND SHE STARTED YAPPIN'.
SHOWBOAT.
SUDDENLY, THEIR VICTORY IS BROKEN BY THE SOUND OF CRASHING PUMPKIN PEELS. COLOSSUSUS SHOOTS INTO THE ROOM, RICOCHETING LIKE A WILD PINBALL!
LOOK OUT, MEIN FREUNDS! THEY HAVE REINFORCEMENTS!
BAMF
CRAWLER'S ALARM IS FOLLOWED BY A SHARP WAVE OF ELECTROMAGNETIC STATIC THAT DROPS THE X-BABIES INSTANTLY AND PAINFULLY!

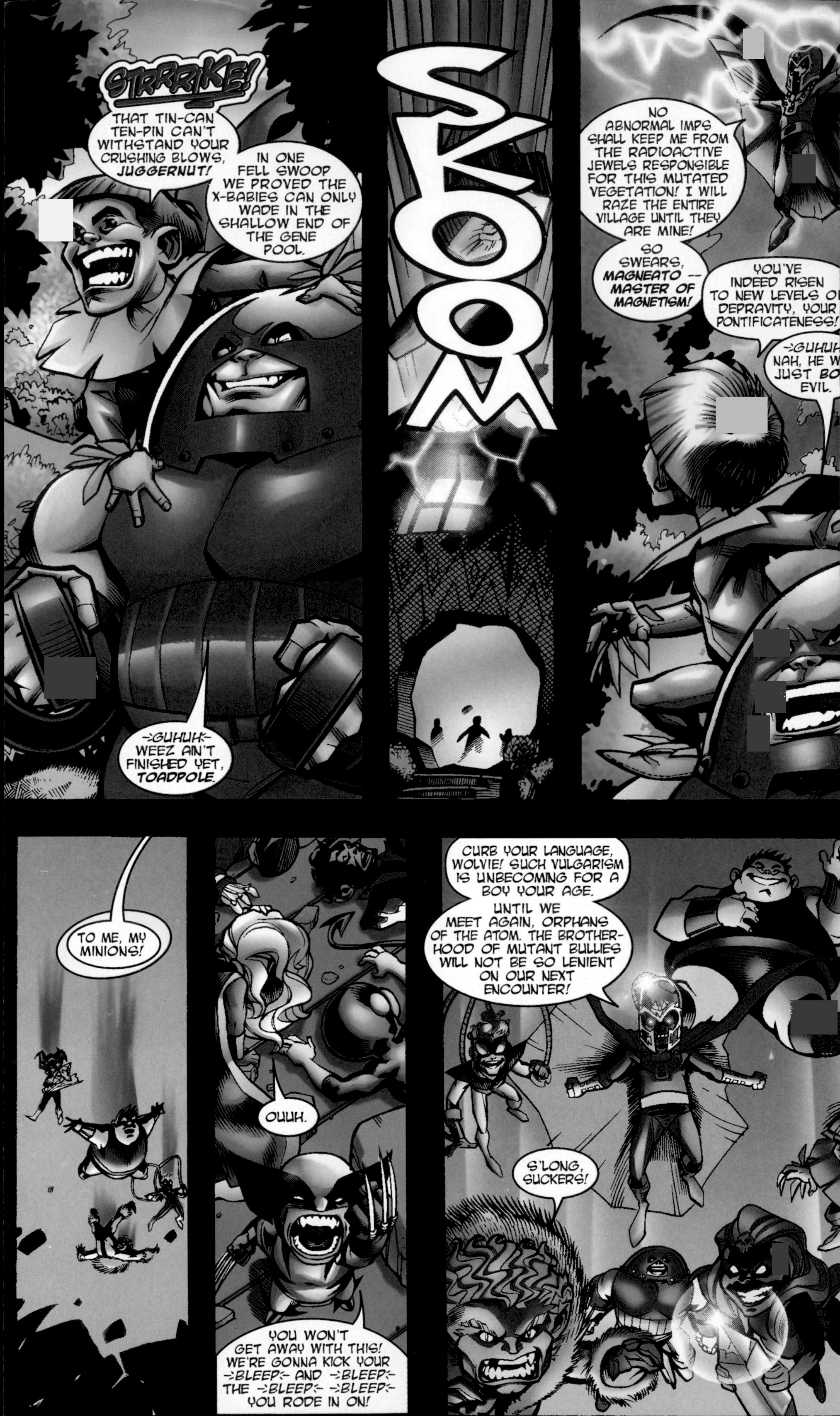
STRRRIKE!
THAT TIN-CAN TEN-PIN CAN'T WITHSTAND YOUR CRUSHING BLOWS, JUGGERNUT!
IN ONE FELL SWOOP WE PROVED THE X-BABIES CAN ONLY WADE IN THE SHALLOW END OF THE GENE POOL.
-GUHUH- WEEZ AIN'T FINISHED YET, TOADPOLE.
SKOOM
NO ABNORMAL IMPS SHALL KEEP ME FROM THE RADIOACTIVE JEWELS RESPONSIBLE FOR THIS MUTATED VEGETATION! I WILL RAZE THE ENTIRE VILLAGE UNTIL THEY ARE MINE!
SO SWEARS, MAGNEATO -- MASTER OF MAGNETISM!
YOU'VE INDEED RISEN TO NEW LEVELS O DEPRAVITY, YOUR PONTIFICATENESS!
-GUHUH NAH, HE W JUST BO EVIL.
TO ME, MY MINIONS!
OUUH.
YOU WON'T GET AWAY WITH THIS! WE'RE GONNA KICK YOUR -BLEEP- AND -BLEEP- THE -BLEEP- -BLEEP- YOU RODE IN ON!
CURB YOUR LANGUAGE, WOLVIE! SUCH VULGARISM IS UNBECOMING FOR A BOY YOUR AGE.
UNTIL WE MEET AGAIN, ORPHANS OF THE ATOM. THE BROTHERHOOD OF MUTANT BULLIES WILL NOT BE SO LENIENT ON OUR NEXT ENCOUNTER!
S'LONG, SUCKERS!

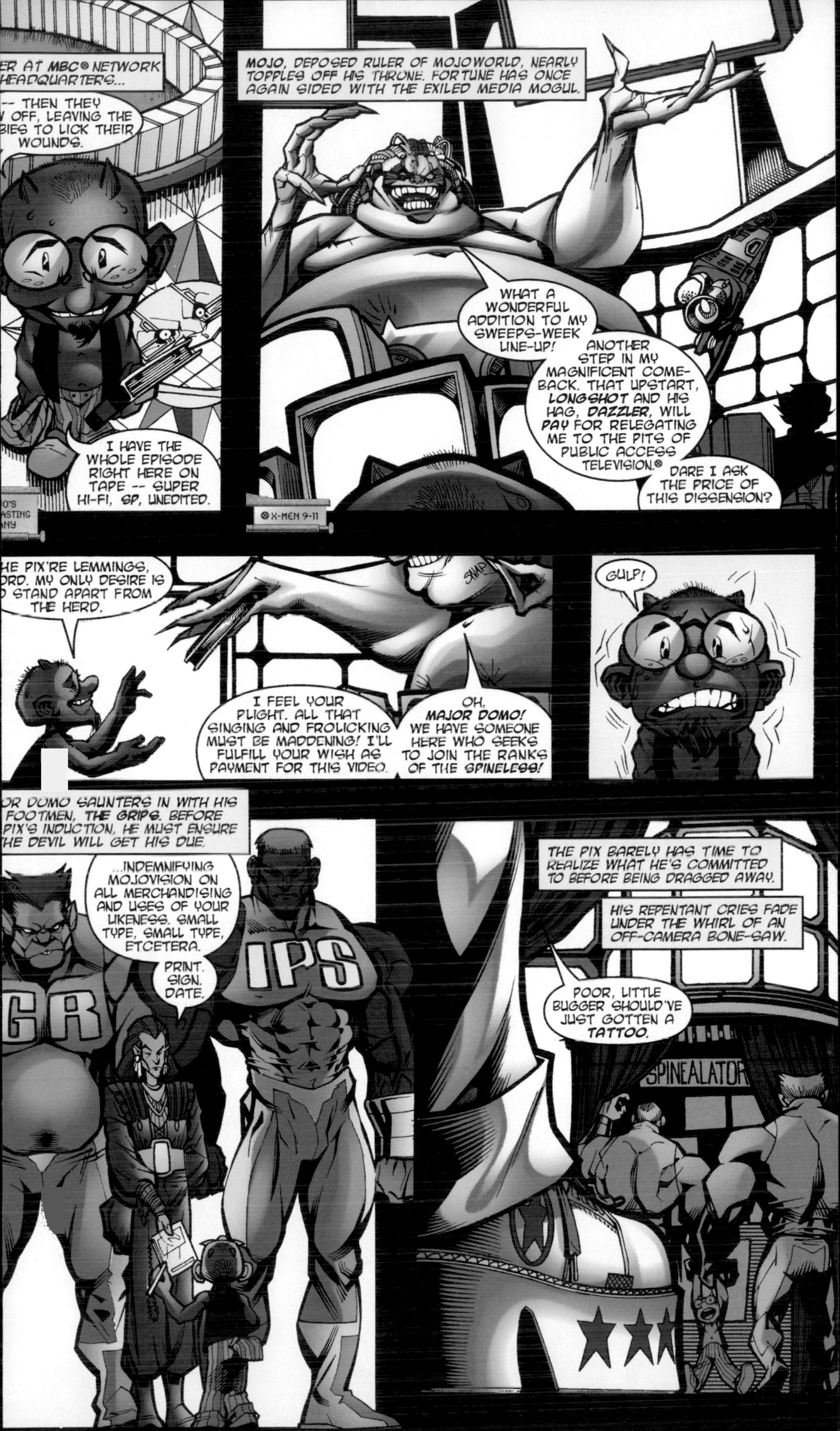
ER AT MBC® NETWORK HEADQUARTERS...
-- THEN THEY W OFF, LEAVING THE BIES TO LICK THEIR WOUNDS.
I HAVE THE WHOLE EPISODE RIGHT HERE ON TAPE -- SUPER HI-FI, SP, UNEDITED.
MOJO, DEPOSED RULER OF MOJOWORLD, NEARLY TOPPLES OFF HIS THRONE. FORTUNE HAS ONCE AGAIN SIDED WITH THE EXILED MEDIA MOGUL.
WHAT A WONDERFUL ADDITION TO MY SWEEPS-WEEK LINE-UP!
ANOTHER STEP IN MY MAGNIFICENT COME-BACK. THAT UPSTART, LONGSHOT AND HIS HAG, DAZZLER, WILL PAY FOR RELEGATING ME TO THE PITS OF PUBLIC ACCESS TELEVISION.®
DARE I ASK THE PRICE OF THIS DISSENSION?
®X-MEN 9-11
HE PIX'RE LEMMINGS, ORD. MY ONLY DESIRE IS STAND APART FROM THE HERD.
SNAP
I FEEL YOUR PLIGHT. ALL THAT SINGING AND FROLICKING MUST BE MADDENING! I'LL FULFILL YOUR WISH AS PAYMENT FOR THIS VIDEO.
OH, MAJOR DOMO! WE HAVE SOMEONE HERE WHO SEEKS TO JOIN THE RANKS OF THE SPINELESS!
GULP!
OR DOMO SAUNTERS IN WITH HIS FOOTMEN, THE GRIPS. BEFORE PIX'S INDUCTION, HE MUST ENSURE HE DEVIL WILL GET HIS DUE.
...INDEMNIFYING MOJOVISION ON ALL MERCHANDISING AND USES OF YOUR LIKENESS. SMALL TYPE, SMALL TYPE, ETCETERA.
PRINT. SIGN. DATE.
THE PIX BARELY HAS TIME TO REALIZE WHAT HE'S COMMITTED TO BEFORE BEING DRAGGED AWAY.
HIS REPENTANT CRIES FADE UNDER THE WHIRL OF AN OFF-CAMERA BONE-SAW.
POOR, LITTLE BUGGER SHOULD'VE JUST GOTTEN A TATTOO.
SPINEALATOR

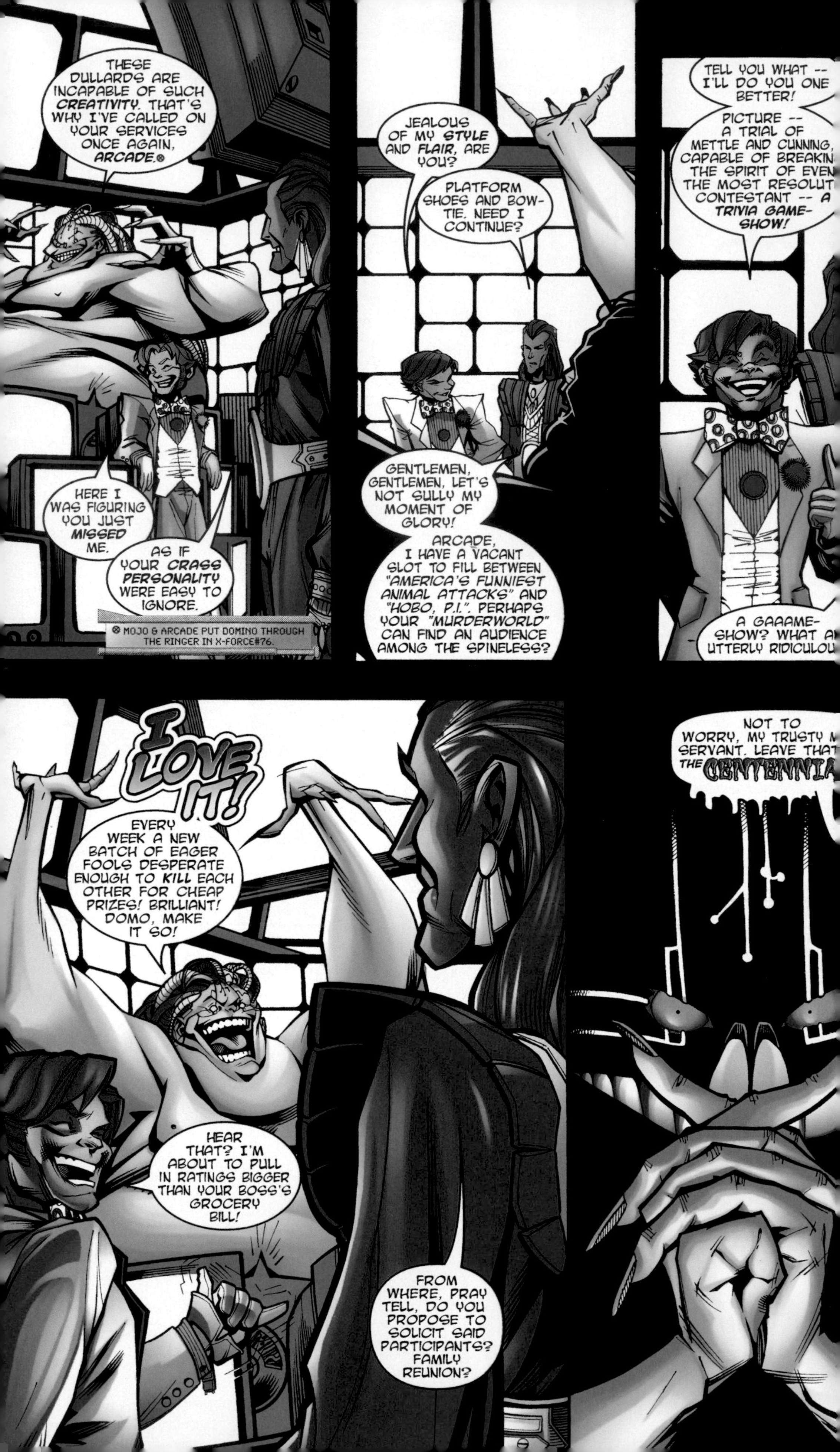

THESE DULLARDS ARE INCAPABLE OF SUCH CREATIVITY. THAT'S WHY I'VE CALLED ON YOUR SERVICES ONCE AGAIN, ARCADE.⊗
HERE I WAS FIGURING YOU JUST MISSED ME.
AS IF YOUR CRASS PERSONALITY WERE EASY TO IGNORE.
⊗ MOJO & ARCADE PUT DOMINO THROUGH THE RINGER IN X-FORCE#76.
JEALOUS OF MY STYLE AND FLAIR, ARE YOU?
PLATFORM SHOES AND BOW-TIE. NEED I CONTINUE?
GENTLEMEN, GENTLEMEN, LET'S NOT SULLY MY MOMENT OF GLORY!
ARCADE, I HAVE A VACANT SLOT TO FILL BETWEEN "AMERICA'S FUNNIEST ANIMAL ATTACKS" AND "HOBO, P.I.". PERHAPS YOUR "MURDERWORLD" CAN FIND AN AUDIENCE AMONG THE SPINELESS?
TELL YOU WHAT -- I'LL DO YOU ONE BETTER!
PICTURE -- A TRIAL OF METTLE AND CUNNING, CAPABLE OF BREAKIN THE SPIRIT OF EVEN THE MOST RESOLUT CONTESTANT -- A TRIVIA GAME-SHOW!
A GAAAME-SHOW? WHAT A UTTERLY RIDICULOU
I LOVE IT!
EVERY WEEK A NEW BATCH OF EAGER FOOLS DESPERATE ENOUGH TO KILL EACH OTHER FOR CHEAP PRIZES! BRILLIANT! DOMO, MAKE IT SO!
HEAR THAT? I'M ABOUT TO PULL IN RATINGS BIGGER THAN YOUR BOSS'S GROCERY BILL!
FROM WHERE, PRAY TELL, DO YOU PROPOSE TO SOLICIT SAID PARTICIPANTS? FAMILY REUNION?
NOT TO WORRY, MY TRUSTY SERVANT. LEAVE THAT THE CENTENNIA

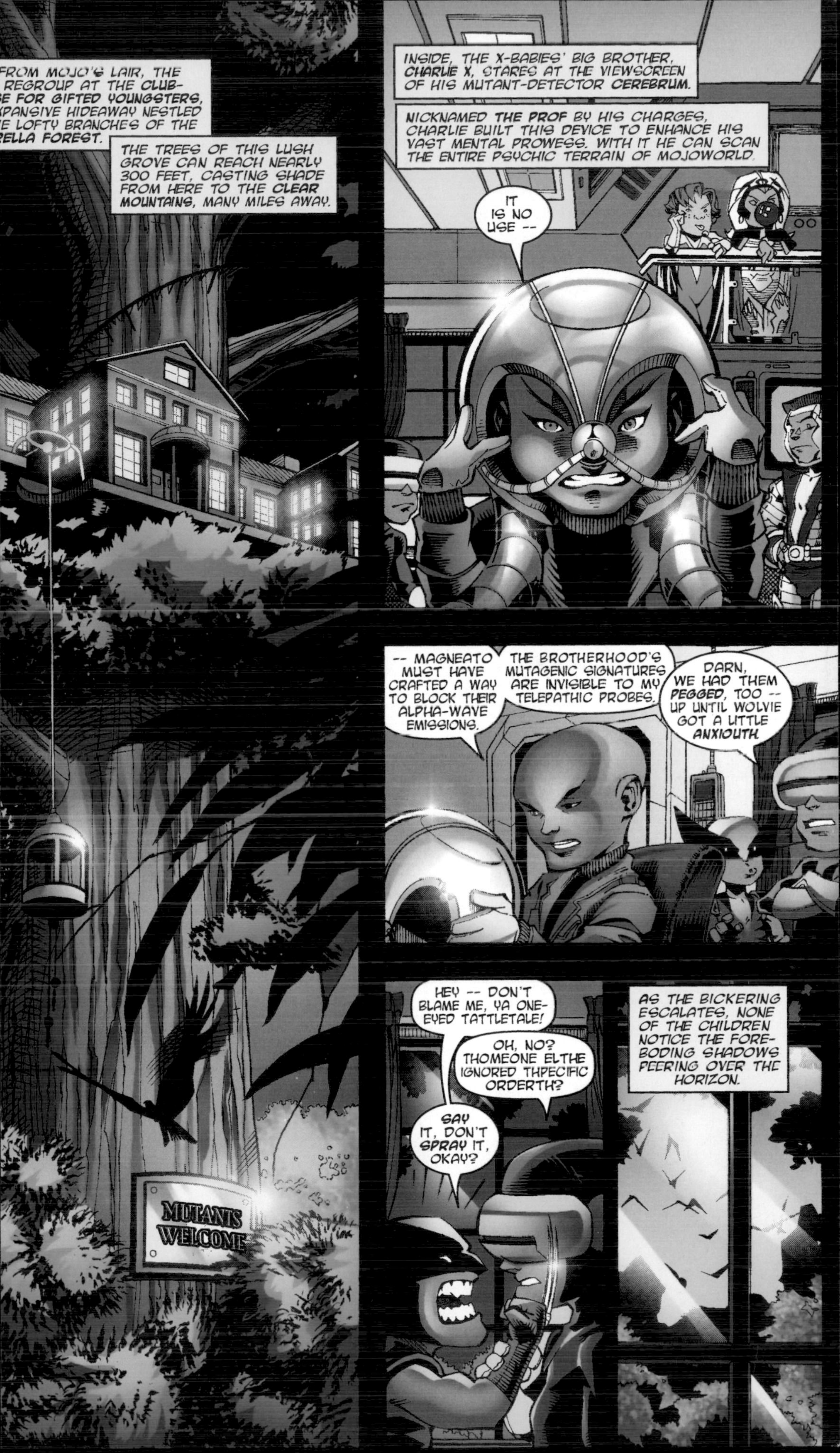
FROM MOJO'S LAIR, THE ... REGROUP AT THE CLUB- ...SE FOR GIFTED YOUNGSTERS, ...XPANSIVE HIDEAWAY NESTLED ...E LOFTY BRANCHES OF THE ...RELLA FOREST.
THE TREES OF THIS LUSH GROVE CAN REACH NEARLY 300 FEET, CASTING SHADE FROM HERE TO THE CLEAR MOUNTAINS, MANY MILES AWAY.
MUTANTS WELCOME
INSIDE, THE X-BABIES' BIG BROTHER, CHARLIE X, STARES AT THE VIEWSCREEN OF HIS MUTANT-DETECTOR CEREBRUM.
NICKNAMED THE PROF BY HIS CHARGES, CHARLIE BUILT THIS DEVICE TO ENHANCE HIS VAST MENTAL PROWESS. WITH IT HE CAN SCAN THE ENTIRE PSYCHIC TERRAIN OF MOJOWORLD.
IT IS NO USE --
-- MAGNEATO MUST HAVE CRAFTED A WAY TO BLOCK THEIR ALPHA-WAVE EMISSIONS.
THE BROTHERHOOD'S MUTAGENIC SIGNATURES ARE INVISIBLE TO MY TELEPATHIC PROBES.
DARN, WE HAD THEM PEGGED, TOO -- UP UNTIL WOLVIE GOT A LITTLE ANXIOUTH.
HEY -- DON'T BLAME ME, YA ONE-EYED TATTLETALE!
OH, NO? THOMEONE ELTHE IGNORED THPECIFIC ORDERTH?
SAY IT, DON'T SPRAY IT, OKAY?
AS THE BICKERING ESCALATES, NONE OF THE CHILDREN NOTICE THE FORE-BODING SHADOWS PEERING OVER THE HORIZON.

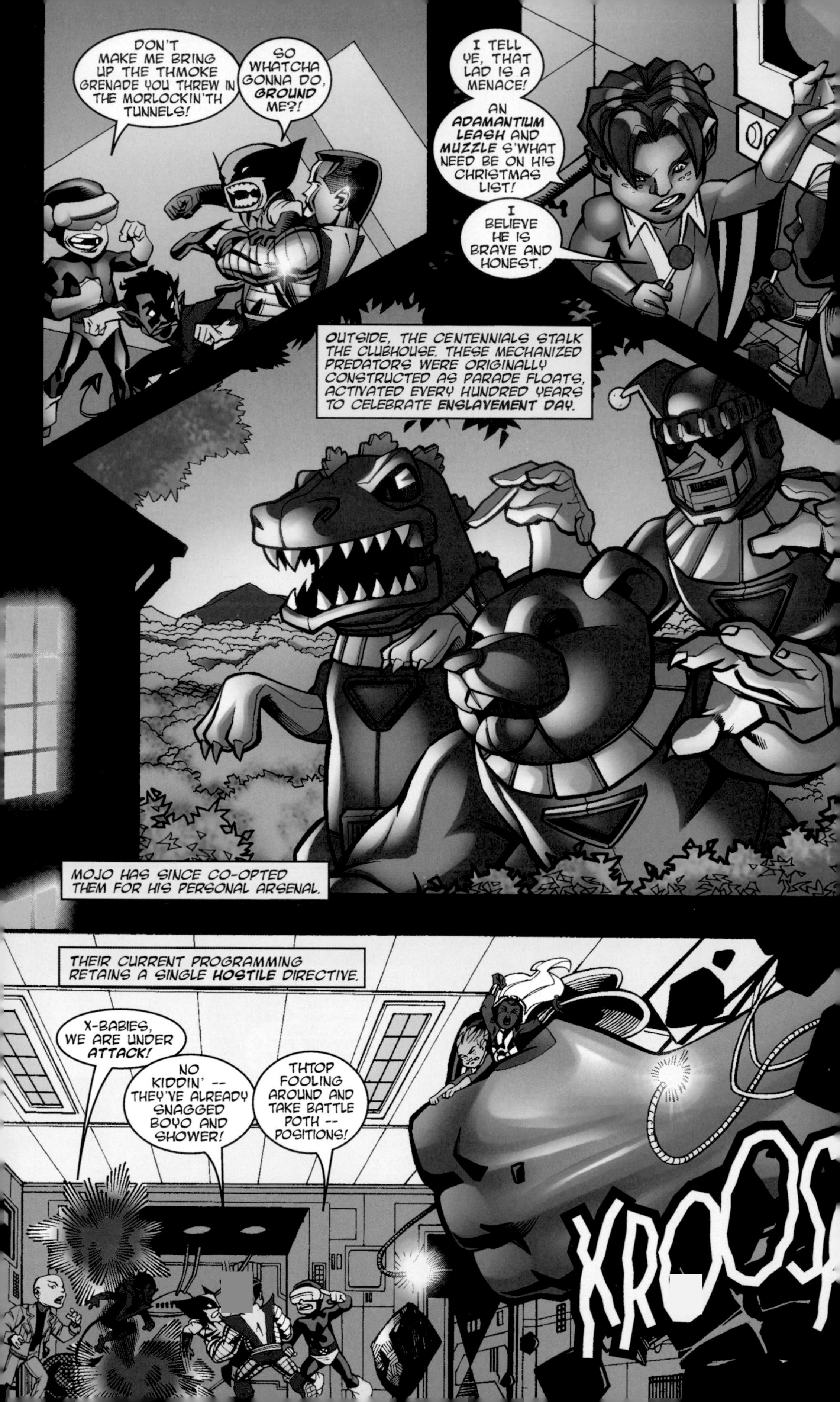
DON'T MAKE ME BRING UP THE THMOKE GRENADE YOU THREW IN THE MORLOCKIN'TH TUNNELS!
SO WHATCHA GONNA DO, GROUND ME?!
I TELL YE, THAT LAD IS A MENACE!
AN ADAMANTIUM LEASH AND MUZZLE S'WHAT NEED BE ON HIS CHRISTMAS LIST!
I BELIEVE HE IS BRAVE AND HONEST.
OUTSIDE, THE CENTENNIALS STALK THE CLUBHOUSE. THESE MECHANIZED PREDATORS WERE ORIGINALLY CONSTRUCTED AS PARADE FLOATS, ACTIVATED EVERY HUNDRED YEARS TO CELEBRATE ENSLAVEMENT DAY.
MOJO HAS SINCE CO-OPTED THEM FOR HIS PERSONAL ARSENAL.
THEIR CURRENT PROGRAMMING RETAINS A SINGLE HOSTILE DIRECTIVE.
X-BABIES, WE ARE UNDER ATTACK!
NO KIDDIN' -- THEY'VE ALREADY SNAGGED BOYO AND SHOWER!
THTOP FOOLING AROUND AND TAKE BATTLE POTH -- POSITIONS!
XROOS

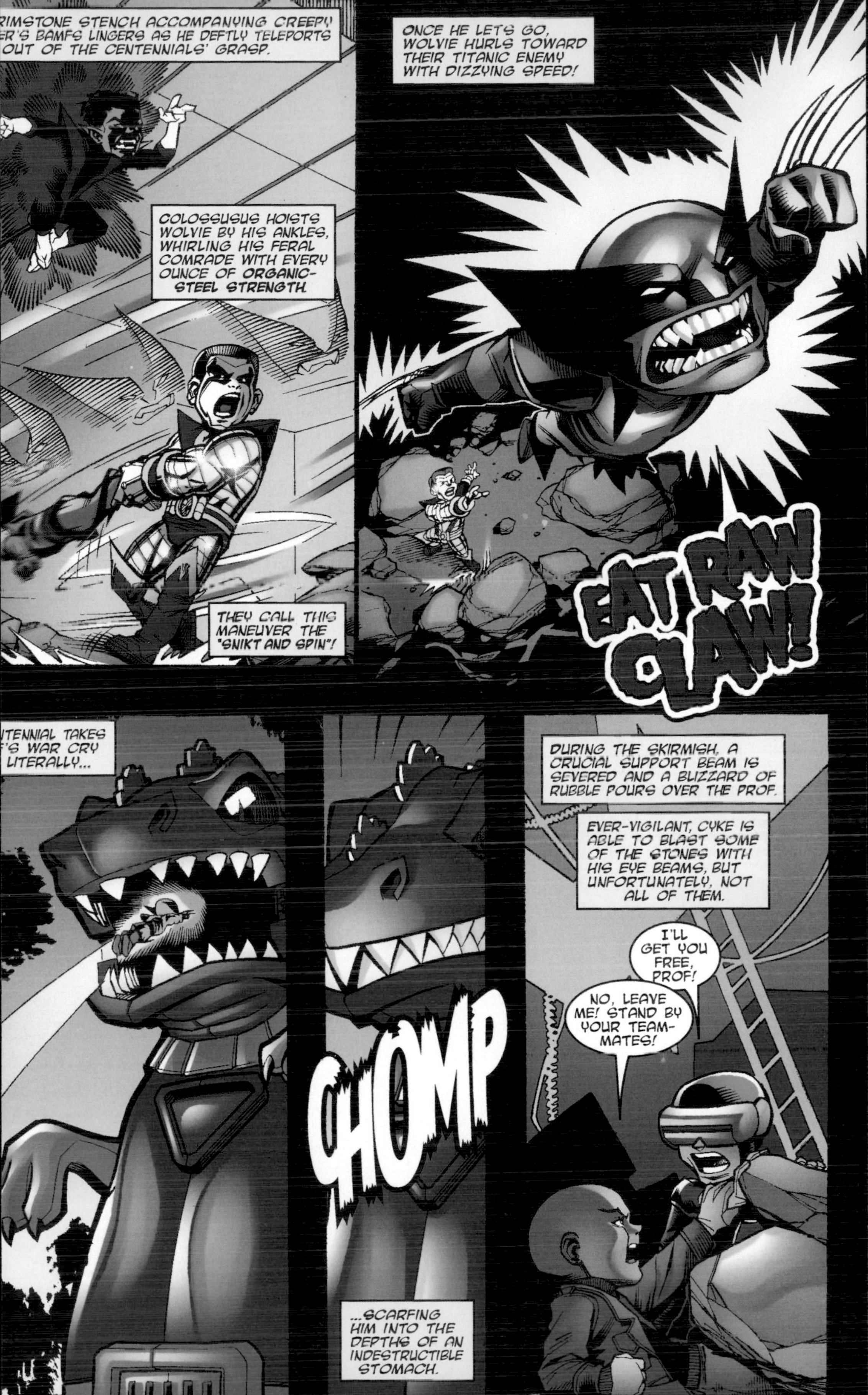
RIMSTONE STENCH ACCOMPANYING CREEPY
ER'S BAMFS LINGERS AS HE DEFTLY TELEPORTS
OUT OF THE CENTENNIALS' GRASP.
COLOSSUSUS HOISTS WOLVIE BY HIS ANKLES, WHIRLING HIS FERAL COMRADE WITH EVERY OUNCE OF ORGANIC-STEEL STRENGTH.
THEY CALL THIS MANEUVER THE "SNIKT AND SPIN"!
ONCE HE LETS GO, WOLVIE HURLS TOWARD THEIR TITANIC ENEMY WITH DIZZYING SPEED!
EAT RAW CLAW!
NTENNIAL TAKES
'S WAR CRY
LITERALLY...
CHOMP
...SCARFING HIM INTO THE DEPTHS OF AN INDESTRUCTIBLE STOMACH.
DURING THE SKIRMISH, A CRUCIAL SUPPORT BEAM IS SEVERED AND A BLIZZARD OF RUBBLE POURS OVER THE PROF.
EVER-VIGILANT, CYKE IS ABLE TO BLAST SOME OF THE STONES WITH HIS EYE BEAMS, BUT UNFORTUNATELY, NOT ALL OF THEM.
I'LL GET YOU FREE, PROF!
NO, LEAVE ME! STAND BY YOUR TEAM-MATES!

COLOSSUSUS STRUGGLES TO BREAK LOOSE FROM CONSTRICTING FINGER-CUFFS, UNTIL HIS MIGHT IS EXHAUSTED.

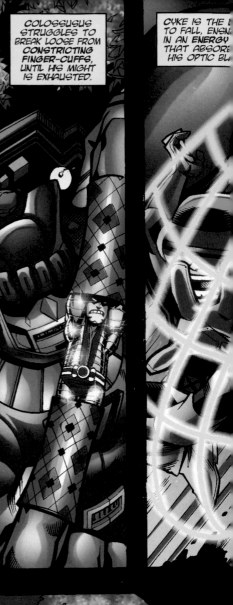

CYKE IS THE [...] TO FALL, ENGN[...] IN AN ENERGY [...] THAT ABSORE[...] HIS OPTIC BL[...]

DESPITE THE X-BABIES' VALIANT RESISTANCE, THE CENTENNIALS STILL PREVAIL.

CREEPY CRAWLER IS SPRAYED WITH A DEBILITATING TOXIN AND EASILY CAPTURED.

A BIO-FEEDBACK FIELD PREVENTS BOYO FROM USING HIS SONIC SCREAM.

NOR CAN SHOWER EMPLOY HER WEATHER-CONTROLLING TALENTS.

ONCE THEIR BOUNTY IS SECURED, THE CENTENNIALS BLAST OFF AND QUICKLY SHRINK INTO THE HORIZON.

PINNED UNDER DEBRIS, LEGS CRUSHED, THE PROF REACHES HOPELESSLY FOR HIS STUDENTS.

CYKE! SHOWER! WOLVIE!

HIS DISTRESSED TELEPATHIC CALLS BUILD INTO A POUNDING MIGRAINE, BUT THE SILENT SKIES YIELD NO RESPONSE.

THE X-BABIES A[...] GONE, AND HE [...] LEFT ALL ALON[...]

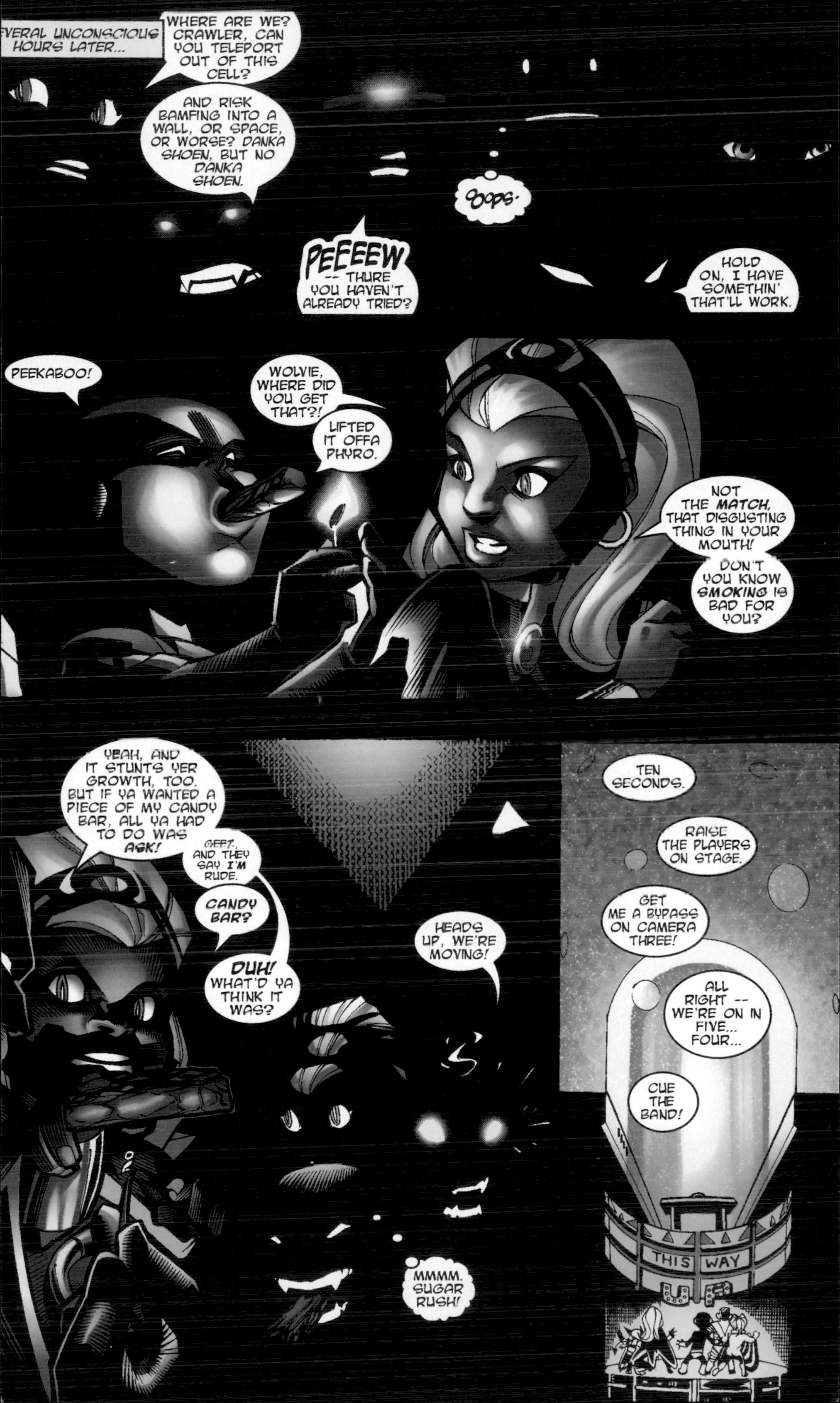

EVERAL UNCONSCIOUS HOURS LATER...
WHERE ARE WE? CRAWLER, CAN YOU TELEPORT OUT OF THIS CELL?
AND RISK BAMFING INTO A WALL, OR SPACE, OR WORSE? DANKA SHOEN, BUT NO DANKA SHOEN.
OOPS.
PEEEEW -- THURE YOU HAVEN'T ALREADY TRIED?
HOLD ON, I HAVE SOMETHIN' THAT'LL WORK.
PEEKABOO!
WOLVIE, WHERE DID YOU GET THAT?!
LIFTED IT OFFA PHYRO.
NOT THE MATCH, THAT DISGUSTING THING IN YOUR MOUTH!
DON'T YOU KNOW SMOKING IS BAD FOR YOU?
YEAH, AND IT STUNTS YER GROWTH, TOO. BUT IF YA WANTED A PIECE OF MY CANDY BAR, ALL YA HAD TO DO WAS ASK!
GEEZ, AND THEY SAY I'M RUDE.
CANDY BAR?
DUH! WHAT'D YA THINK IT WAS?
HEADS UP, WE'RE MOVING!
MMMM. SUGAR RUSH!
TEN SECONDS.
RAISE THE PLAYERS ON STAGE.
GET ME A BYPASS ON CAMERA THREE!
ALL RIGHT -- WE'RE ON IN FIVE... FOUR...
CUE THE BAND!
THIS WAY

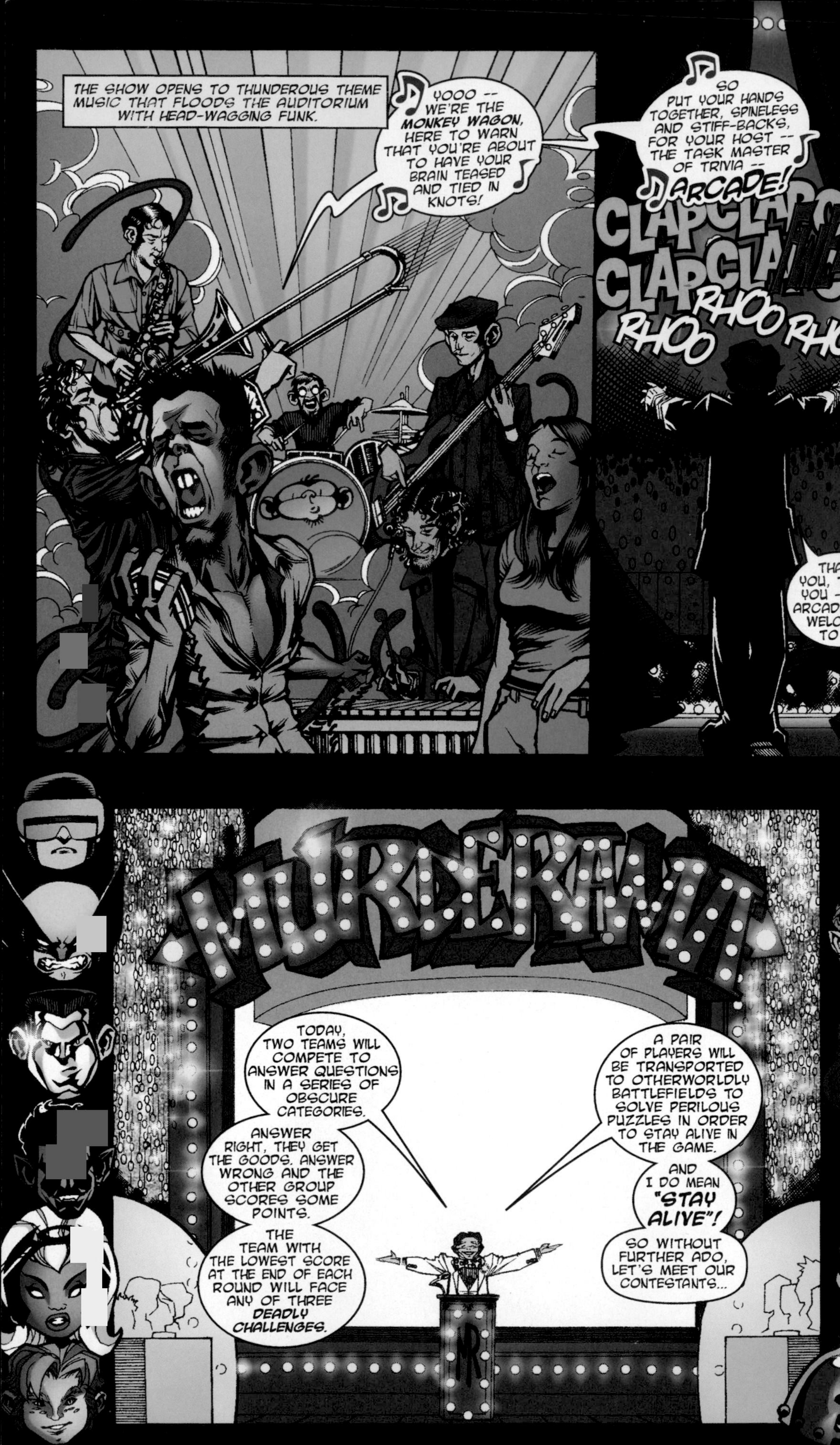
THE SHOW OPENS TO THUNDEROUS THEME MUSIC THAT FLOODS THE AUDITORIUM WITH HEAD-WAGGING FUNK.
YOOO -- WE'RE THE MONKEY WAGON, HERE TO WARN THAT YOU'RE ABOUT TO HAVE YOUR BRAIN TEASED AND TIED IN KNOTS!
SO PUT YOUR HANDS TOGETHER, SPINELESS AND STIFF-BACKS, FOR YOUR HOST -- THE TASK MASTER OF TRIVIA --
ARCADE!
CLAPCLAP
CLAPCLAP
RHOO RHOO
RHOO
MURDERWORLD
TODAY, TWO TEAMS WILL COMPETE TO ANSWER QUESTIONS IN A SERIES OF OBSCURE CATEGORIES.
ANSWER RIGHT, THEY GET THE GOODS. ANSWER WRONG AND THE OTHER GROUP SCORES SOME POINTS.
THE TEAM WITH THE LOWEST SCORE AT THE END OF EACH ROUND WILL FACE ANY OF THREE DEADLY CHALLENGES.
A PAIR OF PLAYERS WILL BE TRANSPORTED TO OTHERWORLDLY BATTLEFIELDS TO SOLVE PERILOUS PUZZLES IN ORDER TO STAY ALIVE IN THE GAME.
AND I DO MEAN "STAY ALIVE"!
SO WITHOUT FURTHER ADO, LET'S MEET OUR CONTESTANTS...

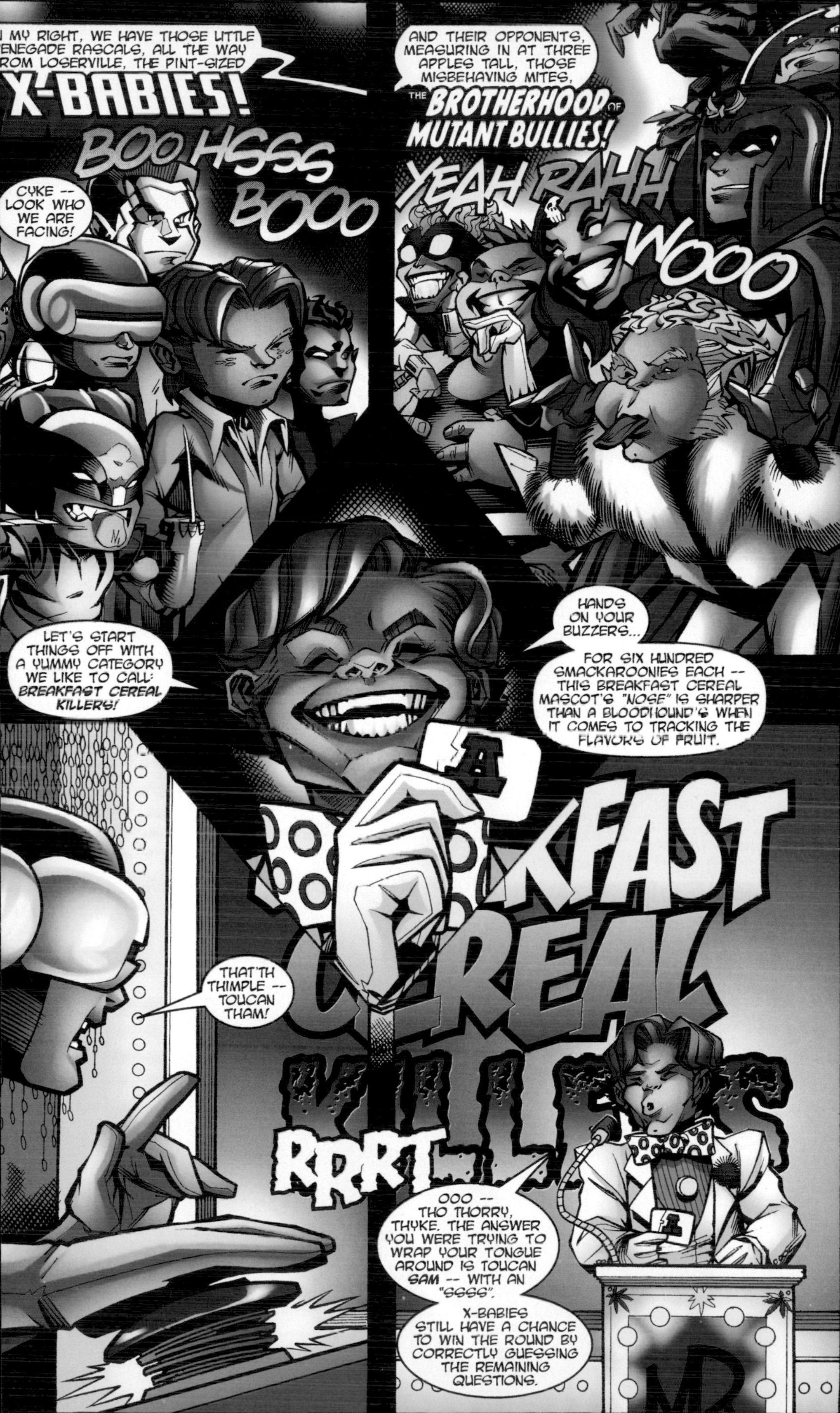
N MY RIGHT, WE HAVE THOSE LITTLE RENEGADE RASCALS, ALL THE WAY FROM LOSERVILLE, THE PINT-SIZED
X-BABIES!
BOO HSSS BOOO
CYKE -- LOOK WHO WE ARE FACING!
AND THEIR OPPONENTS, MEASURING IN AT THREE APPLES TALL, THOSE MISBEHAVING MITES,
THE BROTHERHOOD OF MUTANT BULLIES!
YEAH RAHH WOOO
LET'S START THINGS OFF WITH A YUMMY CATEGORY WE LIKE TO CALL: BREAKFAST CEREAL KILLERS!
HANDS ON YOUR BUZZERS...
FOR SIX HUNDRED SMACKAROONIES EACH -- THIS BREAKFAST CEREAL MASCOT'S "NOSE" IS SHARPER THAN A BLOODHOUND'S WHEN IT COMES TO TRACKING THE FLAVORS OF FRUIT.
THAT'TH THIMPLE -- TOUCAN THAM!
RRRT
OOO -- THO THORRY, THYKE. THE ANSWER YOU WERE TRYING TO WRAP YOUR TONGUE AROUND IS TOUCAN SAM -- WITH AN "SSSS".
X-BABIES STILL HAVE A CHANCE TO WIN THE ROUND BY CORRECTLY GUESSING THE REMAINING QUESTIONS.

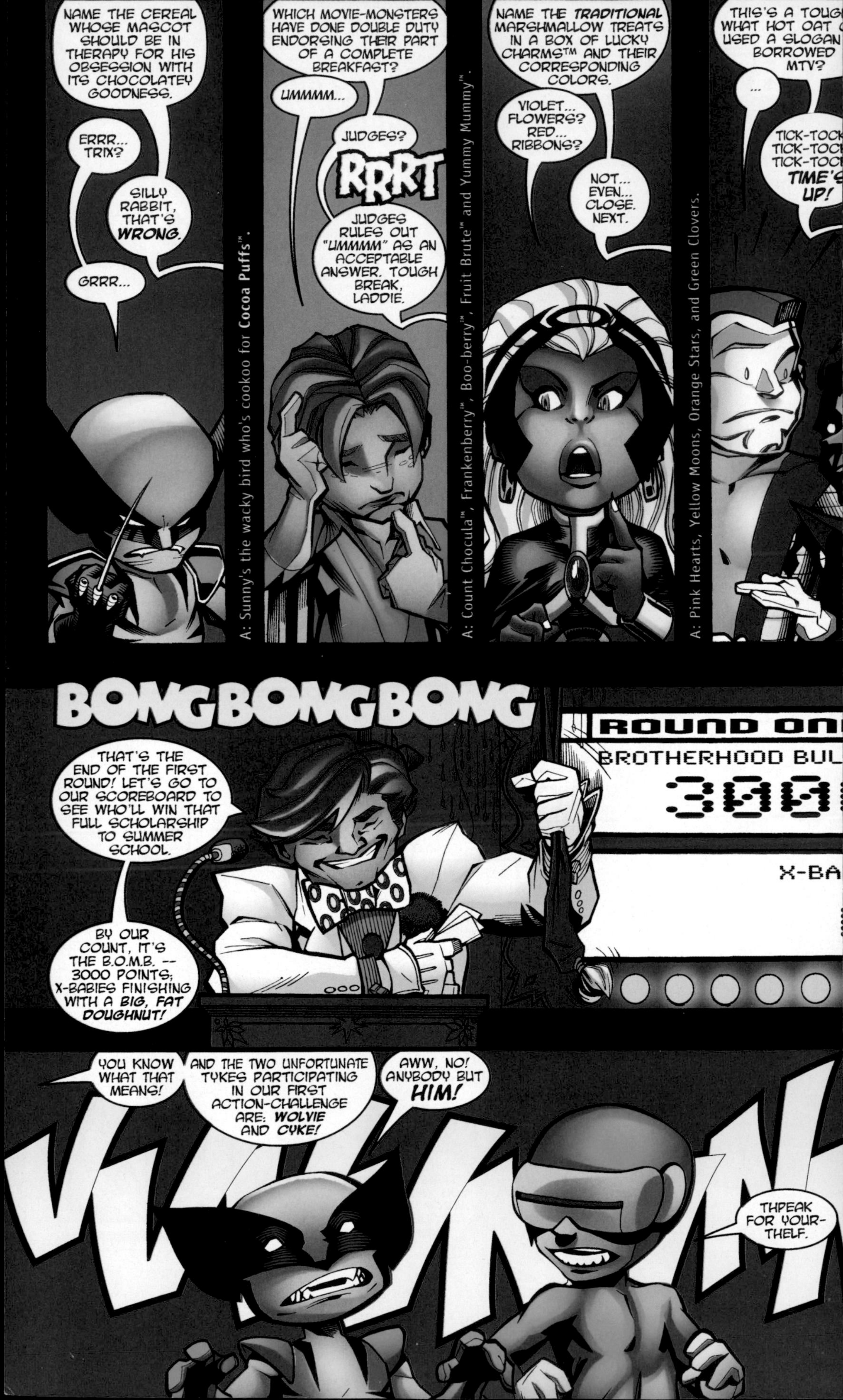

NAME THE CEREAL WHOSE MASCOT SHOULD BE IN THERAPY FOR HIS OBSESSION WITH ITS CHOCOLATEY GOODNESS.
ERRR... TRIX?
SILLY RABBIT, THAT'S WRONG.
GRRR...
A: Sunny's the wacky bird who's cookoo for Cocoa Puffs™.
WHICH MOVIE-MONSTERS HAVE DONE DOUBLE DUTY ENDORSING THEIR PART OF A COMPLETE BREAKFAST?
UMMMM...
JUDGES?
RRRT
JUDGES RULES OUT "UMMMM" AS AN ACCEPTABLE ANSWER. TOUGH BREAK, LADDIE.
A: Count Chocula™, Frankenberry™, Boo-berry™, Fruit Brute™ and Yummy Mummy™.
NAME THE TRADITIONAL MARSHMALLOW TREATS IN A BOX OF LUCKY CHARMS™ AND THEIR CORRESPONDING COLORS.
VIOLET... FLOWERS? RED... RIBBONS?
NOT... EVEN... CLOSE. NEXT.
A: Pink Hearts, Yellow Moons, Orange Stars, and Green Clovers.
THIS'S A TOUG WHAT HOT OAT USED A SLOGAN BORROWED MTV?
...
TICK-TOCK TICK-TOCK TICK-TOCK TIME'S UP!
BONGBONGBONG
ROUND ON
BROTHERHOOD BUL
X-BA
THAT'S THE END OF THE FIRST ROUND! LET'S GO TO OUR SCOREBOARD TO SEE WHO'LL WIN THAT FULL SCHOLARSHIP TO SUMMER SCHOOL.
BY OUR COUNT, IT'S THE B.O.M.B. -- 3000 POINTS; X-BABIES FINISHING WITH A BIG, FAT DOUGHNUT!
YOU KNOW WHAT THAT MEANS!
AND THE TWO UNFORTUNATE TYKES PARTICIPATING IN OUR FIRST ACTION-CHALLENGE ARE: WOLVIE AND CYKE!
AWW, NO! ANYBODY BUT HIM!
THPEAK FOR YOUR-THELF.

THEIR OBJECTIVE, TO SCALE THE MOUNTAIN FORTRESS OF INHOSPITABLE BARBARIANS. FROM ITS DANK BOWELS TO ITS HIGHEST EXIT BEFORE THE COMMERCIAL BREAK.

"FIVE THOUSAND POINTS AND A DECIDED LEAD FOR THE X-BABIES -- IF THEY SURVIVE!"

YIKE TH!

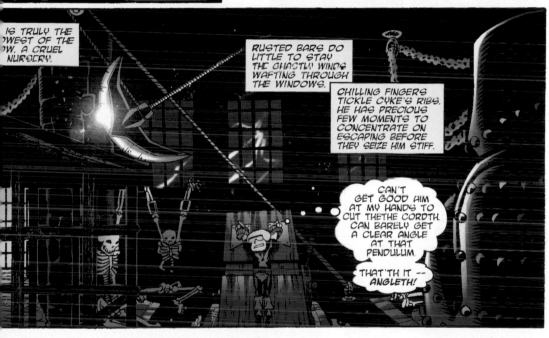

IS TRULY THE OWEST OF THE OW. A CRUEL NURSERY!

RUSTED BARS DO LITTLE TO STAY THE GHASTLY WINDS WAFTING THROUGH THE WINDOWS.

CHILLING FINGERS TICKLE CYKE'S RIBS. HE HAS PRECIOUS FEW MOMENTS TO CONCENTRATE ON ESCAPING BEFORE THEY SEIZE HIM STIFF.

CAN'T GET GOOD AIM AT MY HANDS TO CUT THETHE CORDTH. CAN BARELY GET A CLEAR ANGLE AT THAT PENDULUM.

THAT'TH IT -- ANGLETH!

GENT STUDYING FOR OMETRY CLASS PAYS CYKE BOUNCES A M OFF THE PLATE ON RISONER'S SKULL --

-- DEFLECTING ACROSS THE UNDERBELLY OF A HANGING CAGE, THEN A CRACKED MIRROR --

WHOOSH!

-- SEVERING THE ROPE TO RELEASE THE SWINGING BLADE!

AGH -- MADE IT! THAT WATH WAY TOO CLOSE!

REMIND ME NEVER TO COMPLAIN ABOUT MATH HOME-WORK AGAIN.

GWT MHH OOT RVV HURR! UM HNN DRR UHRN MUHDWN!

WOLVIE, THAT YOU? WHERE ARE YOU?!

UM HNN DRR UHRN NUHDWN!

I'LL FOLLOW THE THOUND OF YOUR VOICE! KEEP TALKING!

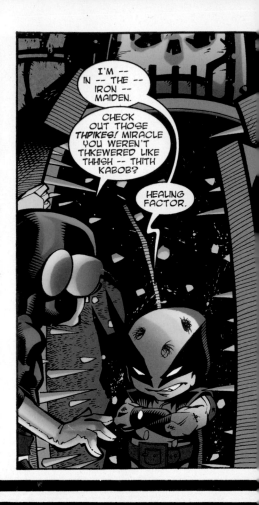

I'M -- IN -- THE -- IRON -- MAIDEN.

CHECK OUT THOSE THPIKES! MIRACLE YOU WEREN'T THKEWERED LIKE THHISH -- THITH KABOB?

HEALING FACTOR.

THE BOYS SCURRY ABOUT THE CATACOMBS, SEARCHING FOR A WAY TO THE SURFACE. THEY'VE MAPPED EVERY DEAD-END AND CIRCULAR CORRIDOR IN THE STRONGHOLD.

RIGHT HERE! FEEL THAT DRAFT UNDERNEATH THITH DOOR. IT MIGHT LEAD UTH --

--NO-WHERE! AND TO PLENTY OF IT!

THEY COME OUT OF A SHAFT. PITCH BLACK FROM TOP TO BOTTOM.

A CARELESS SLIP AND THEY'LL PLUNGE INTO A SEA OF ENDLESS OBLIVION.

NEVERTHELESS, THE CL[U] CONTINUES TO WIND D[O] IN THE FACE OF THIS INSURMOUNTABLE HURDL[E]

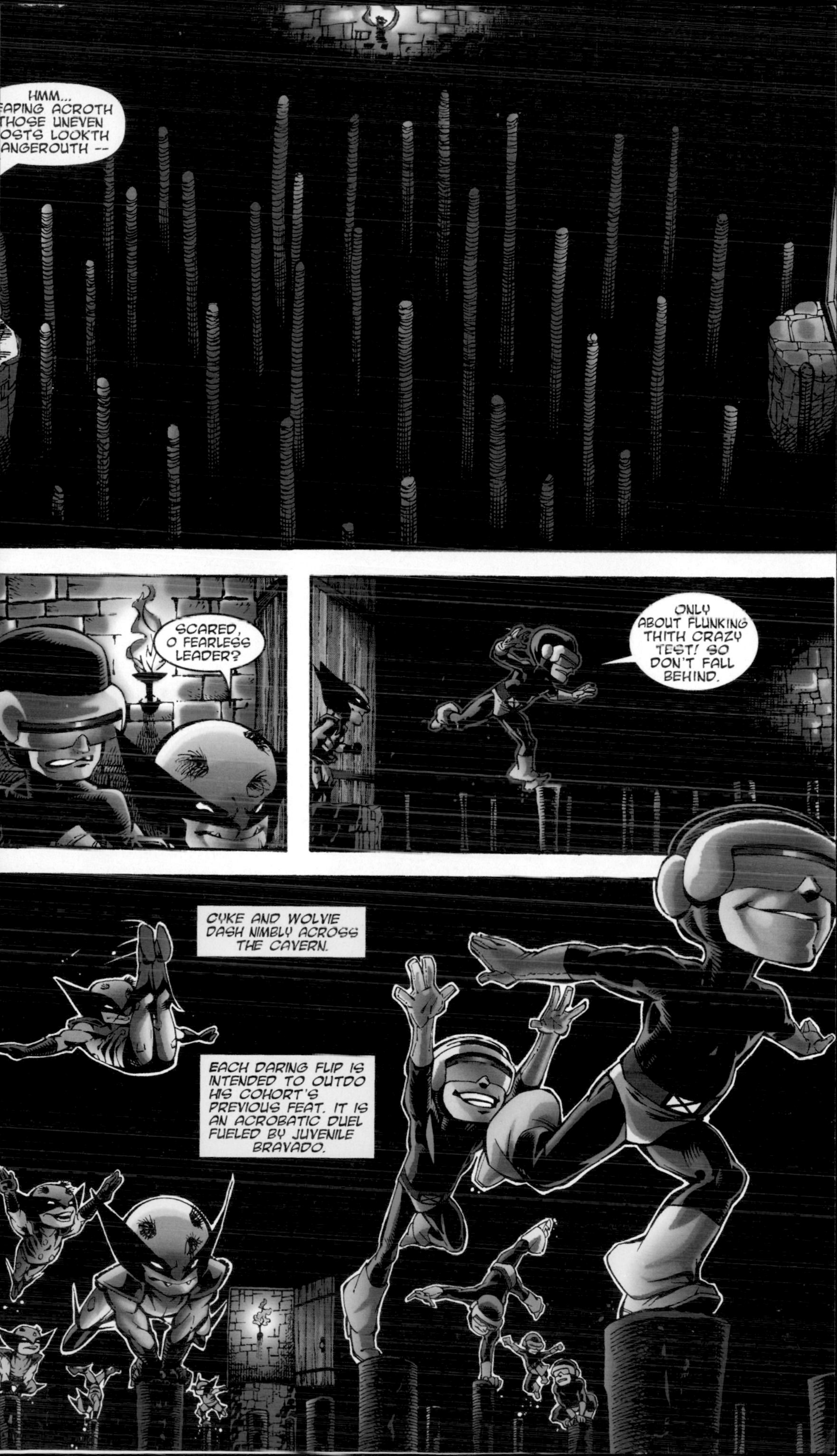
HMM... EAPING ACROTH THOSE UNEVEN OSTS LOOKTH ANGEROUTH --
SCARED, O FEARLESS LEADER?
ONLY ABOUT FLUNKING THITH CRAZY TEST! SO DON'T FALL BEHIND.
CYKE AND WOLVIE DASH NIMBLY ACROSS THE CAVERN.
EACH DARING FLIP IS INTENDED TO OUTDO HIS COHORT'S PREVIOUS FEAT. IT IS AN ACROBATIC DUEL FUELED BY JUVENILE BRAVADO.

YET, A MOMENT OF INDULGENT OVERCONFIDENCE --
LAST MUTANT TO THE OTHER THIDE WEARS UNSTABLE-MOLECULE UNDERWE --
-- INVITES A DIRE MISCALCULATION.
--EEUGH!
CYKE! SIT TIGHT, I'M COMIN'!
MNNFF! CAN'T EXTEND ANY MORE WITHOUT FALLING!
LEDGE WON'T LAST MUCH LONGER'N I WILL!
GRAB MY HAND! C'MON STRETCH!
JUMP IF YOU HAFTA!
HOW 'BOUT NOW!?
SNIKT
A LITTLE -- NNGH -- FURTHER --
GOTCHA!
HANG ON! I WON'T LET YA DROP!
KRMB

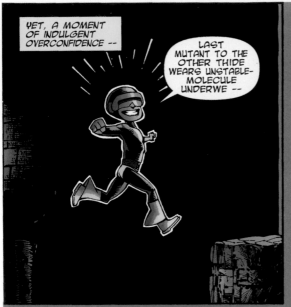

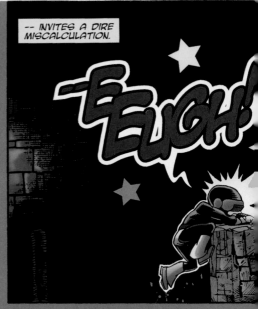

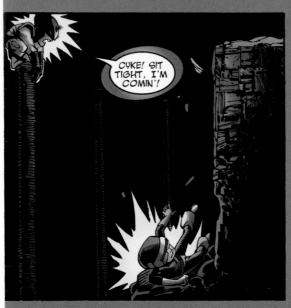

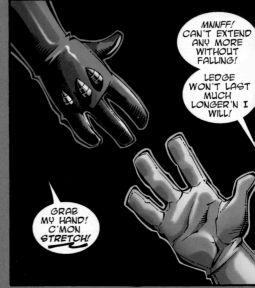

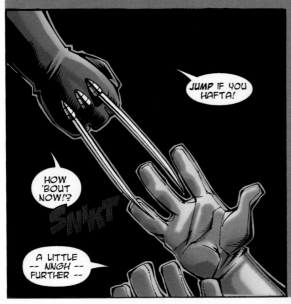

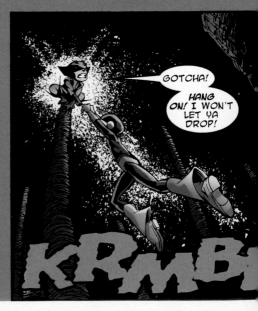

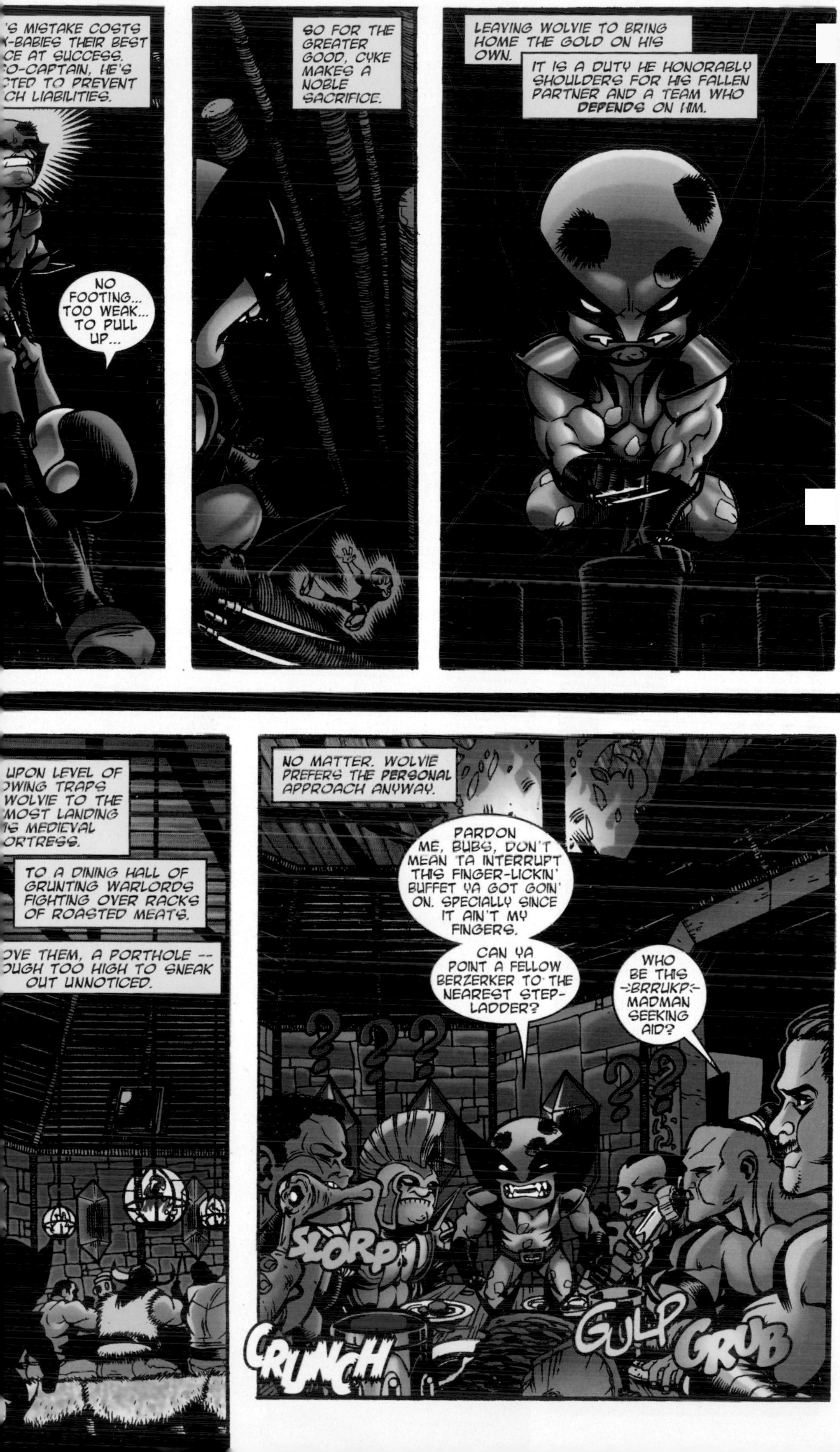
'S MISTAKE COSTS
X-BABIES THEIR BEST
CE AT SUCCESS.
CO-CAPTAIN, HE'S
CTED TO PREVENT
CH LIABILITIES.
NO FOOTING... TOO WEAK... TO PULL UP...
SO FOR THE GREATER GOOD, CYKE MAKES A NOBLE SACRIFICE.
LEAVING WOLVIE TO BRING HOME THE GOLD ON HIS OWN.
IT IS A DUTY HE HONORABLY SHOULDERS FOR HIS FALLEN PARTNER AND A TEAM WHO DEPENDS ON HIM.
UPON LEVEL OF
OWING TRAPS
WOLVIE TO THE
MOST LANDING
IS MEDIEVAL
ORTRESS.
TO A DINING HALL OF GRUNTING WARLORDS FIGHTING OVER RACKS OF ROASTED MEATS.
OVE THEM, A PORTHOLE --
OUGH TOO HIGH TO SNEAK
OUT UNNOTICED.
NO MATTER. WOLVIE PREFERS THE PERSONAL APPROACH ANYWAY.
PARDON ME, BUBS, DON'T MEAN 'TA INTERRUPT THIS FINGER-LICKIN' BUFFET YA GOT GOIN' ON. SPECIALLY SINCE IT AIN'T MY FINGERS.
CAN YA POINT A FELLOW BERZERKER TO THE NEAREST STEP-LADDER?
WHO BE THIS -BRRUKP- MADMAN SEEKING AID?
SLORP
CRUNCH
GULP
GRUB

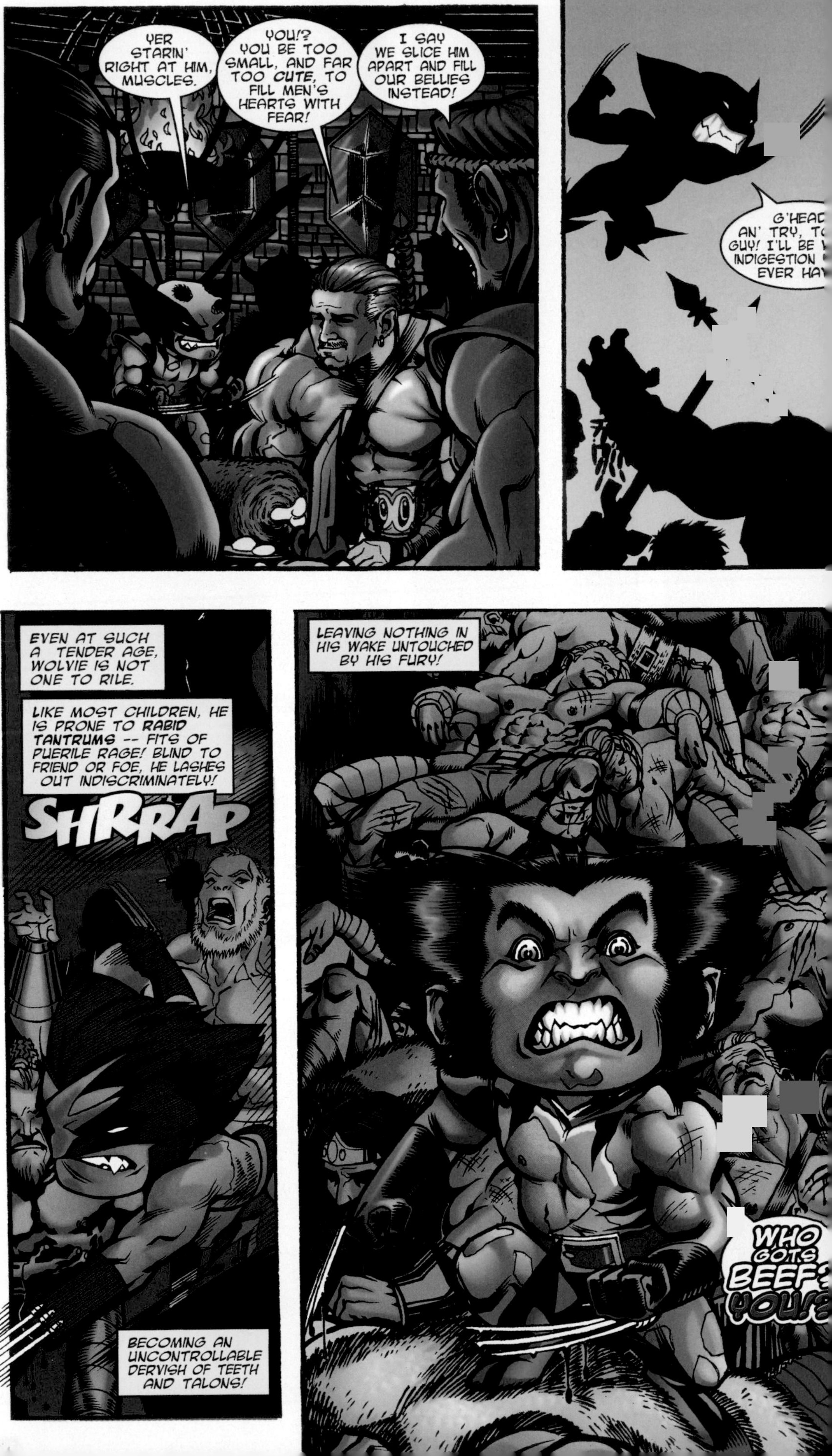

YER STARIN' RIGHT AT HIM, MUSCLES.
YOU!? YOU BE TOO SMALL, AND FAR TOO CUTE, TO FILL MEN'S HEARTS WITH FEAR!
I SAY WE SLICE HIM APART AND FILL OUR BELLIES INSTEAD!
G'HEAD AN' TRY, TO GUY! I'LL BE INDIGESTION EVER HA
EVEN AT SUCH A TENDER AGE, WOLVIE IS NOT ONE TO RILE.
LIKE MOST CHILDREN, HE IS PRONE TO RABID TANTRUMS -- FITS OF PUERILE RAGE! BLIND TO FRIEND OR FOE, HE LASHES OUT INDISCRIMINATELY!
SHRRAP
BECOMING AN UNCONTROLLABLE DERVISH OF TEETH AND TALONS!
LEAVING NOTHING IN HIS WAKE UNTOUCHED BY HIS FURY!
WHO GOTS BEEF? YOU!?

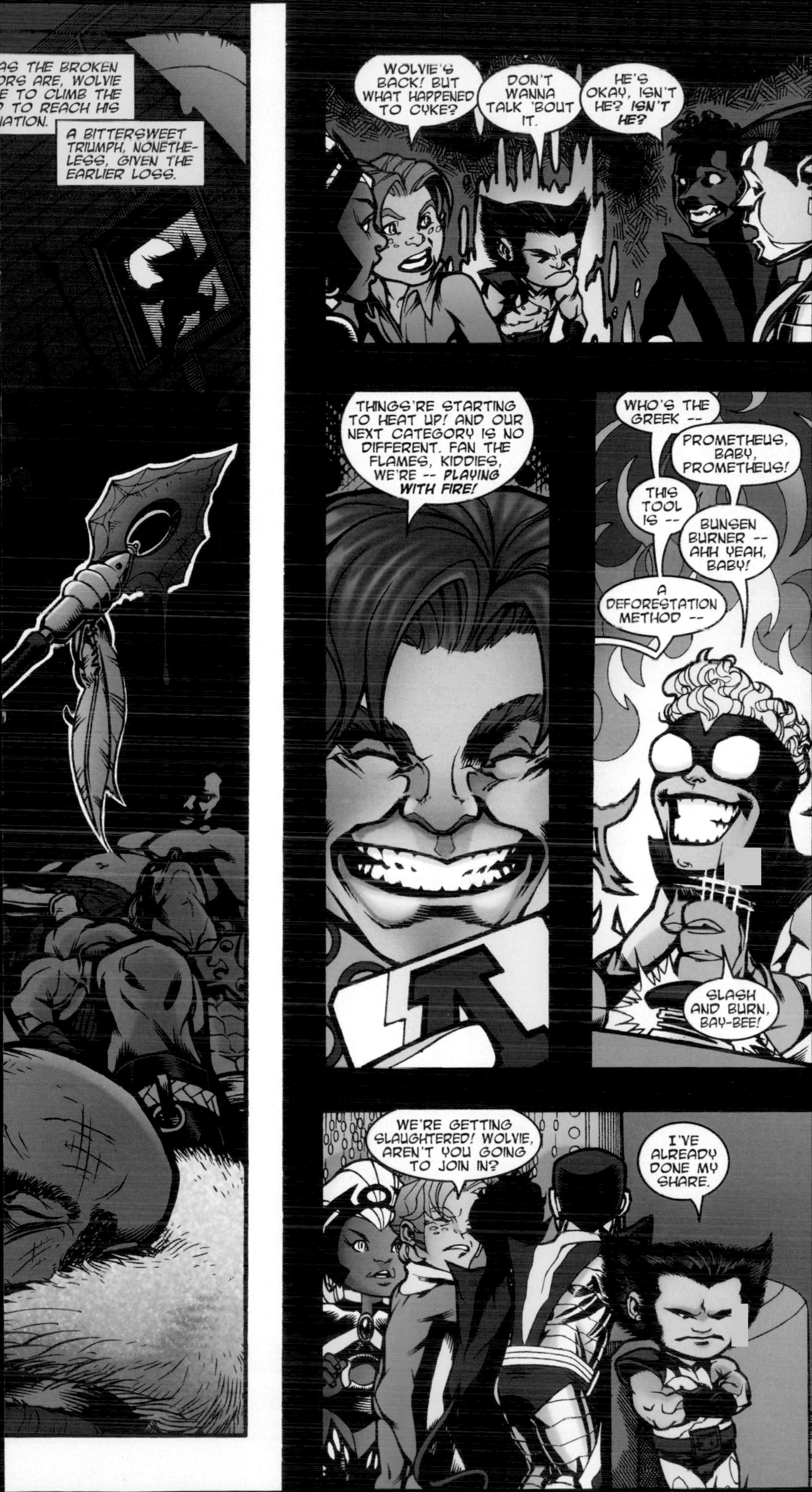

...AS THE BROKEN ...ORS ARE, WOLVIE ...E TO CLIMB THE ...D TO REACH HIS ...NATION.
A BITTERSWEET TRIUMPH, NONETHELESS, GIVEN THE EARLIER LOSS.
WOLVIE'S BACK! BUT WHAT HAPPENED TO CYKE?
DON'T WANNA TALK 'BOUT IT.
HE'S OKAY, ISN'T HE? ISN'T HE?
THINGS'RE STARTING TO HEAT UP! AND OUR NEXT CATEGORY IS NO DIFFERENT. FAN THE FLAMES, KIDDIES, WE'RE -- PLAYING WITH FIRE!
WHO'S THE GREEK --
PROMETHEUS, BABY, PROMETHEUS!
THIS TOOL IS --
BUNSEN BURNER -- AHH YEAH, BABY!
A DEFORESTATION METHOD --
SLASH AND BURN, BAY-BEE!
WE'RE GETTING SLAUGHTERED! WOLVIE, AREN'T YOU GOING TO JOIN IN?
I'VE ALREADY DONE MY SHARE.

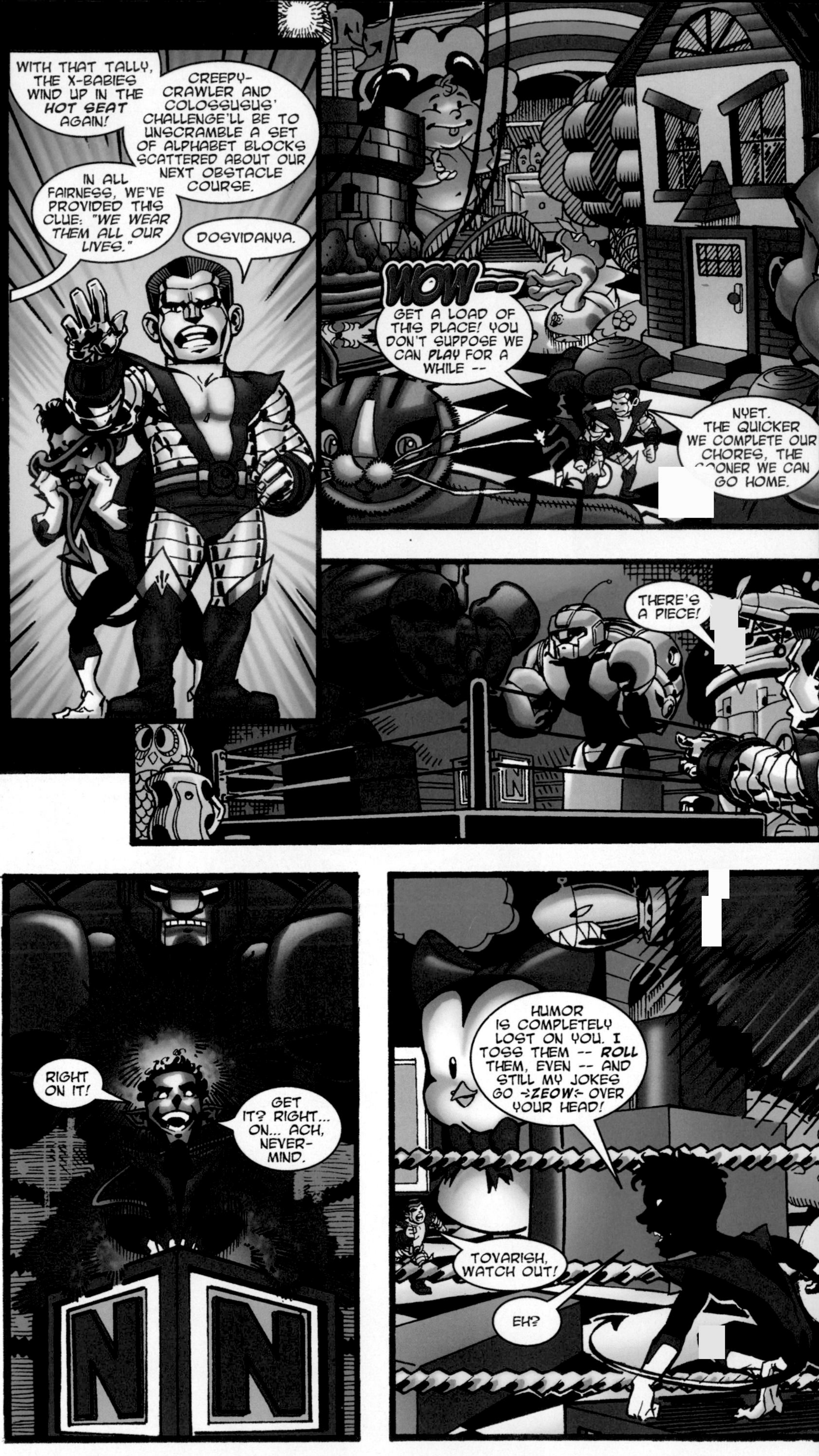

WITH THAT TALLY, THE X-BABIES WIND UP IN THE HOT SEAT AGAIN!
CREEPY-CRAWLER AND COLOSSUSUS' CHALLENGE'LL BE TO UNSCRAMBLE A SET OF ALPHABET BLOCKS SCATTERED ABOUT OUR NEXT OBSTACLE COURSE.
IN ALL FAIRNESS, WE'VE PROVIDED THIS CLUE: "WE WEAR THEM ALL OUR LIVES."
DOSVIDANYA.
WOW--
GET A LOAD OF THIS PLACE! YOU DON'T SUPPOSE WE CAN PLAY FOR A WHILE --
NYET. THE QUICKER WE COMPLETE OUR CHORES, THE SOONER WE CAN GO HOME.
THERE'S A PIECE!
RIGHT ON IT!
GET IT? RIGHT... ON... ACH, NEVER-MIND.
HUMOR IS COMPLETELY LOST ON YOU. I TOSS THEM -- ROLL THEM, EVEN -- AND STILL MY JOKES GO ZEOW OVER YOUR HEAD!
TOVARISH, WATCH OUT!
EH?

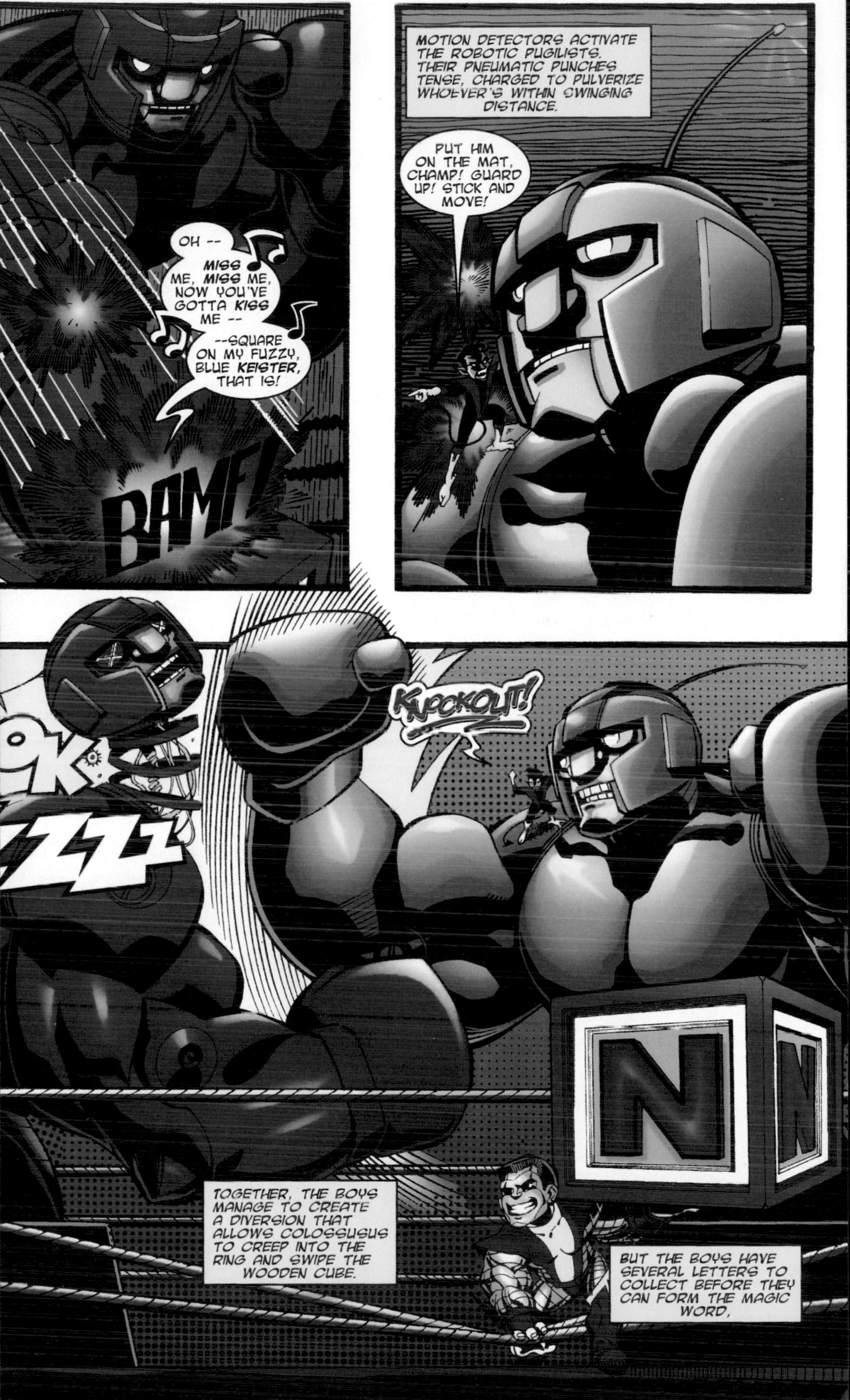
OH --
MISS ME, MISS ME, NOW YOU'VE GOTTA KISS ME --
--SQUARE ON MY FUZZY, BLUE KEISTER, THAT IS!
BAMF!
MOTION DETECTORS ACTIVATE THE ROBOTIC PUGILISTS. THEIR PNEUMATIC PUNCHES TENSE, CHARGED TO PULVERIZE WHOEVER'S WITHIN SWINGING DISTANCE.
PUT HIM ON THE MAT, CHAMP! GUARD UP! STICK AND MOVE!
KNOCKOUT!
ZZZZ
N
TOGETHER, THE BOYS MANAGE TO CREATE A DIVERSION THAT ALLOWS COLOSSUSUS TO CREEP INTO THE RING AND SWIPE THE WOODEN CUBE.
BUT THE BOYS HAVE SEVERAL LETTERS TO COLLECT BEFORE THEY CAN FORM THE MAGIC WORD,

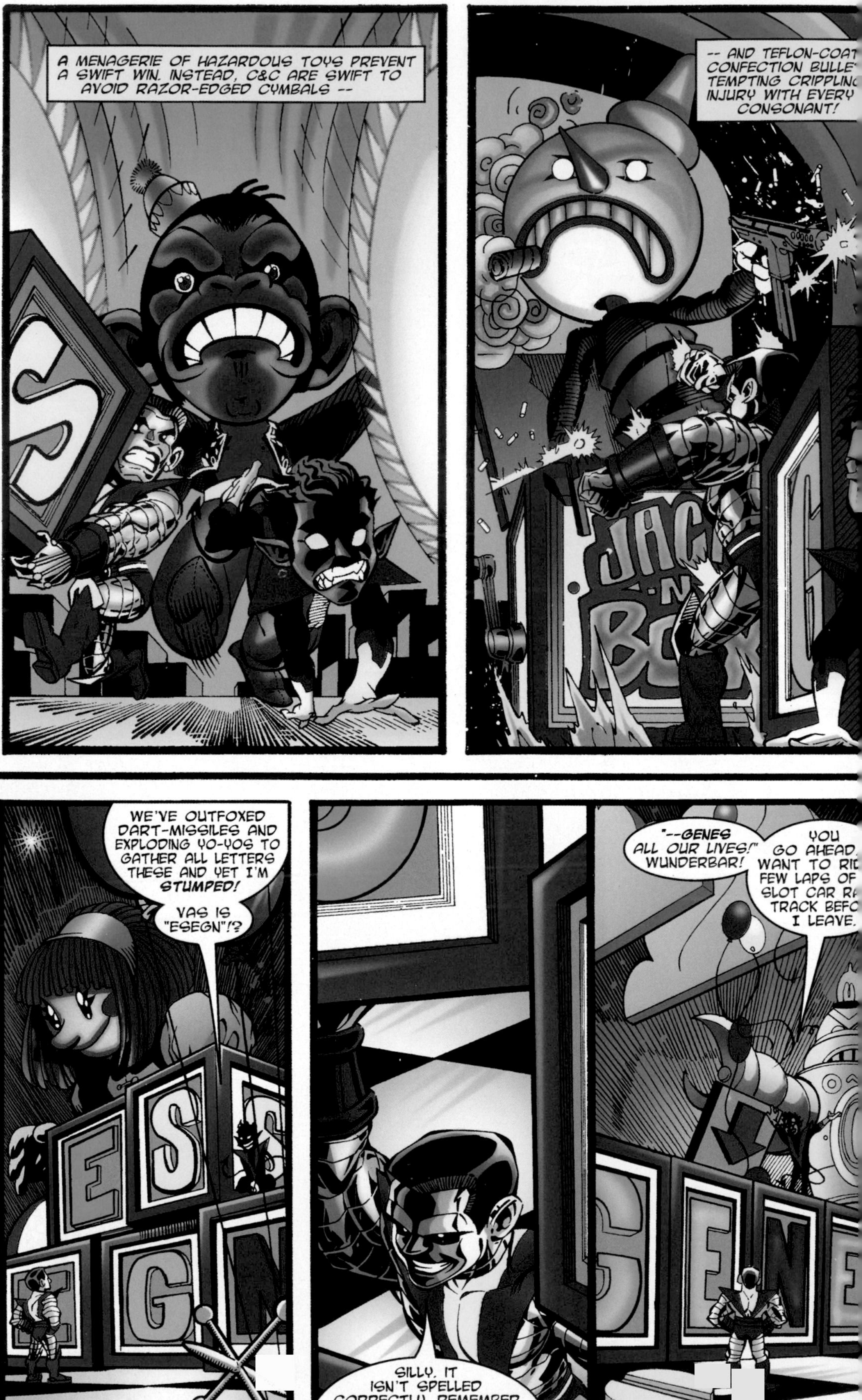
A MENAGERIE OF HAZARDOUS TOYS PREVENT A SWIFT WIN. INSTEAD, C&C ARE SWIFT TO AVOID RAZOR-EDGED CYMBALS --
-- AND TEFLON-COAT CONFECTION BULLE TEMPTING CRIPPLIN INJURY WITH EVERY CONSONANT!
JACK-N-BOX
WE'VE OUTFOXED DART-MISSILES AND EXPLODING YO-YOS TO GATHER ALL LETTERS THESE AND YET I'M STUMPED!
VAS IS "ESEGN"!?
SILLY. IT ISN'T SPELLED CORRECTLY. REMEMBER THE CLUE: "WE WEAR OUR --
"--GENES ALL OUR LIVES!" WUNDERBAR!
YOU GO AHEAD WANT TO RID FEW LAPS OF SLOT CAR R TRACK BEFO I LEAVE.

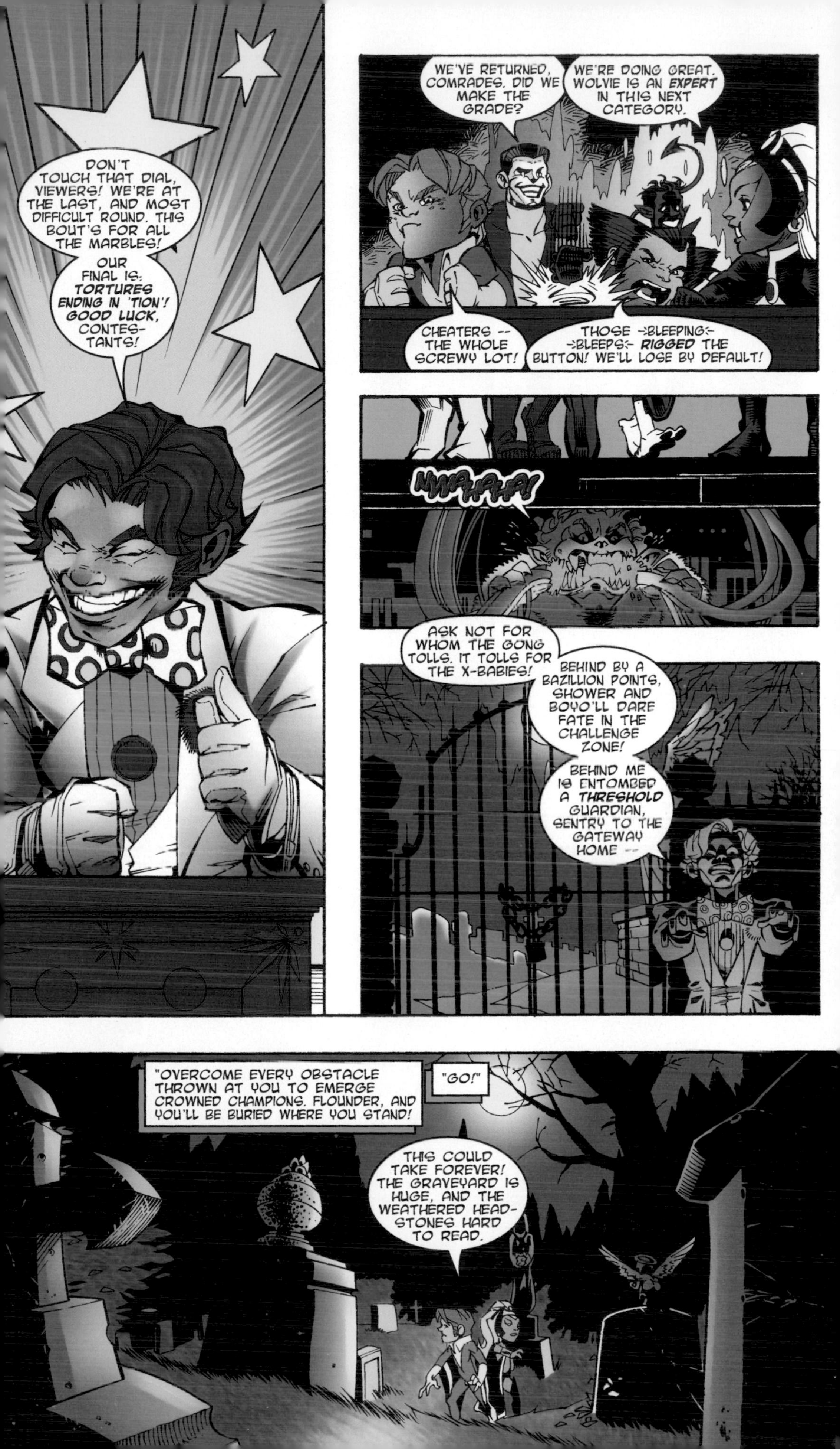
DON'T TOUCH THAT DIAL, VIEWERS! WE'RE AT THE LAST, AND MOST DIFFICULT ROUND. THIS BOUT'S FOR ALL THE MARBLES!
OUR FINAL IS: **TORTURES ENDING IN 'TION'! GOOD LUCK,** CONTESTANTS!
WE'VE RETURNED, COMRADES. DID WE MAKE THE GRADE?
WE'RE DOING GREAT. WOLVIE IS AN *EXPERT* IN THIS NEXT CATEGORY.
CHEATERS -- THE WHOLE SCREWY LOT!
THOSE -BLEEPING- -BLEEPS- **RIGGED** THE BUTTON! WE'LL LOSE BY DEFAULT!
NWAHAHA!
ASK NOT FOR WHOM THE GONG TOLLS. IT TOLLS FOR THE X-BABIES!
BEHIND BY A BAZILLION POINTS, SHOWER AND BOYO'LL DARE FATE IN THE CHALLENGE ZONE!
BEHIND ME IS ENTOMBED A **THRESHOLD** GUARDIAN, SENTRY TO THE GATEWAY HOME --
"OVERCOME EVERY OBSTACLE THROWN AT YOU TO EMERGE CROWNED CHAMPIONS. FLOUNDER, AND YOU'LL BE BURIED WHERE YOU STAND!
"GO!"
THIS COULD TAKE FOREVER! THE GRAVEYARD IS HUGE, AND THE WEATHERED HEADSTONES HARD TO READ.

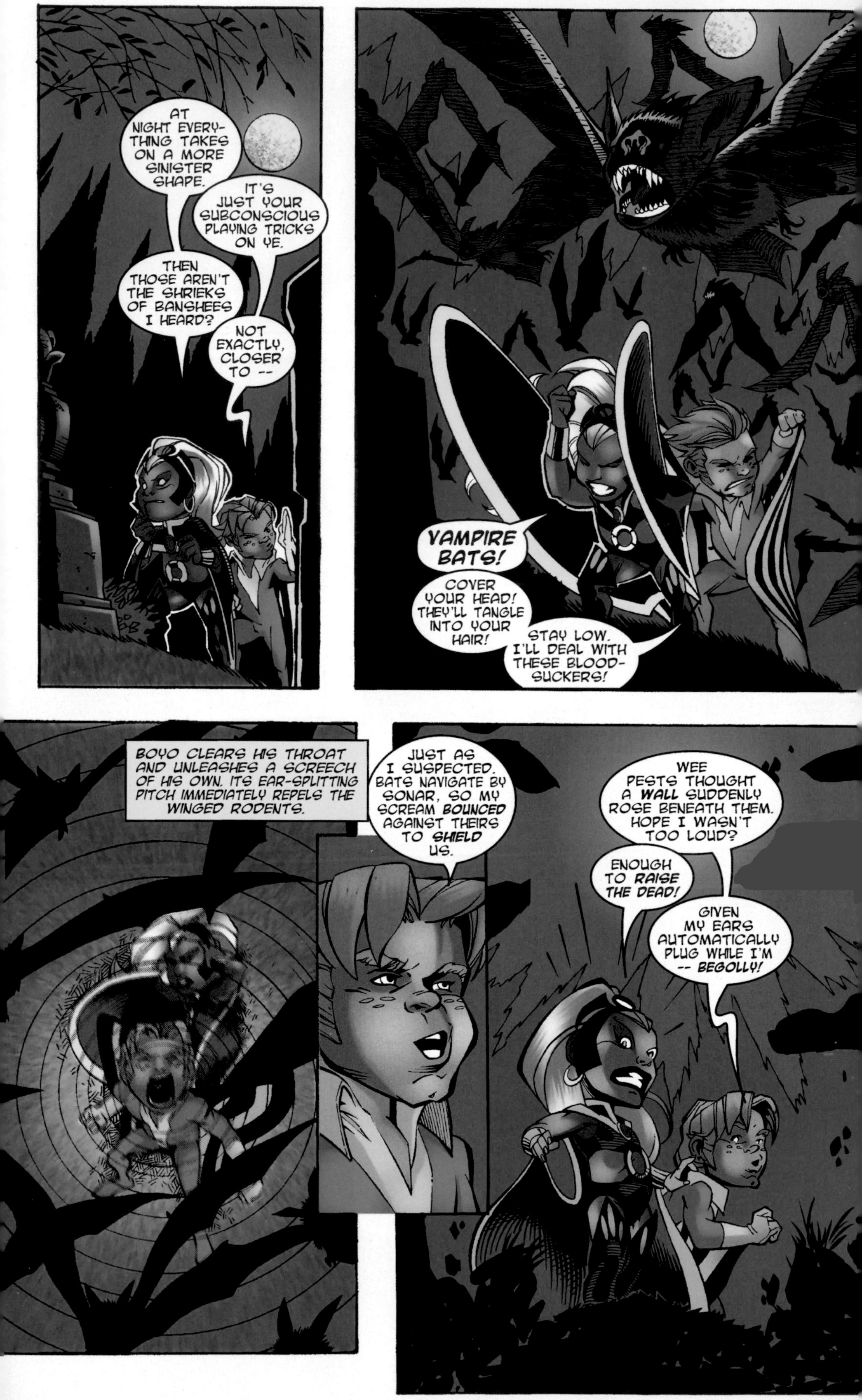
AT NIGHT EVERYTHING TAKES ON A MORE SINISTER SHAPE.
IT'S JUST YOUR SUBCONSCIOUS PLAYING TRICKS ON YE.
THEN THOSE AREN'T THE SHRIEKS OF BANSHEES I HEARD?
NOT EXACTLY, CLOSER TO --
VAMPIRE BATS!
COVER YOUR HEAD! THEY'LL TANGLE INTO YOUR HAIR!
STAY LOW. I'LL DEAL WITH THESE BLOOD-SUCKERS!
BOYO CLEARS HIS THROAT AND UNLEASHES A SCREECH OF HIS OWN. ITS EAR-SPLITTING PITCH IMMEDIATELY REPELS THE WINGED RODENTS.
JUST AS I SUSPECTED. BATS NAVIGATE BY SONAR, SO MY SCREAM BOUNCED AGAINST THEIRS TO SHIELD US.
WEE PESTS THOUGHT A WALL SUDDENLY ROSE BENEATH THEM. HOPE I WASN'T TOO LOUD?
ENOUGH TO RAISE THE DEAD!
GIVEN MY EARS AUTOMATICALLY PLUG WHILE I'M -- BEGOLLY!

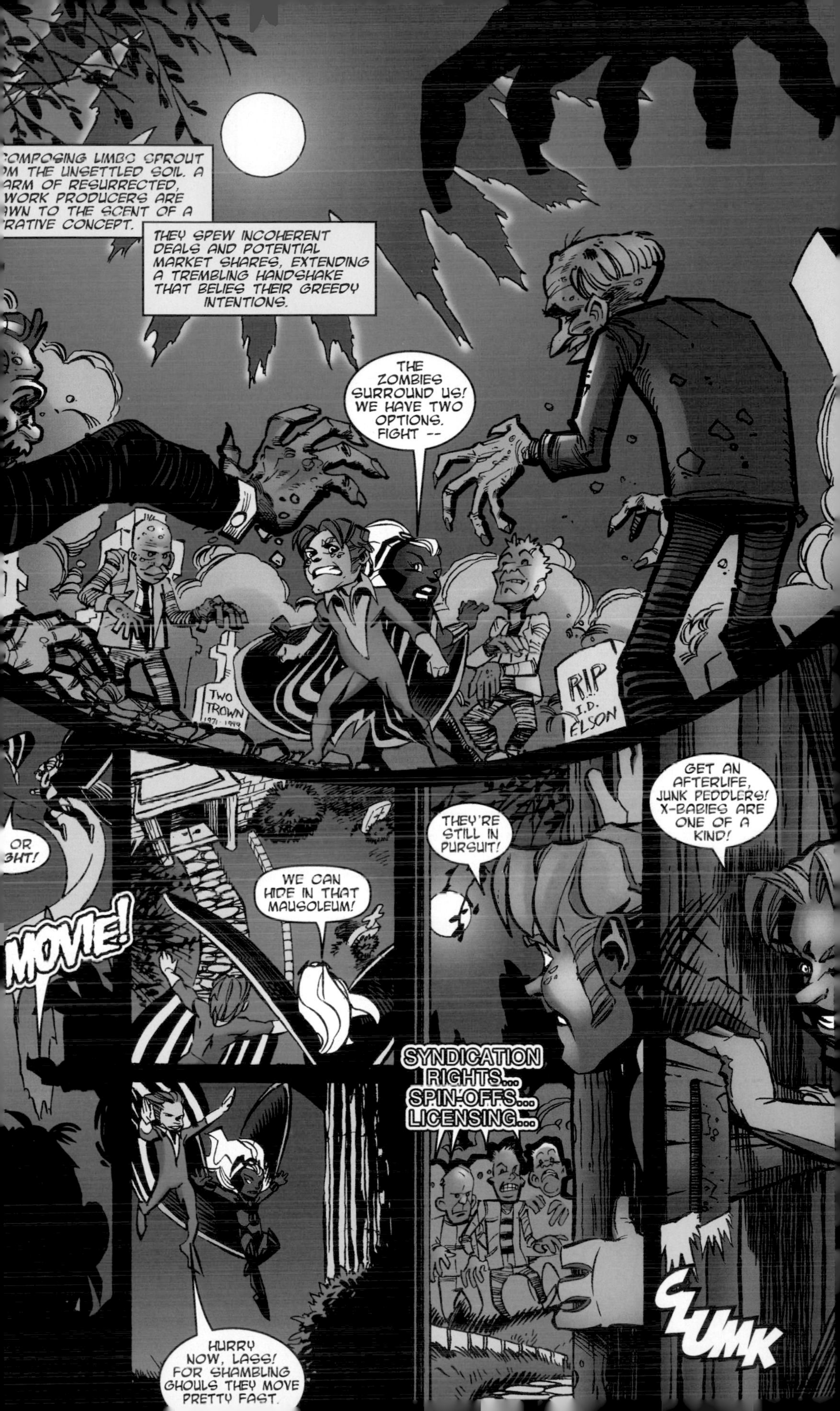

COMPOSING LIMBS SPROUT
OM THE UNSETTLED SOIL. A
ARM OF RESURRECTED,
WORK PRODUCERS ARE
AWN TO THE SCENT OF A
RATIVE CONCEPT.
THEY SPEW INCOHERENT DEALS AND POTENTIAL MARKET SHARES, EXTENDING A TREMBLING HANDSHAKE THAT BELIES THEIR GREEDY INTENTIONS.
THE ZOMBIES SURROUND US! WE HAVE TWO OPTIONS. FIGHT --
TWO TROWN 1971-1999
RIP I.D. ELSON
OR
GHT!
MOVIE!
WE CAN HIDE IN THAT MAUSOLEUM!
THEY'RE STILL IN PURSUIT!
GET AN AFTERLIFE, JUNK PEDDLERS! X-BABIES ARE ONE OF A KIND!
HURRY NOW, LASS! FOR SHAMBLING GHOULS THEY MOVE PRETTY FAST.
SYNDICATION RIGHTS... SPIN-OFFS... LICENSING...
CLUMK

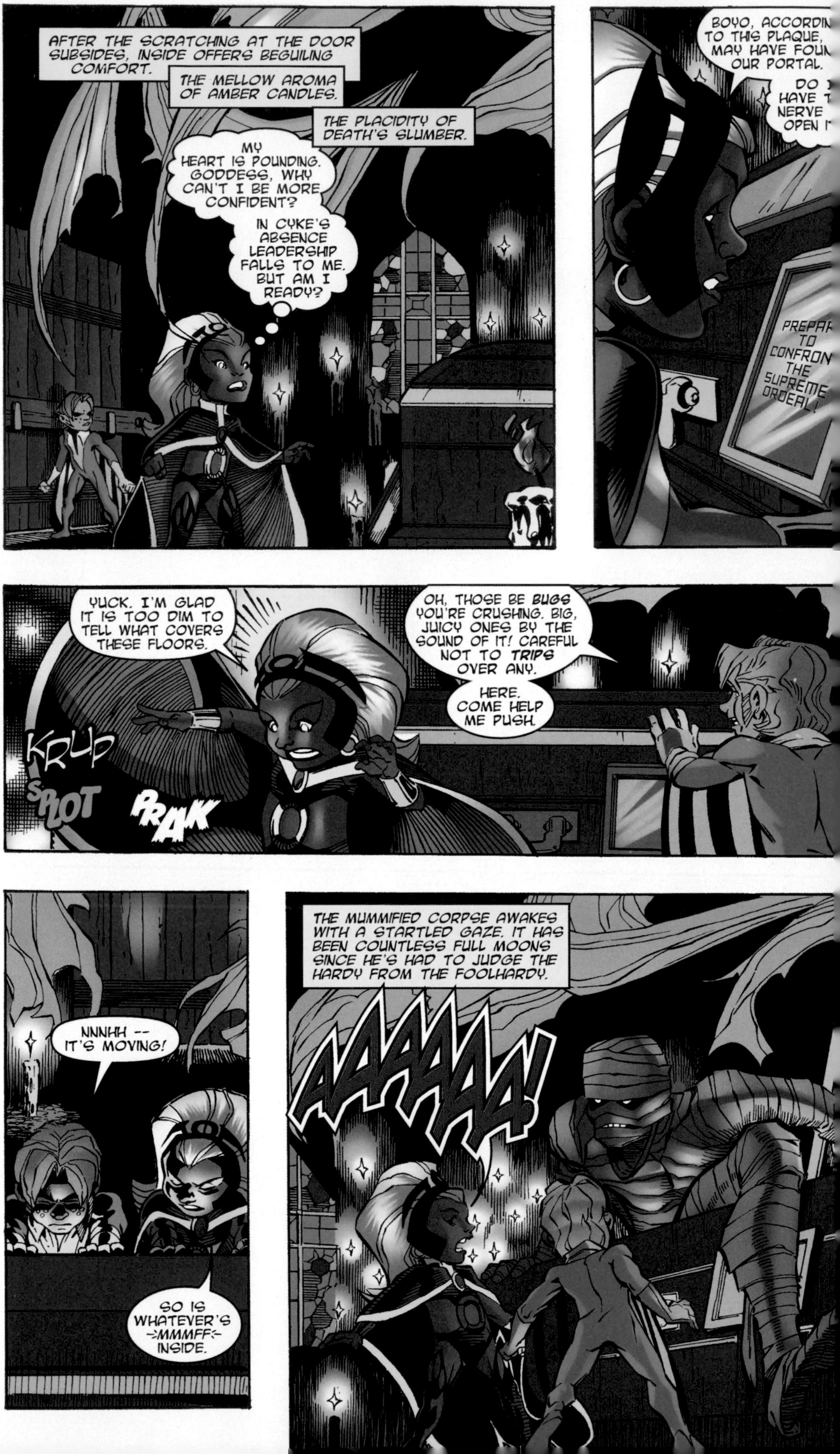
AFTER THE SCRATCHING AT THE DOOR SUBSIDES, INSIDE OFFERS BEGUILING COMFORT.
THE MELLOW AROMA OF AMBER CANDLES.
THE PLACIDITY OF DEATH'S SLUMBER.
MY HEART IS POUNDING. GODDESS, WHY CAN'T I BE MORE CONFIDENT?
IN CYKE'S ABSENCE LEADERSHIP FALLS TO ME. BUT AM I READY?
BOYO, ACCORDIN TO THIS PLAQUE, MAY HAVE FOUN OUR PORTAL.
DO HAVE NERVE OPEN I
PREPAR TO CONFRON THE SUPREME ORDEAL!
YUCK. I'M GLAD IT IS TOO DIM TO TELL WHAT COVERS THESE FLOORS.
KRUP
SPLOT
PRAK
OH, THOSE BE BUGS YOU'RE CRUSHING. BIG, JUICY ONES BY THE SOUND OF IT! CAREFUL NOT TO TRIPS OVER ANY.
HERE. COME HELP ME PUSH.
NNNHH -- IT'S MOVING!
SO IS WHATEVER'S -MMMFF- INSIDE.
THE MUMMIFIED CORPSE AWAKES WITH A STARTLED GAZE. IT HAS BEEN COUNTLESS FULL MOONS SINCE HE'S HAD TO JUDGE THE HARDY FROM THE FOOLHARDY.
AAAAAA!

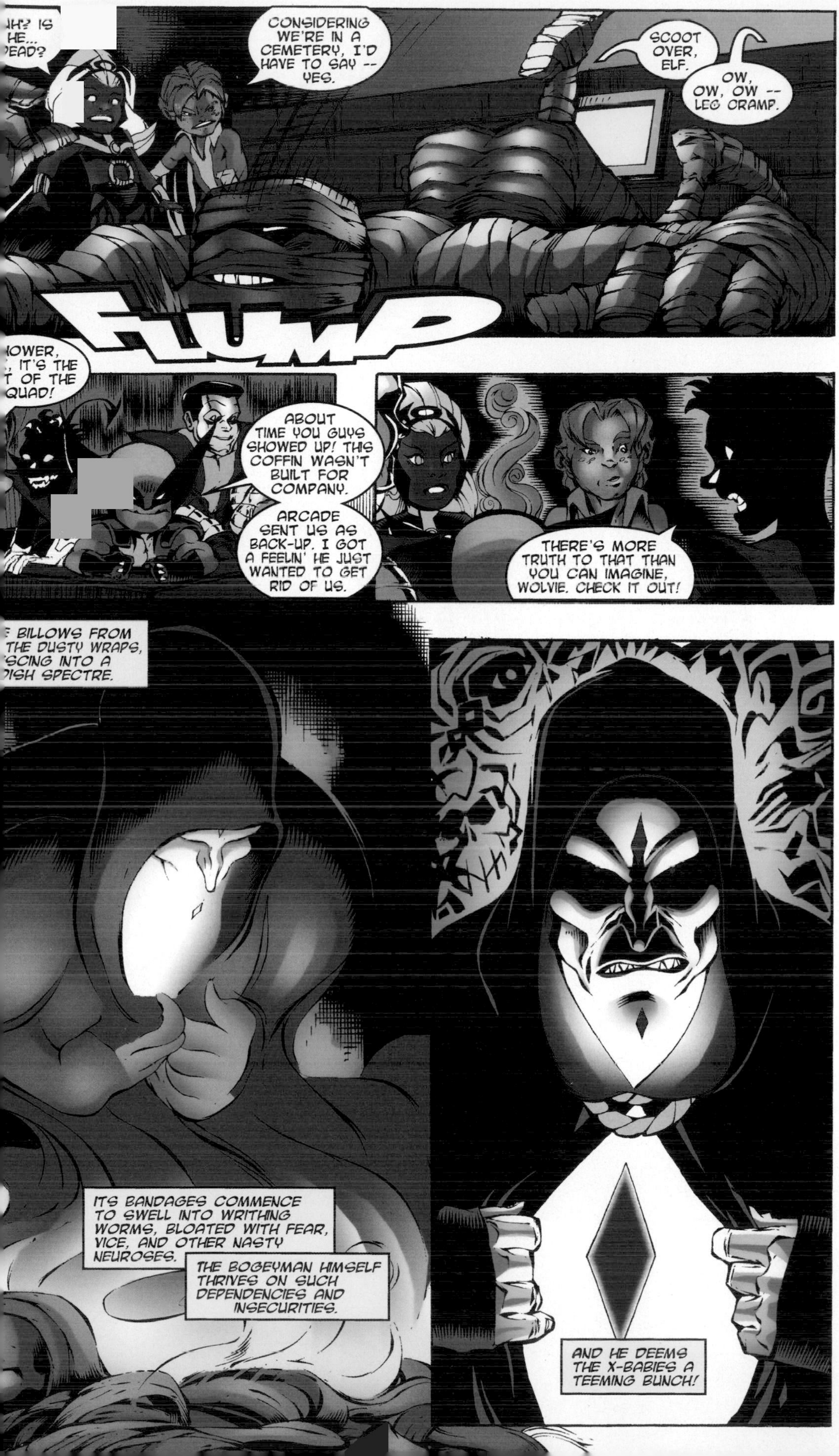

HE...
CONSIDERING WE'RE IN A CEMETERY, I'D HAVE TO SAY -- YES.
SCOOT OVER, ELF.
OW, OW, OW -- LEG CRAMP.
FLUMP
IT'S THE
OF THE
QUAD!
ABOUT TIME YOU GUYS SHOWED UP! THIS COFFIN WASN'T BUILT FOR COMPANY.
ARCADE SENT US AS BACK-UP. I GOT A FEELIN' HE JUST WANTED TO GET RID OF US.
THERE'S MORE TRUTH TO THAT THAN YOU CAN IMAGINE, WOLVIE. CHECK IT OUT!
BILLOWS FROM THE DUSTY WRAPS,
SPECTRE.
ITS BANDAGES COMMENCE TO SWELL INTO WRITHING WORMS, BLOATED WITH FEAR, VICE, AND OTHER NASTY NEUROSES.
THE BOGEYMAN HIMSELF THRIVES ON SUCH DEPENDENCIES AND INSECURITIES.
AND HE DEEMS THE X-BABIES A TEEMING BUNCH!

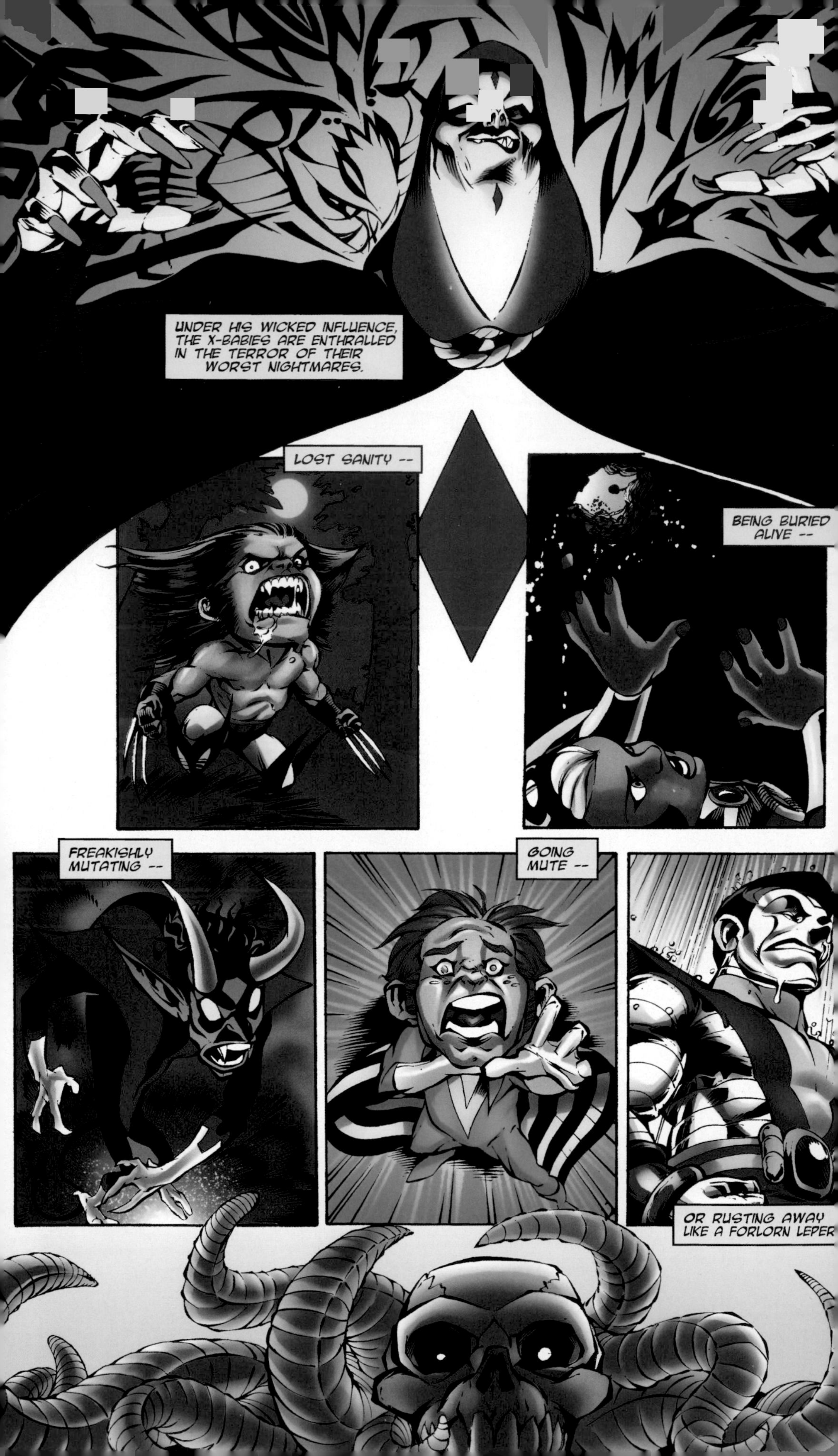
UNDER HIS WICKED INFLUENCE, THE X-BABIES ARE ENTHRALLED IN THE TERROR OF THEIR WORST NIGHTMARES.
LOST SANITY --
BEING BURIED ALIVE --
FREAKISHLY MUTATING --
GOING MUTE --
OR RUSTING AWAY LIKE A FORLORN LEPER

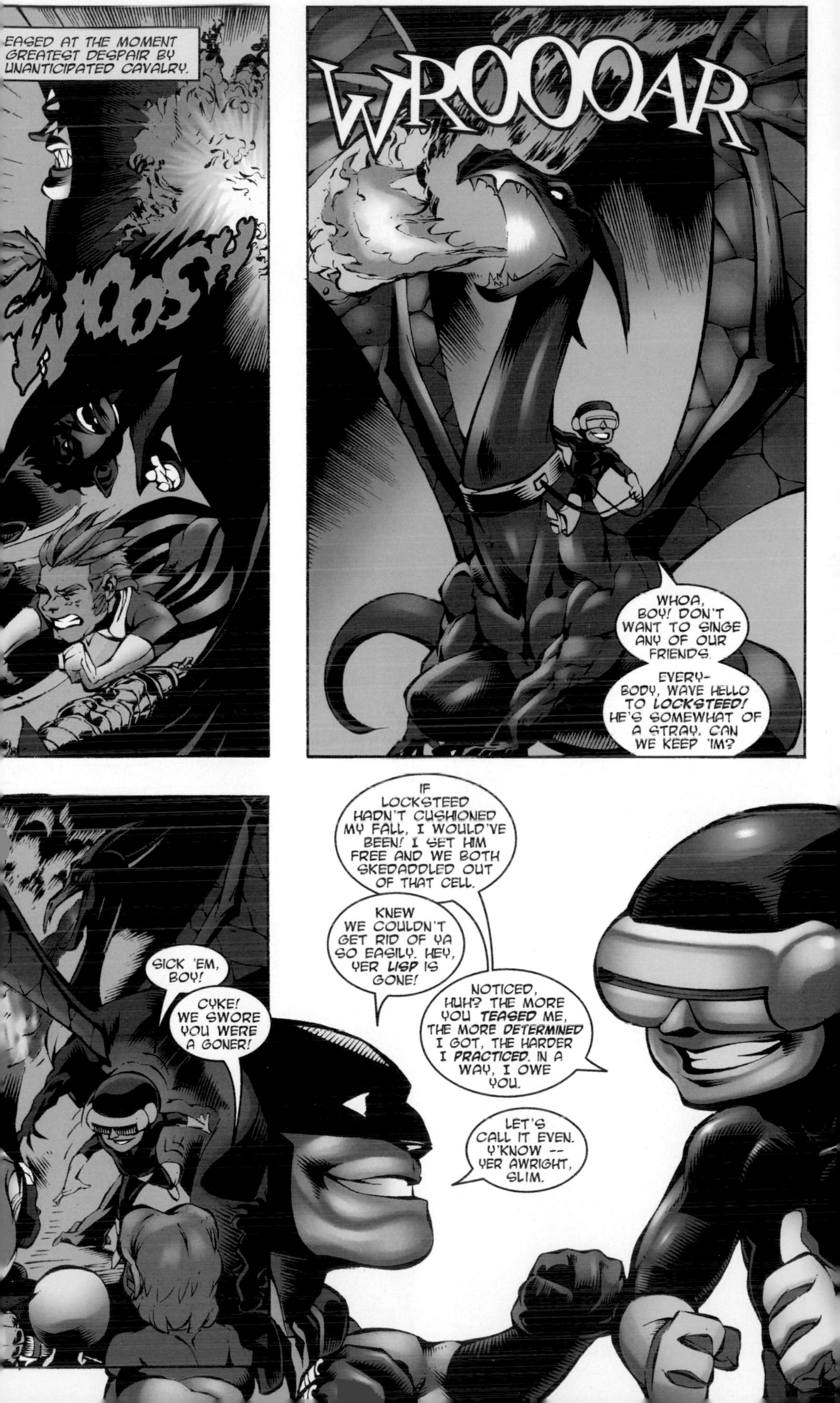
EASED AT THE MOMENT
GREATEST DESPAIR BY
UNANTICIPATED CAVALRY.
WHOOSH
WROOOAR
WHOA, BOY! DON'T WANT TO SINGE ANY OF OUR FRIENDS.
EVERY-BODY, WAVE HELLO TO LOCKSTEED! HE'S SOMEWHAT OF A STRAY. CAN WE KEEP 'IM?
SICK 'EM, BOY!
CYKE! WE SWORE YOU WERE A GONER!
IF LOCKSTEED HADN'T CUSHIONED MY FALL, I WOULD'VE BEEN! I SET HIM FREE AND WE BOTH SKEDADDLED OUT OF THAT CELL.
KNEW WE COULDN'T GET RID OF YA SO EASILY. HEY, YER LISP IS GONE!
NOTICED, HUH? THE MORE YOU TEASED ME, THE MORE DETERMINED I GOT, THE HARDER I PRACTICED. IN A WAY, I OWE YOU.
LET'S CALL IT EVEN. Y'KNOW -- YER AWRIGHT, SLIM.

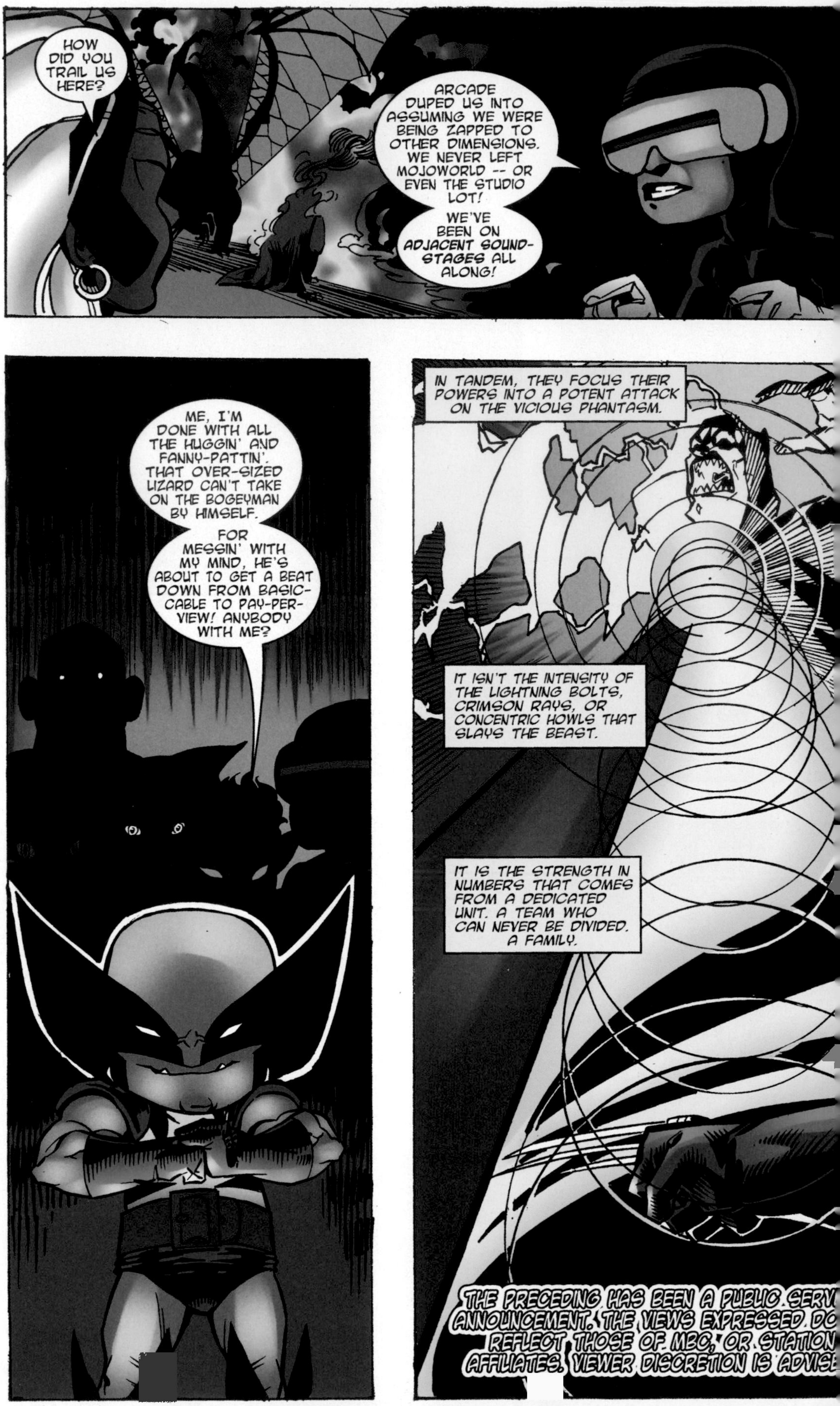
HOW DID YOU TRAIL US HERE?
ARCADE DUPED US INTO ASSUMING WE WERE BEING ZAPPED TO OTHER DIMENSIONS. WE NEVER LEFT MOJOWORLD -- OR EVEN THE STUDIO LOT!
WE'VE BEEN ON ADJACENT SOUND-STAGES ALL ALONG!
ME, I'M DONE WITH ALL THE HUGGIN' AND FANNY-PATTIN'. THAT OVER-SIZED LIZARD CAN'T TAKE ON THE BOGEYMAN BY HIMSELF.
FOR MESSIN' WITH MY MIND, HE'S ABOUT TO GET A BEAT DOWN FROM BASIC-CABLE TO PAY-PER-VIEW! ANYBODY WITH ME?
IN TANDEM, THEY FOCUS THEIR POWERS INTO A POTENT ATTACK ON THE VICIOUS PHANTASM.
IT ISN'T THE INTENSITY OF THE LIGHTNING BOLTS, CRIMSON RAYS, OR CONCENTRIC HOWLS THAT SLAYS THE BEAST.
IT IS THE STRENGTH IN NUMBERS THAT COMES FROM A DEDICATED UNIT. A TEAM WHO CAN NEVER BE DIVIDED. A FAMILY.
THE PRECEDING HAS BEEN A PUBLIC SERV ANNOUNCEMENT. THE VIEWS EXPRESSED DO REFLECT THOSE OF MBC, OR STATION AFFILIATES. VIEWER DISCRETION IS ADVISE

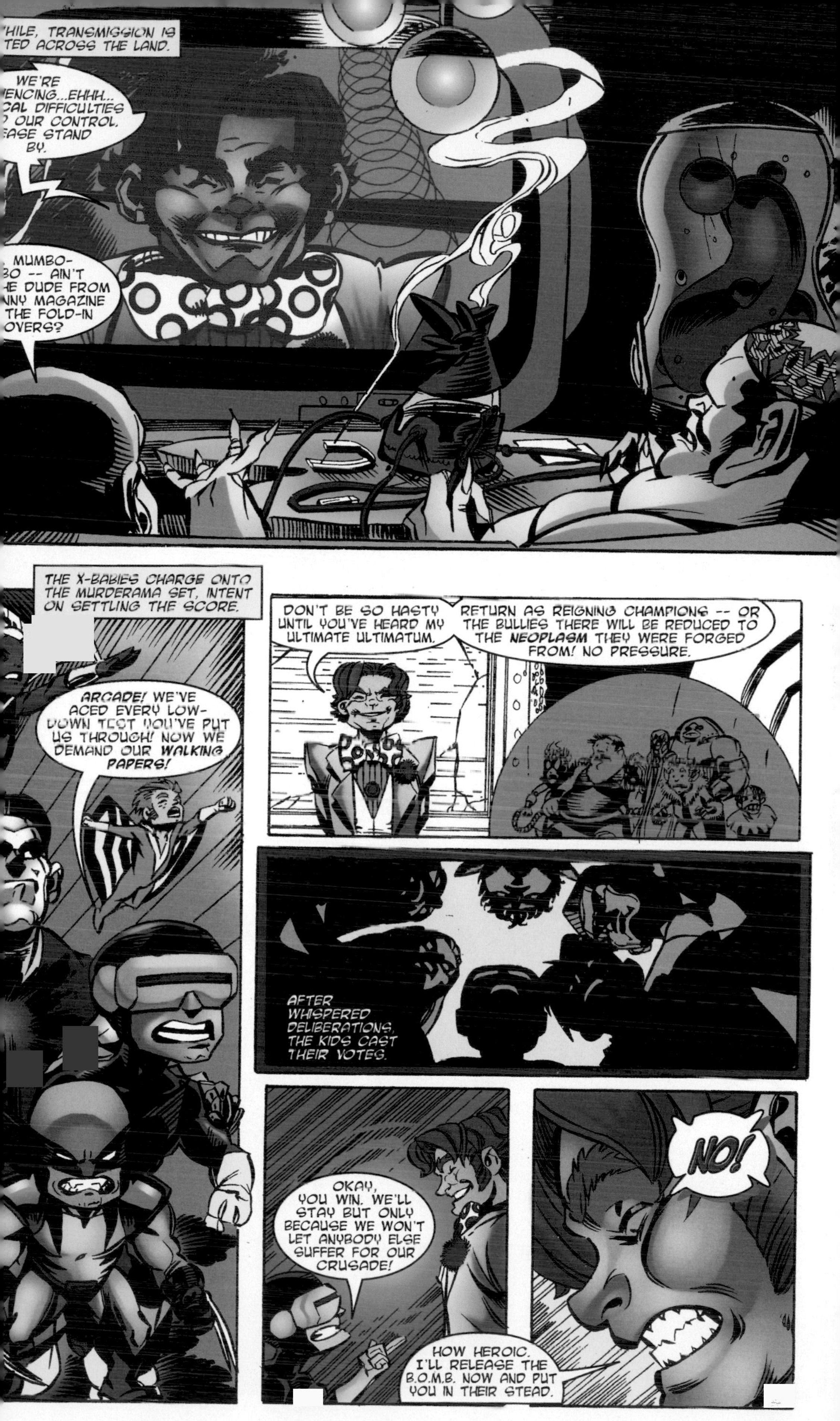

...HILE, TRANSMISSION IS ...TED ACROSS THE LAND.
WE'RE ...ENCING...EHHH... ...CAL DIFFICULTIES ... OUR CONTROL. ...EASE STAND BY.
... MUMBO-...O -- AIN'T ...HE DUDE FROM ...NNY MAGAZINE ... THE FOLD-IN ...OVERS?
THE X-BABIES CHARGE ONTO THE MURDERAMA SET, INTENT ON SETTLING THE SCORE.
ARCADE! WE'VE ACED EVERY LOW-DOWN TEST YOU'VE PUT US THROUGH! NOW WE DEMAND OUR WALKING PAPERS!
DON'T BE SO HASTY UNTIL YOU'VE HEARD MY ULTIMATE ULTIMATUM.
RETURN AS REIGNING CHAMPIONS -- OR THE BULLIES THERE WILL BE REDUCED TO THE NEOPLASM THEY WERE FORGED FROM! NO PRESSURE.
AFTER WHISPERED DELIBERATIONS, THE KIDS CAST THEIR VOTES.
OKAY, YOU WIN. WE'LL STAY BUT ONLY BECAUSE WE WON'T LET ANYBODY ELSE SUFFER FOR OUR CRUSADE!
HOW HEROIC. I'LL RELEASE THE B.O.M.B. NOW AND PUT YOU IN THEIR STEAD.
NO!

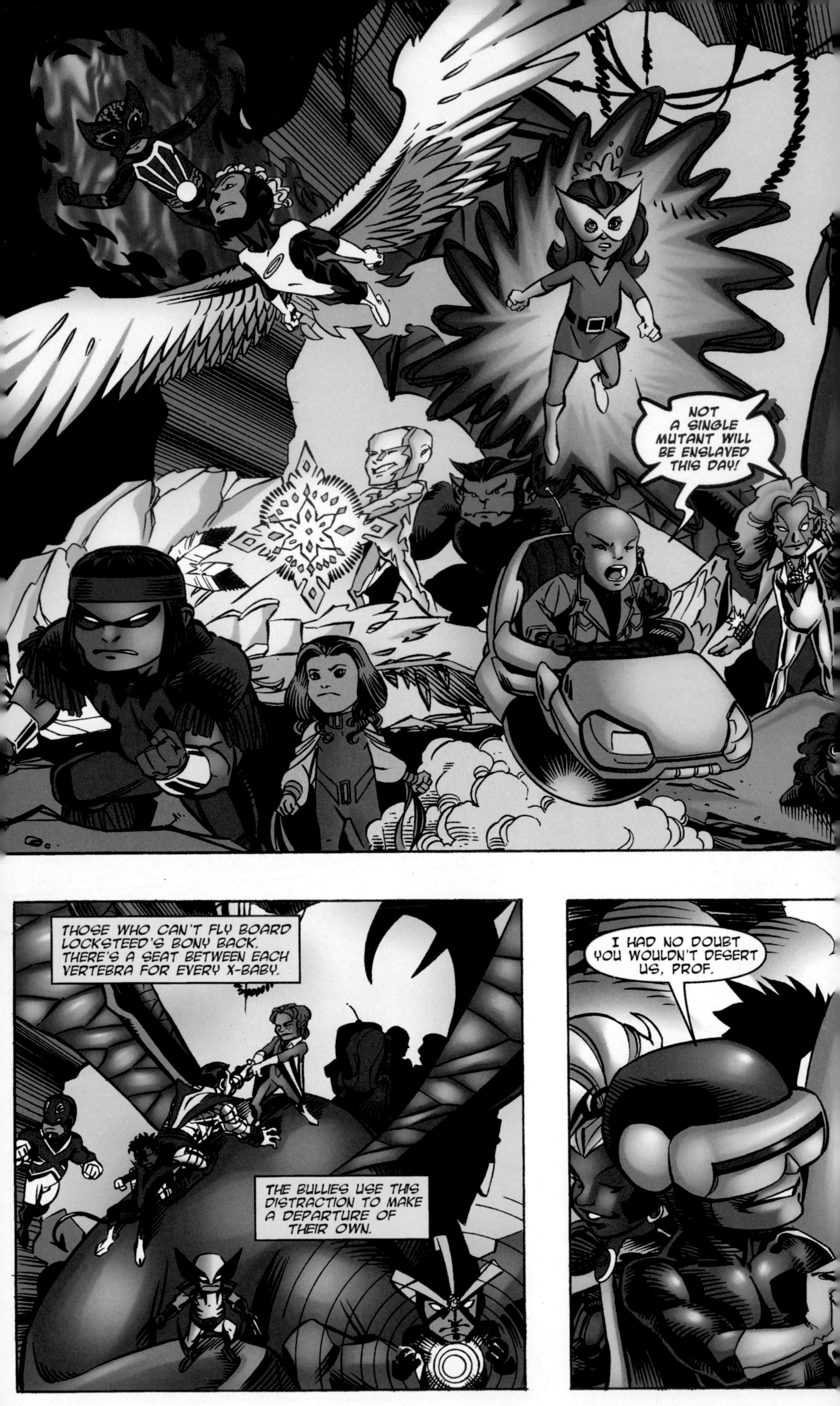
NOT A SINGLE MUTANT WILL BE ENSLAVED THIS DAY!
THOSE WHO CAN'T FLY BOARD LOCKSTEED'S BONY BACK. THERE'S A SEAT BETWEEN EACH VERTEBRA FOR EVERY X-BABY.
THE BULLIES USE THIS DISTRACTION TO MAKE A DEPARTURE OF THEIR OWN.
I HAD NO DOUBT YOU WOULDN'T DESERT US, PROF.

AS DID I. I IMMEDIATELY ROUSED A FEW AVAILABLE ALLIES TO MOUNT A SEARCH. PROMISED THEM A *PARTY* AFTERWARDS.

WELL, THERE'S ALWAYS SPACE IN THE CLUBHOUSE, BESIDES A MASSIVE *PAJAMA-THON* --

HA HA HA HA HA HA HA HA HA HA HA HA HA HA

-- WHAT ELSE ARE WE GOING TO DO WITH ALL THESE X-BABIES?

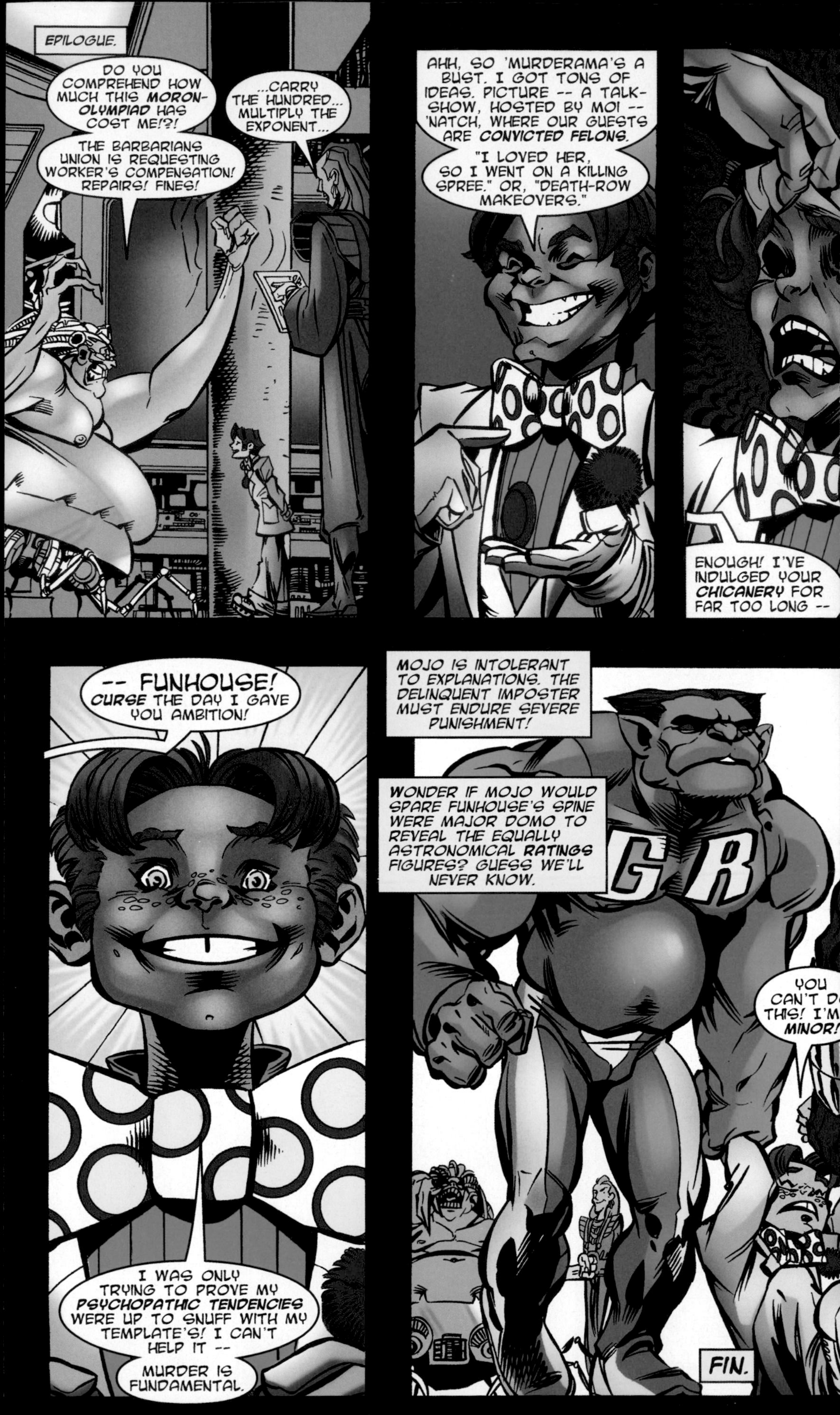
EPILOGUE.
DO YOU COMPREHEND HOW MUCH THIS MORON-OLYMPIAD HAS COST ME!?!
THE BARBARIANS UNION IS REQUESTING WORKER'S COMPENSATION! REPAIRS! FINES!
...CARRY THE HUNDRED... MULTIPLY THE EXPONENT...
AHH, SO 'MURDERAMA'S A BUST. I GOT TONS OF IDEAS. PICTURE -- A TALK-SHOW, HOSTED BY MOI -- 'NATCH, WHERE OUR GUESTS ARE CONVICTED FELONS.
"I LOVED HER, SO I WENT ON A KILLING SPREE." OR, "DEATH-ROW MAKEOVERS."
ENOUGH! I'VE INDULGED YOUR CHICANERY FOR FAR TOO LONG --
-- FUNHOUSE! CURSE THE DAY I GAVE YOU AMBITION!
I WAS ONLY TRYING TO PROVE MY PSYCHOPATHIC TENDENCIES WERE UP TO SNUFF WITH MY TEMPLATE'S! I CAN'T HELP IT --
MURDER IS FUNDAMENTAL.
MOJO IS INTOLERANT TO EXPLANATIONS. THE DELINQUENT IMPOSTER MUST ENDURE SEVERE PUNISHMENT!
WONDER IF MOJO WOULD SPARE FUNHOUSE'S SPINE WERE MAJOR DOMO TO REVEAL THE EQUALLY ASTRONOMICAL RATINGS FIGURES? GUESS WE'LL NEVER KNOW.
GR
FIN.

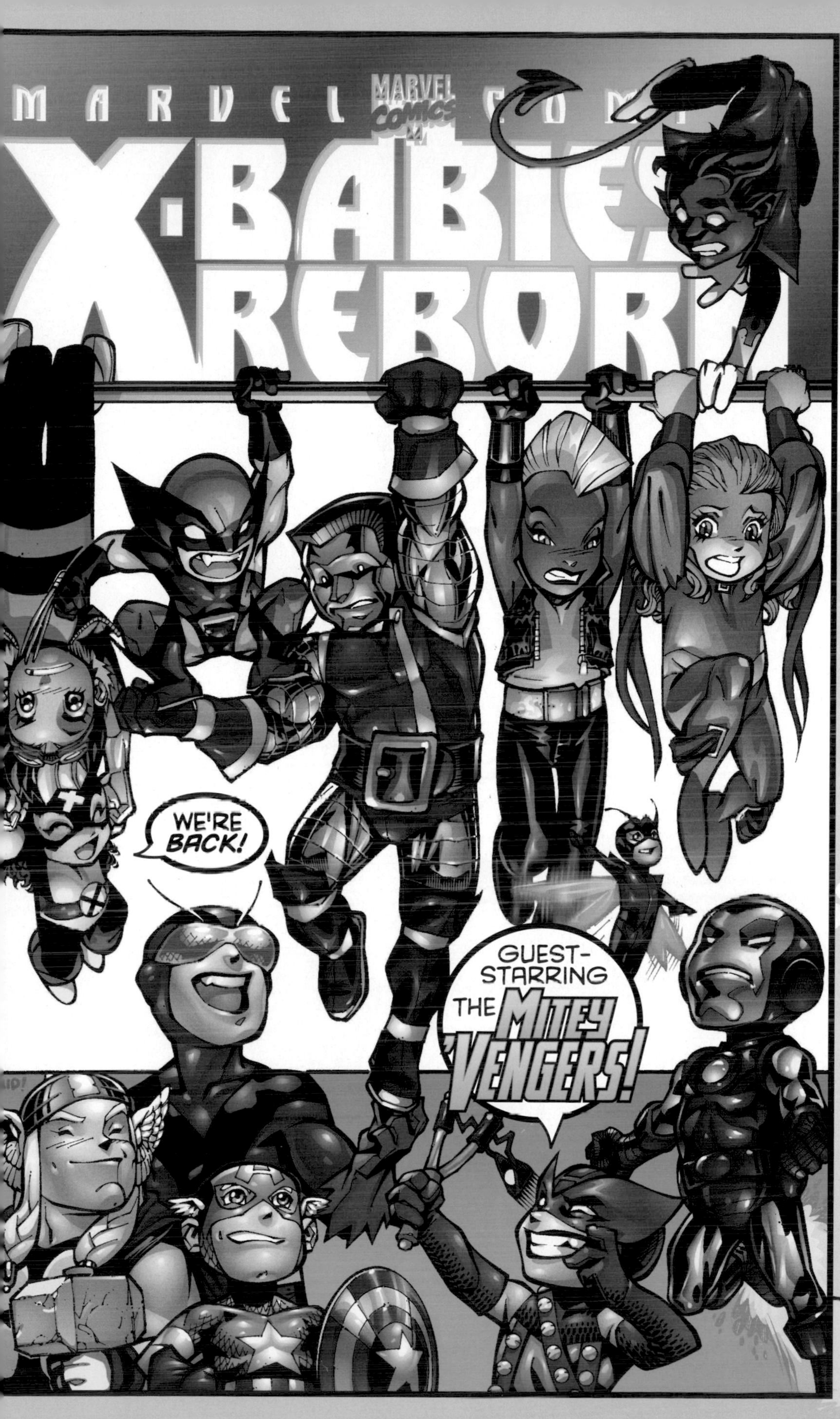
MARVEL
X-BABIES
WE'RE BACK!
GUEST-STARRING THE MITEY 'VENGERS!

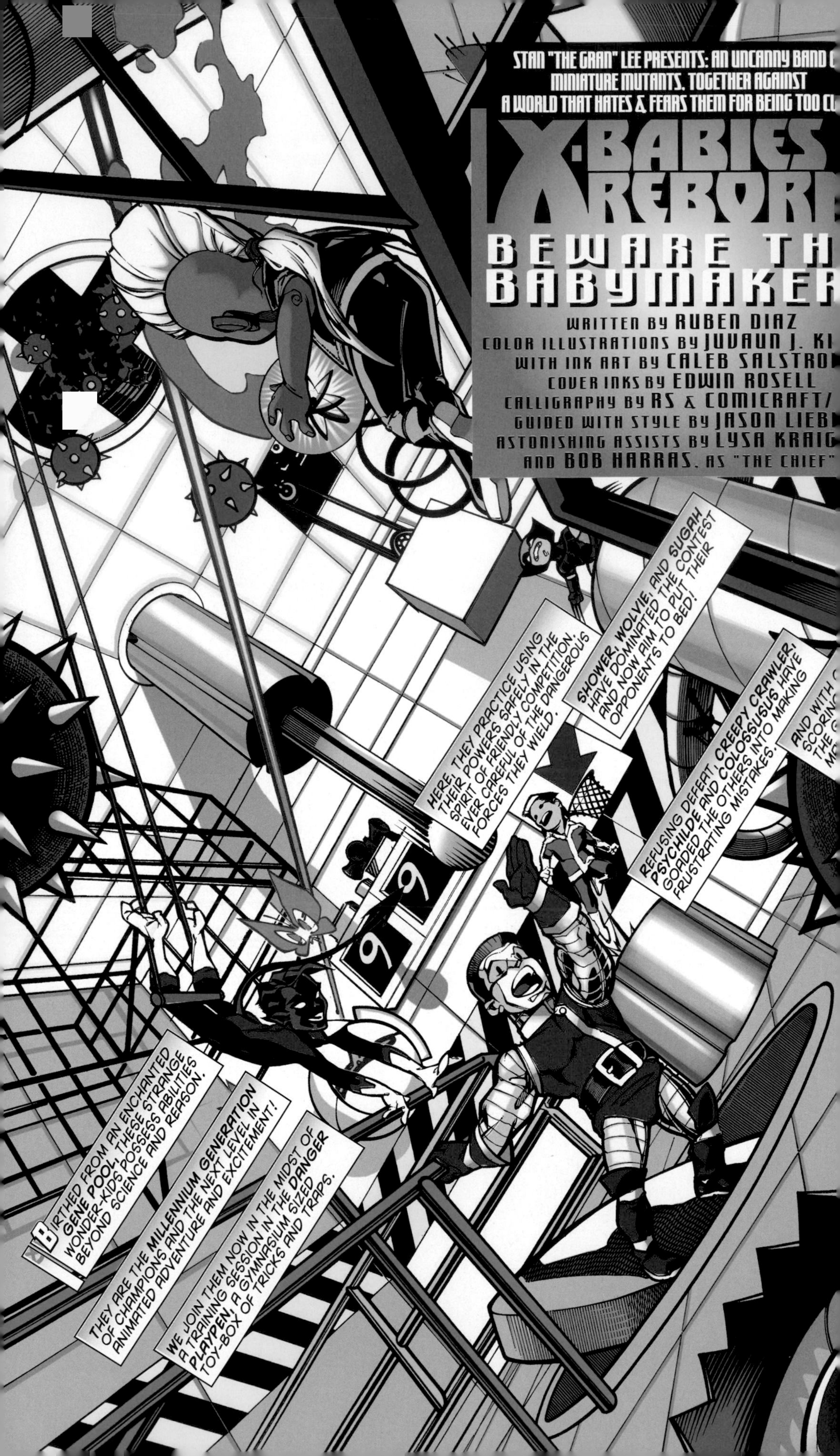

STAN "THE GRAN" LEE PRESENTS: AN UNCANNY BAND
MINIATURE MUTANTS, TOGETHER AGAINST
A WORLD THAT HATES & FEARS THEM FOR BEING TOO
X-BABIES
BEWARE TH
BABYMAKER
WRITTEN BY RUBEN DIAZ
COLOR ILLUSTRATIONS BY JUVAUN J. KI
WITH INK ART BY CALEB SALSTRO
COVER INKS BY EDWIN ROSELL
CALLIGRAPHY BY RS & COMICRAFT/
GUIDED WITH STYLE BY JASON LIEB
ASTONISHING ASSISTS BY LYSA KRAIG
AND BOB HARRAS, AS "THE CHIEF"
BIRTHED FROM AN ENCHANTED GENE POOL, THESE STRANGE WONDER-KIDS POSSESS ABILITIES BEYOND SCIENCE AND REASON.
THEY ARE THE MILLENNIUM GENERATION OF CHAMPIONS AND THE NEXT LEVEL IN ANIMATED ADVENTURE AND EXCITEMENT!
WE JOIN THEM NOW IN THE MIDST OF A TRAINING SESSION IN THE DANGER PLAYPEN, A GYMNASIUM SIZED TOY-BOX OF TRICKS AND TRAPS.
HERE, THEY PRACTICE USING THEIR POWERS SAFELY IN THE SPIRIT OF FRIENDLY COMPETITION, EVER CAREFUL OF THE DANGEROUS FORCES THEY WIELD.
SHOWER, WOLVIE, AND SUGAH HAVE DOMINATED THE CONTEST AND NOW AIM TO PUT THEIR OPPONENTS TO BED!
REFUSING DEFEAT, CREEPY CRAWLER, PSYCHILDE AND COLOSSUSUS HAVE GOADED THE OTHERS INTO MAKING FRUSTRATING MISTAKES.

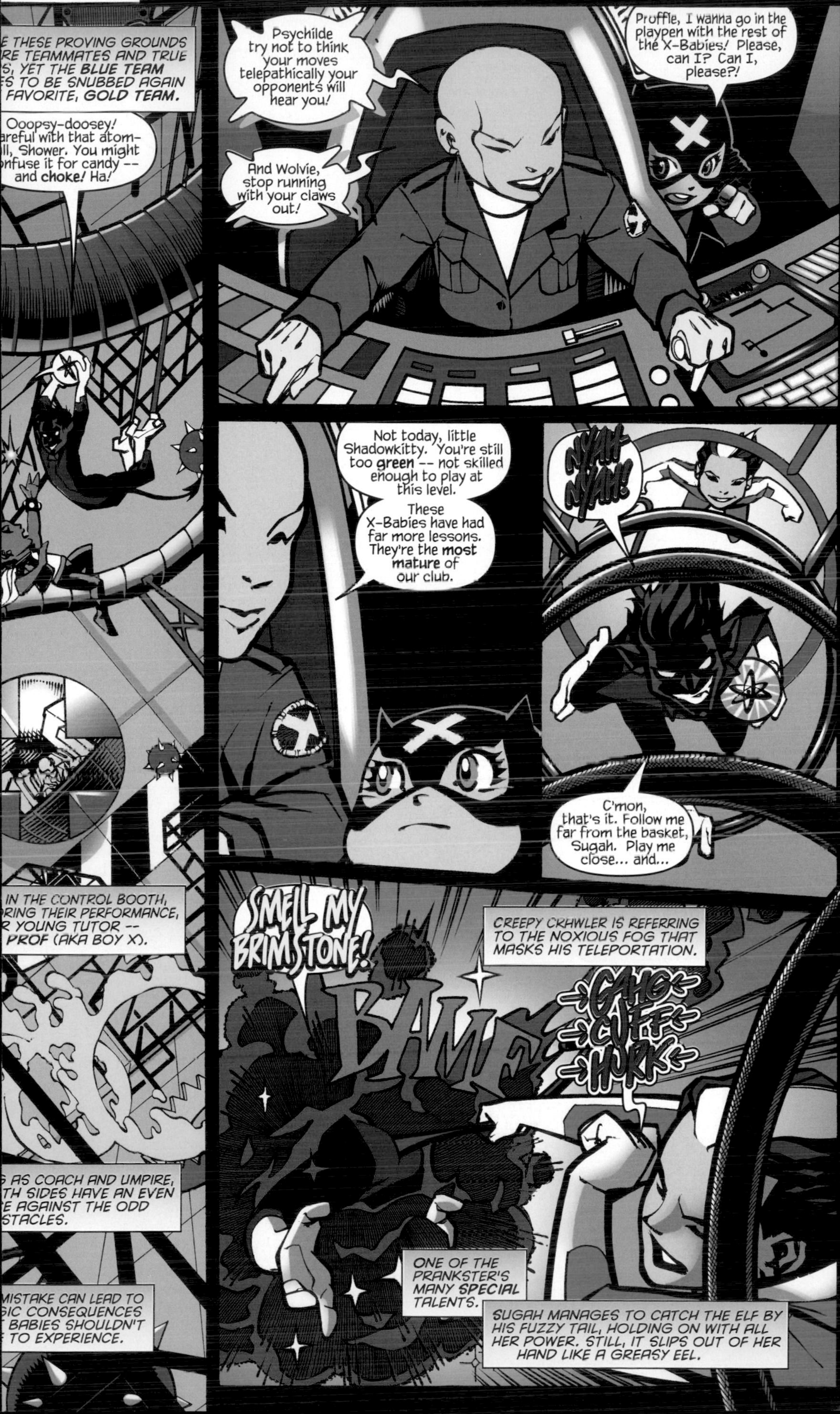

E THESE PROVING GROUNDS RE TEAMMATES AND TRUE S, YET THE BLUE TEAM ES TO BE SNUBBED AGAIN FAVORITE, GOLD TEAM.
Ooopsy-doosey! areful with that atom- ll, Shower. You might onfuse it for candy -- and choke! Ha!
Psychilde try not to think your moves telepathically your opponents will hear you!
And Wolvie, stop running with your claws out!
Proffle, I wanna go in the playpen with the rest of the X-Babies! Please, can I? Can I, please?!
IN THE CONTROL BOOTH, RING THEIR PERFORMANCE, R YOUNG TUTOR -- PROF (AKA BOY X).
Not today, little Shadowkitty. You're still too green -- not skilled enough to play at this level.
These X-Babies have had far more lessons. They're the most mature of our club.
NYAH NYAH!
C'mon, that's it. Follow me far from the basket, Sugah. Play me close... and...
S AS COACH AND UMPIRE, TH SIDES HAVE AN EVEN E AGAINST THE ODD STACLES.
MISTAKE CAN LEAD TO GIC CONSEQUENCES BABIES SHOULDN'T E TO EXPERIENCE.
SMELL MY BRIMSTONE!
CREEPY CRAWLER IS REFERRING TO THE NOXIOUS FOG THAT MASKS HIS TELEPORTATION.
BAMF
GAHG CUFF HURK
ONE OF THE PRANKSTER'S MANY SPECIAL TALENTS.
SUGAH MANAGES TO CATCH THE ELF BY HIS FUZZY TAIL, HOLDING ON WITH ALL HER POWER. STILL, IT SLIPS OUT OF HER HAND LIKE A GREASY EEL.

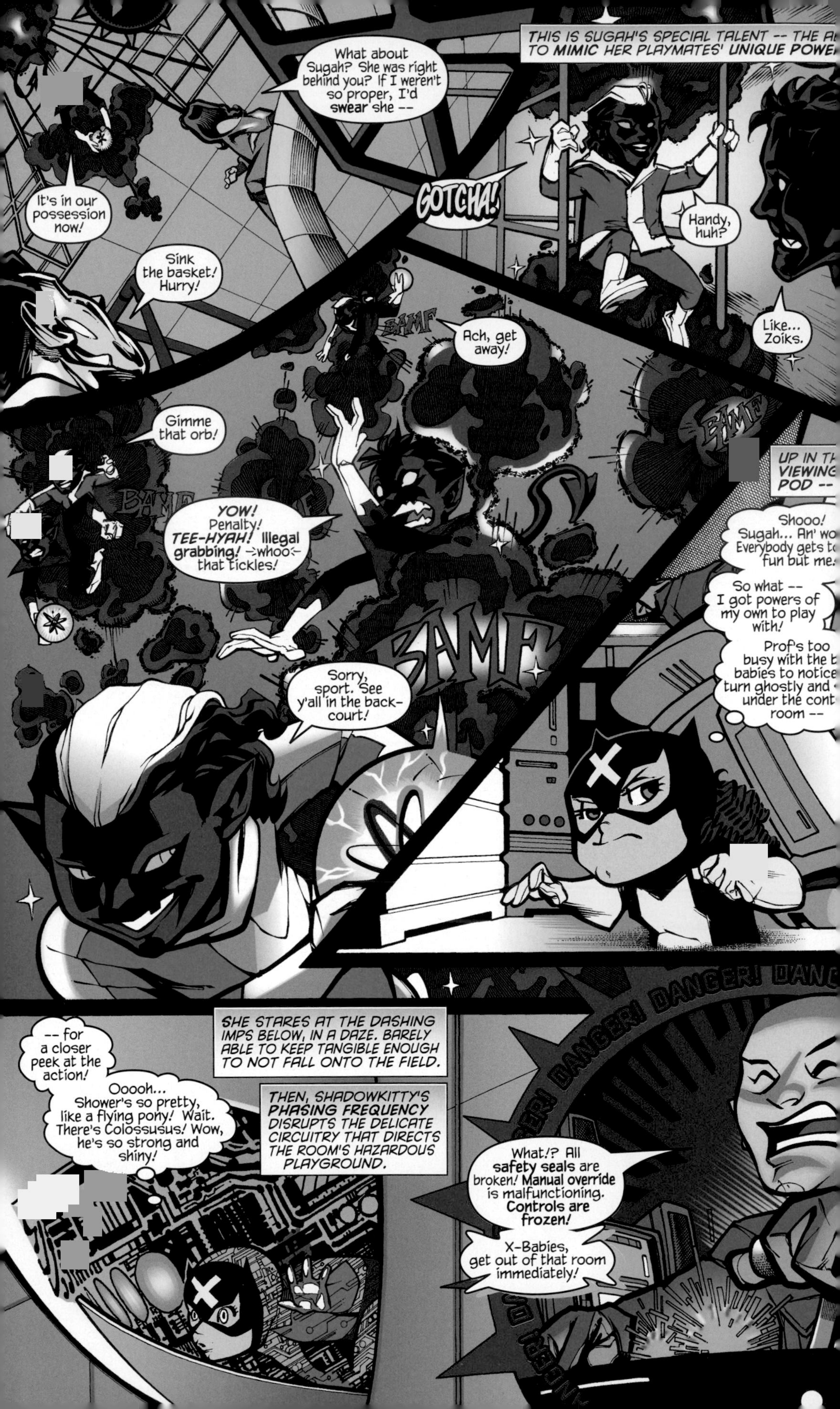

What about Sugah? She was right behind you? If I weren't so proper, I'd swear she --
It's in our possession now!
THIS IS SUGAH'S SPECIAL TALENT -- THE A
TO MIMIC HER PLAYMATES' UNIQUE POWE
GOTCHA!
Handy, huh?
Like... Zoiks.
Sink the basket! Hurry!
BAMF
Ach, get away!
Gimme that orb!
BAMF
YOW! Penalty! TEE-HYAH! Illegal grabbing! ~whoo~ that tickles!
BAMF
BAMF
Sorry, sport. See y'all in the back-court!
UP IN TH
VIEWING
POD --
Shooo! Sugah... An' wo
Everybody gets t
fun but me.
So what -- I got powers of my own to play with!
Prof's too busy with the b
babies to notice
turn ghostly and
under the cont
room --
-- for a closer peek at the action!
Ooooh... Shower's so pretty, like a flying pony! Wait. There's Colossusus! Wow, he's so strong and shiny!
SHE STARES AT THE DASHING IMPS BELOW, IN A DAZE. BARELY ABLE TO KEEP TANGIBLE ENOUGH TO NOT FALL ONTO THE FIELD.
THEN, SHADOWKITTY'S PHASING FREQUENCY DISRUPTS THE DELICATE CIRCUITRY THAT DIRECTS THE ROOM'S HAZARDOUS PLAYGROUND.
DANGER! DANGER! DANGER! DANG
What!? All safety seals are broken! Manual override is malfunctioning. Controls are frozen!
X-Babies, get out of that room immediately!

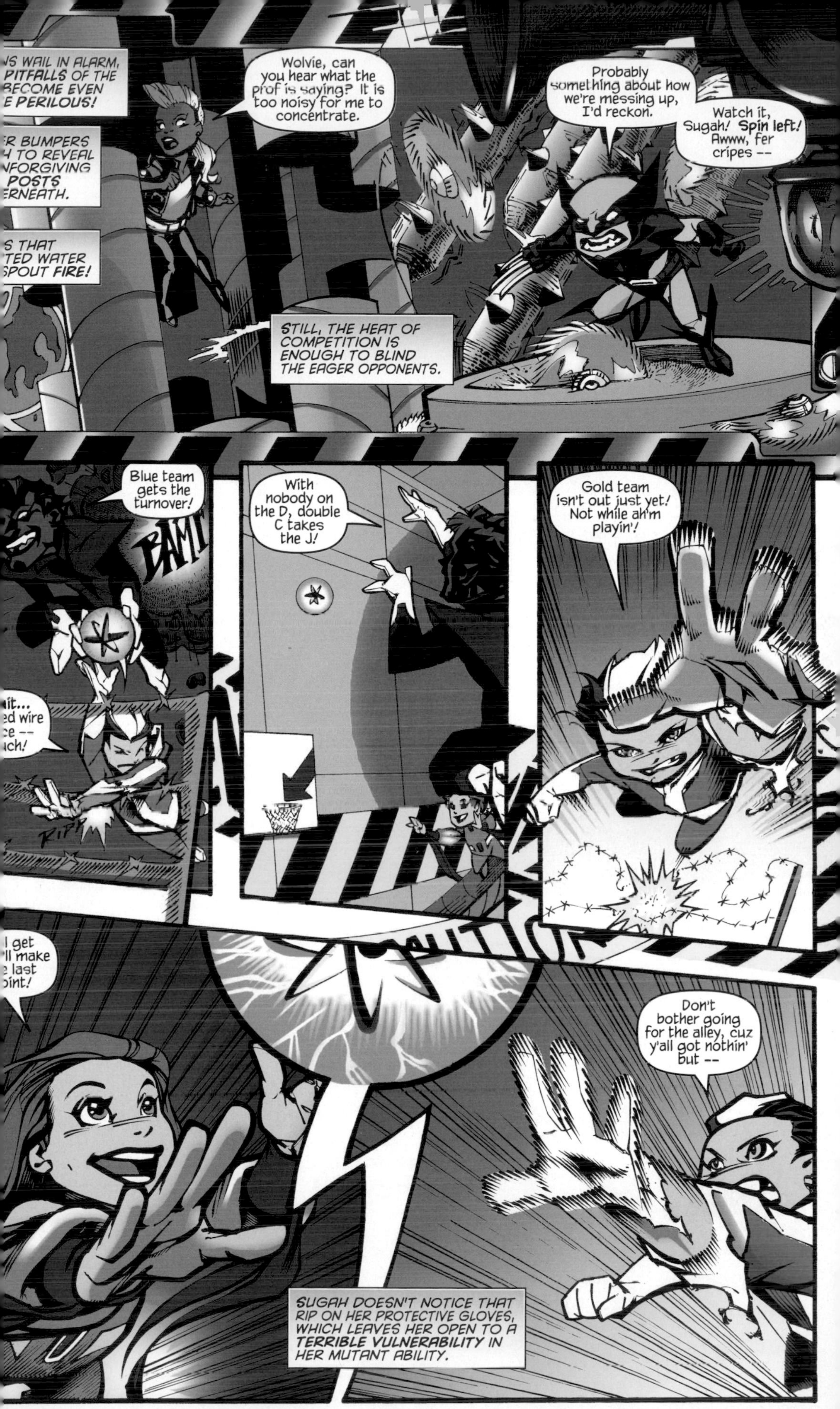

WS WAIL IN ALARM, PITFALLS OF THE BECOME EVEN E PERILOUS!
Wolvie, can you hear what the prof is saying? It is too noisy for me to concentrate.
Probably something about how we're messing up, I'd reckon.
Watch it, Sugah! Spin left! Awww, fer cripes --
ER BUMPERS H TO REVEAL NFORGIVING POSTS ERNEATH.
S THAT TED WATER SPOUT FIRE!
STILL, THE HEAT OF COMPETITION IS ENOUGH TO BLIND THE EAGER OPPONENTS.
Blue team gets the turnover!
BAM!
ait... ed wire ce -- ch!
RIP
With nobody on the D, double C takes the J!
Gold team isn't out just yet! Not while ah'm playin'!
l get 'll make e last oint!
Don't bother going for the alley, cuz y'all got nothin' but --
SUGAH DOESN'T NOTICE THAT RIP ON HER PROTECTIVE GLOVES, WHICH LEAVES HER OPEN TO A TERRIBLE VULNERABILITY IN HER MUTANT ABILITY.

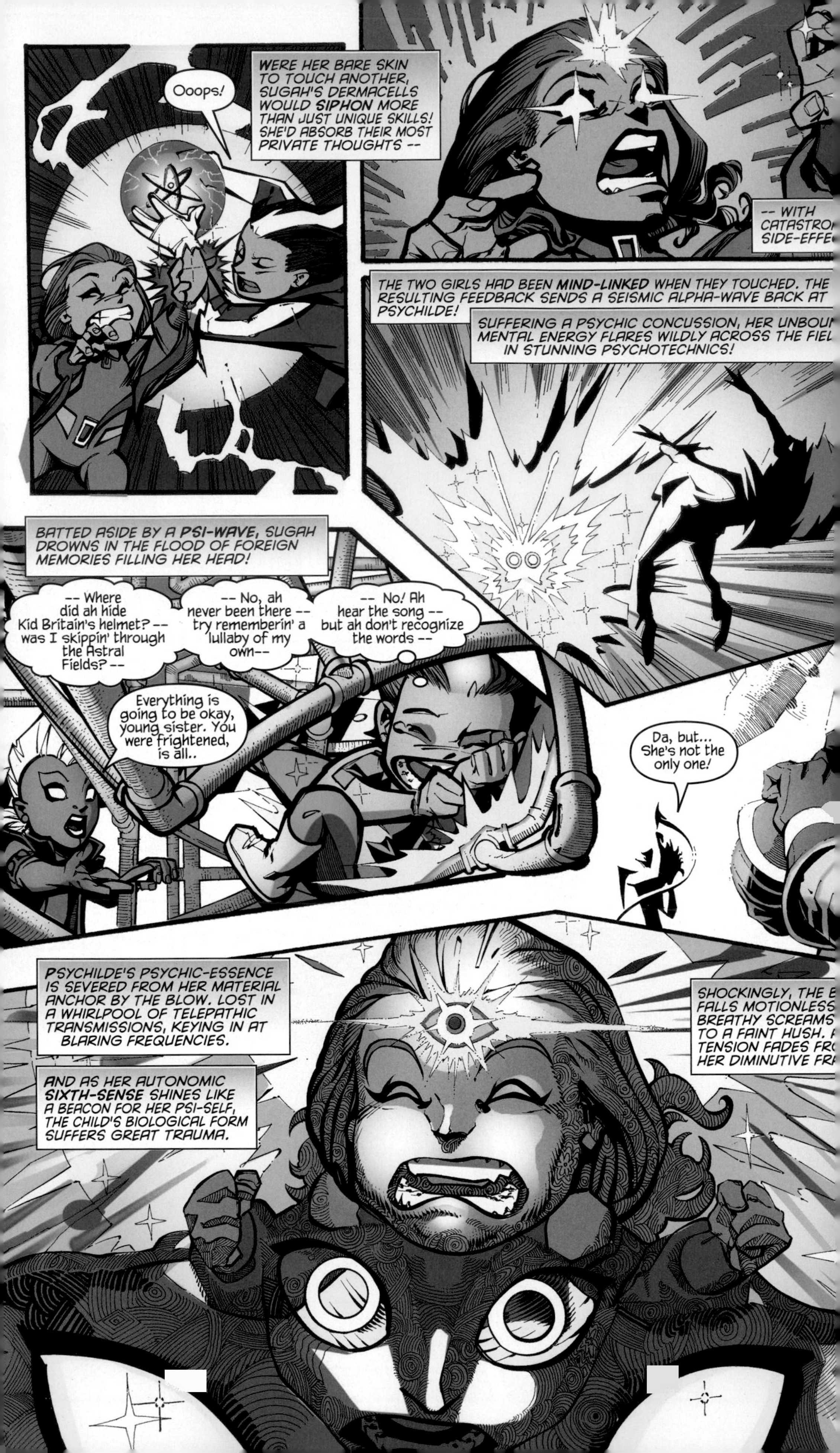
Ooops!
WERE HER BARE SKIN TO TOUCH ANOTHER, SUGAH'S DERMACELLS WOULD SIPHON MORE THAN JUST UNIQUE SKILLS! SHE'D ABSORB THEIR MOST PRIVATE THOUGHTS --
-- WITH CATASTRO SIDE-EFFE
THE TWO GIRLS HAD BEEN MIND-LINKED WHEN THEY TOUCHED. THE RESULTING FEEDBACK SENDS A SEISMIC ALPHA-WAVE BACK AT PSYCHILDE!
SUFFERING A PSYCHIC CONCUSSION, HER UNBOU MENTAL ENERGY FLARES WILDLY ACROSS THE FIEL IN STUNNING PSYCHOTECHNICS!
BATTED ASIDE BY A PSI-WAVE, SUGAH DROWNS IN THE FLOOD OF FOREIGN MEMORIES FILLING HER HEAD!
-- Where did ah hide Kid Britain's helmet? -- was I skippin' through the Astral Fields? --
-- No, ah never been there -- try rememberin' a lullaby of my own--
-- No! Ah hear the song -- but ah don't recognize the words --
Everything is going to be okay, young sister. You were frightened, is all..
Da, but... She's not the only one!
PSYCHILDE'S PSYCHIC-ESSENCE IS SEVERED FROM HER MATERIAL ANCHOR BY THE BLOW. LOST IN A WHIRLPOOL OF TELEPATHIC TRANSMISSIONS, KEYING IN AT BLARING FREQUENCIES.
AND AS HER AUTONOMIC SIXTH-SENSE SHINES LIKE A BEACON FOR HER PSI-SELF, THE CHILD'S BIOLOGICAL FORM SUFFERS GREAT TRAUMA.
SHOCKINGLY, THE FALLS MOTIONLESS BREATHY SCREAMS TO A FAINT HUSH. TENSION FADES FR HER DIMINUTIVE FR

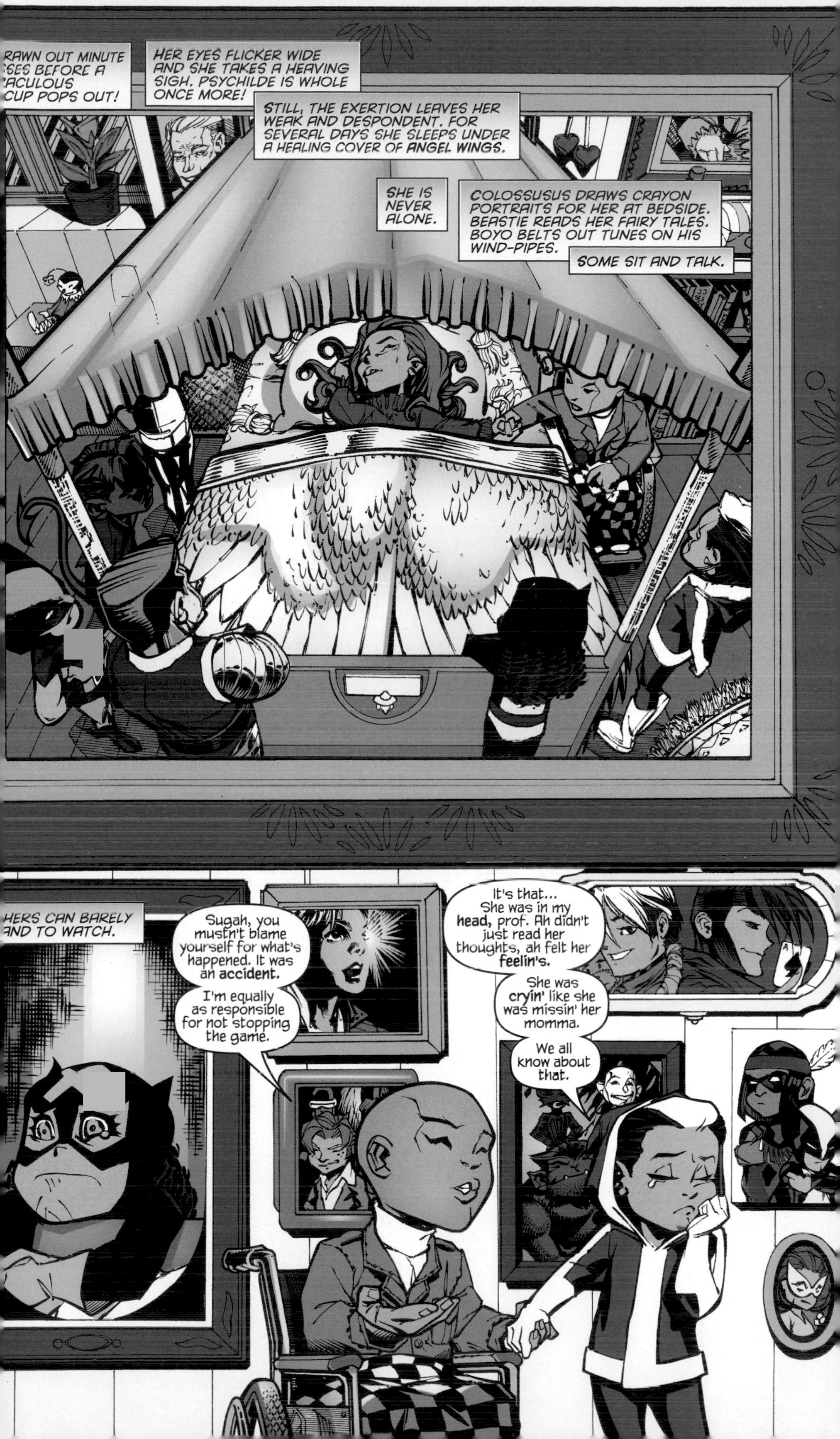

RAWN OUT MINUTE SES BEFORE A ACULOUS CUP POPS OUT!
HER EYES FLICKER WIDE AND SHE TAKES A HEAVING SIGH. PSYCHILDE IS WHOLE ONCE MORE!
STILL, THE EXERTION LEAVES HER WEAK AND DESPONDENT. FOR SEVERAL DAYS SHE SLEEPS UNDER A HEALING COVER OF ANGEL WINGS.
SHE IS NEVER ALONE.
COLOSSUSUS DRAWS CRAYON PORTRAITS FOR HER AT BEDSIDE. BEASTIE READS HER FAIRY TALES. BOYO BELTS OUT TUNES ON HIS WIND-PIPES.
SOME SIT AND TALK.
HERS CAN BARELY AND TO WATCH.
Sugah, you mustn't blame yourself for what's happened. It was an accident.
I'm equally as responsible for not stopping the game.
It's that... She was in my head, prof. Ah didn't just read her thoughts, ah felt her feelin's.
She was cryin' like she was missin' her momma.
We all know about that.

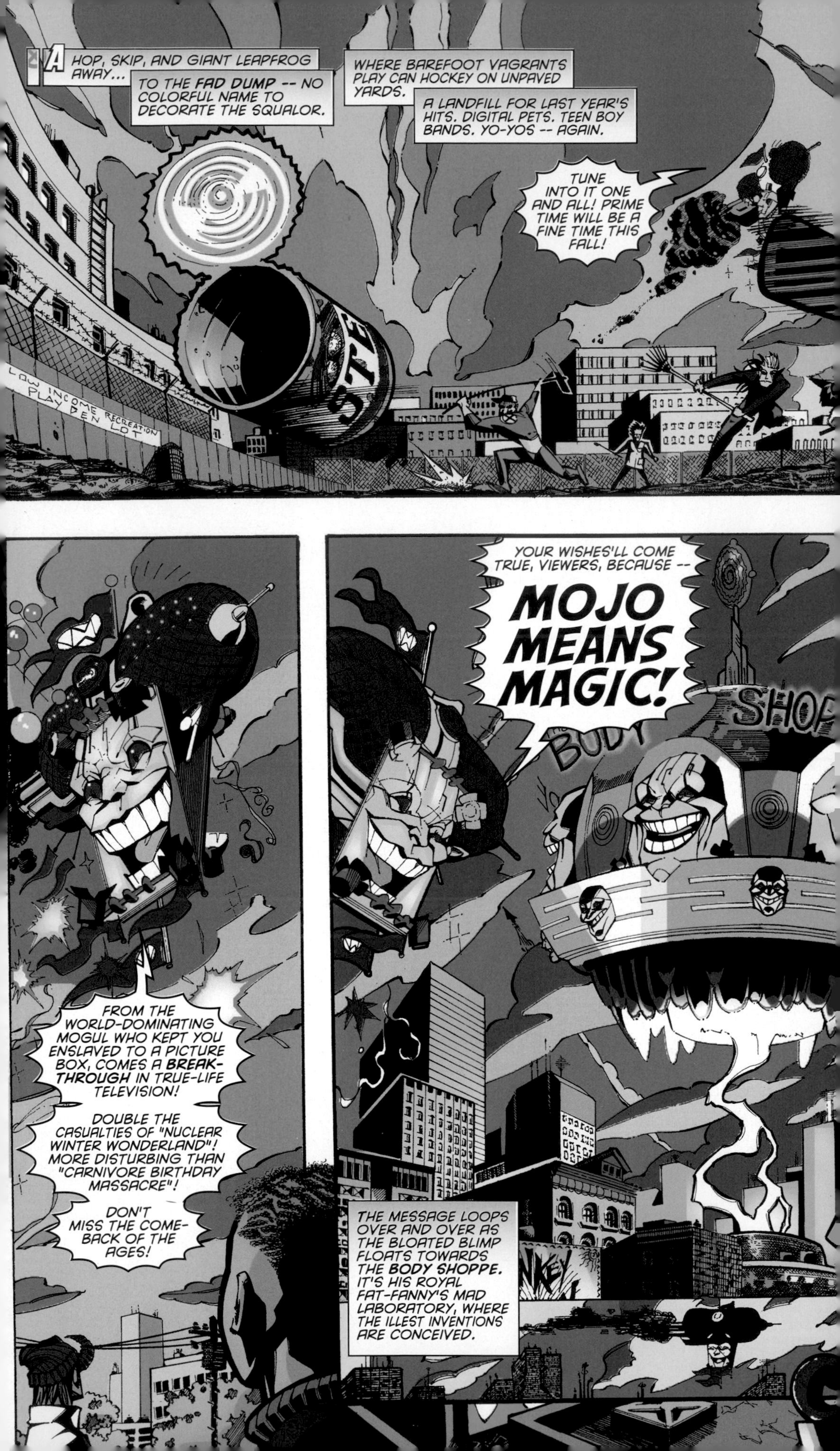

HOP, SKIP, AND GIANT LEAPFROG AWAY...
TO THE **FAD DUMP** -- NO COLORFUL NAME TO DECORATE THE SQUALOR.
WHERE BAREFOOT VAGRANTS PLAY CAN HOCKEY ON UNPAVED YARDS.
A LANDFILL FOR LAST YEAR'S HITS. DIGITAL PETS. TEEN BOY BANDS. YO-YOS -- AGAIN.
TUNE INTO IT ONE AND ALL! PRIME TIME WILL BE A FINE TIME THIS FALL!
LOW INCOME RECREATION PLAY PEN LOT
FROM THE WORLD-DOMINATING MOGUL WHO KEPT YOU ENSLAVED TO A PICTURE BOX, COMES A **BREAK-THROUGH** IN TRUE-LIFE TELEVISION!
DOUBLE THE CASUALTIES OF "NUCLEAR WINTER WONDERLAND"! MORE DISTURBING THAN "CARNIVORE BIRTHDAY MASSACRE"!
DON'T MISS THE COME-BACK OF THE AGES!
YOUR WISHES'LL COME TRUE, VIEWERS, BECAUSE --
MOJO MEANS MAGIC!
THE MESSAGE LOOPS OVER AND OVER AS THE BLOATED BLIMP FLOATS TOWARDS THE **BODY SHOPPE.** IT'S HIS ROYAL FAT-FANNY'S MAD LABORATORY, WHERE THE ILLEST INVENTIONS ARE CONCEIVED.

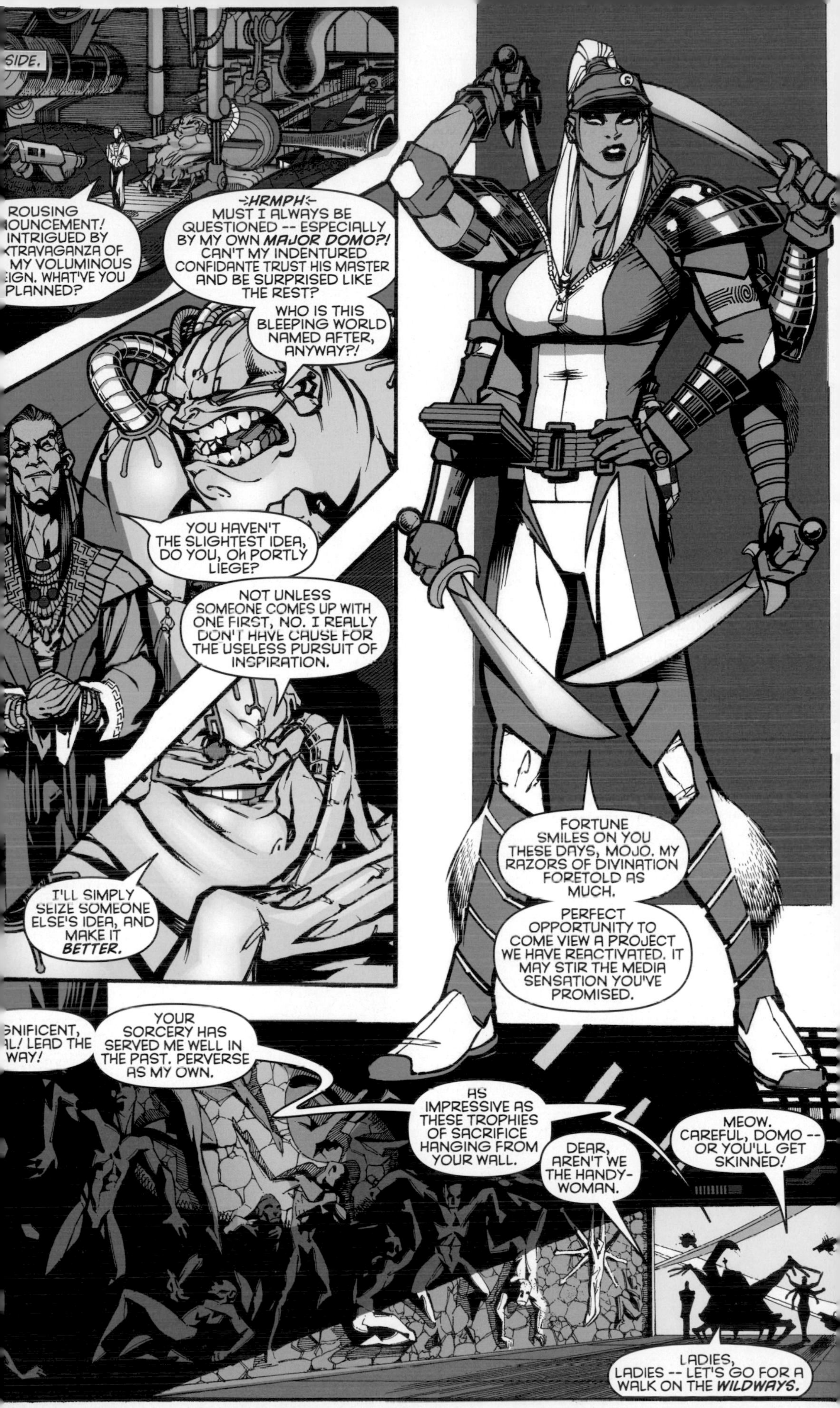
SIDE.
ROUSING
OUNCEMENT! INTRIGUED BY
XTRAVAGANZA OF
MY VOLUMINOUS
EIGN. WHAT'VE YOU
PLANNED?
HRMPH
MUST I ALWAYS BE QUESTIONED -- ESPECIALLY BY MY OWN MAJOR DOMO?! CAN'T MY INDENTURED CONFIDANTE TRUST HIS MASTER AND BE SURPRISED LIKE THE REST?
WHO IS THIS BLEEPING WORLD NAMED AFTER, ANYWAY?!
YOU HAVEN'T THE SLIGHTEST IDEA, DO YOU, Oh PORTLY LIEGE?
NOT UNLESS SOMEONE COMES UP WITH ONE FIRST, NO. I REALLY DON'T HAVE CAUSE FOR THE USELESS PURSUIT OF INSPIRATION.
I'LL SIMPLY SEIZE SOMEONE ELSE'S IDEA, AND MAKE IT BETTER.
FORTUNE SMILES ON YOU THESE DAYS, MOJO. MY RAZORS OF DIVINATION FORETOLD AS MUCH.
PERFECT OPPORTUNITY TO COME VIEW A PROJECT WE HAVE REACTIVATED. IT MAY STIR THE MEDIA SENSATION YOU'VE PROMISED.
GNIFICENT,
AL! LEAD THE
WAY!
YOUR SORCERY HAS SERVED ME WELL IN THE PAST. PERVERSE AS MY OWN.
AS IMPRESSIVE AS THESE TROPHIES OF SACRIFICE HANGING FROM YOUR WALL.
DEAR, AREN'T WE THE HANDY-WOMAN.
MEOW. CAREFUL, DOMO -- OR YOU'LL GET SKINNED!
LADIES, LADIES -- LET'S GO FOR A WALK ON THE WILDWAYS.

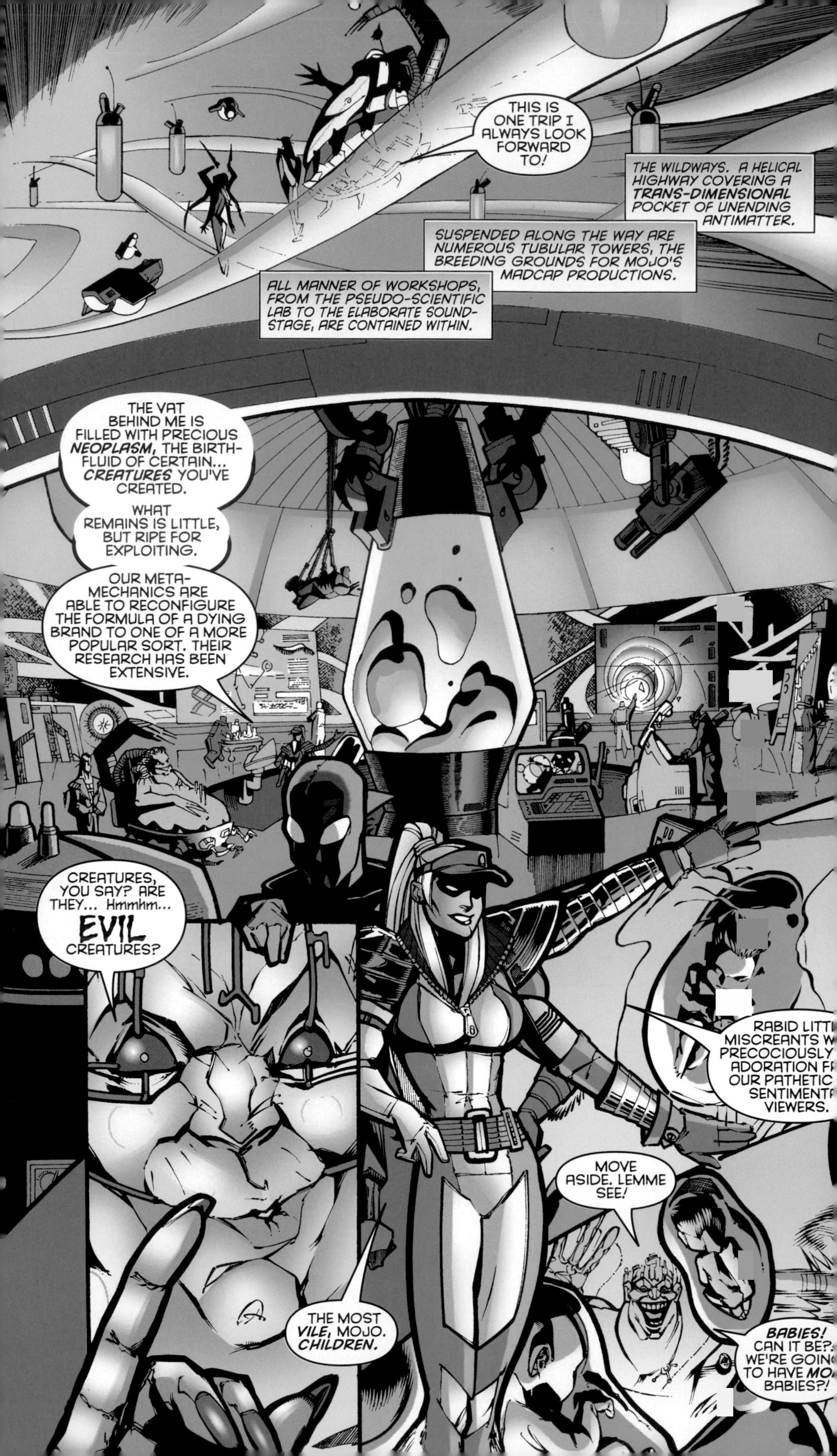
THIS IS ONE TRIP I ALWAYS LOOK FORWARD TO!
THE WILDWAYS. A HELICAL HIGHWAY COVERING A TRANS-DIMENSIONAL POCKET OF UNENDING ANTIMATTER.
SUSPENDED ALONG THE WAY ARE NUMEROUS TUBULAR TOWERS, THE BREEDING GROUNDS FOR MOJO'S MADCAP PRODUCTIONS.
ALL MANNER OF WORKSHOPS, FROM THE PSEUDO-SCIENTIFIC LAB TO THE ELABORATE SOUND-STAGE, ARE CONTAINED WITHIN.
THE VAT BEHIND ME IS FILLED WITH PRECIOUS NEOPLASM, THE BIRTH-FLUID OF CERTAIN... CREATURES YOU'VE CREATED.
WHAT REMAINS IS LITTLE, BUT RIPE FOR EXPLOITING.
OUR META-MECHANICS ARE ABLE TO RECONFIGURE THE FORMULA OF A DYING BRAND TO ONE OF A MORE POPULAR SORT. THEIR RESEARCH HAS BEEN EXTENSIVE.
CREATURES, YOU SAY? ARE THEY... Hmmhm... EVIL CREATURES?
RABID LITT
MISCREANTS W
PRECOCIOUSLY
ADORATION F
OUR PATHETIC
SENTIMENT
VIEWERS.
THE MOST VILE, MOJO. CHILDREN.
MOVE ASIDE. LEMME SEE!
BABIES! CAN IT BE?.. WE'RE GOIN TO HAVE MO BABIES?!

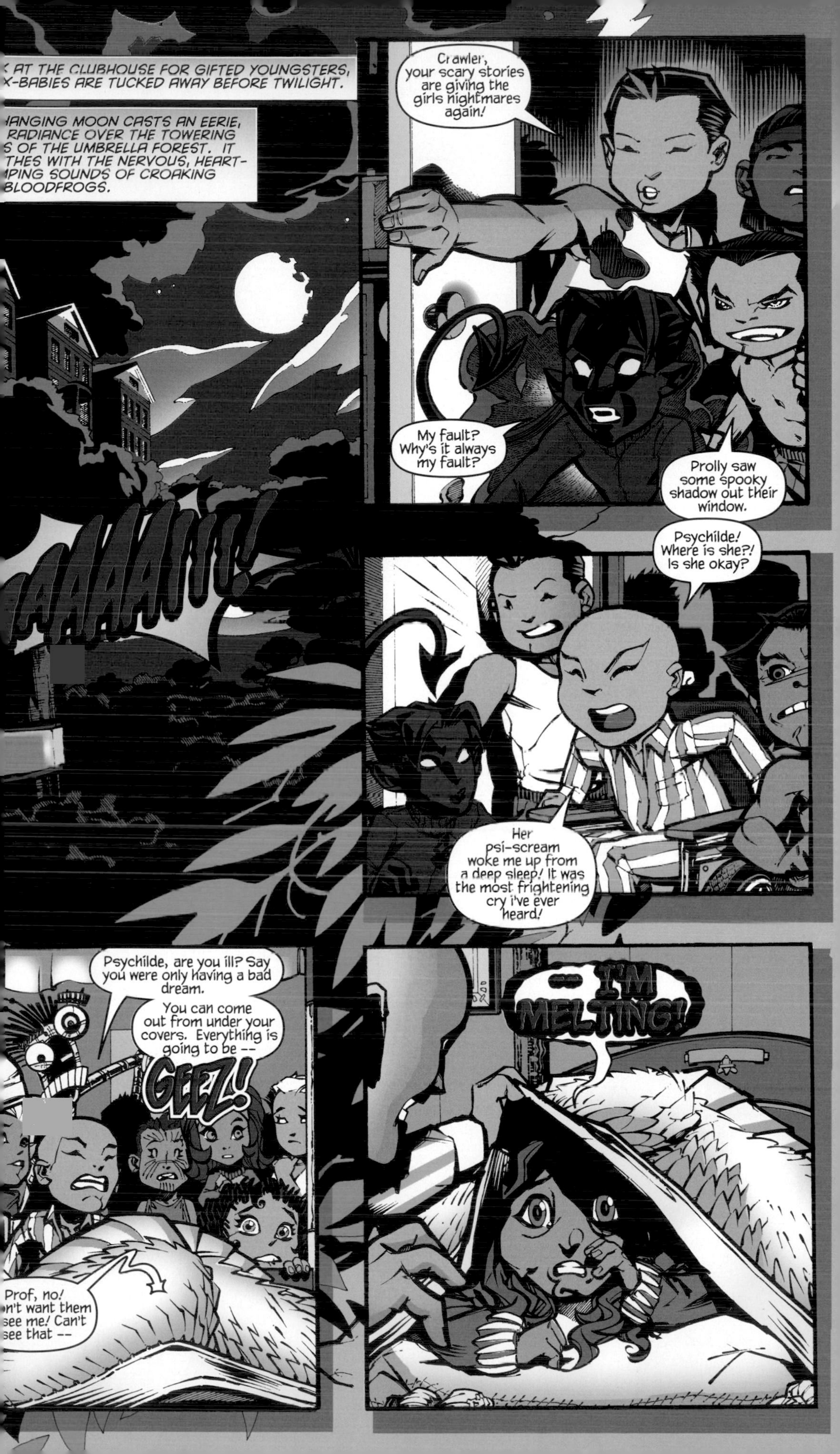
K AT THE CLUBHOUSE FOR GIFTED YOUNGSTERS, X-BABIES ARE TUCKED AWAY BEFORE TWILIGHT.
HANGING MOON CASTS AN EERIE, RADIANCE OVER THE TOWERING S OF THE UMBRELLA FOREST. IT THES WITH THE NERVOUS, HEART-MPING SOUNDS OF CROAKING BLOODFROGS.
Crawler, your scary stories are giving the girls nightmares again!
My fault? Why's it always my fault?
Prolly saw some spooky shadow out their window.
Psychilde! Where is she?! Is she okay?
Her psi-scream woke me up from a deep sleep! It was the most frightening cry I've ever heard!
Psychilde, are you ill? Say you were only having a bad dream.
You can come out from under your covers. Everything is going to be --
GEEZ!
Prof, no! n't want them see me! Can't see that --
-- I'M MELTING!

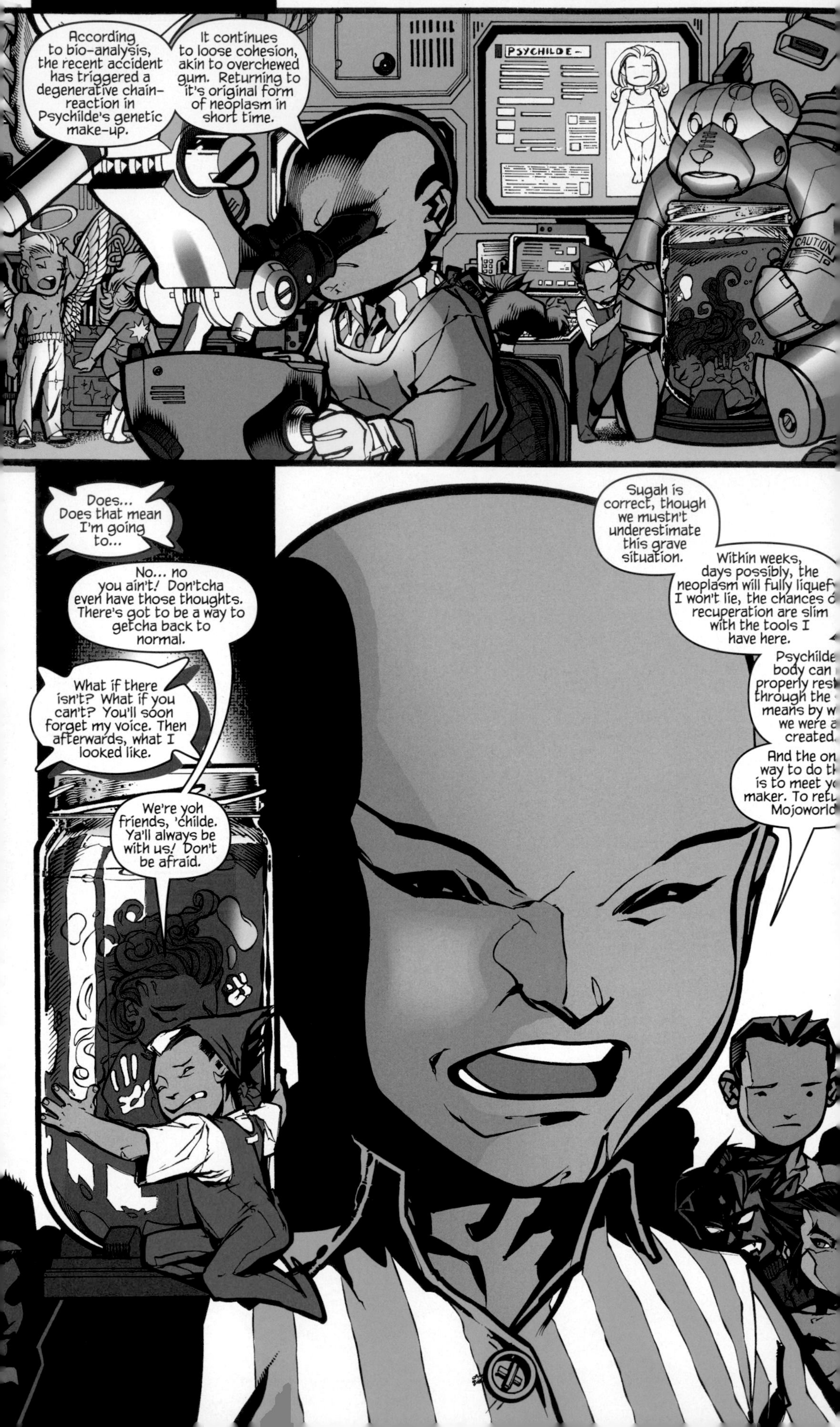
According to bio-analysis, the recent accident has triggered a degenerative chain-reaction in Psychilde's genetic make-up.
It continues to loose cohesion, akin to overchewed gum. Returning to it's original form of neoplasm in short time.
PSYCHILDE-
CAUTION
Does... Does that mean I'm going to...
No... no you ain't! Don'tcha even have those thoughts. There's got to be a way to getcha back to normal.
What if there isn't? What if you can't? You'll soon forget my voice. Then afterwards, what I looked like.
We're yoh friends, 'childe. Ya'll always be with us! Don't be afraid.
Sugah is correct, though we mustn't underestimate this grave situation.
Within weeks, days possibly, the neoplasm will fully liquef I won't lie, the chances o recuperation are slim with the tools I have here.
Psychilde body can properly res through the means by w we were a created.
And the on way to do t is to meet y maker. To ret Mojoworld

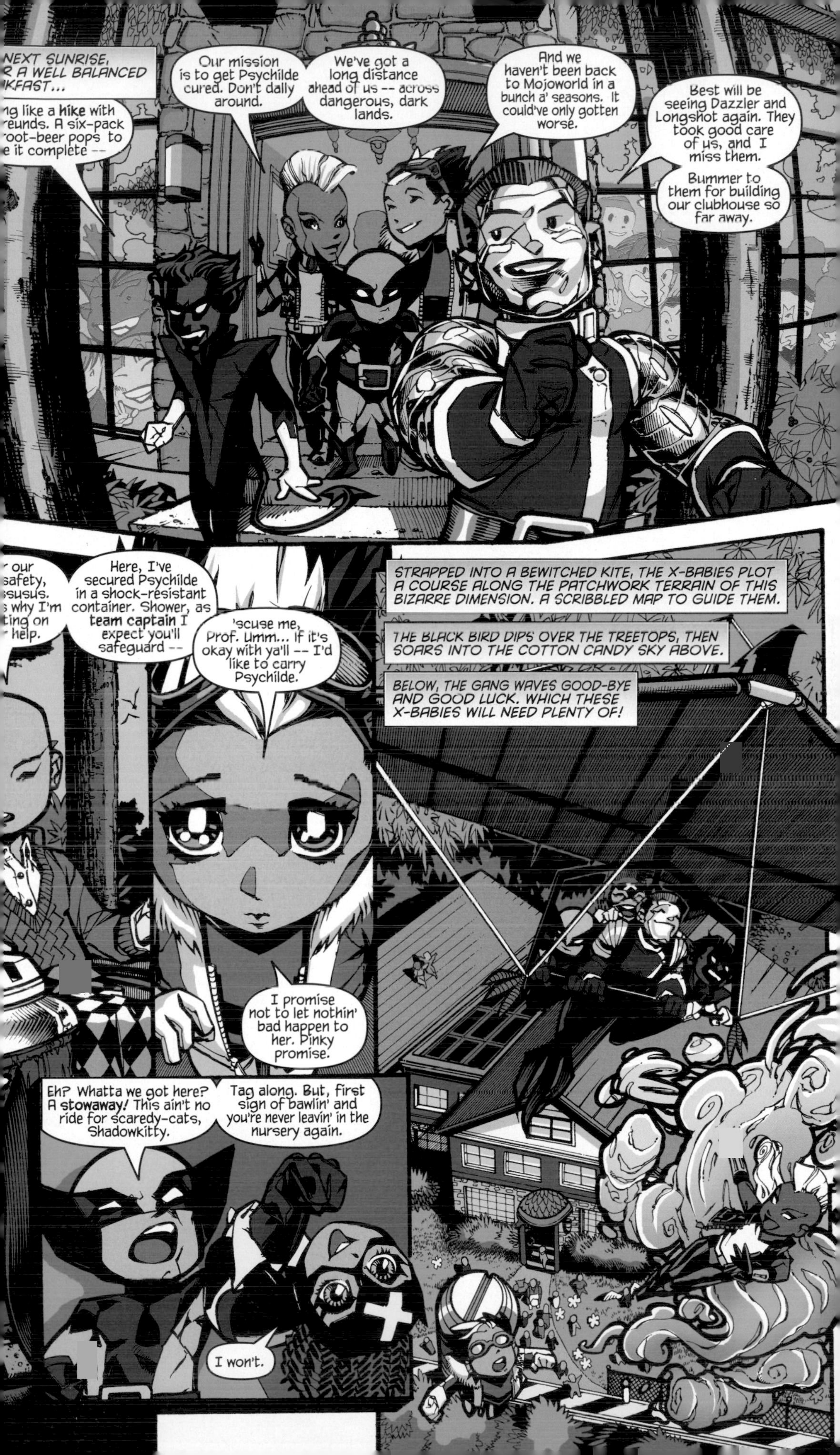

NEXT SUNRISE, R A WELL BALANCED KFAST...
ng like a hike with reunds. A six-pack root-beer pops to e it complete --
Our mission is to get Psychilde cured. Don't dally around.
We've got a long distance ahead of us -- across dangerous, dark lands.
And we haven't been back to Mojoworld in a bunch a' seasons. It could've only gotten worse.
Best will be seeing Dazzler and Longshot again. They took good care of us, and I miss them.
Bummer to them for building our clubhouse so far away.
r our safety, ssusus. s why I'm ting on help.
Here, I've secured Psychilde in a shock-resistant container. Shower, as team captain I expect you'll safeguard --
'scuse me, Prof. Umm... If it's okay with ya'll -- I'd like to carry Psychilde.
I promise not to let nothin' bad happen to her. Pinky promise.
Eh? Whatta we got here? A stowaway! This ain't no ride for scaredy-cats, Shadowkitty.
Tag along. But, first sign of bawlin' and you're never leavin' in the nursery again.
I won't.
STRAPPED INTO A BEWITCHED KITE, THE X-BABIES PLOT A COURSE ALONG THE PATCHWORK TERRAIN OF THIS BIZARRE DIMENSION. A SCRIBBLED MAP TO GUIDE THEM.
THE BLACK BIRD DIPS OVER THE TREETOPS, THEN SOARS INTO THE COTTON CANDY SKY ABOVE.
BELOW, THE GANG WAVES GOOD-BYE AND GOOD LUCK. WHICH THESE X-BABIES WILL NEED PLENTY OF!

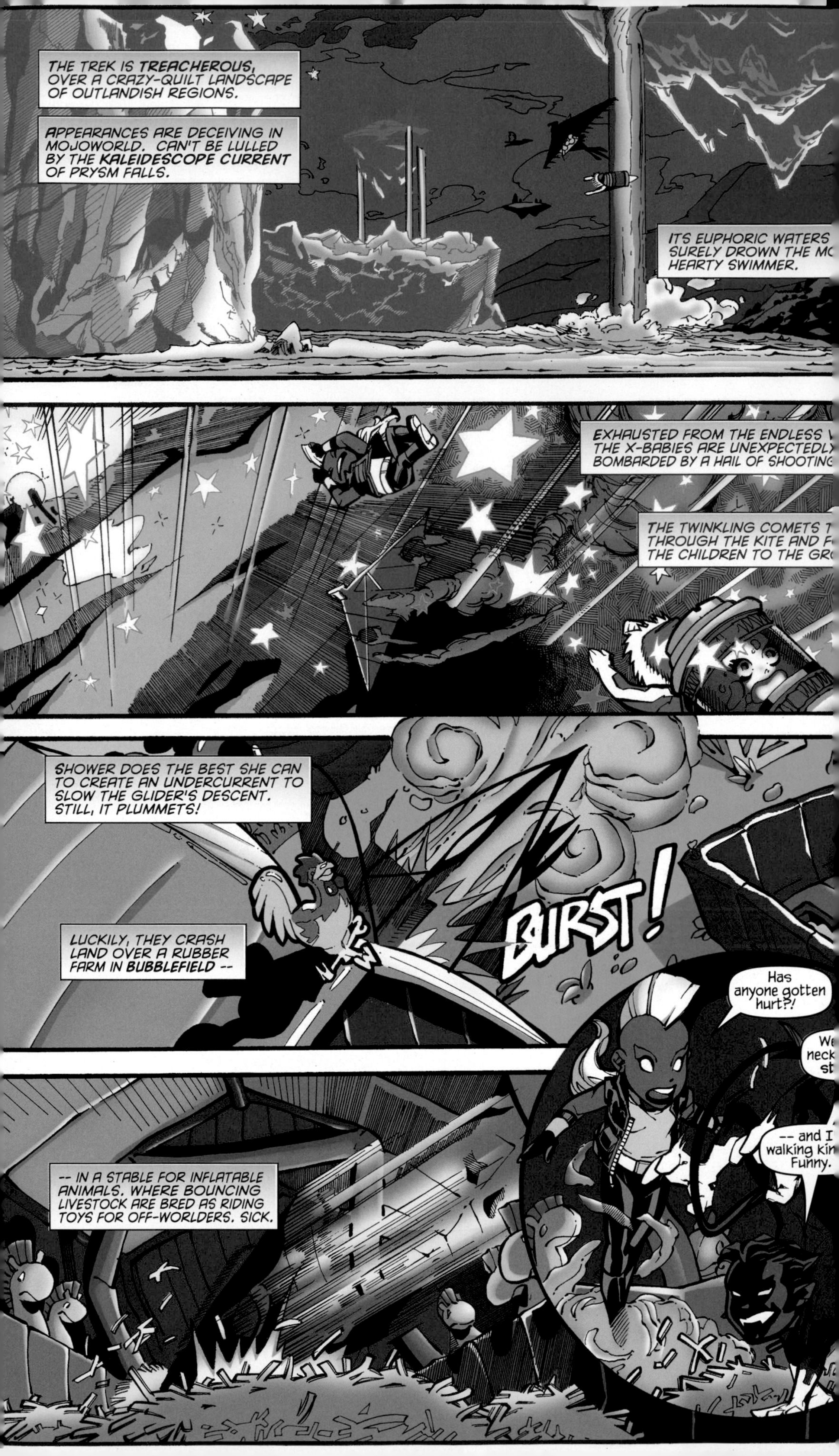
THE TREK IS TREACHEROUS, OVER A CRAZY-QUILT LANDSCAPE OF OUTLANDISH REGIONS.
APPEARANCES ARE DECEIVING IN MOJOWORLD. CAN'T BE LULLED BY THE KALEIDESCOPE CURRENT OF PRYSM FALLS.
ITS EUPHORIC WATERS SURELY DROWN THE MO HEARTY SWIMMER.
EXHAUSTED FROM THE ENDLESS THE X-BABIES ARE UNEXPECTEDLY BOMBARDED BY A HAIL OF SHOOTING
THE TWINKLING COMETS THROUGH THE KITE AND THE CHILDREN TO THE GR
SHOWER DOES THE BEST SHE CAN TO CREATE AN UNDERCURRENT TO SLOW THE GLIDER'S DESCENT. STILL, IT PLUMMETS!
BURST!
LUCKILY, THEY CRASH LAND OVER A RUBBER FARM IN BUBBLEFIELD --
Has anyone gotten hurt?!
-- IN A STABLE FOR INFLATABLE ANIMALS. WHERE BOUNCING LIVESTOCK ARE BRED AS RIDING TOYS FOR OFF-WORLDERS. SICK.
-- and I walking ki Funny.

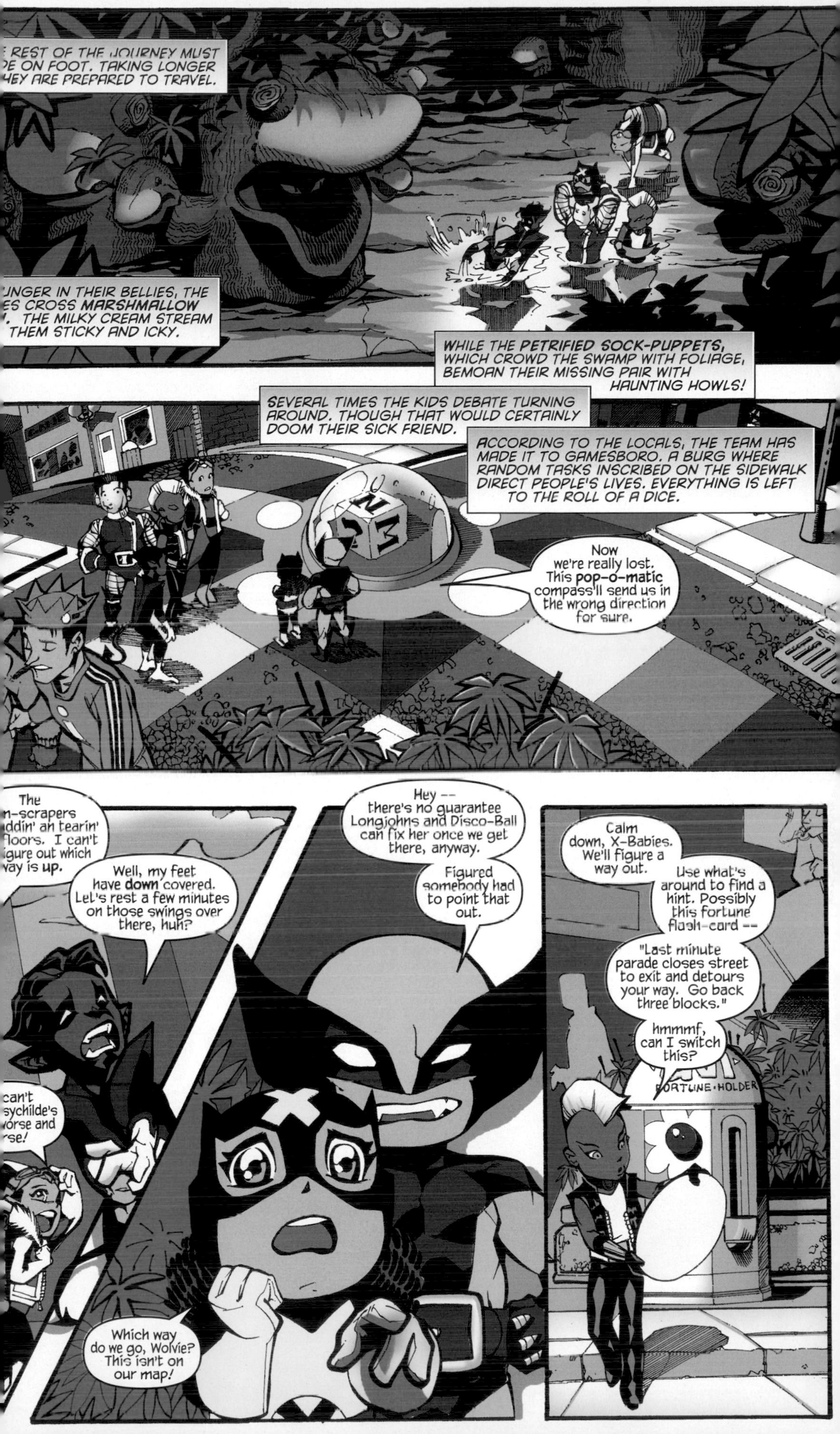
E REST OF THE JOURNEY MUST E ON FOOT. TAKING LONGER HEY ARE PREPARED TO TRAVEL.
UNGER IN THEIR BELLIES, THE ES CROSS MARSHMALLOW . THE MILKY CREAM STREAM THEM STICKY AND ICKY.
WHILE THE PETRIFIED SOCK-PUPPETS, WHICH CROWD THE SWAMP WITH FOLIAGE, BEMOAN THEIR MISSING PAIR WITH HAUNTING HOWLS!
SEVERAL TIMES THE KIDS DEBATE TURNING AROUND. THOUGH THAT WOULD CERTAINLY DOOM THEIR SICK FRIEND.
ACCORDING TO THE LOCALS, THE TEAM HAS MADE IT TO GAMESBORO. A BURG WHERE RANDOM TASKS INSCRIBED ON THE SIDEWALK DIRECT PEOPLE'S LIVES. EVERYTHING IS LEFT TO THE ROLL OF A DICE.
Now we're really lost. This pop-o-matic compass'll send us in the wrong direction for sure.
The n-scrapers ddin' an tearin' floors. I can't igure out which vay is up.
Well, my feet have down covered. Let's rest a few minutes on those swings over there, huh?
can't sychilde's vorse and rse!
Which way do we go, Wolvie? This isn't on our map!
Hey -- there's no guarantee Longjohns and Disco-Ball can fix her once we get there, anyway.
Figured somebody had to point that out.
Calm down, X-Babies. We'll figure a way out.
Use what's around to find a hint. Possibly this fortune flash-card --
"Last minute parade closes street to exit and detours your way. Go back three blocks."
hmmmf, can I switch this?
FORTUNE·HOLDER

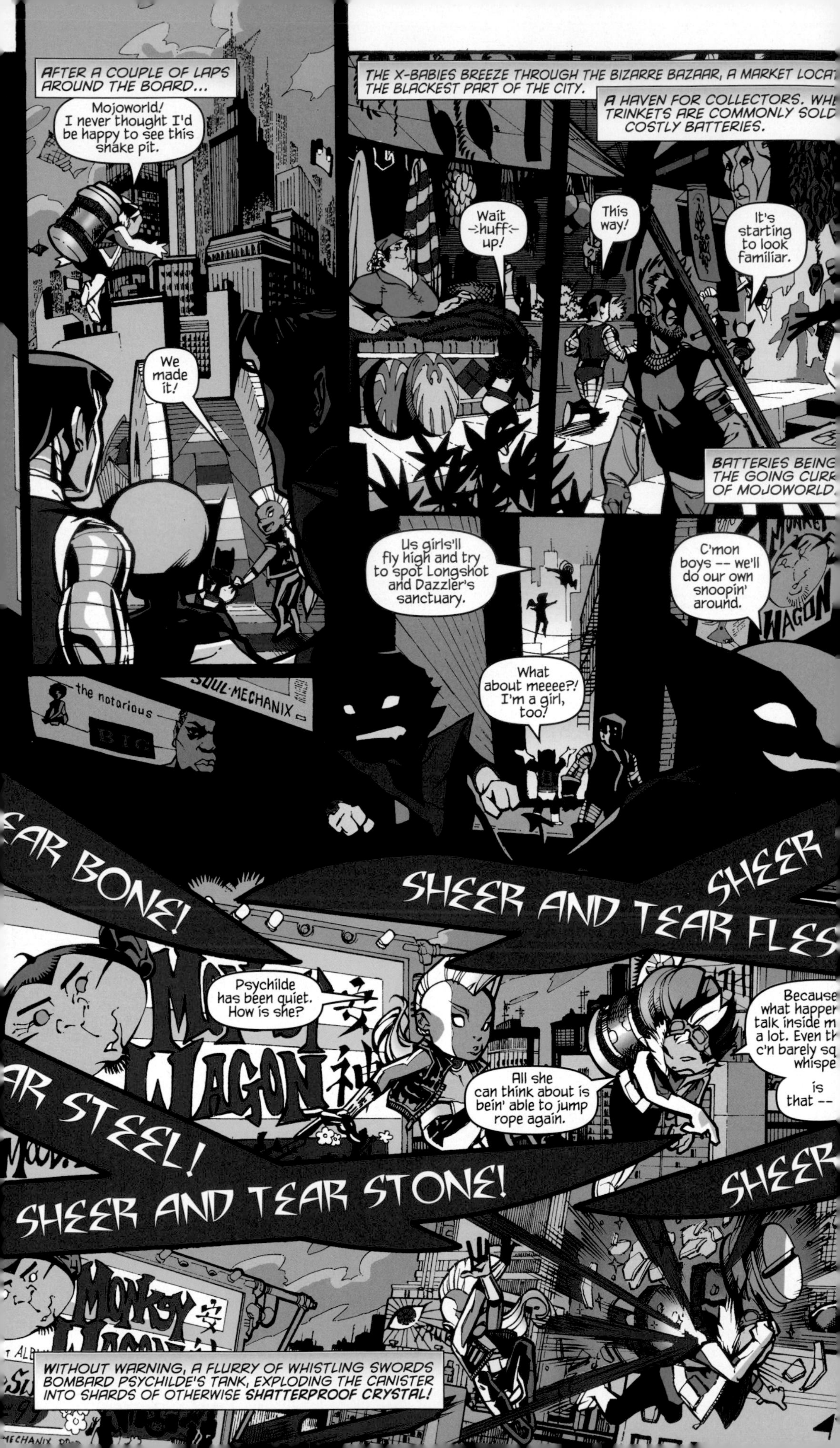

AFTER A COUPLE OF LAPS AROUND THE BOARD...
Mojoworld! I never thought I'd be happy to see this snake pit.
We made it!
THE X-BABIES BREEZE THROUGH THE BIZARRE BAZAAR, A MARKET LOCAT
THE BLACKEST PART OF THE CITY.
A HAVEN FOR COLLECTORS. WHE
TRINKETS ARE COMMONLY SOLD
COSTLY BATTERIES.
Wait -huff- up!
This way!
It's starting to look familiar.
BATTERIES BEING
THE GOING CURR
OF MOJOWORLD.
Us girls'll fly high and try to spot Longshot and Dazzler's sanctuary.
C'mon boys -- we'll do our own snoopin' around.
the notarious
BIG
SOUL·MECHANIX
What about meeee?! I'm a girl, too!
EAR BONE!
SHEER AND TEAR FLES
SHEER
WAGON
Psychilde has been quiet. How is she?
Because
what happe
talk inside m
a lot. Even th
c'n barely sq
whispe
All she can think about is bein' able to jump rope again.
is that --
AR STEEL!
SHEER AND TEAR STONE!
SHEER
WITHOUT WARNING, A FLURRY OF WHISTLING SWORDS BOMBARD PSYCHILDE'S TANK, EXPLODING THE CANISTER INTO SHARDS OF OTHERWISE SHATTERPROOF CRYSTAL!

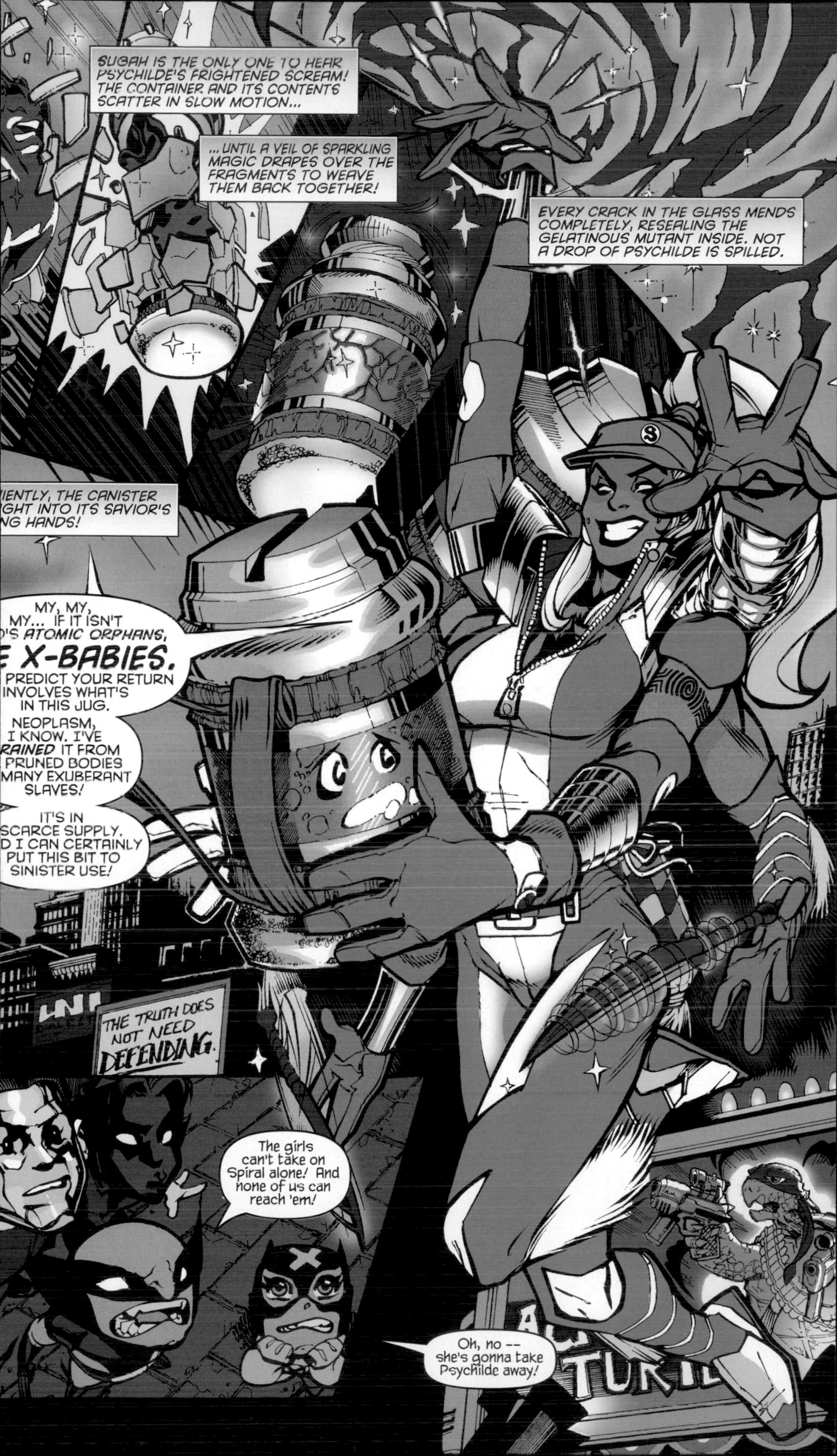
SUGAH IS THE ONLY ONE TO HEAR PSYCHILDE'S FRIGHTENED SCREAM! THE CONTAINER AND ITS CONTENTS SCATTER IN SLOW MOTION...
...UNTIL A VEIL OF SPARKLING MAGIC DRAPES OVER THE FRAGMENTS TO WEAVE THEM BACK TOGETHER!
EVERY CRACK IN THE GLASS MENDS COMPLETELY, RESEALING THE GELATINOUS MUTANT INSIDE. NOT A DROP OF PSYCHILDE IS SPILLED.
IENTLY, THE CANISTER GHT INTO ITS SAVIOR'S NG HANDS!
MY, MY, MY... IF IT ISN'T 'S ATOMIC ORPHANS, E X-BABIES. PREDICT YOUR RETURN INVOLVES WHAT'S IN THIS JUG.
NEOPLASM, I KNOW. I'VE RAINED IT FROM PRUNED BODIES MANY EXUBERANT SLAVES!
IT'S IN SCARCE SUPPLY. D I CAN CERTAINLY PUT THIS BIT TO SINISTER USE!
THE TRUTH DOES NOT NEED DEFENDING.
The girls can't take on Spiral alone! And none of us can reach 'em!
Oh, no -- she's gonna take Psychilde away!

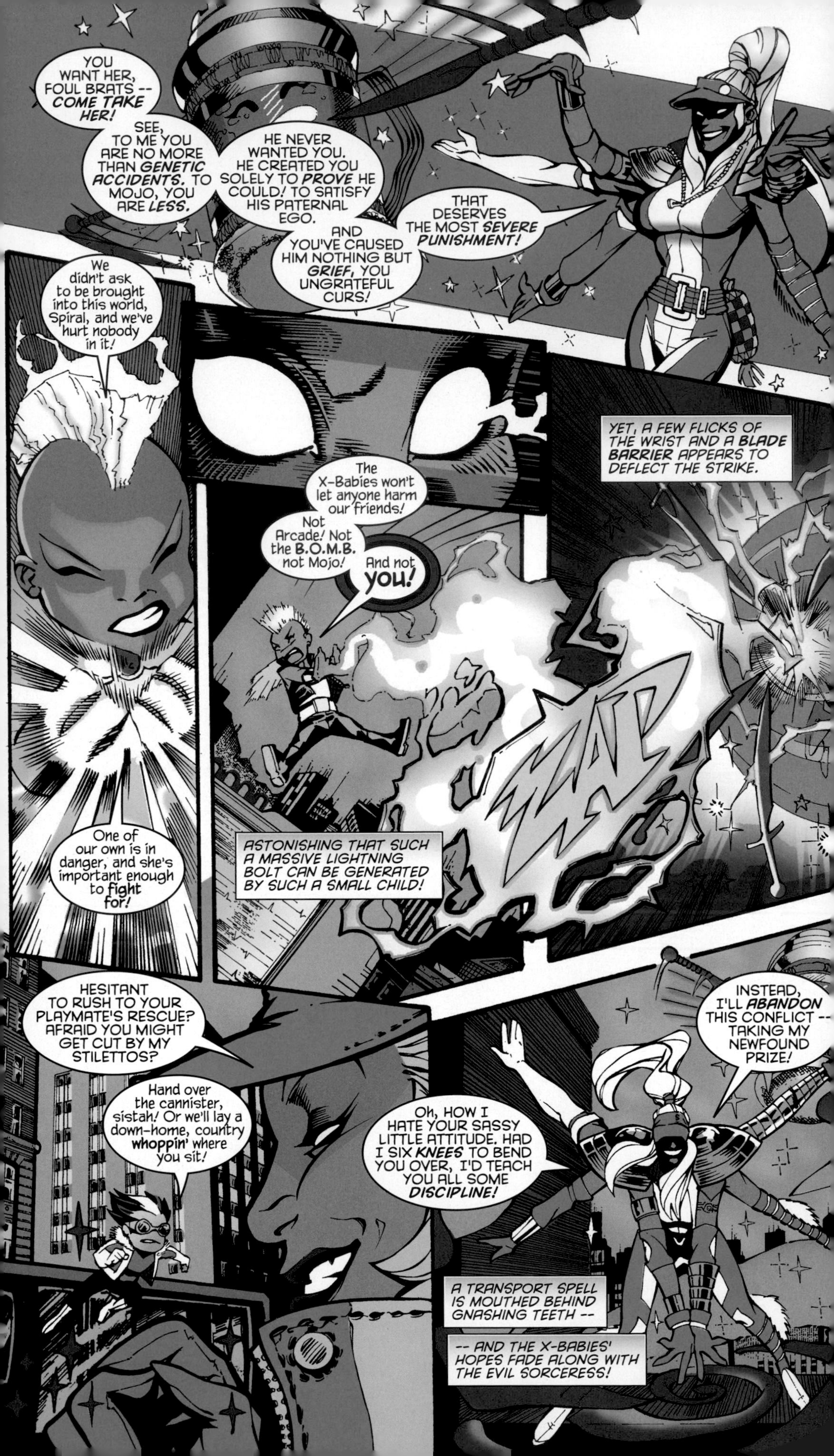
YOU WANT HER, FOUL BRATS -- COME TAKE HER!
SEE, TO ME YOU ARE NO MORE THAN GENETIC ACCIDENTS. TO MOJO, YOU ARE LESS.
HE NEVER WANTED YOU. HE CREATED YOU SOLELY TO PROVE HE COULD! TO SATISFY HIS PATERNAL EGO.
AND YOU'VE CAUSED HIM NOTHING BUT GRIEF, YOU UNGRATEFUL CURS!
THAT DESERVES THE MOST SEVERE PUNISHMENT!
We didn't ask to be brought into this world, Spiral, and we've hurt nobody in it!
One of our own is in danger, and she's important enough to fight for!
The X-Babies won't let anyone harm our friends!
Not Arcade! Not the B.O.M.B. not Mojo!
And not you!
ASTONISHING THAT SUCH A MASSIVE LIGHTNING BOLT CAN BE GENERATED BY SUCH A SMALL CHILD!
YET, A FEW FLICKS OF THE WRIST AND A BLADE BARRIER APPEARS TO DEFLECT THE STRIKE.
HESITANT TO RUSH TO YOUR PLAYMATE'S RESCUE? AFRAID YOU MIGHT GET CUT BY MY STILETTOS?
Hand over the cannister, sistah! Or we'll lay a down-home, country whoppin' where you sit!
Oh, HOW I HATE YOUR SASSY LITTLE ATTITUDE. HAD I SIX KNEES TO BEND YOU OVER, I'D TEACH YOU ALL SOME DISCIPLINE!
INSTEAD, I'LL ABANDON THIS CONFLICT -- TAKING MY NEWFOUND PRIZE!
A TRANSPORT SPELL IS MOUTHED BEHIND GNASHING TEETH --
-- AND THE X-BABIES' HOPES FADE ALONG WITH THE EVIL SORCERESS!

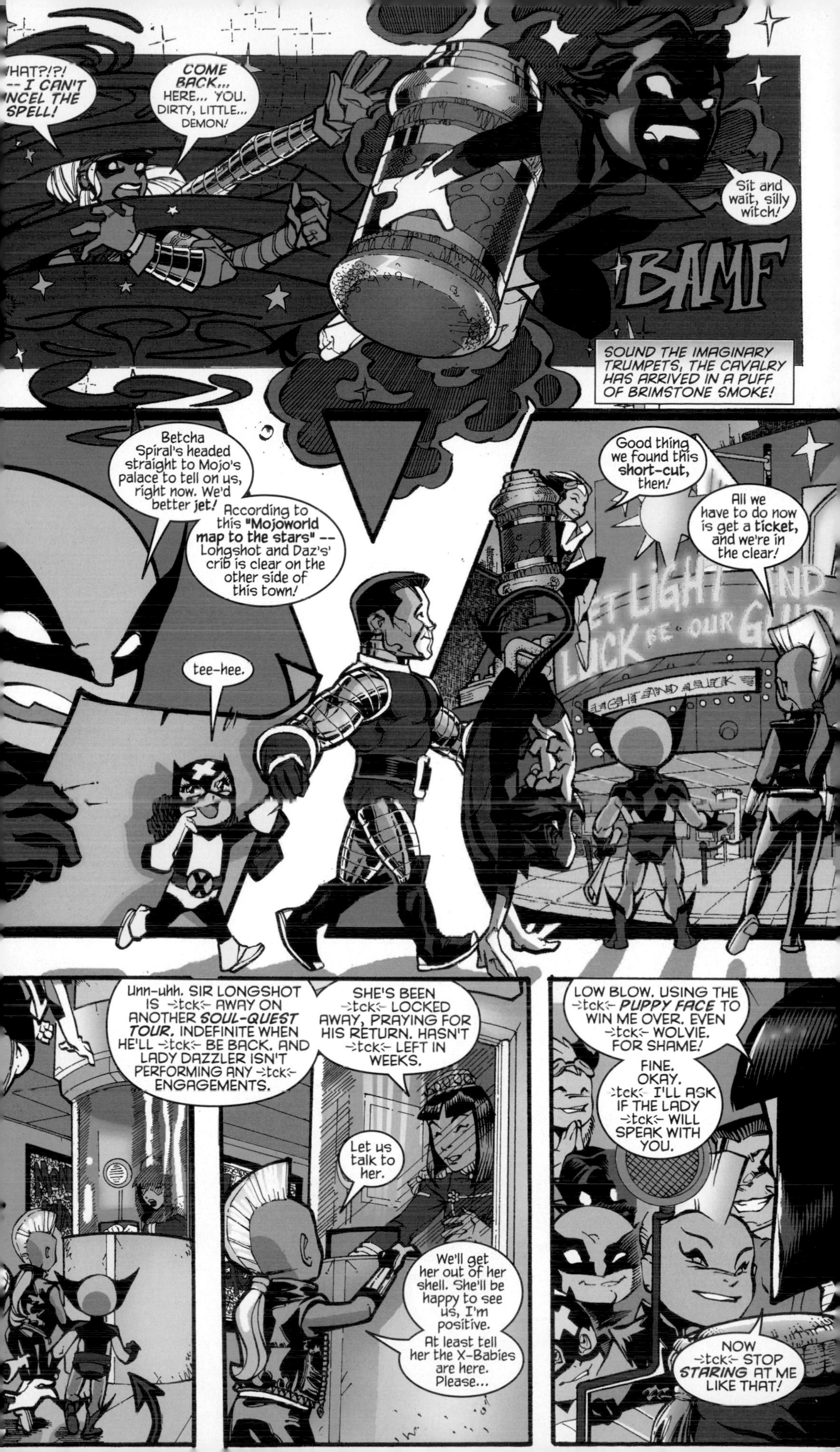

HAT?!?! -- I CAN'T NCEL THE SPELL!
COME BACK... HERE... YOU. DIRTY, LITTLE... DEMON!
Sit and wait, silly witch!
BAMF
SOUND THE IMAGINARY TRUMPETS, THE CAVALRY HAS ARRIVED IN A PUFF OF BRIMSTONE SMOKE!
Betcha Spiral's headed straight to Mojo's palace to tell on us, right now. We'd better jet!
According to this "Mojoworld map to the stars" -- Longshot and Daz's' crib is clear on the other side of this town!
tee-hee.
Good thing we found this short-cut, then!
All we have to do now is get a ticket, and we're in the clear!
LUCK BE OUR
Unn-uhh. SIR LONGSHOT IS -tck- AWAY ON ANOTHER SOUL-QUEST TOUR. INDEFINITE WHEN HE'LL -tck- BE BACK. AND LADY DAZZLER ISN'T PERFORMING ANY -tck- ENGAGEMENTS.
SHE'S BEEN -tck- LOCKED AWAY, PRAYING FOR HIS RETURN. HASN'T -tck- LEFT IN WEEKS.
Let us talk to her.
We'll get her out of her shell. She'll be happy to see us, I'm positive.
At least tell her the X-Babies are here. Please...
LOW BLOW. USING THE -tck- PUPPY FACE TO WIN ME OVER. EVEN -tck- WOLVIE. FOR SHAME!
FINE. OKAY. -tck- I'LL ASK IF THE LADY -tck- WILL SPEAK WITH YOU.
NOW -tck- STOP STARING AT ME LIKE THAT!

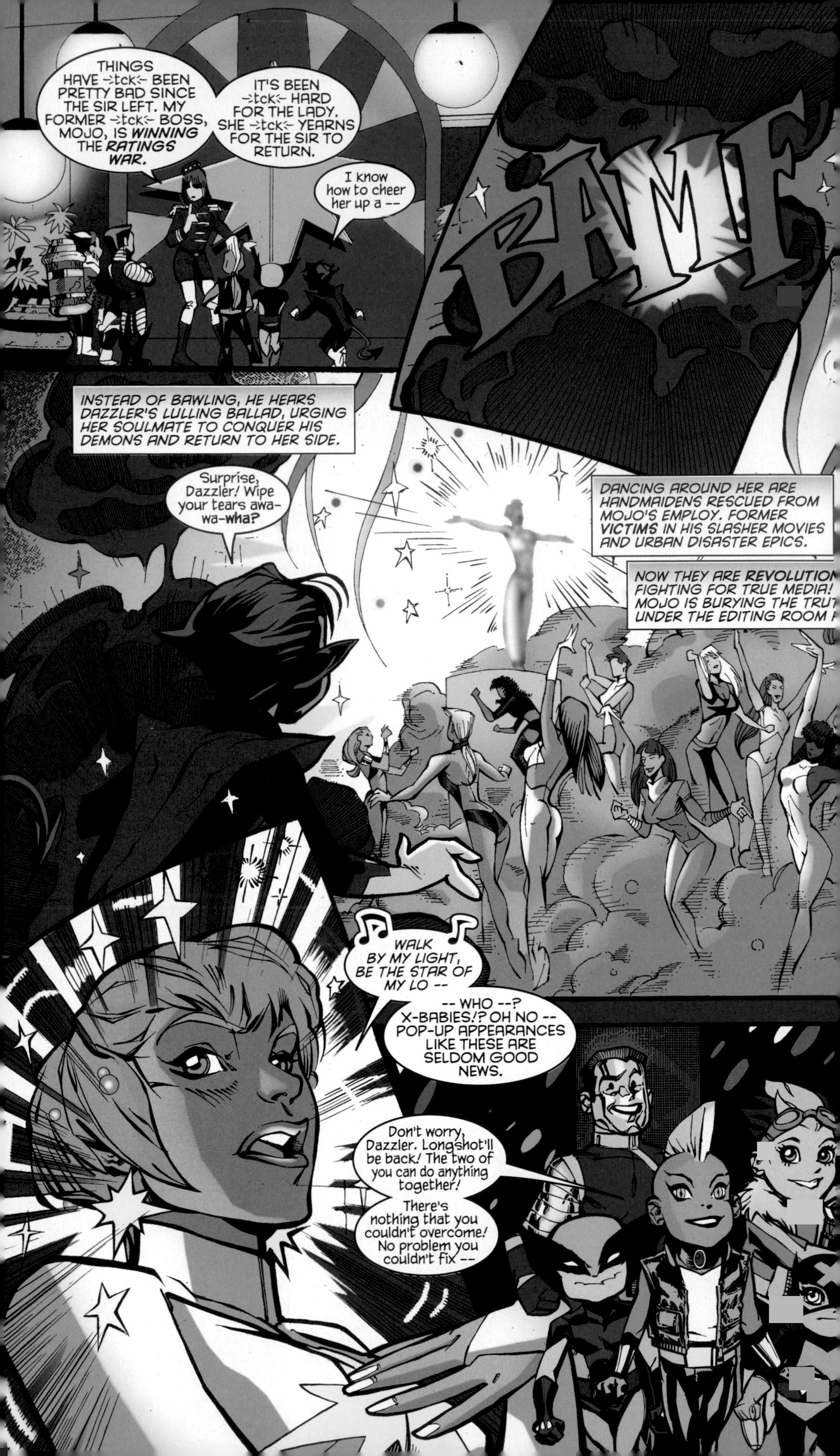
THINGS HAVE -tck- BEEN PRETTY BAD SINCE THE SIR LEFT. MY FORMER -tck- BOSS, MOJO, IS WINNING THE RATINGS WAR.
IT'S BEEN -tck- HARD FOR THE LADY. SHE -tck- YEARNS FOR THE SIR TO RETURN.
I know how to cheer her up a --
BAMF
INSTEAD OF BAWLING, HE HEARS DAZZLER'S LULLING BALLAD, URGING HER SOULMATE TO CONQUER HIS DEMONS AND RETURN TO HER SIDE.
Surprise, Dazzler! Wipe your tears awa-wa-wha?
DANCING AROUND HER ARE HANDMAIDENS RESCUED FROM MOJO'S EMPLOY. FORMER VICTIMS IN HIS SLASHER MOVIES AND URBAN DISASTER EPICS.
WALK BY MY LIGHT, BE THE STAR OF MY LO --
-- WHO --? X-BABIES!? OH NO -- POP-UP APPEARANCES LIKE THESE ARE SELDOM GOOD NEWS.
Don't worry, Dazzler. Longshot'll be back! The two of you can do anything together!
There's nothing that you couldn't overcome! No problem you couldn't fix --

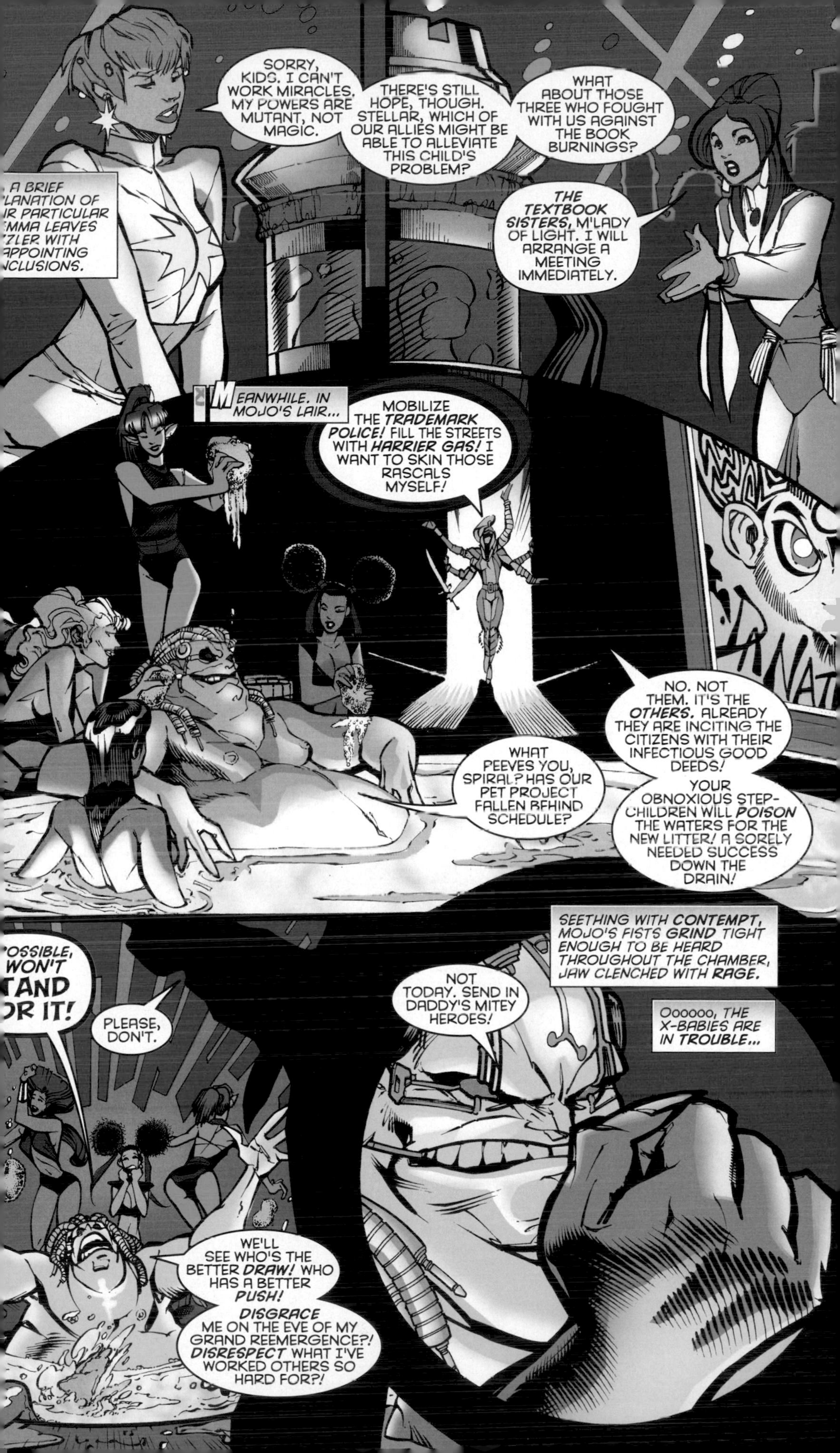
A BRIEF
PLANATION OF
IR PARTICULAR
EMMA LEAVES
ZLER WITH
APPOINTING
NCLUSIONS.
SORRY, KIDS. I CAN'T WORK MIRACLES. MY POWERS ARE MUTANT, NOT MAGIC.
THERE'S STILL HOPE, THOUGH. STELLAR, WHICH OF OUR ALLIES MIGHT BE ABLE TO ALLEVIATE THIS CHILD'S PROBLEM?
WHAT ABOUT THOSE THREE WHO FOUGHT WITH US AGAINST THE BOOK BURNINGS?
THE TEXTBOOK SISTERS, M'LADY OF LIGHT. I WILL ARRANGE A MEETING IMMEDIATELY.
MEANWHILE, IN MOJO'S LAIR...
MOBILIZE THE TRADEMARK POLICE! FILL THE STREETS WITH HARRIER GAS! I WANT TO SKIN THOSE RASCALS MYSELF!
WHAT PEEVES YOU, SPIRAL? HAS OUR PET PROJECT FALLEN BEHIND SCHEDULE?
NO. NOT THEM. IT'S THE OTHERS. ALREADY THEY ARE INCITING THE CITIZENS WITH THEIR INFECTIOUS GOOD DEEDS!
YOUR OBNOXIOUS STEP-CHILDREN WILL POISON THE WATERS FOR THE NEW LITTER! A SORELY NEEDED SUCCESS DOWN THE DRAIN!
OSSIBLE, WON'T TAND OR IT!
PLEASE, DON'T.
WE'LL SEE WHO'S THE BETTER DRAW! WHO HAS A BETTER PUSH!
DISGRACE ME ON THE EVE OF MY GRAND REEMERGENCE?! DISRESPECT WHAT I'VE WORKED OTHERS SO HARD FOR?!
SEETHING WITH CONTEMPT, MOJO'S FISTS GRIND TIGHT ENOUGH TO BE HEARD THROUGHOUT THE CHAMBER, JAW CLENCHED WITH RAGE.
NOT TODAY. SEND IN DADDY'S MITEY HEROES!
Oooooo, THE X-BABIES ARE IN TROUBLE...

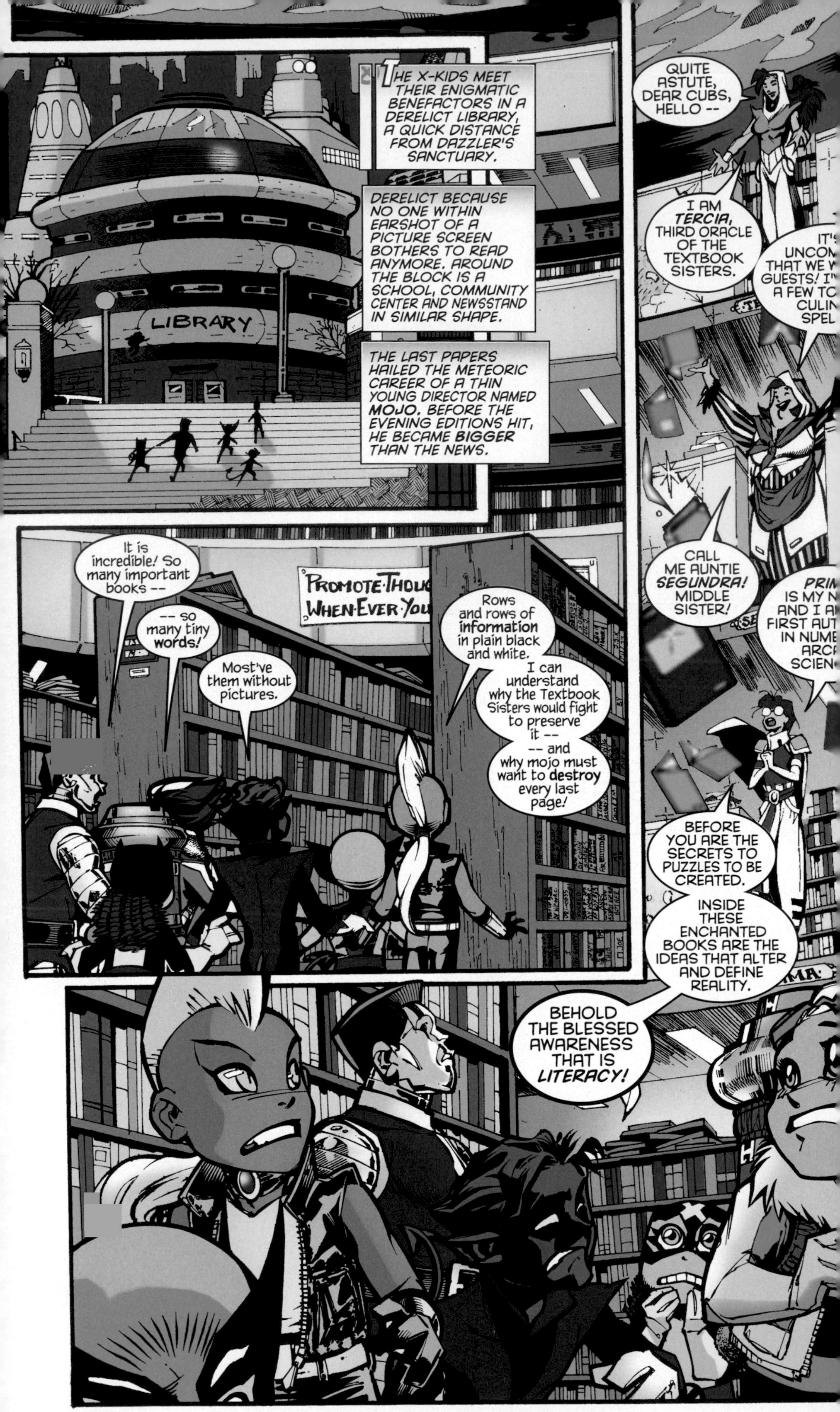

THE X-KIDS MEET THEIR ENIGMATIC BENEFACTORS IN A DERELICT LIBRARY, A QUICK DISTANCE FROM DAZZLER'S SANCTUARY.
DERELICT BECAUSE NO ONE WITHIN EARSHOT OF A PICTURE SCREEN BOTHERS TO READ ANYMORE. AROUND THE BLOCK IS A SCHOOL, COMMUNITY CENTER AND NEWSSTAND IN SIMILAR SHAPE.
THE LAST PAPERS HAILED THE METEORIC CAREER OF A THIN YOUNG DIRECTOR NAMED MOJO. BEFORE THE EVENING EDITIONS HIT, HE BECAME BIGGER THAN THE NEWS.
LIBRARY
QUITE ASTUTE, DEAR CUBS, HELLO --
I AM TERCIA, THIRD ORACLE OF THE TEXTBOOK SISTERS.
It is incredible! So many important books --
-- so many tiny words!
Most've them without pictures.
PROMOTE·THOU
WHEN·EVER·YOU
Rows and rows of information in plain black and white.
I can understand why the Textbook Sisters would fight to preserve it --
-- and why mojo must want to destroy every last page!
CALL ME AUNTIE SEGUNDRA! MIDDLE SISTER!
BEFORE YOU ARE THE SECRETS TO PUZZLES TO BE CREATED.
INSIDE THESE ENCHANTED BOOKS ARE THE IDEAS THAT ALTER AND DEFINE REALITY.
BEHOLD THE BLESSED AWARENESS THAT IS LITERACY!

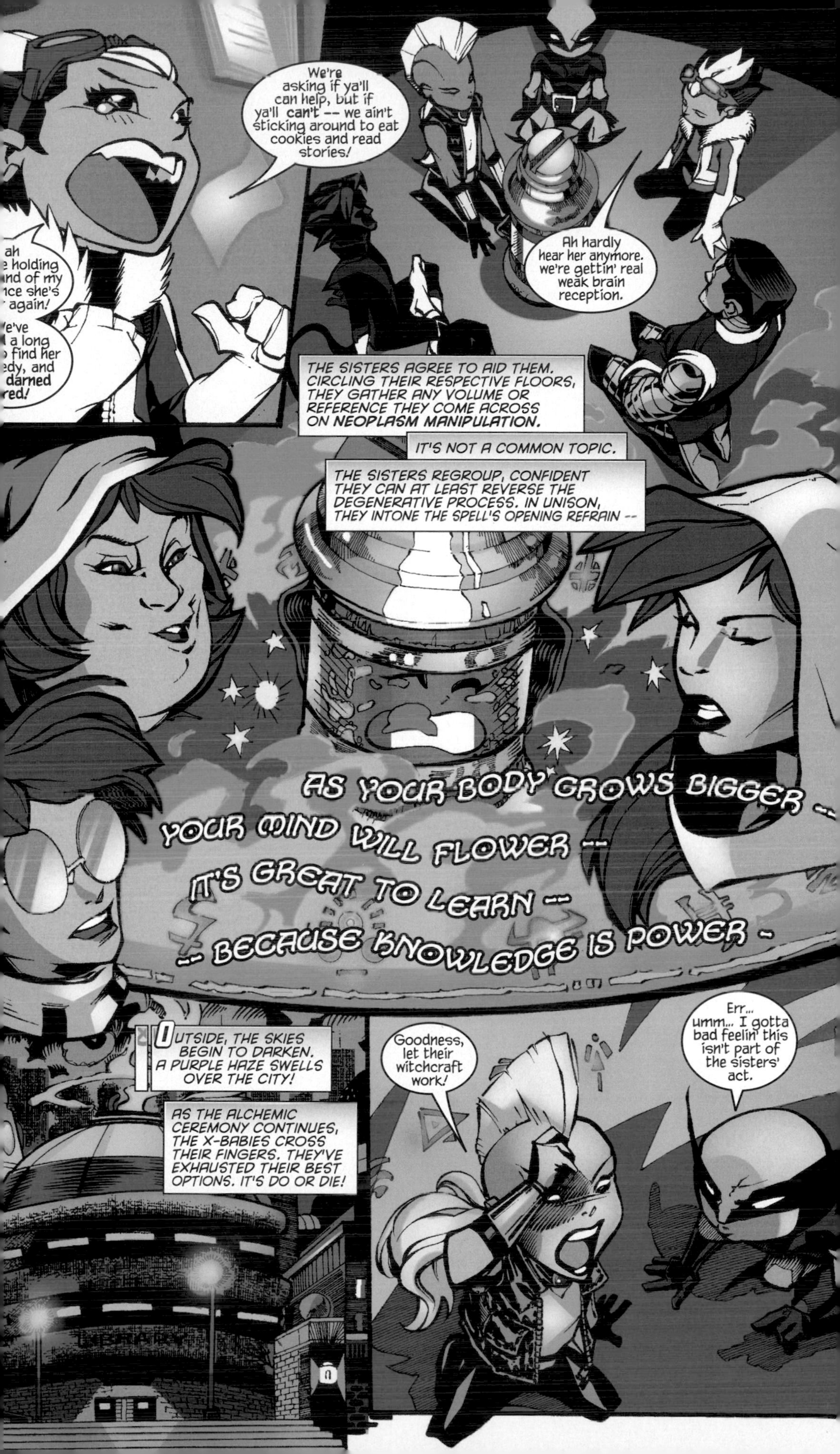

We're asking if ya'll can help, but if ya'll **can't** -- we ain't sticking around to eat cookies and read stories!
ah e holding nd of my nce she's again! e've a long find her dy, and darned red!
Ah hardly hear her anymore. we're gettin' real weak brain reception.
THE SISTERS AGREE TO AID THEM. CIRCLING THEIR RESPECTIVE FLOORS, THEY GATHER ANY VOLUME OR REFERENCE THEY COME ACROSS ON **NEOPLASM MANIPULATION.**
IT'S NOT A COMMON TOPIC.
THE SISTERS REGROUP, CONFIDENT THEY CAN AT LEAST REVERSE THE DEGENERATIVE PROCESS. IN UNISON, THEY INTONE THE SPELL'S OPENING REFRAIN --
AS YOUR BODY GROWS BIGGER --
YOUR MIND WILL FLOWER --
IT'S GREAT TO LEARN --
-- BECAUSE KNOWLEDGE IS POWER -
OUTSIDE, THE SKIES BEGIN TO DARKEN. A PURPLE HAZE SWELLS OVER THE CITY!
AS THE ALCHEMIC CEREMONY CONTINUES, THE X-BABIES CROSS THEIR FINGERS. THEY'VE EXHAUSTED THEIR BEST OPTIONS. IT'S DO OR DIE!
LIBRARY
Goodness, let their witchcraft work!
Err... umm... I gotta bad feelin' this isn't part of the sisters' act.

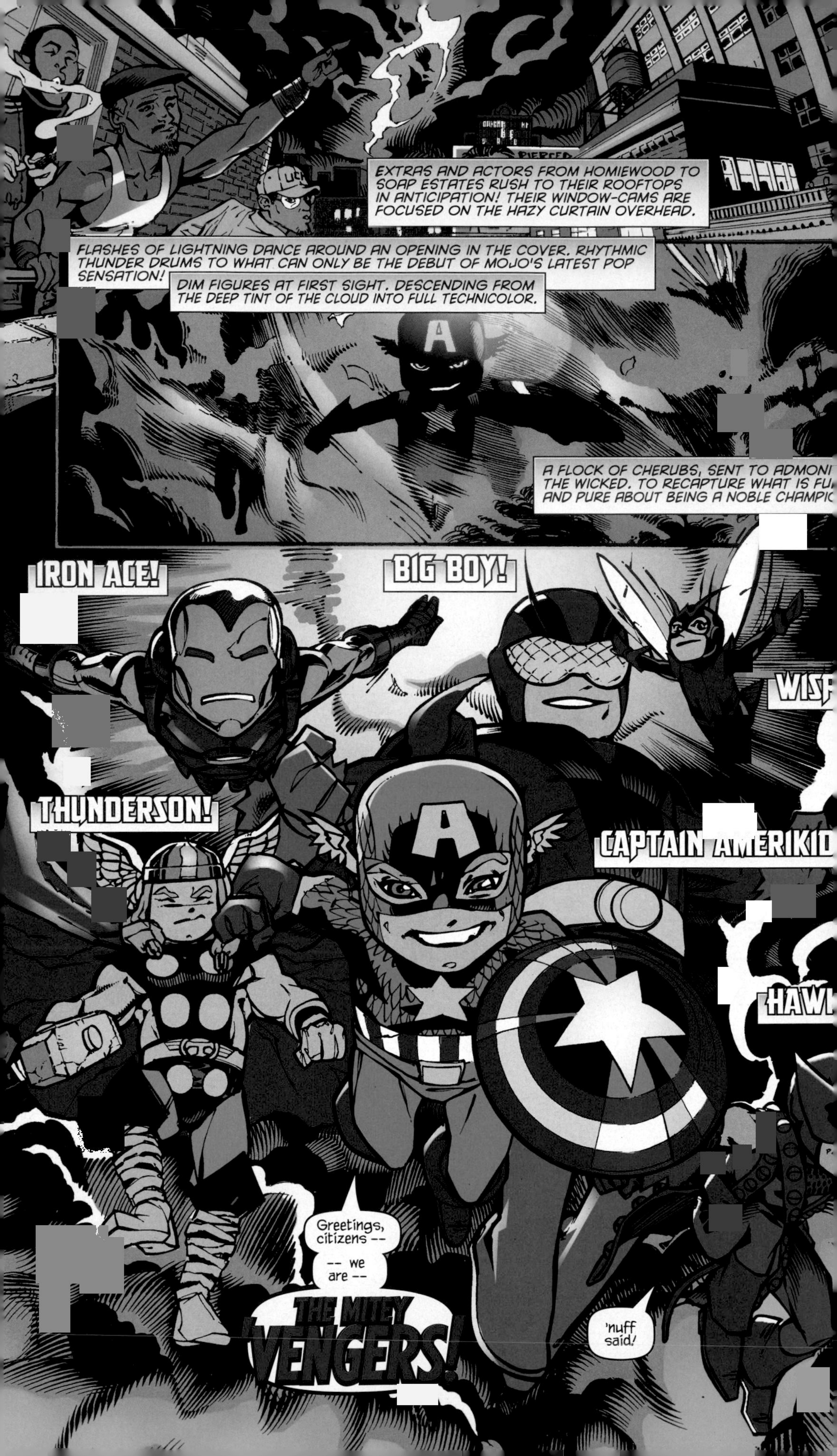

EXTRAS AND ACTORS FROM HOMIEWOOD TO SOAP ESTATES RUSH TO THEIR ROOFTOPS IN ANTICIPATION! THEIR WINDOW-CAMS ARE FOCUSED ON THE HAZY CURTAIN OVERHEAD.
FLASHES OF LIGHTNING DANCE AROUND AN OPENING IN THE COVER. RHYTHMIC THUNDER DRUMS TO WHAT CAN ONLY BE THE DEBUT OF MOJO'S LATEST POP SENSATION!
DIM FIGURES AT FIRST SIGHT. DESCENDING FROM THE DEEP TINT OF THE CLOUD INTO FULL TECHNICOLOR.
A FLOCK OF CHERUBS, SENT TO ADMONI THE WICKED. TO RECAPTURE WHAT IS FU AND PURE ABOUT BEING A NOBLE CHAMPIC
IRON ACE!
BIG BOY!
WIS
THUNDERSON!
CAPTAIN AMERIKID
HAW
Greetings, citizens --
-- we are --
THE MITEY VENGERS!
'nuff said!

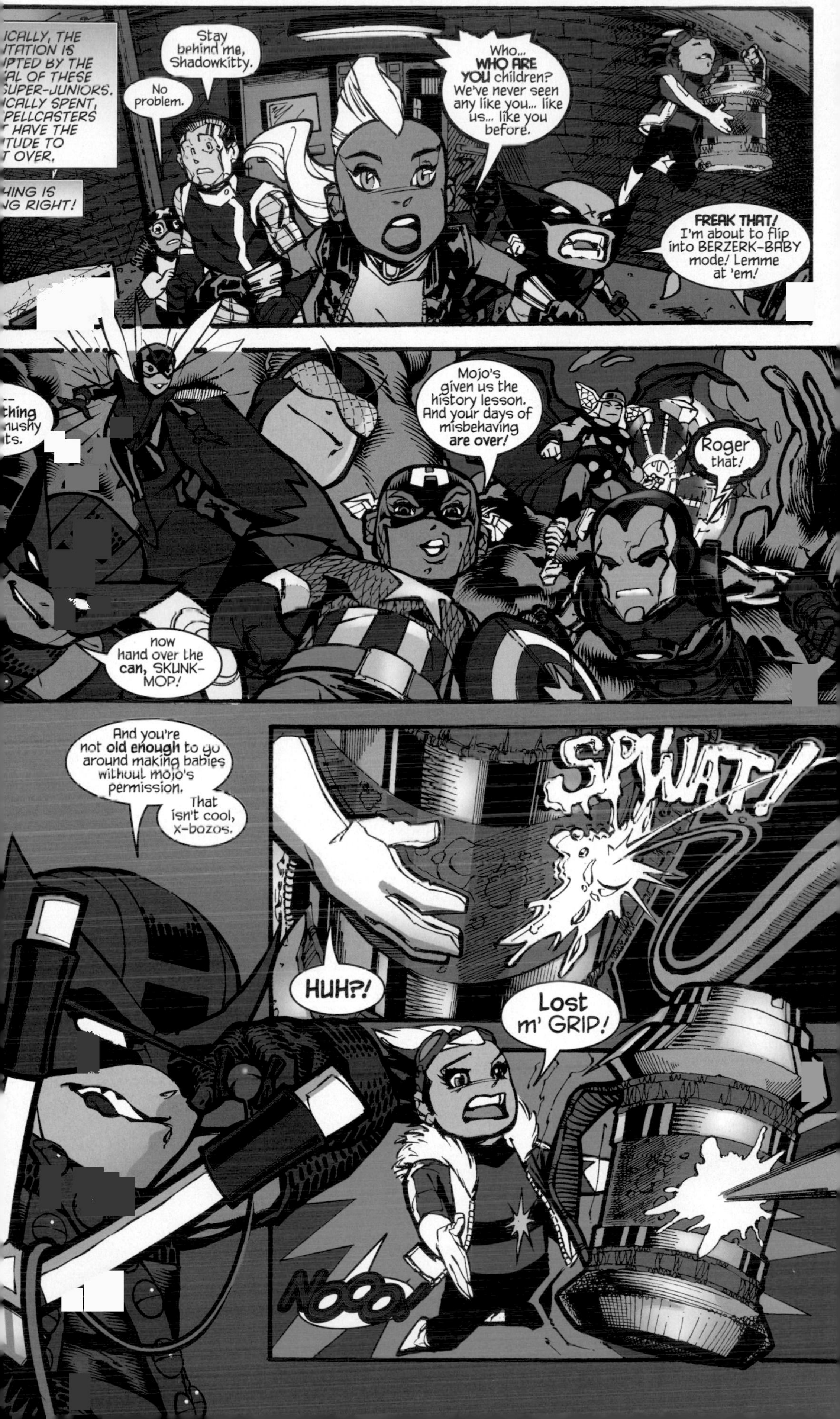

ICALLY, THE
NTATION IS
UPTED BY THE
AL OF THESE
SUPER-JUNIORS.
ICALLY SPENT,
PELLCASTERS
T HAVE THE
TUDE TO
T OVER.
HING IS
NG RIGHT!
Stay behind me, Shadowkitty.
No problem.
Who... WHO ARE YOU children? We've never seen any like you... like us... like you before.
FREAK THAT! I'm about to flip into BERZERK-BABY mode! Lemme at 'em!
thing
nushy
ts.
Mojo's given us the history lesson. And your days of misbehaving are over!
Roger that!
now hand over the can, SKUNK-MOP!
And you're not old enough to go around making babies without mojo's permission.
That isn't cool, x-bozos.
SPWAT!
HUH?!
Lost m' GRIP!
NOOO!

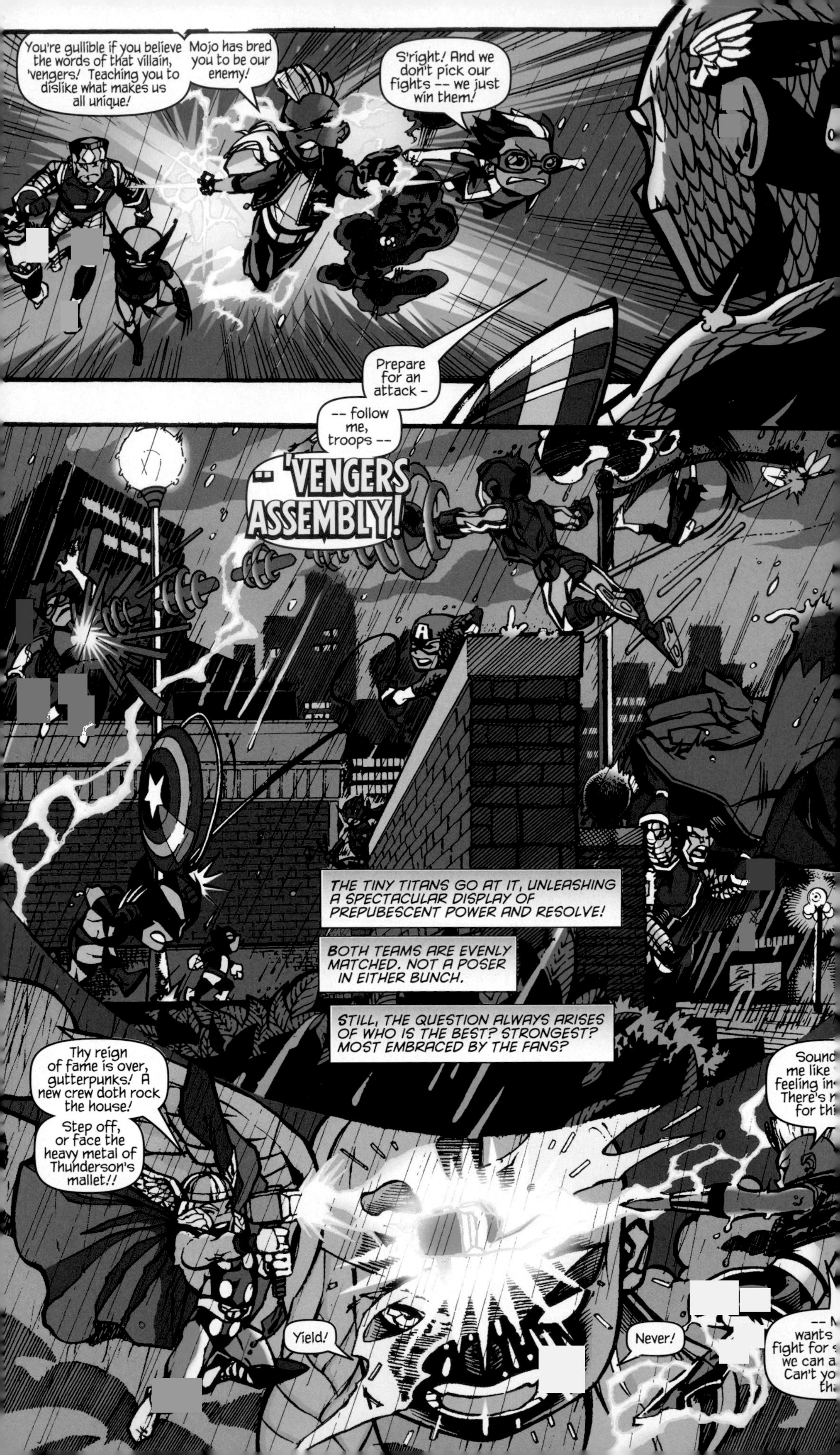

You're gullible if you believe the words of that villain, 'vengers! Teaching you to dislike what makes us all unique!
Mojo has bred you to be our enemy!
S'right! And we don't pick our fights -- we just win them!
Prepare for an attack -
-- follow me, troops --
-- 'VENGERS ASSEMBLY!
THE TINY TITANS GO AT IT, UNLEASHING A SPECTACULAR DISPLAY OF PREPUBESCENT POWER AND RESOLVE!
BOTH TEAMS ARE EVENLY MATCHED. NOT A POSER IN EITHER BUNCH.
STILL, THE QUESTION ALWAYS ARISES OF WHO IS THE BEST? STRONGEST? MOST EMBRACED BY THE FANS?
Thy reign of fame is over, gutterpunks! A new crew doth rock the house!
Step off, or face the heavy metal of Thunderson's mallet!!
Yield!
Never!

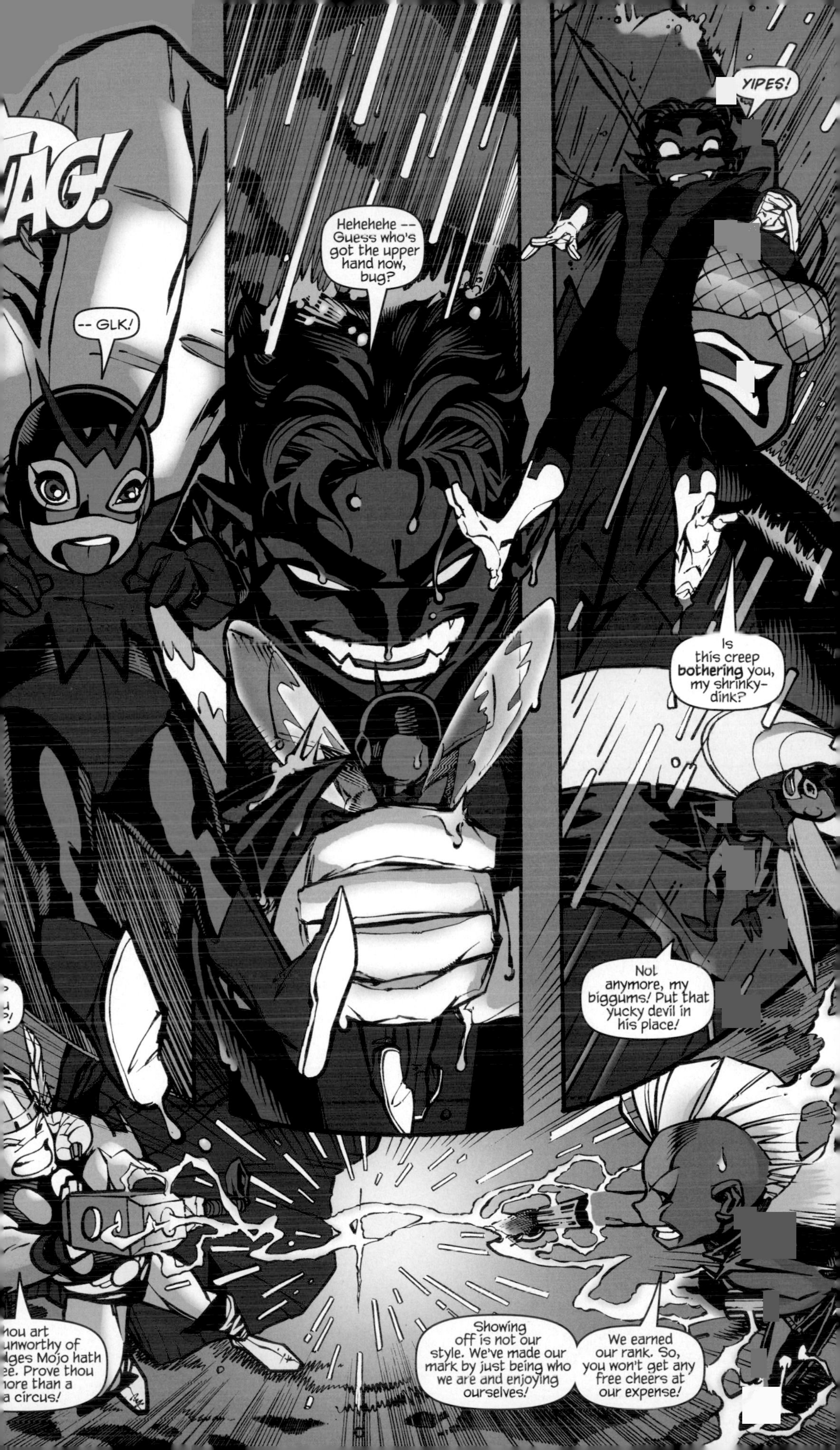

AG!
-- GLK!
Hehehehe -- Guess who's got the upper hand now, bug?
YIPES!
Is this creep **bothering** you, my shrinky-dink?
No! anymore, my biggums! Put that yucky devil in his place!
hou art
unworthy of
dges Mojo hath
ee. Prove thou
nore than a
a circus!
Showing off is not our style. We've made our mark by just being who we are and enjoying ourselves!
We earned our rank. So, you won't get any free cheers at our expense!

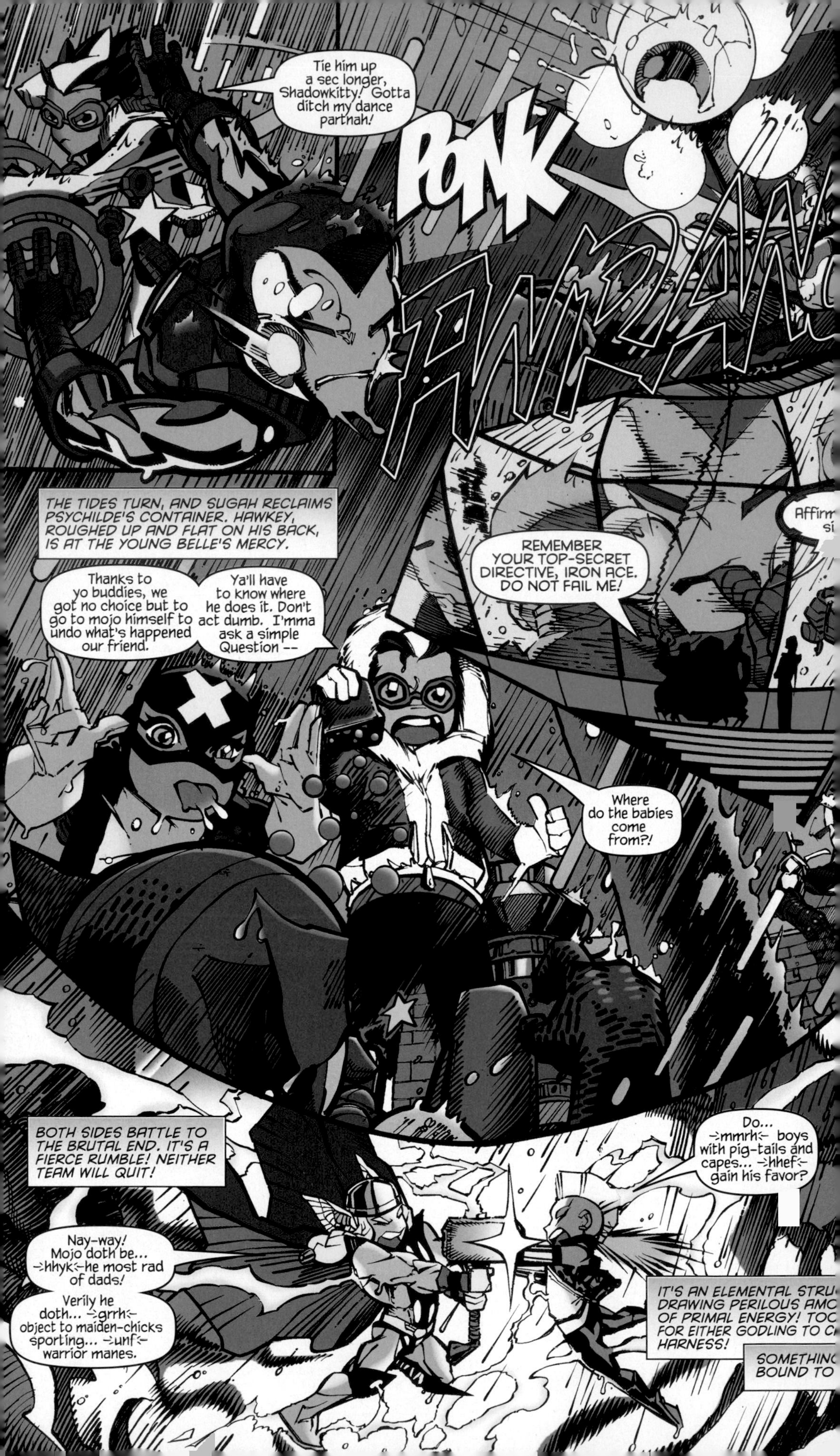
Tie him up a sec longer, Shadowkitty! Gotta ditch my dance partnah!
PONK
THE TIDES TURN, AND SUGAH RECLAIMS PSYCHILDE'S CONTAINER. HAWKEY, ROUGHED UP AND FLAT ON HIS BACK, IS AT THE YOUNG BELLE'S MERCY.
Thanks to yo buddies, we got no choice but to go to mojo himself to undo what's happened our friend.
Ya'll have to know where he does it. Don't act dumb. I'mma ask a simple Question --
REMEMBER YOUR TOP-SECRET DIRECTIVE, IRON ACE. DO NOT FAIL ME!
Where do the babies come from?!
BOTH SIDES BATTLE TO THE BRUTAL END. IT'S A FIERCE RUMBLE! NEITHER TEAM WILL QUIT!
Do... -mmrh- boys with pig-tails and capes... -hhef- gain his favor?
Nay-way! Mojo doth be... -hhyk- he most rad of dads!
Verily he doth... -grrh- object to maiden-chicks sporting... -unf- warrior manes.

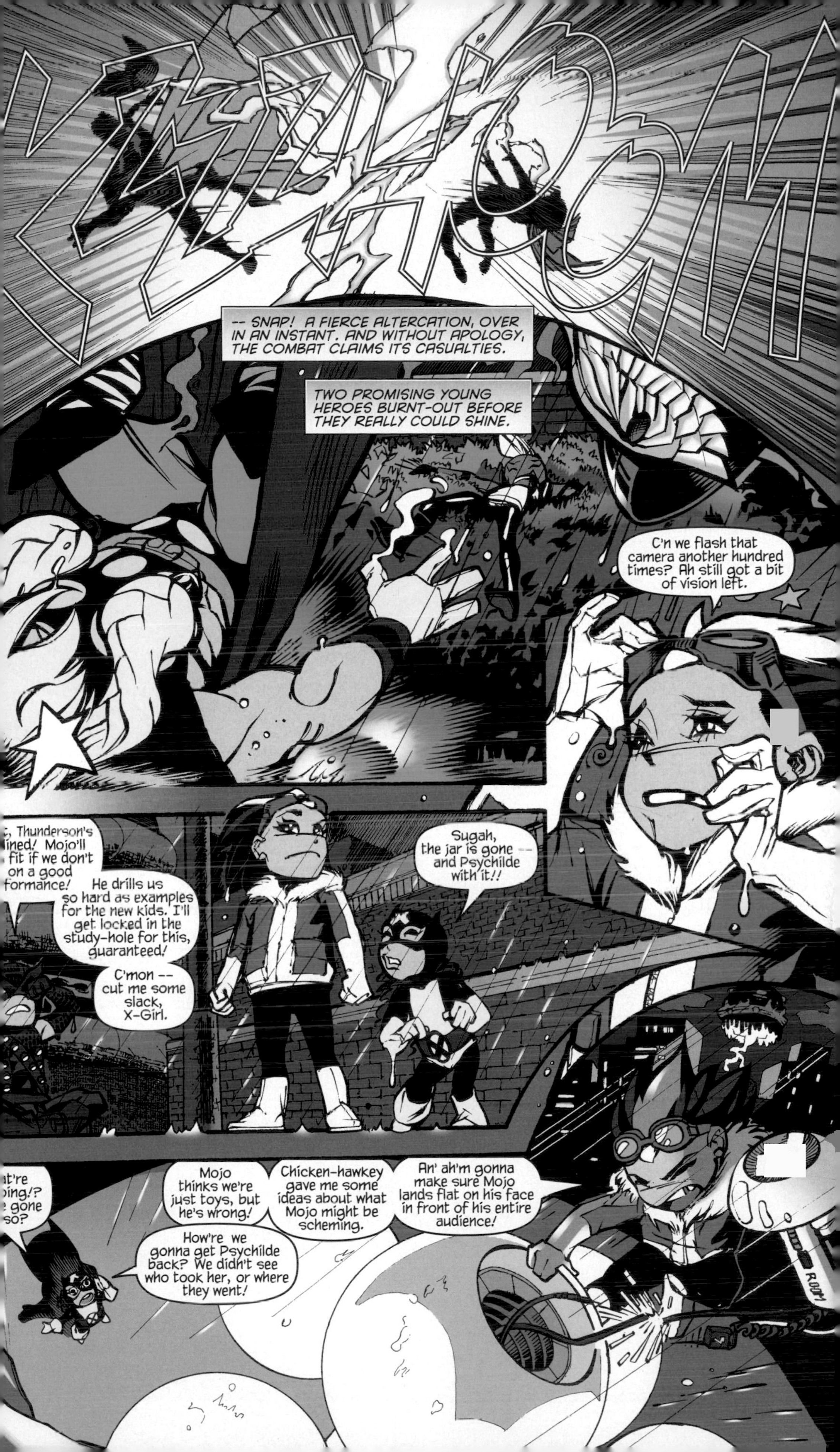

-- SNAP! A FIERCE ALTERCATION, OVER IN AN INSTANT. AND WITHOUT APOLOGY, THE COMBAT CLAIMS ITS CASUALTIES.
TWO PROMISING YOUNG HEROES BURNT-OUT BEFORE THEY REALLY COULD SHINE.
C'n we flash that camera another hundred times? Ah still got a bit of vision left.
t, Thunderson's lined! Mojo'll fit if we don't on a good formance!
He drills us so hard as examples for the new kids. I'll get locked in the study-hole for this, guaranteed!
C'mon -- cut me some slack, X-Girl.
Sugah, the jar is gone -- and Psychilde with it!!
at're oing!? e gone so?
Mojo thinks we're just toys, but he's wrong!
How're we gonna get Psychilde back? We didn't see who took her, or where they went!
Chicken-hawkey gave me some ideas about what Mojo might be scheming.
An' ah'm gonna make sure Mojo lands flat on his face in front of his entire audience!

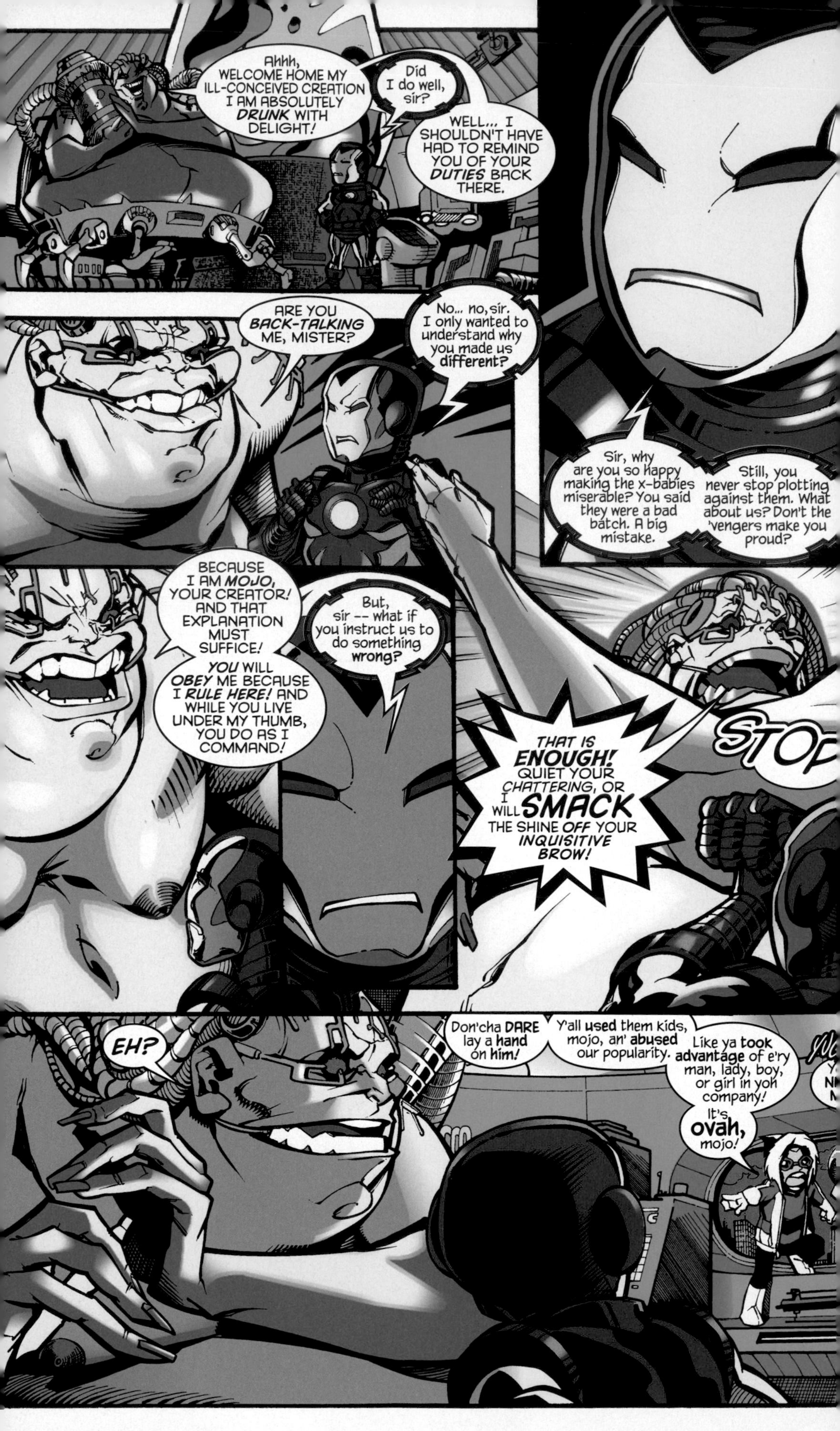
Ahhh, WELCOME HOME MY ILL-CONCEIVED CREATION I AM ABSOLUTELY DRUNK WITH DELIGHT!
Did I do well, sir?
WELL... I SHOULDN'T HAVE HAD TO REMIND YOU OF YOUR DUTIES BACK THERE.
ARE YOU BACK-TALKING ME, MISTER?
No... no, sir. I only wanted to understand why you made us different?
Sir, why are you so happy making the x-babies miserable? You said they were a bad batch. A big mistake.
Still, you never stop plotting against them. What about us? Don't the 'vengers make you proud?
BECAUSE I AM MOJO, YOUR CREATOR! AND THAT EXPLANATION MUST SUFFICE!
YOU WILL OBEY ME BECAUSE I RULE HERE! AND WHILE YOU LIVE UNDER MY THUMB, YOU DO AS I COMMAND!
But, sir -- what if you instruct us to do something wrong?
THAT IS ENOUGH! QUIET YOUR CHATTERING, OR I WILL SMACK THE SHINE OFF YOUR INQUISITIVE BROW!
EH?
Don'cha DARE lay a hand on him!
Y'all used them kids, mojo, an' abused our popularity.
Like ya took advantage of e'ry man, lady, boy, or girl in yoh company!
It's ovah, mojo!

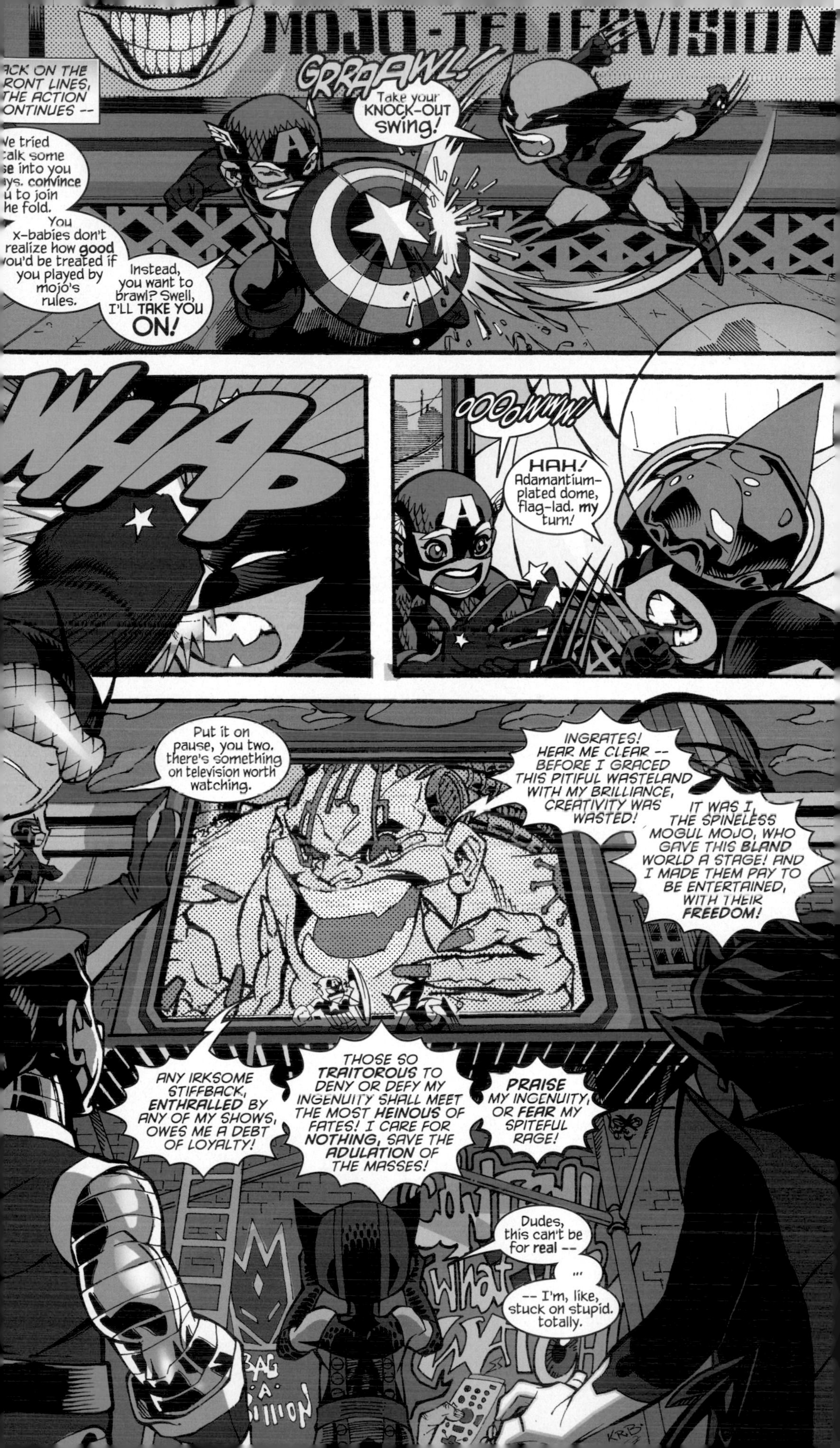
MOJO-TELEVISION
ACK ON THE RONT LINES, THE ACTION ONTINUES --
GRRAAWL!
Take your KNOCK-OUT swing!
We tried talk some se into you ys. convince u to join he fold.
You x-babies don't realize how good you'd be treated if you played by mojo's rules.
Instead, you want to brawl? Swell, I'LL TAKE YOU ON!
WHAP
OOOMMM!
HAH! Adamantium-plated dome, flag-lad. my turn!
Put it on pause, you two. there's something on television worth watching.
INGRATES! HEAR ME CLEAR -- BEFORE I GRACED THIS PITIFUL WASTELAND WITH MY BRILLIANCE, CREATIVITY WAS WASTED!
IT WAS I, THE SPINELESS MOGUL MOJO, WHO GAVE THIS BLAND WORLD A STAGE! AND I MADE THEM PAY TO BE ENTERTAINED, WITH THEIR FREEDOM!
ANY IRKSOME STIFFBACK, ENTHRALLED BY ANY OF MY SHOWS, OWES ME A DEBT OF LOYALTY!
THOSE SO TRAITOROUS TO DENY OR DEFY MY INGENUITY SHALL MEET THE MOST HEINOUS OF FATES! I CARE FOR NOTHING, SAVE THE ADULATION OF THE MASSES!
PRAISE MY INGENUITY, OR FEAR MY SPITEFUL RAGE!
Dudes, this can't be for real --
...
-- I'm, like, stuck on stupid. totally.

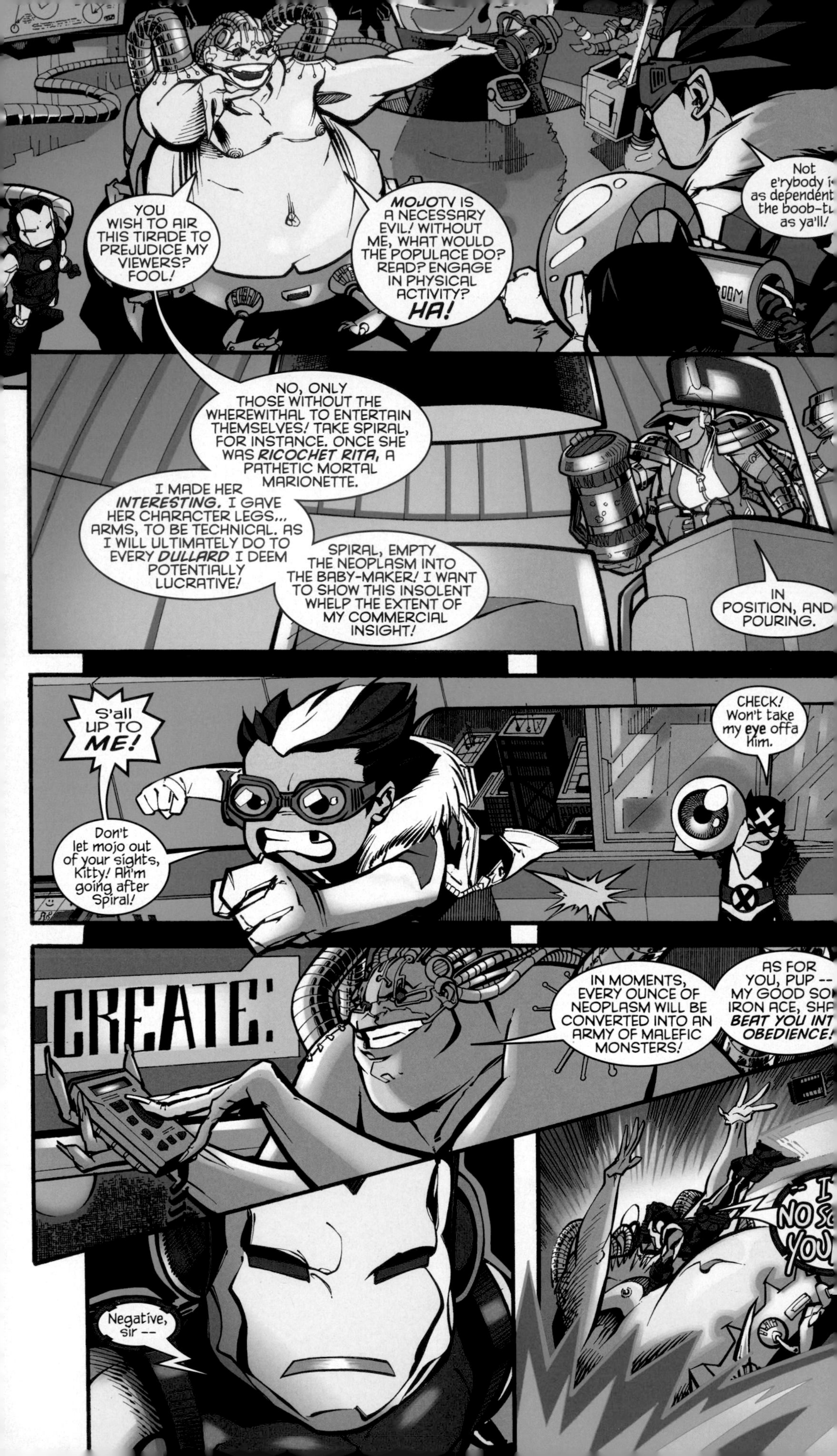
YOU WISH TO AIR THIS TIRADE TO PREJUDICE MY VIEWERS? FOOL!
MOJOTV IS A NECESSARY EVIL! WITHOUT ME, WHAT WOULD THE POPULACE DO? READ? ENGAGE IN PHYSICAL ACTIVITY? HA!
Not e'rybody is as dependent on the boob-tube as ya'll!
NO, ONLY THOSE WITHOUT THE WHEREWITHAL TO ENTERTAIN THEMSELVES! TAKE SPIRAL, FOR INSTANCE. ONCE SHE WAS RICOCHET RITA, A PATHETIC MORTAL MARIONETTE.
I MADE HER INTERESTING. I GAVE HER CHARACTER LEGS... ARMS, TO BE TECHNICAL. AS I WILL ULTIMATELY DO TO EVERY DULLARD I DEEM POTENTIALLY LUCRATIVE!
SPIRAL, EMPTY THE NEOPLASM INTO THE BABY-MAKER! I WANT TO SHOW THIS INSOLENT WHELP THE EXTENT OF MY COMMERCIAL INSIGHT!
IN POSITION, AND POURING.
S'all UP TO ME!
Don't let mojo out of your sights, Kitty! Ah'm going after Spiral!
CHECK! Won't take my eye offa him.
CREATE:
IN MOMENTS, EVERY OUNCE OF NEOPLASM WILL BE CONVERTED INTO AN ARMY OF MALEFIC MONSTERS!
AS FOR YOU, PUP -- MY GOOD SO IRON ACE, SH BEAT YOU INT OBEDIENCE!
Negative, sir --

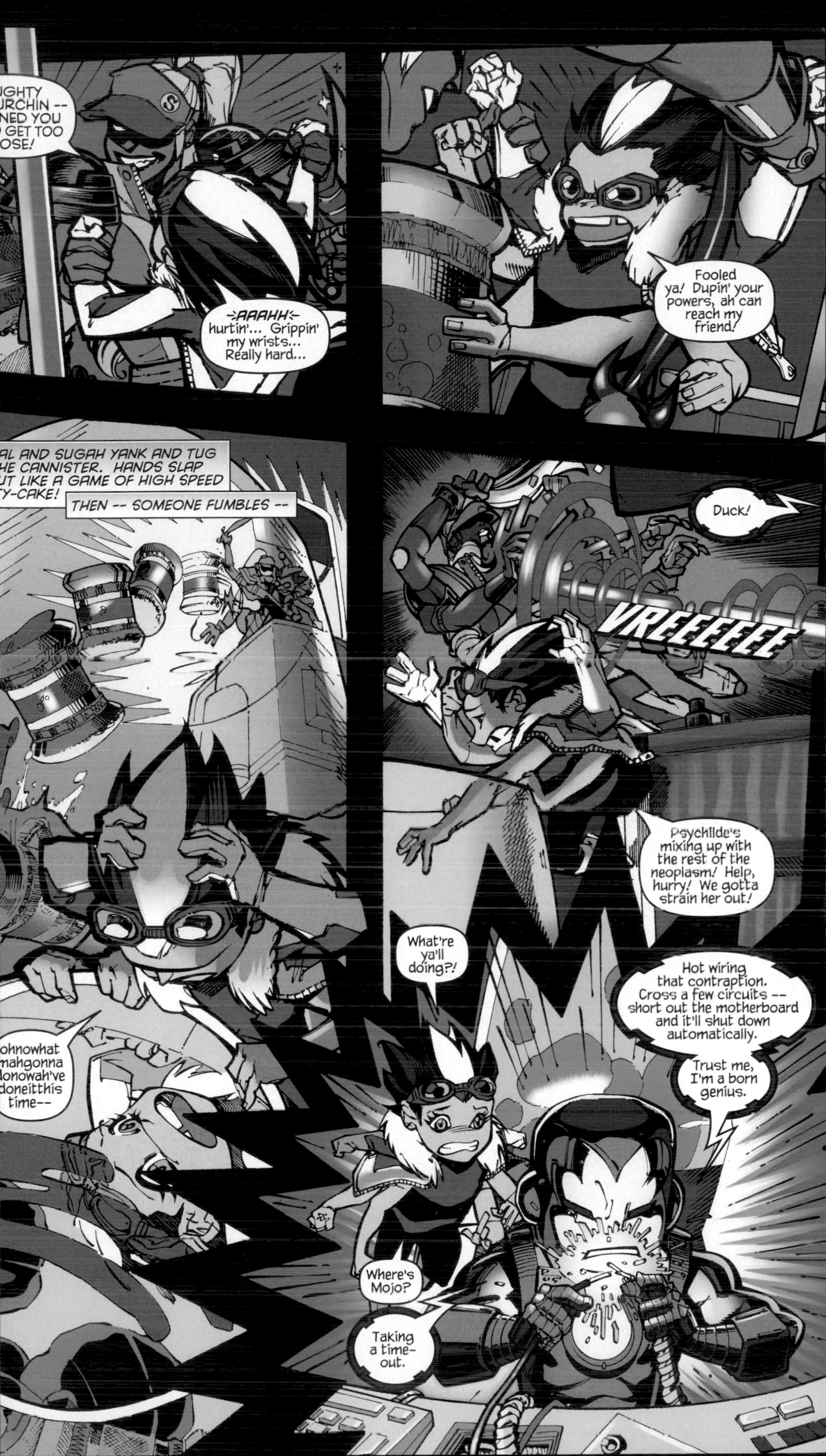
UGHTY URCHIN -- NED YOU GET TOO OSE!
-AAAHH- hurtin'... Grippin' my wrists... Really hard...
Fooled ya! Dupin' your powers, ah can reach my friend!
AL AND SUGAH YANK AND TUG HE CANNISTER. HANDS SLAP UT LIKE A GAME OF HIGH SPEED TY-CAKE!
THEN -- SOMEONE FUMBLES --
ohnowhat mahgonna donowah've doneitthis time--
Duck!
VREEEEEEE
Psychilde's mixing up with the rest of the neoplasm! Help, hurry! We gotta strain her out!
What're ya'll doing?!
Hot wiring that contraption. Cross a few circuits -- short out the motherboard and it'll shut down automatically.
Trust me, I'm a born genius.
Where's Mojo?
Taking a time-out.

THE MACHINE SLOWS... SPUTTERS... NEARLY HALTS... THEN CHURNS UP ONCE AGAIN!

RAPIDLY, IT DRAINS THE NEOPLASM. TRANSFORMING IT INTO MORE AND MORE DEVIANT HATCHLINGS.

It's **not** working! Psychilde'll be changed into some ugly, flyin' monkey and ah'm ta blame!

Ah promised ah wouldn't let her get into any harm! On my pinky, ah promised!

Why'd ya'll have to start trouble? **Why?!**

I'm... I'm sorry...

All the neoplasm is near tapped! Not a gene'll be left if we don't turn it off!

Sugah, it's creating more life-pods than the tank can fit! Look, the glass is straining!

But, aborting now will **jeopardize** the newbies growing inside.

NO! >HRRFF< **DON'T HURT MY BABIES!**

Oh-sho Mojo's bonkers! go ghos

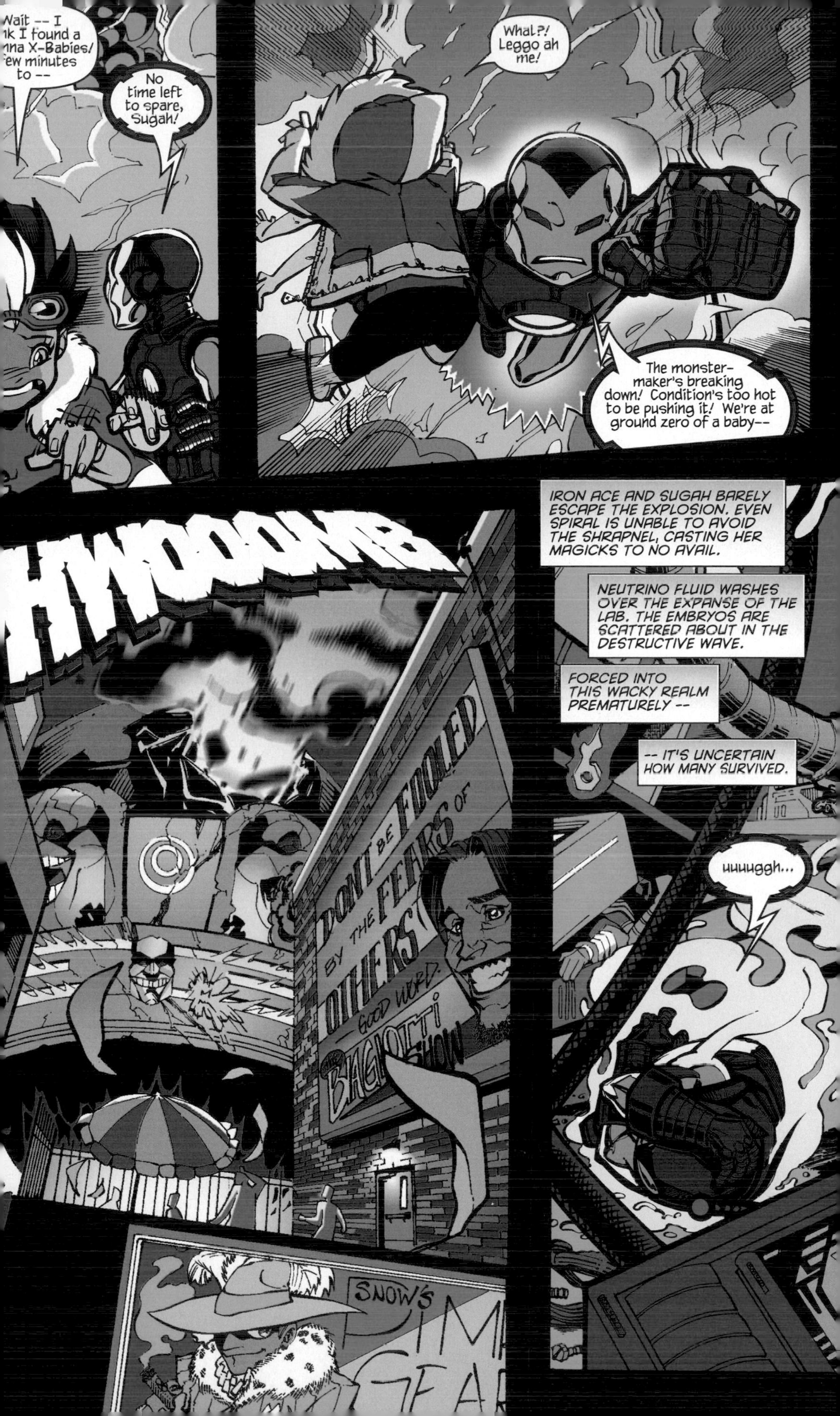
Wait -- I
nk I found a
nna X-Babies!
few minutes
to --
No time left to spare, Sugah!
What?! Leggo ah me!
The monster-maker's breaking down! Condition's too hot to be pushing it! We're at ground zero of a baby--
IRON ACE AND SUGAH BARELY ESCAPE THE EXPLOSION. EVEN SPIRAL IS UNABLE TO AVOID THE SHRAPNEL, CASTING HER MAGICKS TO NO AVAIL.
NEUTRINO FLUID WASHES OVER THE EXPANSE OF THE LAB. THE EMBRYOS ARE SCATTERED ABOUT IN THE DESTRUCTIVE WAVE.
FORCED INTO THIS WACKY REALM PREMATURELY --
-- IT'S UNCERTAIN HOW MANY SURVIVED.
HWOOOMB
DON'T BE FOOLED BY THE FEARS OF OTHERS
GOOD WORD.
SNOW'S
uuuuggh...

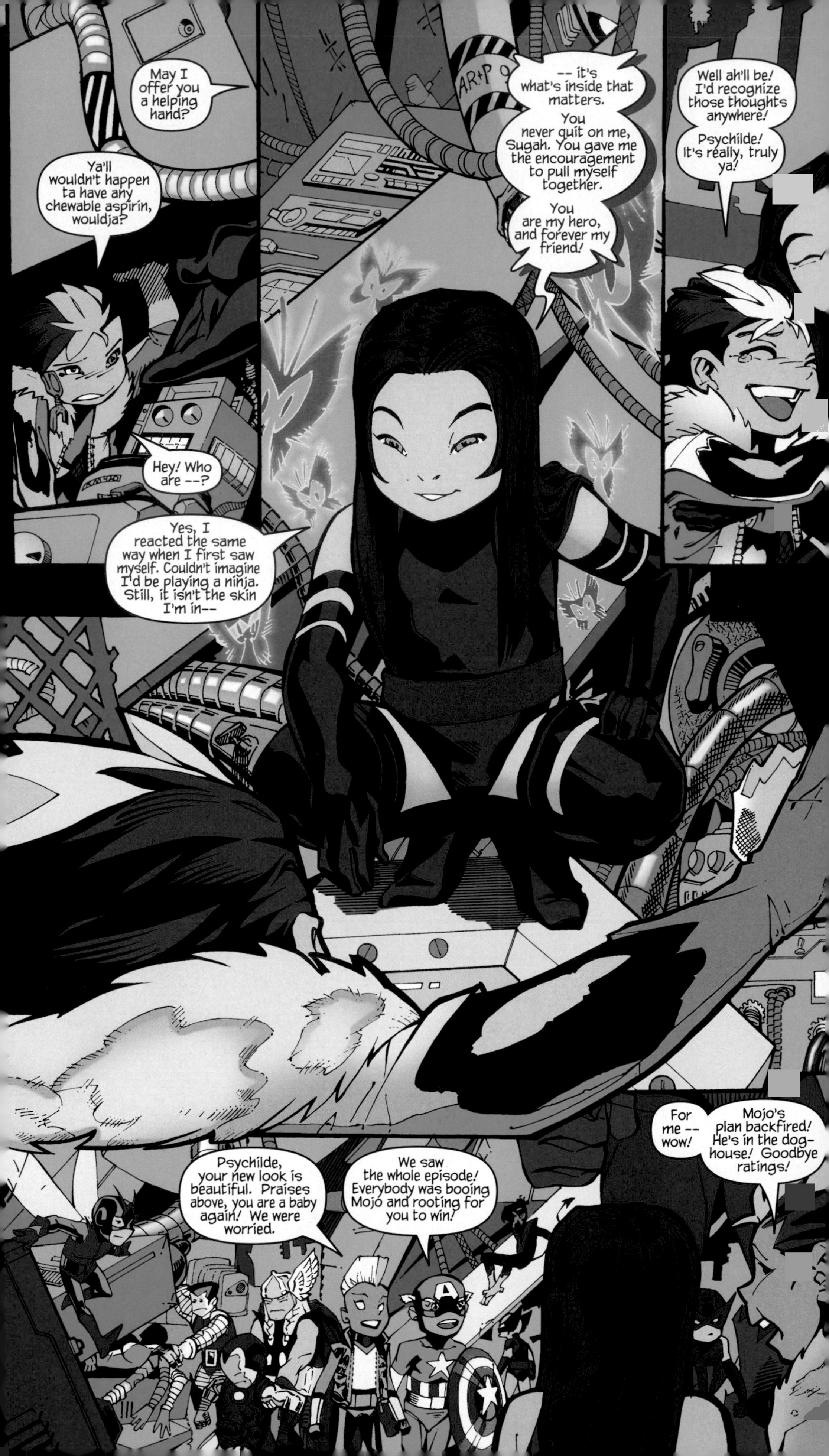
May I offer you a helping hand?
Ya'll wouldn't happen ta have any chewable aspirin, wouldja?
Hey! Who are --?
Yes, I reacted the same way when I first saw myself. Couldn't imagine I'd be playing a ninja. Still, it isn't the skin I'm in--
-- it's what's inside that matters.
You never quit on me, Sugah. You gave me the encouragement to pull myself together.
You are my hero, and forever my friend!
Well ah'll be! I'd recognize those thoughts anywhere!
Psychilde! It's really, truly ya!
Psychilde, your new look is beautiful. Praises above, you are a baby again! We were worried.
We saw the whole episode! Everybody was booing Mojo and rooting for you to win!
For me -- wow!
Mojo's plan backfired! He's in the dog-house! Goodbye ratings!

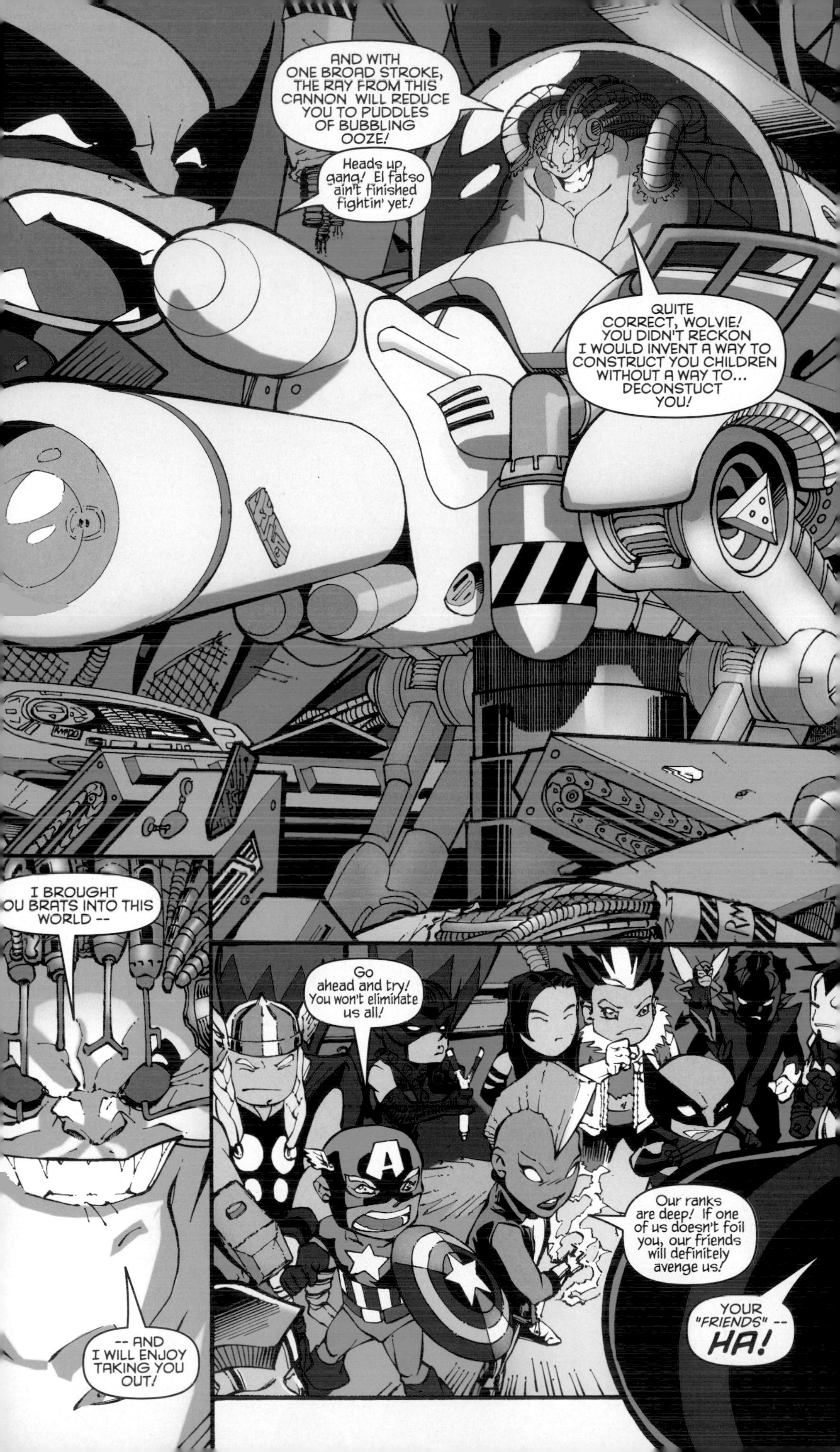
AND WITH ONE BROAD STROKE, THE RAY FROM THIS CANNON WILL REDUCE YOU TO PUDDLES OF BUBBLING OOZE!
Heads up, gang! El fatso ain't finished fightin' yet!
QUITE CORRECT, WOLVIE! YOU DIDN'T RECKON I WOULD INVENT A WAY TO CONSTRUCT YOU CHILDREN WITHOUT A WAY TO... DECONSTUCT YOU!
I BROUGHT OU BRATS INTO THIS WORLD --
-- AND I WILL ENJOY TAKING YOU OUT!
Go ahead and try! You won't eliminate us all!
Our ranks are deep! If one of us doesn't foil you, our friends will definitely avenge us!
YOUR "FRIENDS" -- HA!

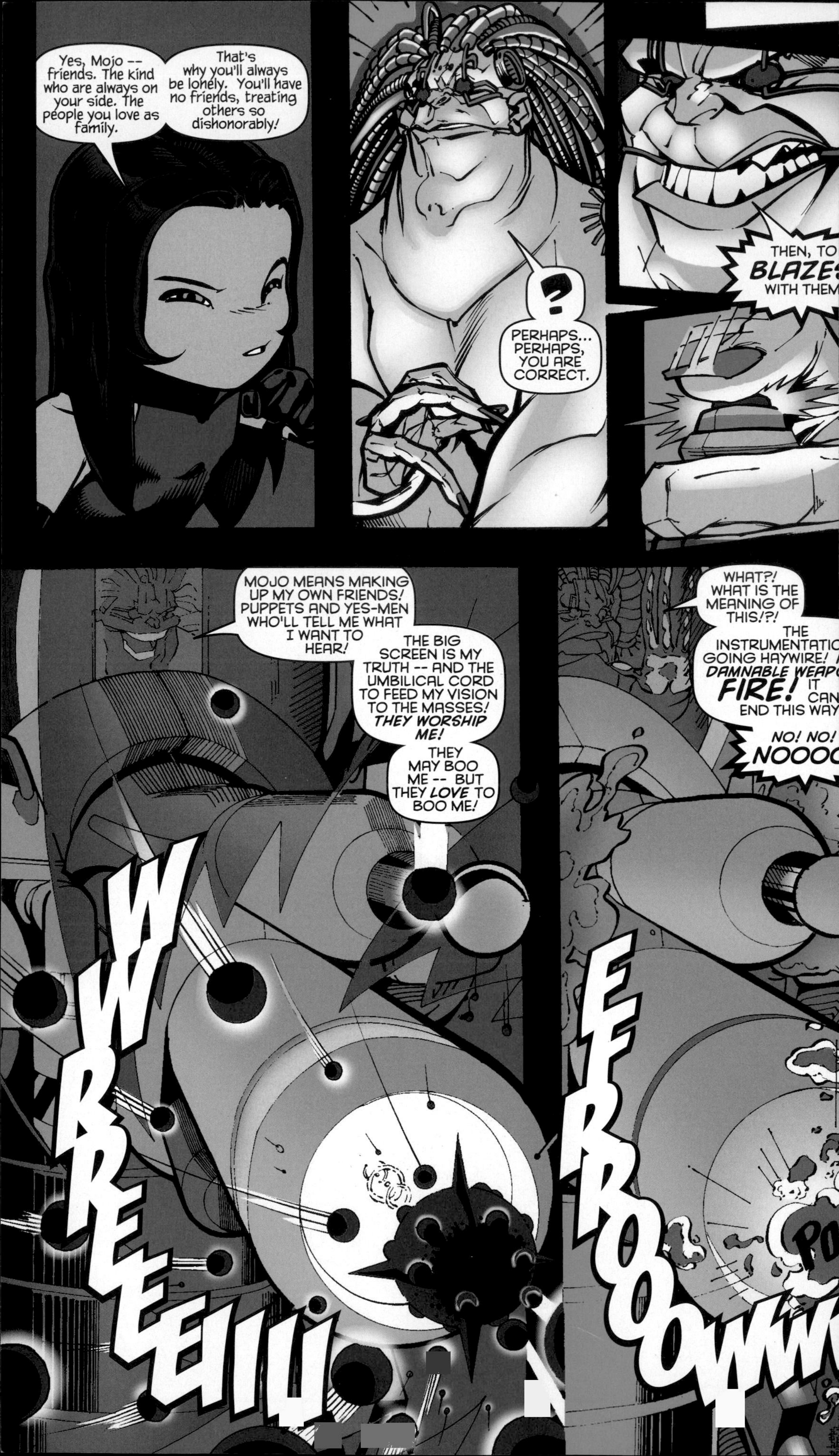
Yes, Mojo -- friends. The kind who are always on your side. The people you love as family.
That's why you'll always be lonely. You'll have no friends, treating others so dishonorably!
?
PERHAPS... PERHAPS, YOU ARE CORRECT.
THEN, TO BLAZES WITH THEM
MOJO MEANS MAKING UP MY OWN FRIENDS! PUPPETS AND YES-MEN WHO'LL TELL ME WHAT I WANT TO HEAR!
THE BIG SCREEN IS MY TRUTH -- AND THE UMBILICAL CORD TO FEED MY VISION TO THE MASSES! THEY WORSHIP ME!
THEY MAY BOO ME -- BUT THEY LOVE TO BOO ME!
WHAT?! WHAT IS THE MEANING OF THIS!?!
THE INSTRUMENTATIO GOING HAYWIRE! DAMNABLE WEAPO FIRE! IT CAN END THIS WAY
NO! NO! NOOOO

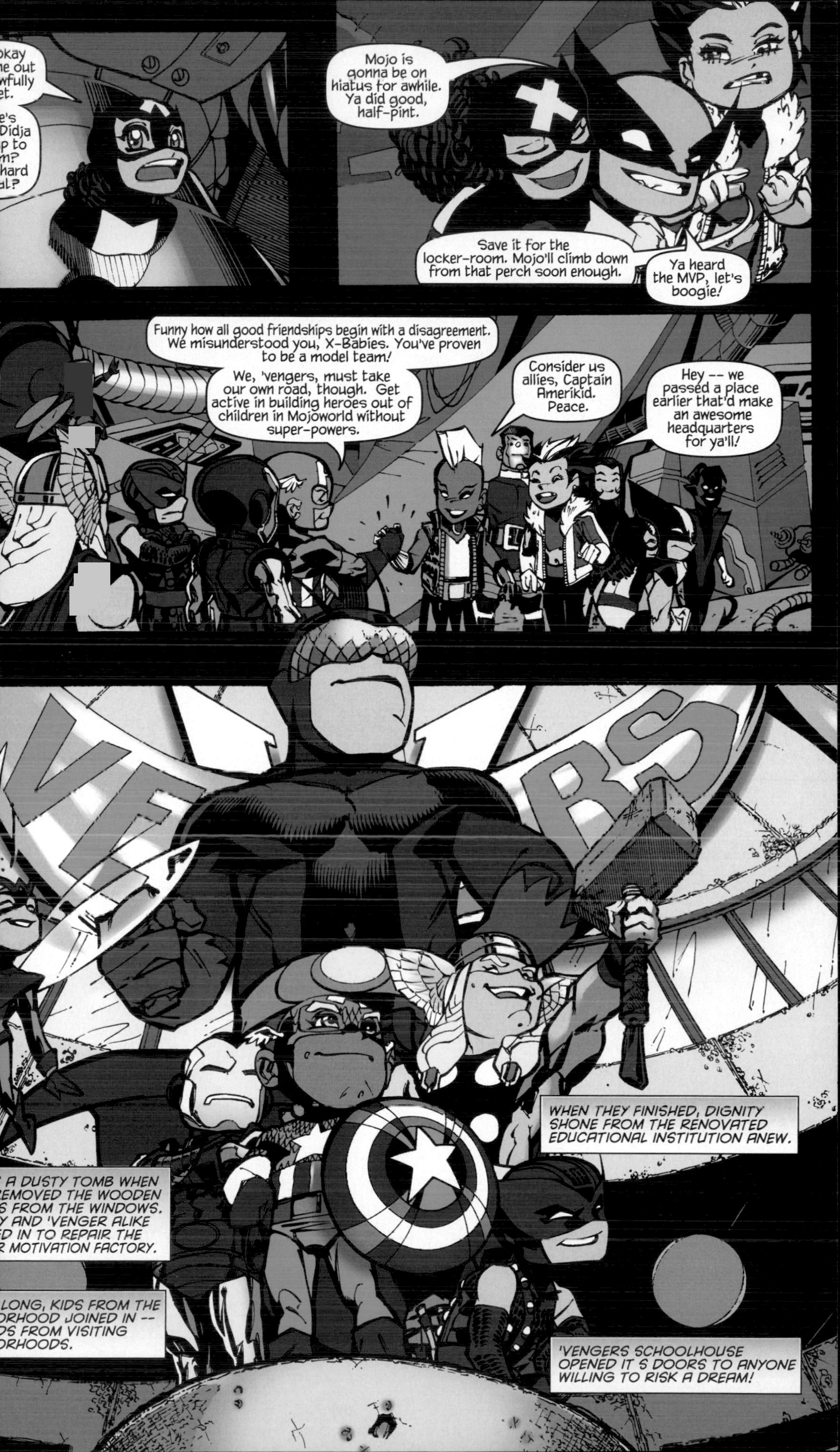

okay he out wfully et.
e's Didja p to m? hard al?
Mojo is gonna be on hiatus for awhile. Ya did good, half-pint.
Save it for the locker-room. Mojo'll climb down from that perch soon enough.
Ya heard the MVP, let's boogie!
Funny how all good friendships begin with a disagreement. We misunderstood you, X-Babies. You've proven to be a model team!
We, 'vengers, must take our own road, though. Get active in building heroes out of children in Mojoworld without super-powers.
Consider us allies, Captain Amerikid. Peace.
Hey -- we passed a place earlier that'd make an awesome headquarters for ya'll!
VE
RS
A DUSTY TOMB WHEN REMOVED THE WOODEN S FROM THE WINDOWS. Y AND 'VENGER ALIKE ED IN TO REPAIR THE R MOTIVATION FACTORY.
LONG, KIDS FROM THE ORHOOD JOINED IN -- DS FROM VISITING ORHOODS.
WHEN THEY FINISHED, DIGNITY SHONE FROM THE RENOVATED EDUCATIONAL INSTITUTION ANEW.
'VENGERS SCHOOLHOUSE OPENED IT S DOORS TO ANYONE WILLING TO RISK A DREAM!

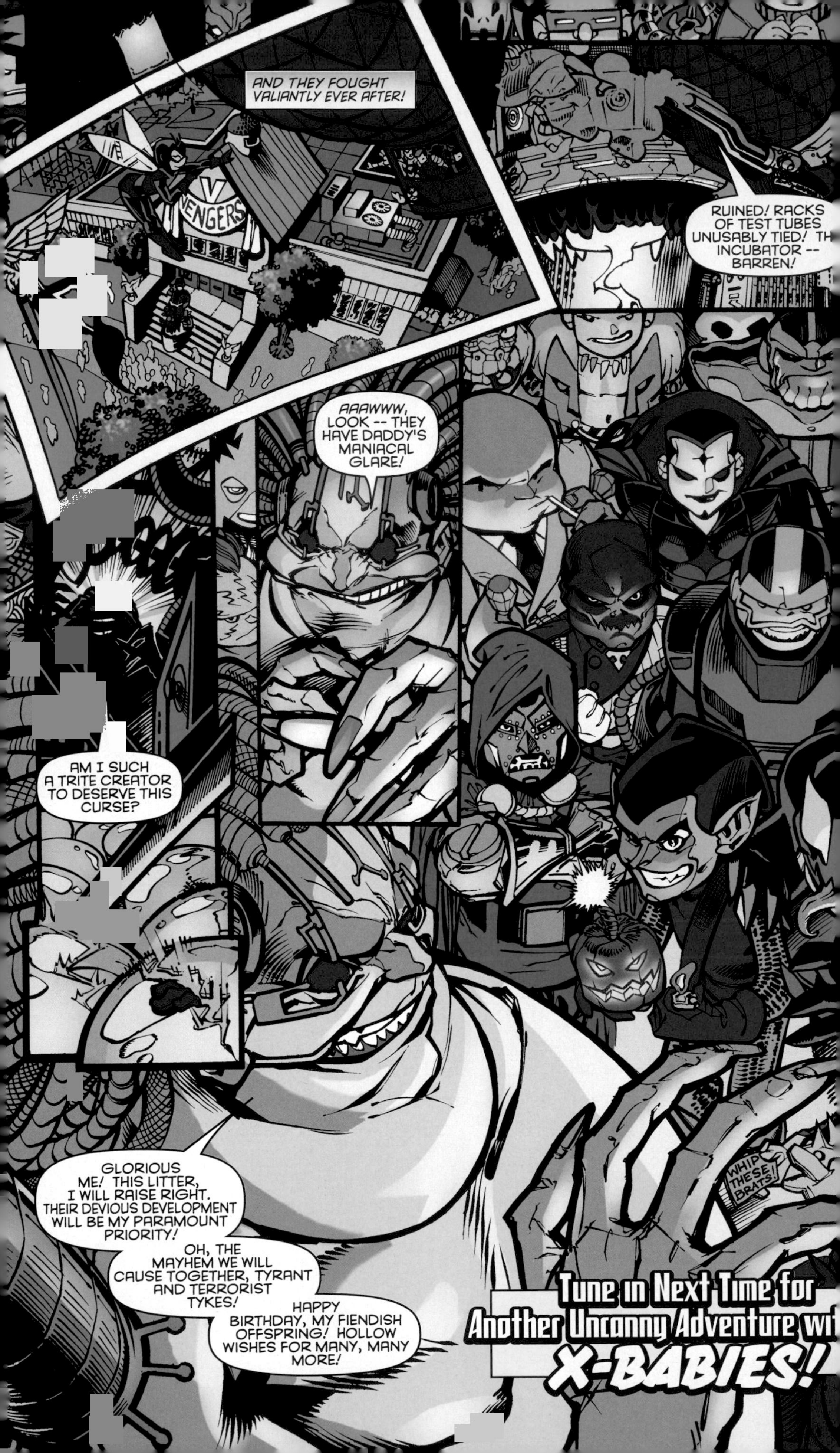
AND THEY FOUGHT VALIANTLY EVER AFTER!
VENGERS
RUINED! RACKS OF TEST TUBES UNUSABLY TIED! TH INCUBATOR -- BARREN!
AAAWWW, LOOK -- THEY HAVE DADDY'S MANIACAL GLARE!
AM I SUCH A TRITE CREATOR TO DESERVE THIS CURSE?
GLORIOUS ME! THIS LITTER, I WILL RAISE RIGHT. THEIR DEVIOUS DEVELOPMENT WILL BE MY PARAMOUNT PRIORITY!
OH, THE MAYHEM WE WILL CAUSE TOGETHER, TYRANT AND TERRORIST TYKES!
HAPPY BIRTHDAY, MY FIENDISH OFFSPRING! HOLLOW WISHES FOR MANY, MANY MORE!
WHIP THESE BRATS!
Tune in Next Time for Another Uncanny Adventure wit
X-BABIES!

With the original X-Babies no longer under his control, Mojo decided to create new baby X-Men — by
tering the real things! During a time when a reformed Juggernaut and the interdimensional Exiles member
octurne had allied with the team, Mojo and Spiral attacked the X-Mansion during a Danger Room session...

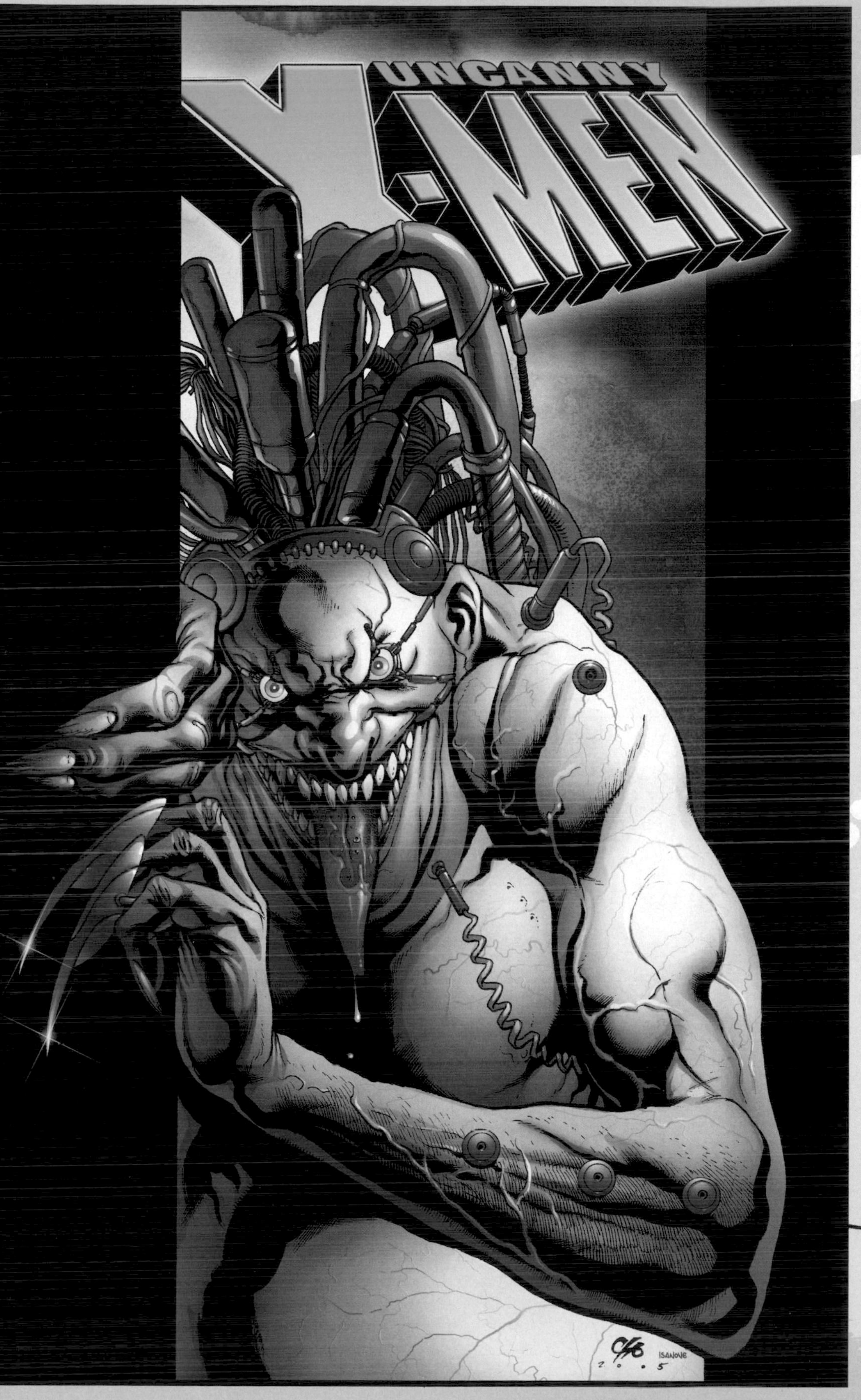
UNCANNY
X-MEN

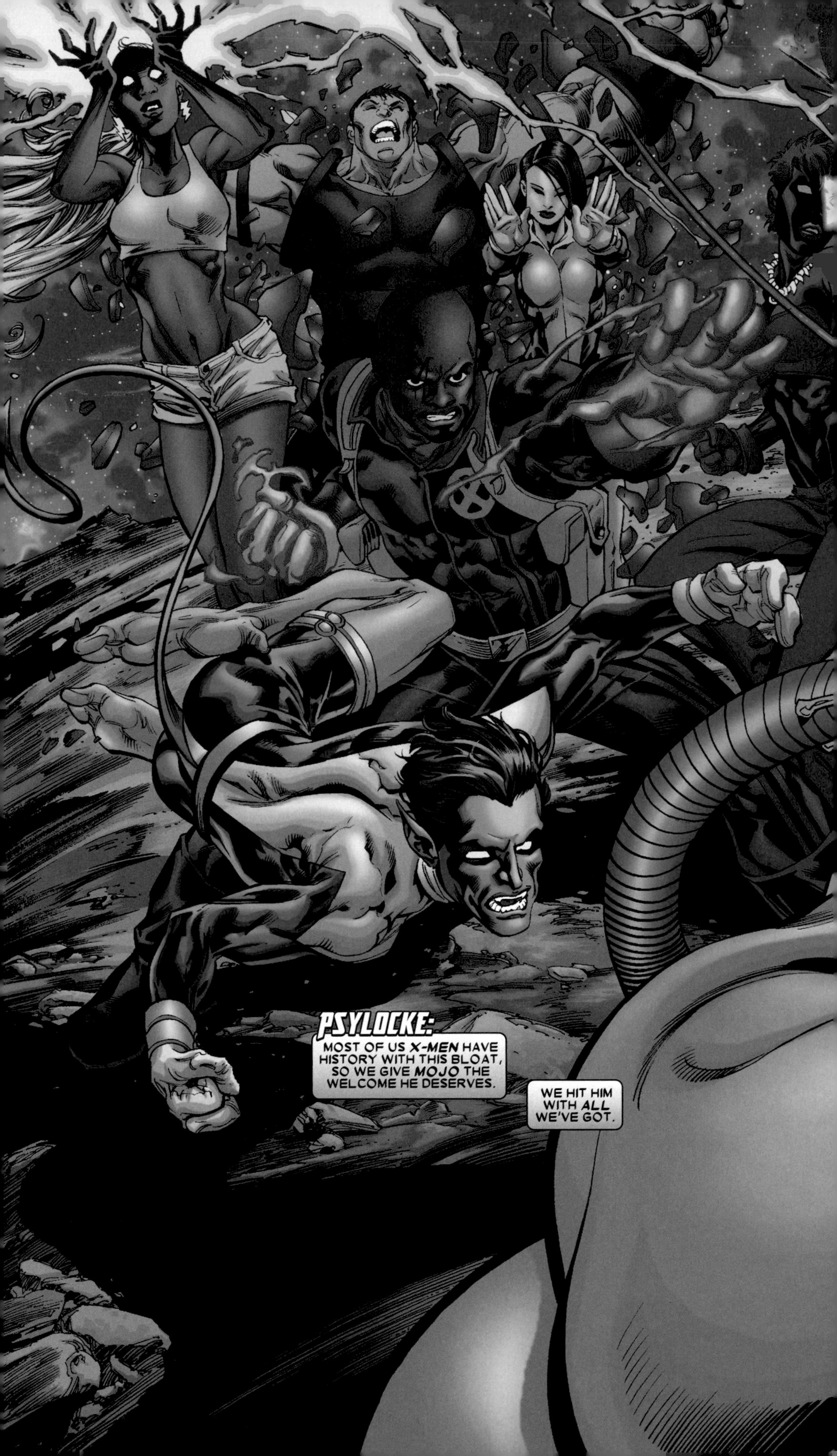
PSYLOCKE:
MOST OF US X-MEN HAVE HISTORY WITH THIS BLOAT, SO WE GIVE MOJO THE WELCOME HE DESERVES.
WE HIT HIM WITH ALL WE'VE GOT.

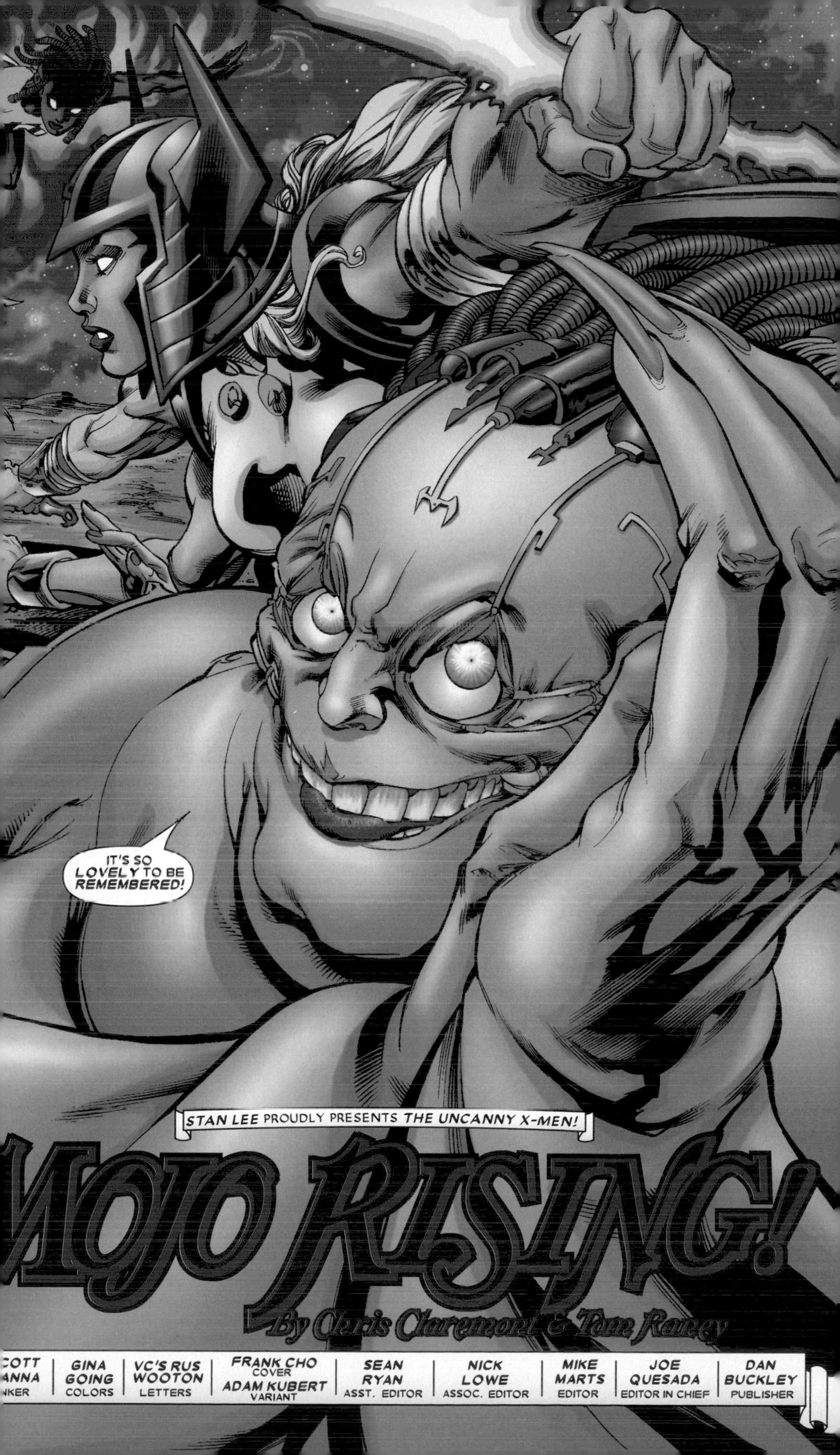
IT'S SO LOVELY TO BE REMEMBERED!
STAN LEE PROUDLY PRESENTS THE UNCANNY X-MEN!
MOJO RISING!
By Chris Claremont & Tom Raney
COTT ANNA INKER
GINA GOING COLORS
VC'S RUS WOOTON LETTERS
FRANK CHO COVER
ADAM KUBERT VARIANT
SEAN RYAN ASST. EDITOR
NICK LOWE ASSOC. EDITOR
MIKE MARTS EDITOR
JOE QUESADA EDITOR IN CHIEF
DAN BUCKLEY PUBLISHER

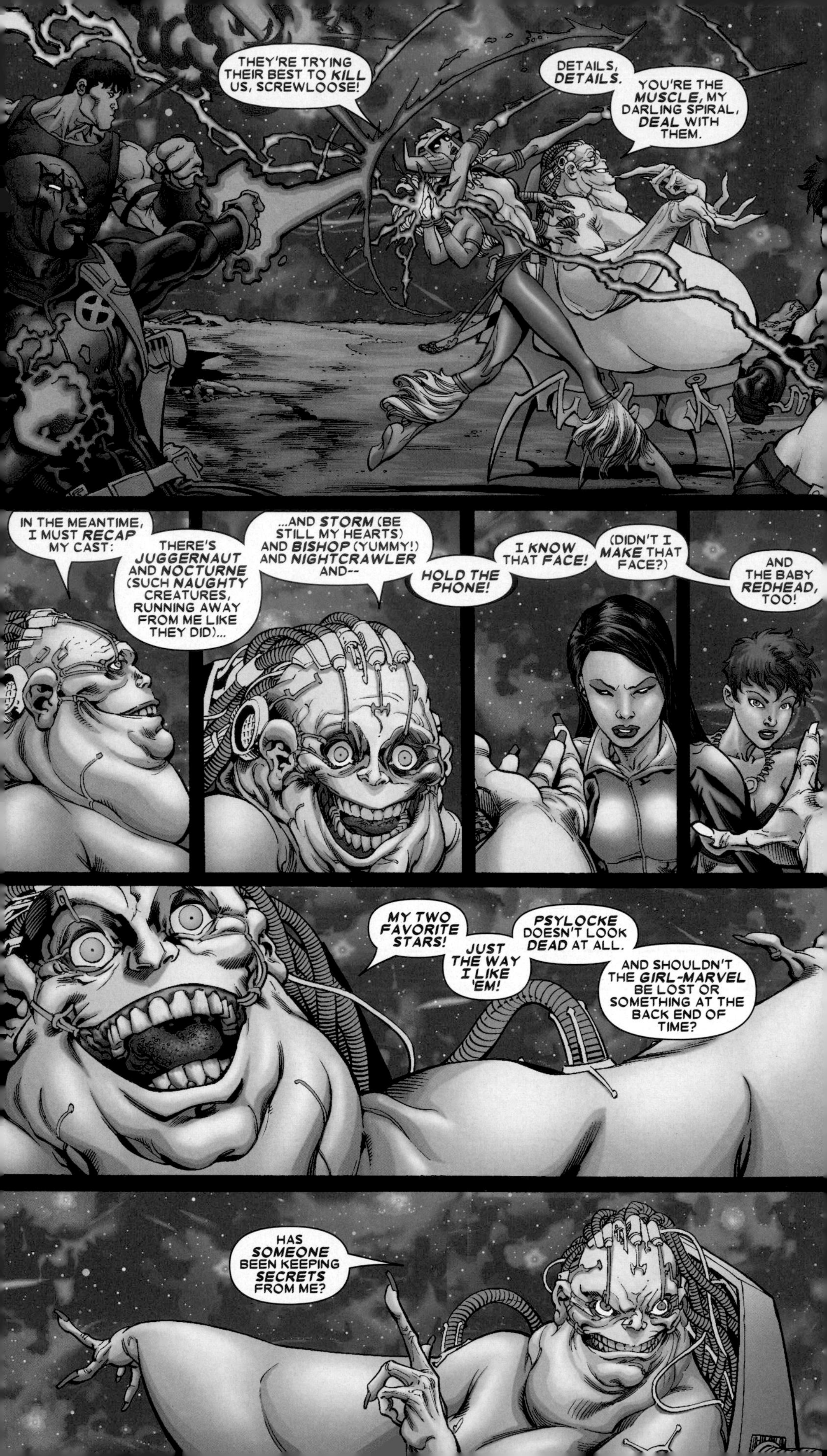
THEY'RE TRYING THEIR BEST TO KILL US, SCREWLOOSE!
DETAILS, DETAILS.
YOU'RE THE MUSCLE, MY DARLING SPIRAL, DEAL WITH THEM.
IN THE MEANTIME, I MUST RECAP MY CAST:
THERE'S JUGGERNAUT AND NOCTURNE (SUCH NAUGHTY CREATURES, RUNNING AWAY FROM ME LIKE THEY DID)...
...AND STORM (BE STILL MY HEARTS) AND BISHOP (YUMMY!) AND NIGHTCRAWLER AND--
HOLD THE PHONE!
I KNOW THAT FACE!
(DIDN'T I MAKE THAT FACE?)
AND THE BABY REDHEAD, TOO!
MY TWO FAVORITE STARS!
JUST THE WAY I LIKE 'EM!
PSYLOCKE DOESN'T LOOK DEAD AT ALL.
AND SHOULDN'T THE GIRL-MARVEL BE LOST OR SOMETHING AT THE BACK END OF TIME?
HAS SOMEONE BEEN KEEPING SECRETS FROM ME?

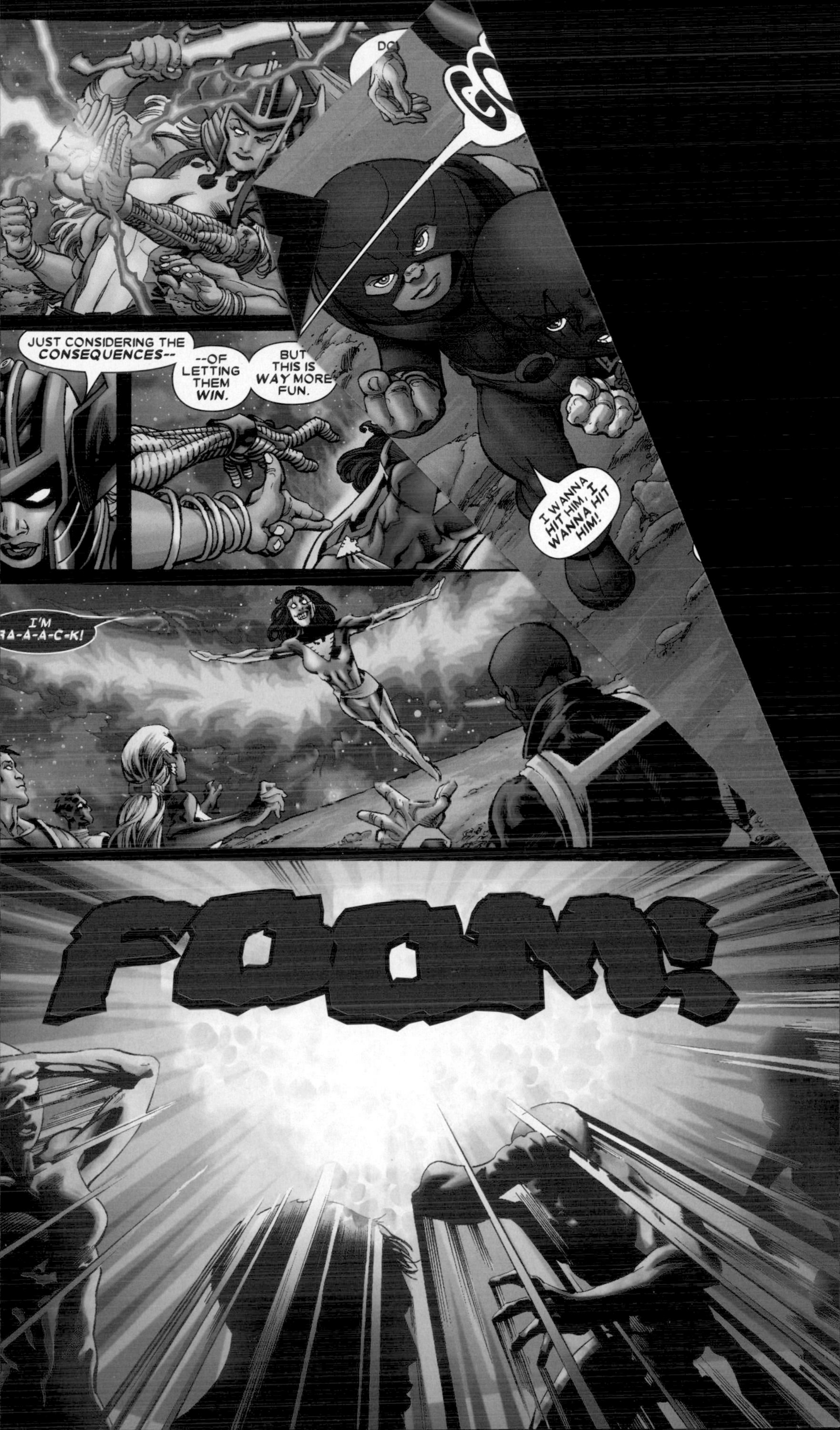
JUST CONSIDERING THE CONSEQUENCES--
--OF LETTING THEM WIN.
BUT THIS IS WAY MORE FUN.
I WANNA HIT HIM, I WANNA HIT HIM!
I'M BA-A-A-C-K!
FOOM!

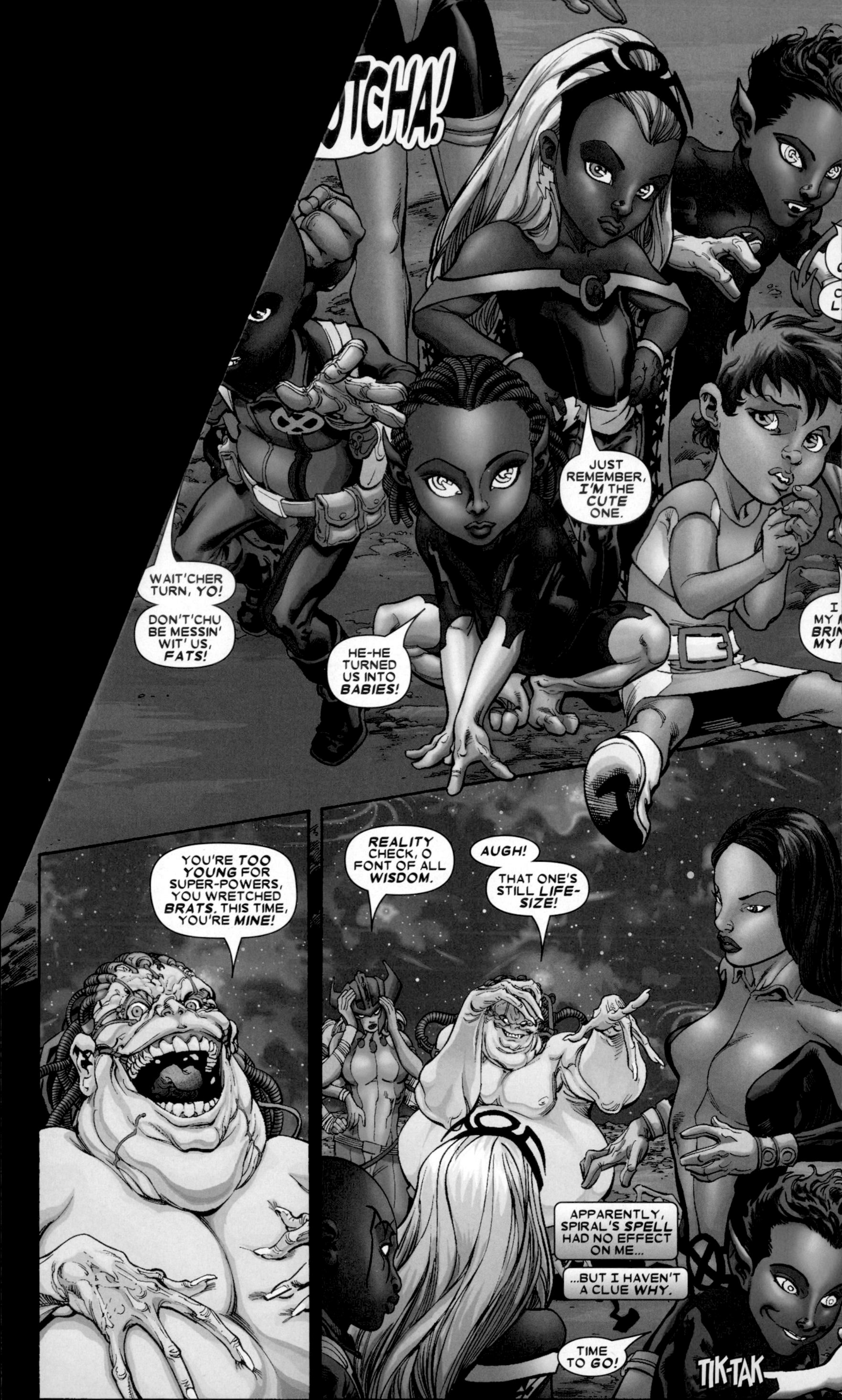
TCHA!
JUST REMEMBER, I'M THE CUTE ONE.
WAIT'CHER TURN, YO!
DON'T'CHU BE MESSIN' WIT' US, FATS!
HE-HE TURNED US INTO BABIES!
YOU'RE TOO YOUNG FOR SUPER-POWERS, YOU WRETCHED BRATS. THIS TIME, YOU'RE MINE!
REALITY CHECK, O FONT OF ALL WISDOM.
AUGH!
THAT ONE'S STILL LIFE-SIZE!
APPARENTLY, SPIRAL'S SPELL HAD NO EFFECT ON ME...
...BUT I HAVEN'T A CLUE WHY.
TIME TO GO!
TIK-TAK

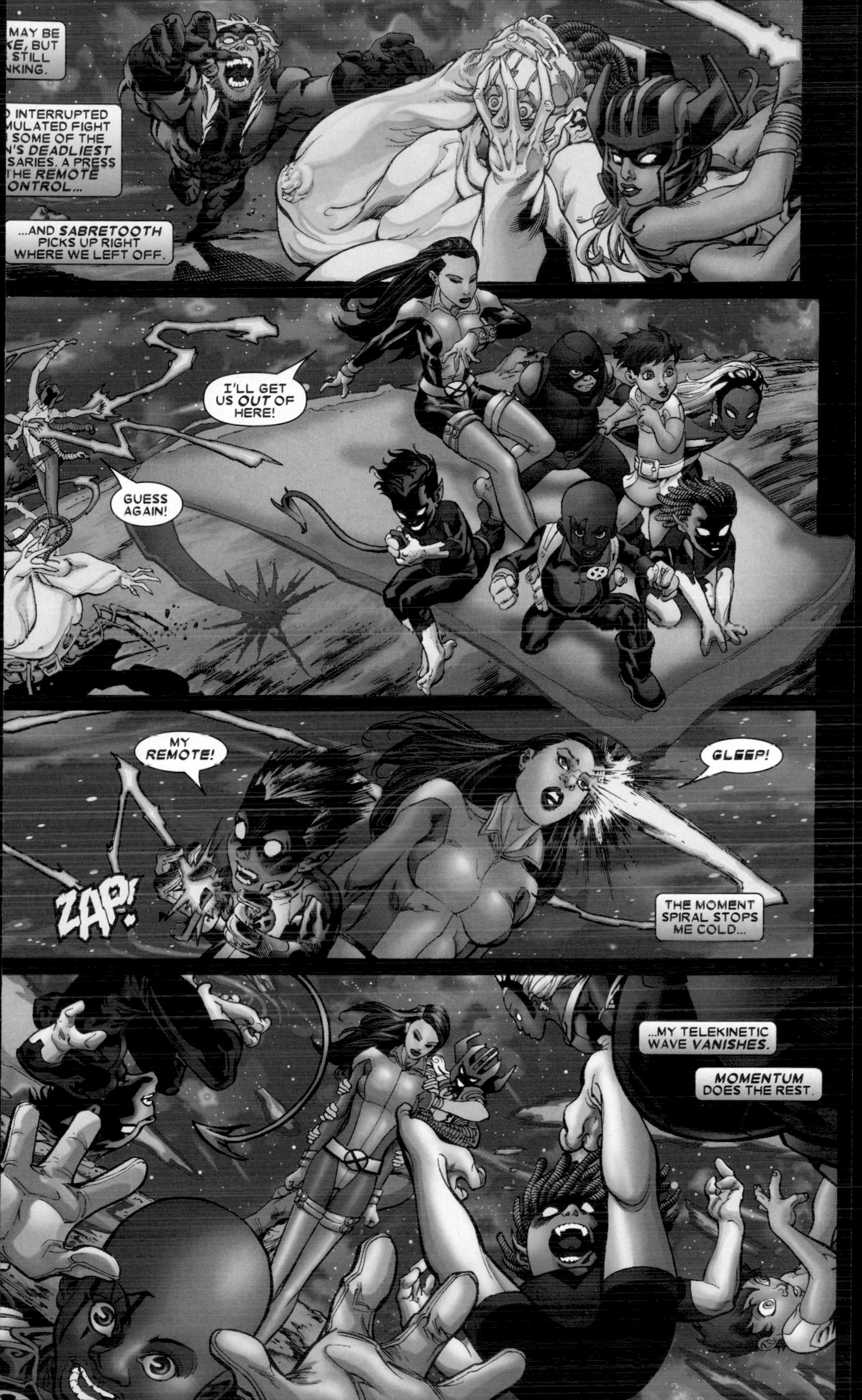
MAY BE
KE, BUT
STILL
NKING.
D INTERRUPTED
MULATED FIGHT
SOME OF THE
N'S DEADLIEST
SARIES. A PRESS
THE REMOTE
ONTROL...
...AND SABRETOOTH PICKS UP RIGHT WHERE WE LEFT OFF.
I'LL GET US OUT OF HERE!
GUESS AGAIN!
MY REMOTE!
GLEEP!
ZAP!
THE MOMENT SPIRAL STOPS ME COLD...
...MY TELEKINETIC WAVE VANISHES.
MOMENTUM DOES THE REST.

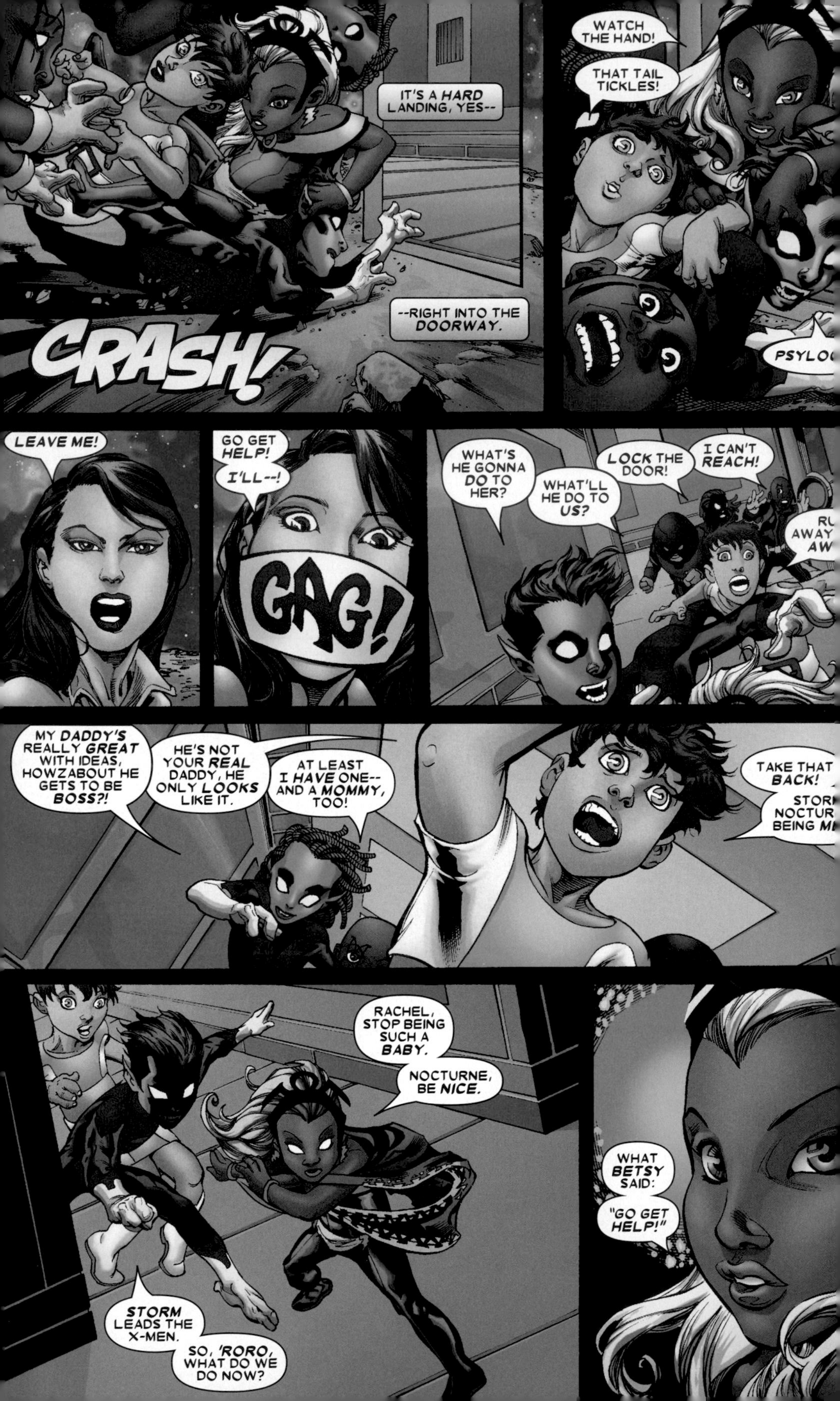
IT'S A HARD LANDING, YES--
--RIGHT INTO THE DOORWAY.
CRASH!
WATCH THE HAND!
THAT TAIL TICKLES!
PSYLOC
LEAVE ME!
GO GET HELP!
I'LL--!
GAG!
WHAT'S HE GONNA DO TO HER?
WHAT'LL HE DO TO US?
LOCK THE DOOR!
I CAN'T REACH!
RU AWAY AW
MY DADDY'S REALLY GREAT WITH IDEAS, HOWZABOUT HE GETS TO BE BOSS?!
HE'S NOT YOUR REAL DADDY, HE ONLY LOOKS LIKE IT.
AT LEAST I HAVE ONE-- AND A MOMMY, TOO!
TAKE THAT BACK!
STOR NOCTUR BEING M
RACHEL, STOP BEING SUCH A BABY.
NOCTURNE, BE NICE.
STORM LEADS THE X-MEN.
SO, 'RORO, WHAT DO WE DO NOW?
WHAT BETSY SAID:
"GO GET HELP!"

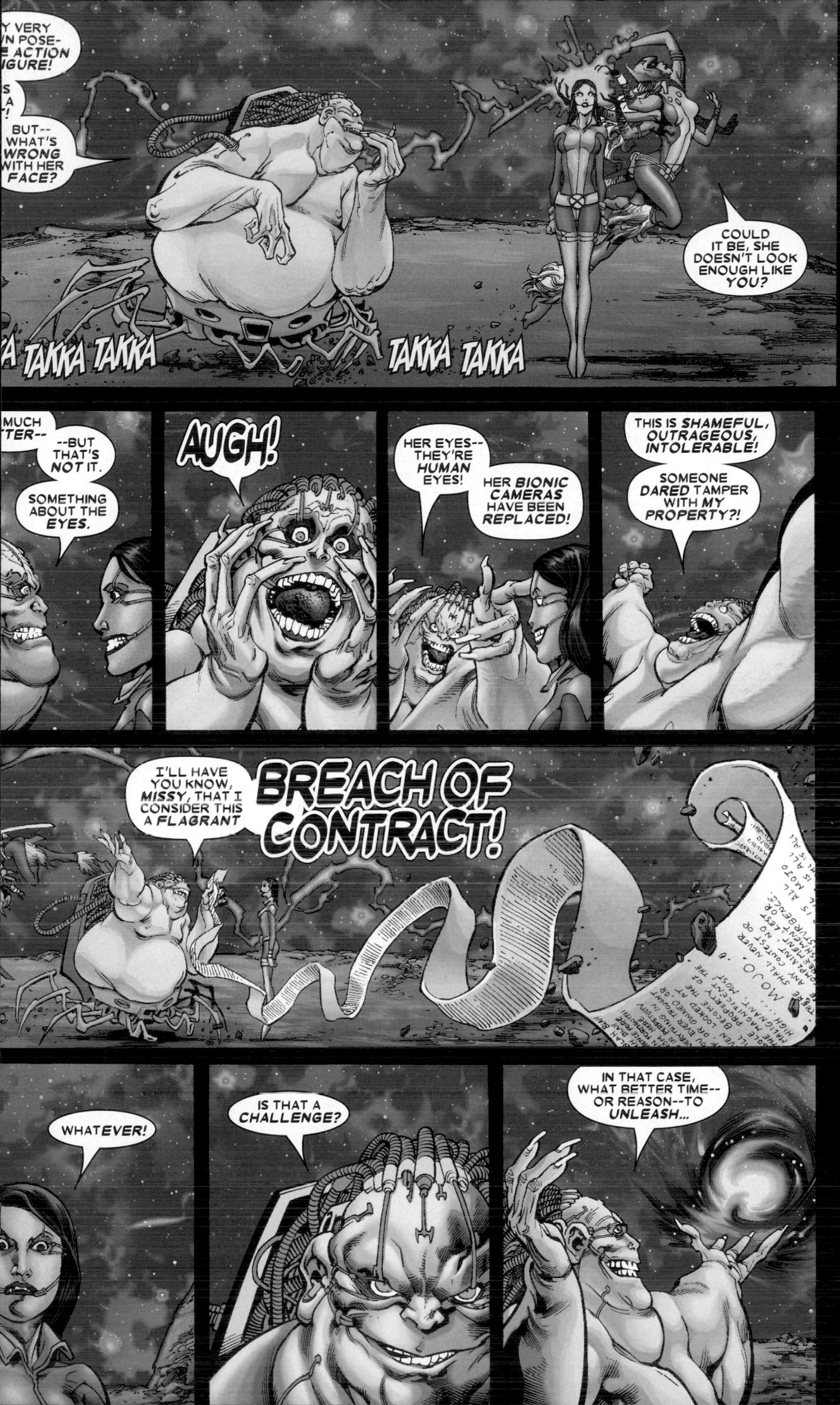

Y VERY N POSE- E ACTION IGURE!
BUT-- WHAT'S WRONG WITH HER FACE?
COULD IT BE, SHE DOESN'T LOOK ENOUGH LIKE YOU?
TAKKA TAKKA
TAKKA TAKKA
MUCH TTER--
--BUT THAT'S NOT IT.
SOMETHING ABOUT THE EYES.
AUGH!
HER EYES-- THEY'RE HUMAN EYES!
HER BIONIC CAMERAS HAVE BEEN REPLACED!
THIS IS SHAMEFUL, OUTRAGEOUS, INTOLERABLE!
SOMEONE DARED TAMPER WITH MY PROPERTY?!
I'LL HAVE YOU KNOW, MISSY, THAT I CONSIDER THIS A FLAGRANT
BREACH OF CONTRACT!
MOJO
WHATEVER!
IS THAT A CHALLENGE?
IN THAT CASE, WHAT BETTER TIME-- OR REASON--TO UNLEASH...

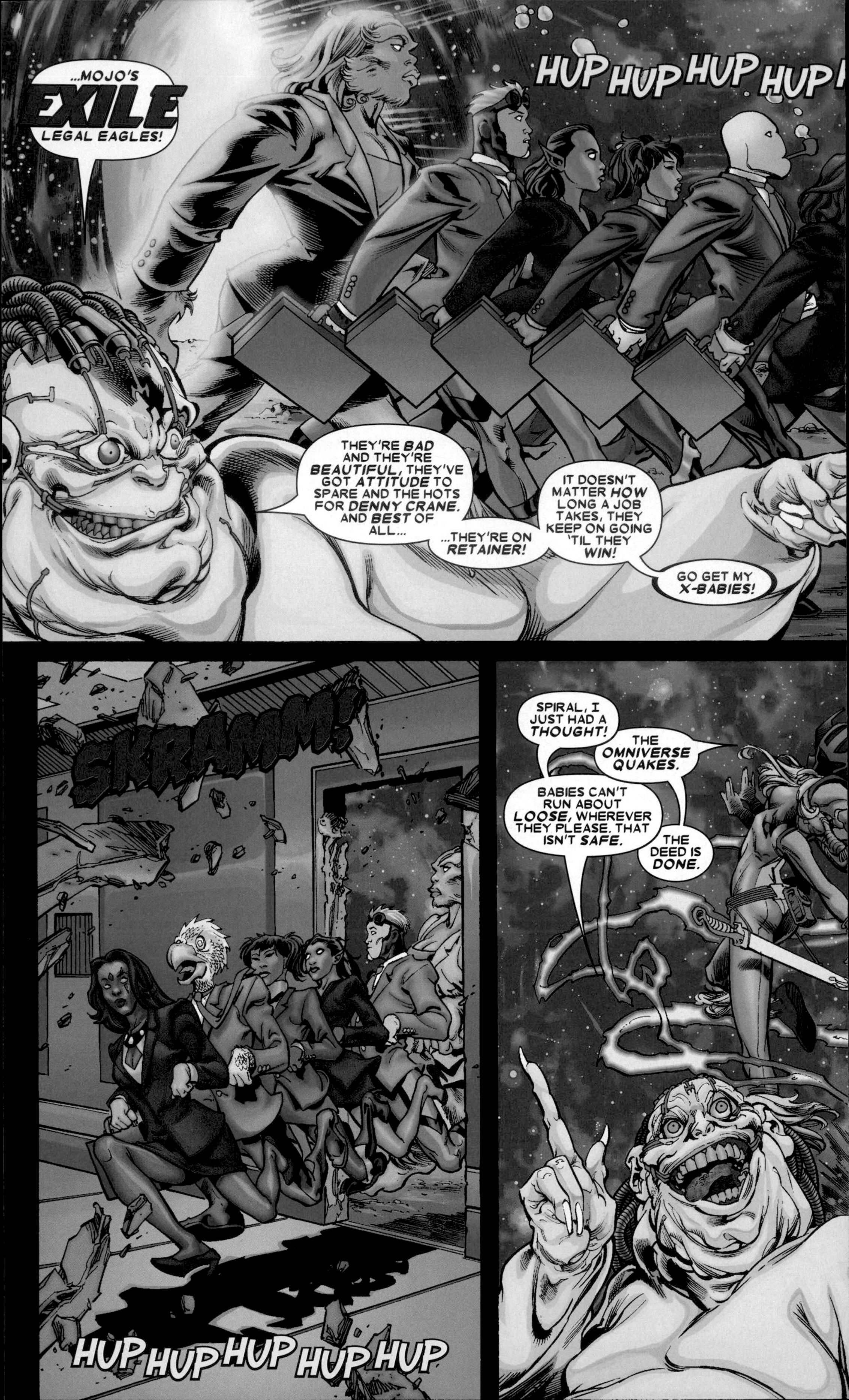
...MOJO'S EXILE LEGAL EAGLES!
HUP HUP HUP HUP HUP
THEY'RE BAD AND THEY'RE BEAUTIFUL, THEY'VE GOT ATTITUDE TO SPARE AND THE HOTS FOR DENNY CRANE. AND BEST OF ALL...
...THEY'RE ON RETAINER!
IT DOESN'T MATTER HOW LONG A JOB TAKES, THEY KEEP ON GOING 'TIL THEY WIN!
GO GET MY X-BABIES!
SKRAMM!
HUP HUP HUP HUP HUP
SPIRAL, I JUST HAD A THOUGHT!
THE OMNIVERSE QUAKES.
BABIES CAN'T RUN ABOUT LOOSE, WHEREVER THEY PLEASE. THAT ISN'T SAFE.
THE DEED IS DONE.

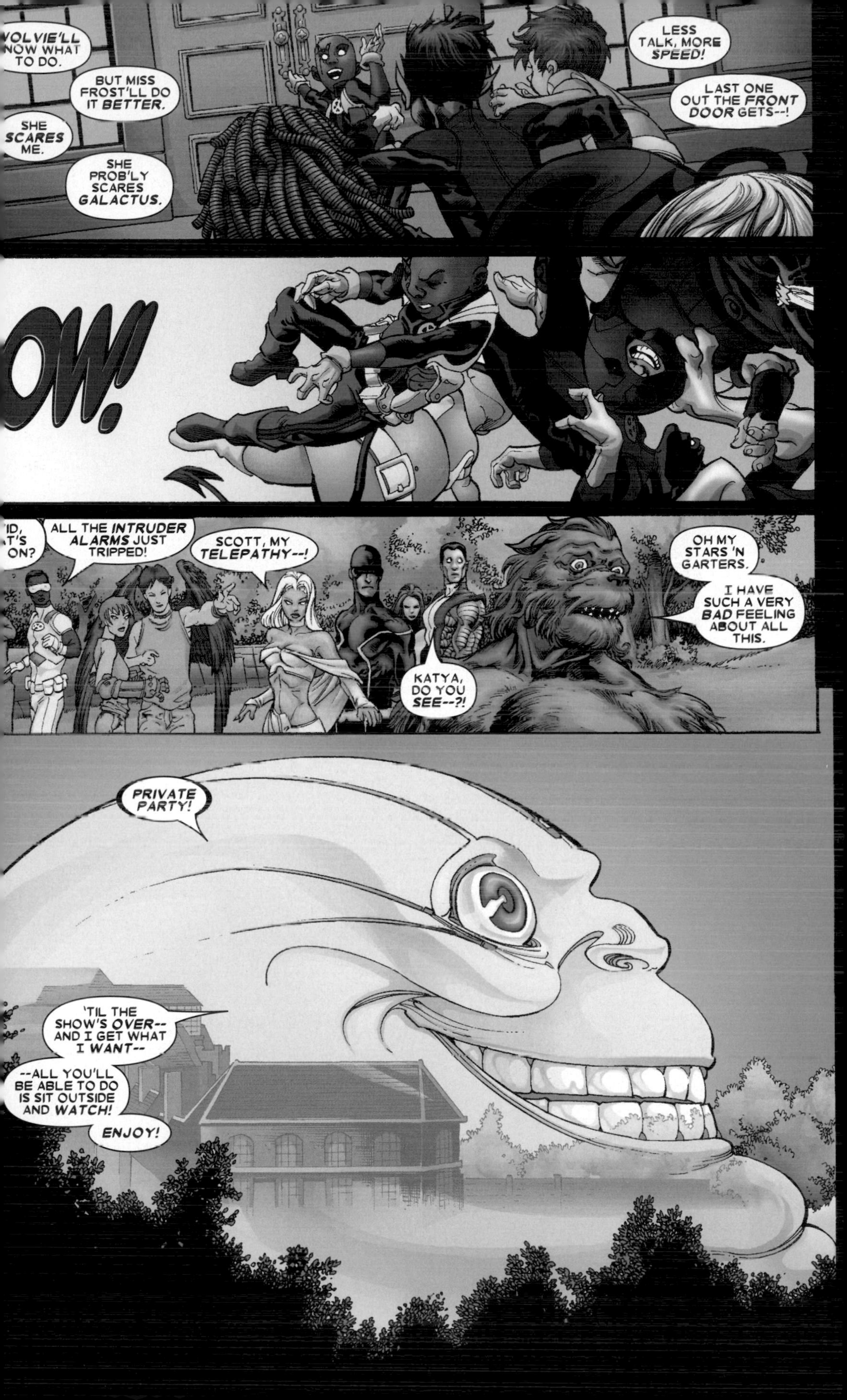

WOLVIE'LL
NOW WHAT
TO DO.
BUT MISS
FROST'LL DO
IT BETTER.
SHE
SCARES
ME.
SHE
PROB'LY
SCARES
GALACTUS.
LESS
TALK, MORE
SPEED!
LAST ONE
OUT THE FRONT
DOOR GETS--!
OW!
ID,
T'S
ON?
ALL THE INTRUDER
ALARMS JUST
TRIPPED!
SCOTT, MY
TELEPATHY--!
KATYA,
DO YOU
SEE--?!
OH MY
STARS 'N
GARTERS.
I HAVE
SUCH A VERY
BAD FEELING
ABOUT ALL
THIS.
PRIVATE
PARTY!
'TIL THE
SHOW'S OVER--
AND I GET WHAT
I WANT--
--ALL YOU'LL
BE ABLE TO DO
IS SIT OUTSIDE
AND WATCH!
ENJOY!

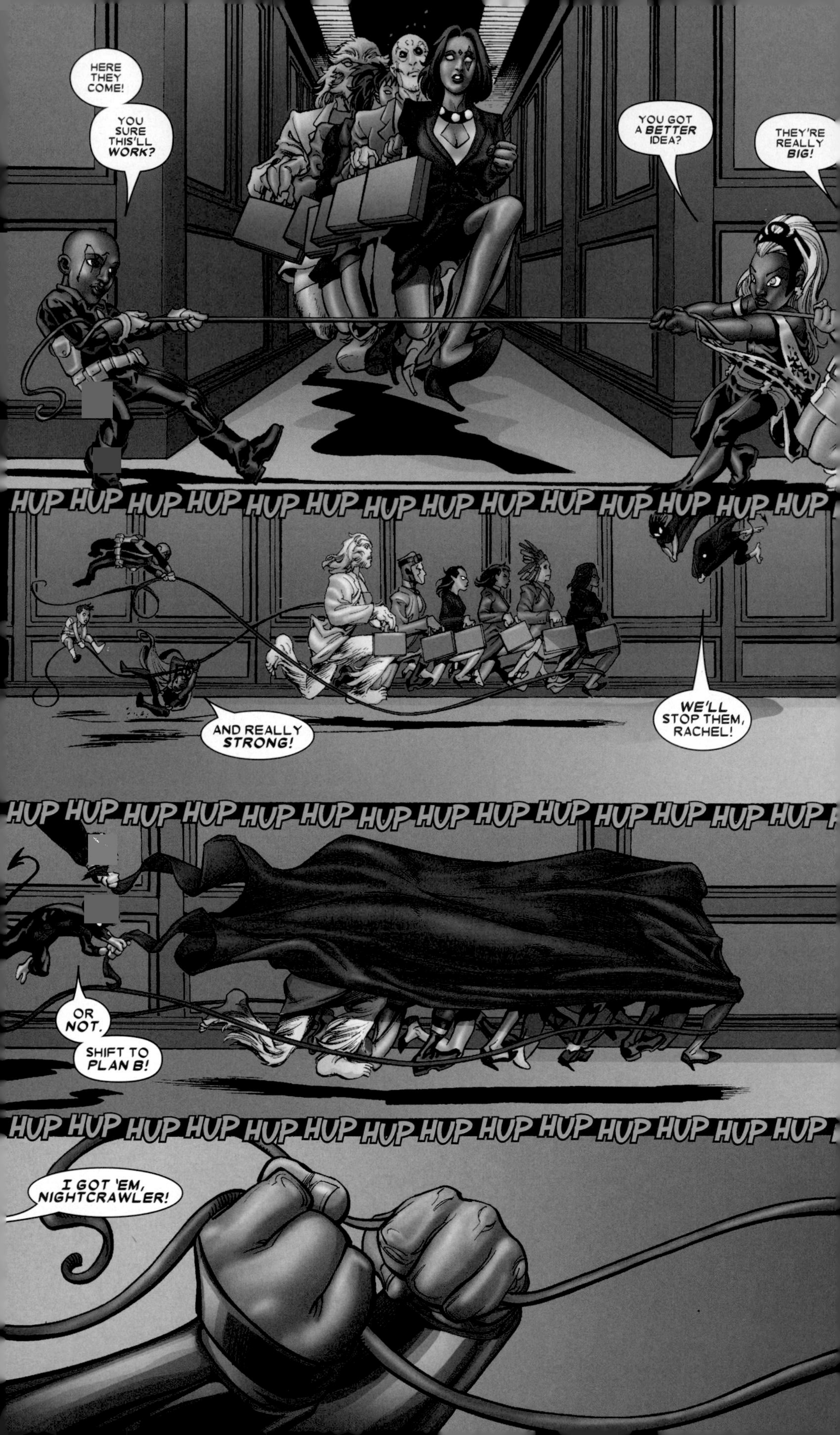
HERE THEY COME!
YOU SURE THIS'LL WORK?
YOU GOT A BETTER IDEA?
THEY'RE REALLY BIG!
HUP HUP HUP HUP HUP HUP HUP HUP HUP HUP HUP HUP HUP HUP
AND REALLY STRONG!
WE'LL STOP THEM, RACHEL!
HUP HUP HUP HUP HUP HUP HUP HUP HUP HUP HUP HUP HUP HUP
OR NOT.
SHIFT TO PLAN B!
HUP HUP HUP HUP HUP HUP HUP HUP HUP HUP HUP HUP HUP HUP
I GOT 'EM, NIGHTCRAWLER!

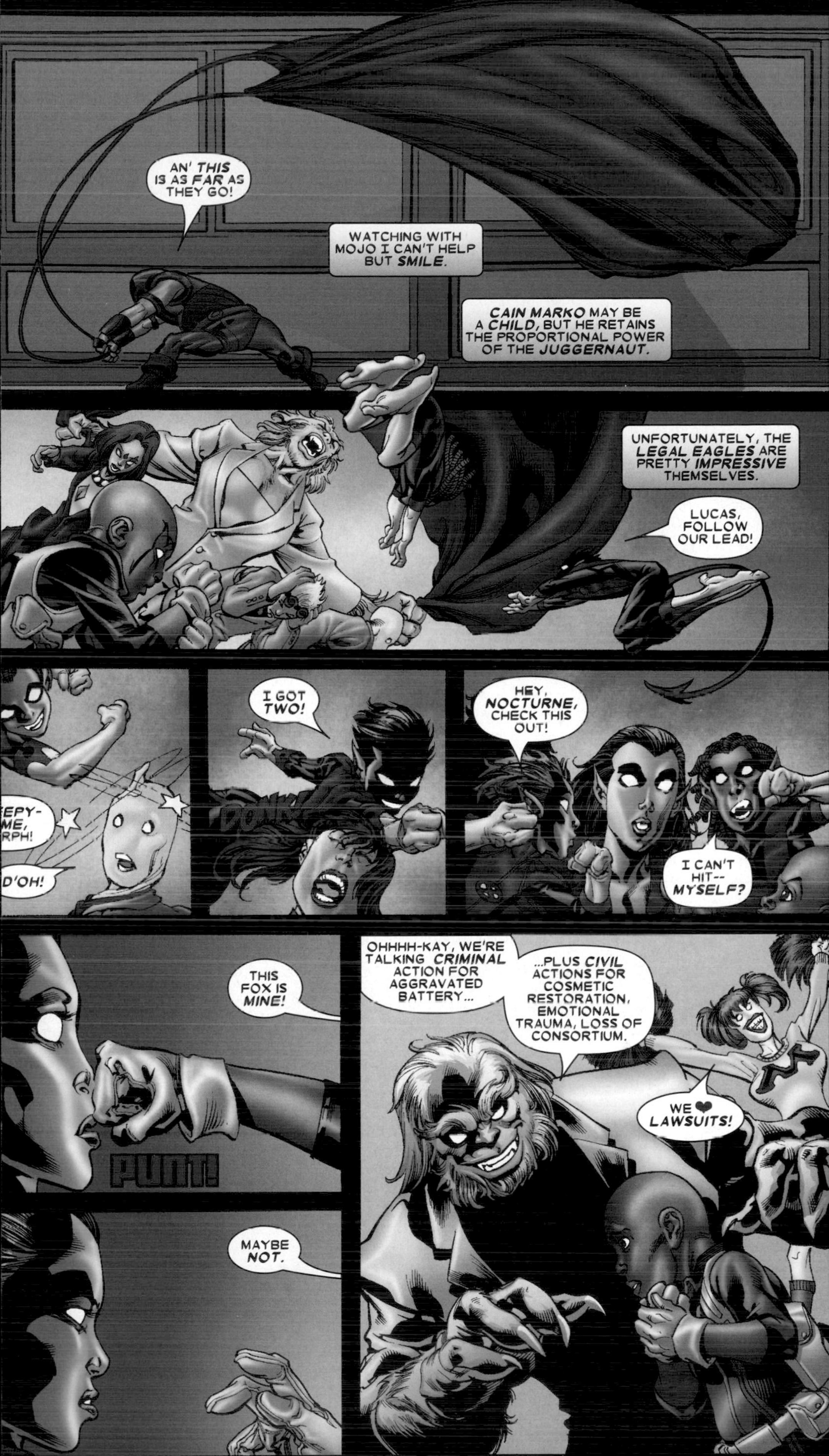

AN' THIS IS AS FAR AS THEY GO!
WATCHING WITH MOJO I CAN'T HELP BUT SMILE.
CAIN MARKO MAY BE A CHILD, BUT HE RETAINS THE PROPORTIONAL POWER OF THE JUGGERNAUT.
UNFORTUNATELY, THE LEGAL EAGLES ARE PRETTY IMPRESSIVE THEMSELVES.
LUCAS, FOLLOW OUR LEAD!
D'OH!
I GOT TWO!
HEY, NOCTURNE, CHECK THIS OUT!
I CAN'T HIT-- MYSELF?
THIS FOX IS MINE!
PUNT!
MAYBE NOT.
OHHHH-KAY, WE'RE TALKING CRIMINAL ACTION FOR AGGRAVATED BATTERY...
...PLUS CIVIL ACTIONS FOR COSMETIC RESTORATION, EMOTIONAL TRAUMA, LOSS OF CONSORTIUM.
WE ❤ LAWSUITS!

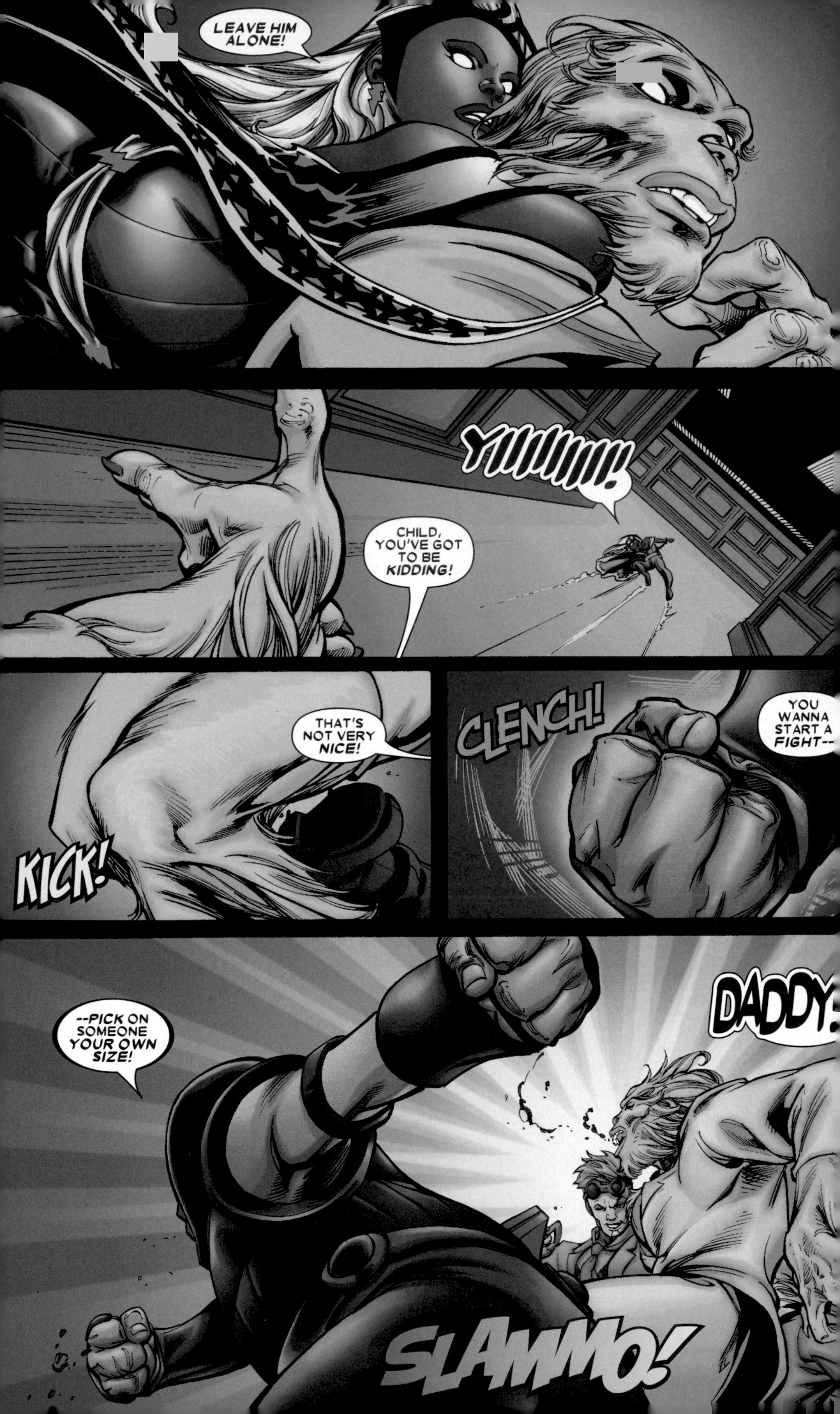
LEAVE HIM ALONE!
YIIIIIIIII!
CHILD, YOU'VE GOT TO BE KIDDING!
THAT'S NOT VERY NICE!
KICK!
CLENCH!
YOU WANNA START A FIGHT--
--PICK ON SOMEONE YOUR OWN SIZE!
DADDY!
SLAMMO!

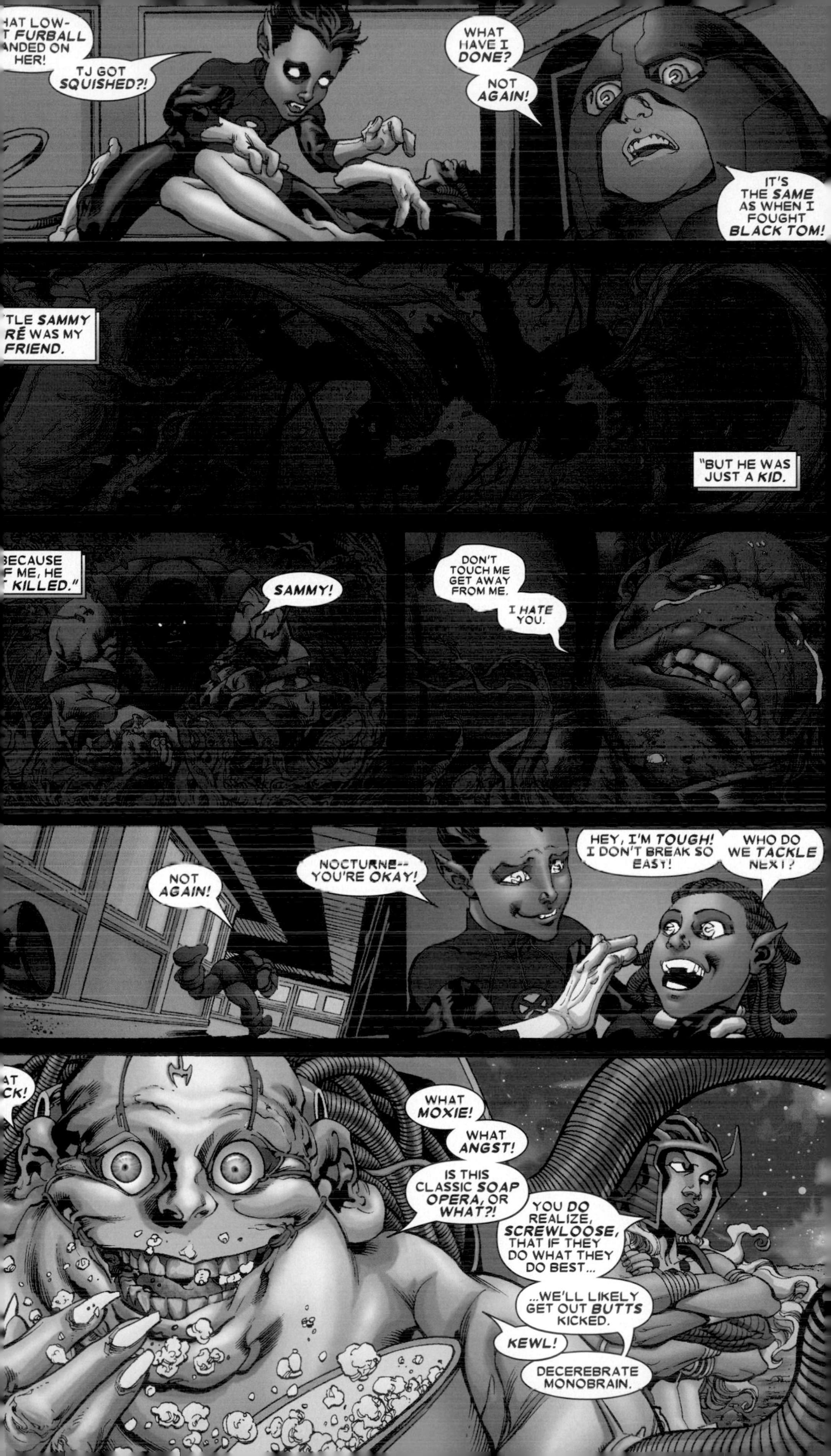
HAT LOW- T FURBALL ANDED ON HER!
TJ GOT SQUISHED?!
WHAT HAVE I DONE?
NOT AGAIN!
IT'S THE SAME AS WHEN I FOUGHT BLACK TOM!
TLE SAMMY RÉ WAS MY FRIEND.
"BUT HE WAS JUST A KID.
BECAUSE F ME, HE T KILLED."
SAMMY!
DON'T TOUCH ME GET AWAY FROM ME.
I HATE YOU.
NOT AGAIN!
NOCTURNE-- YOU'RE OKAY!
HEY, I'M TOUGH! I DON'T BREAK SO EASY!
WHO DO WE TACKLE NEXT?
AT CK!
WHAT MOXIE!
WHAT ANGST!
IS THIS CLASSIC SOAP OPERA, OR WHAT?!
YOU DO REALIZE, SCREWLOOSE, THAT IF THEY DO WHAT THEY DO BEST...
...WE'LL LIKELY GET OUT BUTTS KICKED.
KEWL!
DECEREBRATE MONOBRAIN.

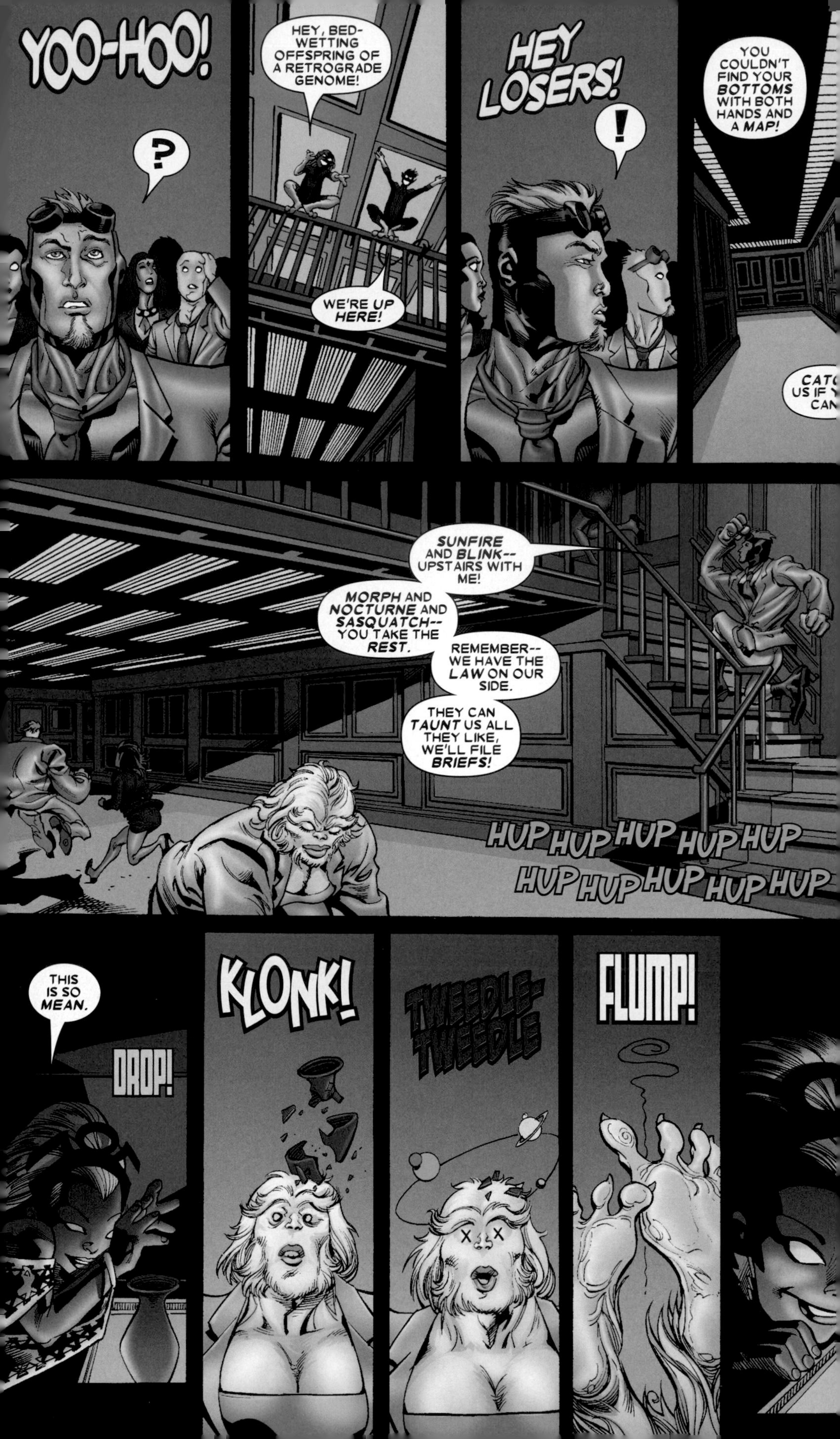

YOO-HOO!
?
HEY, BED-WETTING OFFSPRING OF A RETROGRADE GENOME!
WE'RE UP HERE!
HEY LOSERS!
!
YOU COULDN'T FIND YOUR BOTTOMS WITH BOTH HANDS AND A MAP!
SUNFIRE AND BLINK-- UPSTAIRS WITH ME!
MORPH AND NOCTURNE AND SASQUATCH-- YOU TAKE THE REST.
REMEMBER-- WE HAVE THE LAW ON OUR SIDE.
THEY CAN TAUNT US ALL THEY LIKE, WE'LL FILE BRIEFS!
HUP HUP HUP HUP HUP
HUP HUP HUP HUP HUP
THIS IS SO MEAN.
DROP!
KLONK!
TWEEDLE-TWEEDLE
FLUMP!

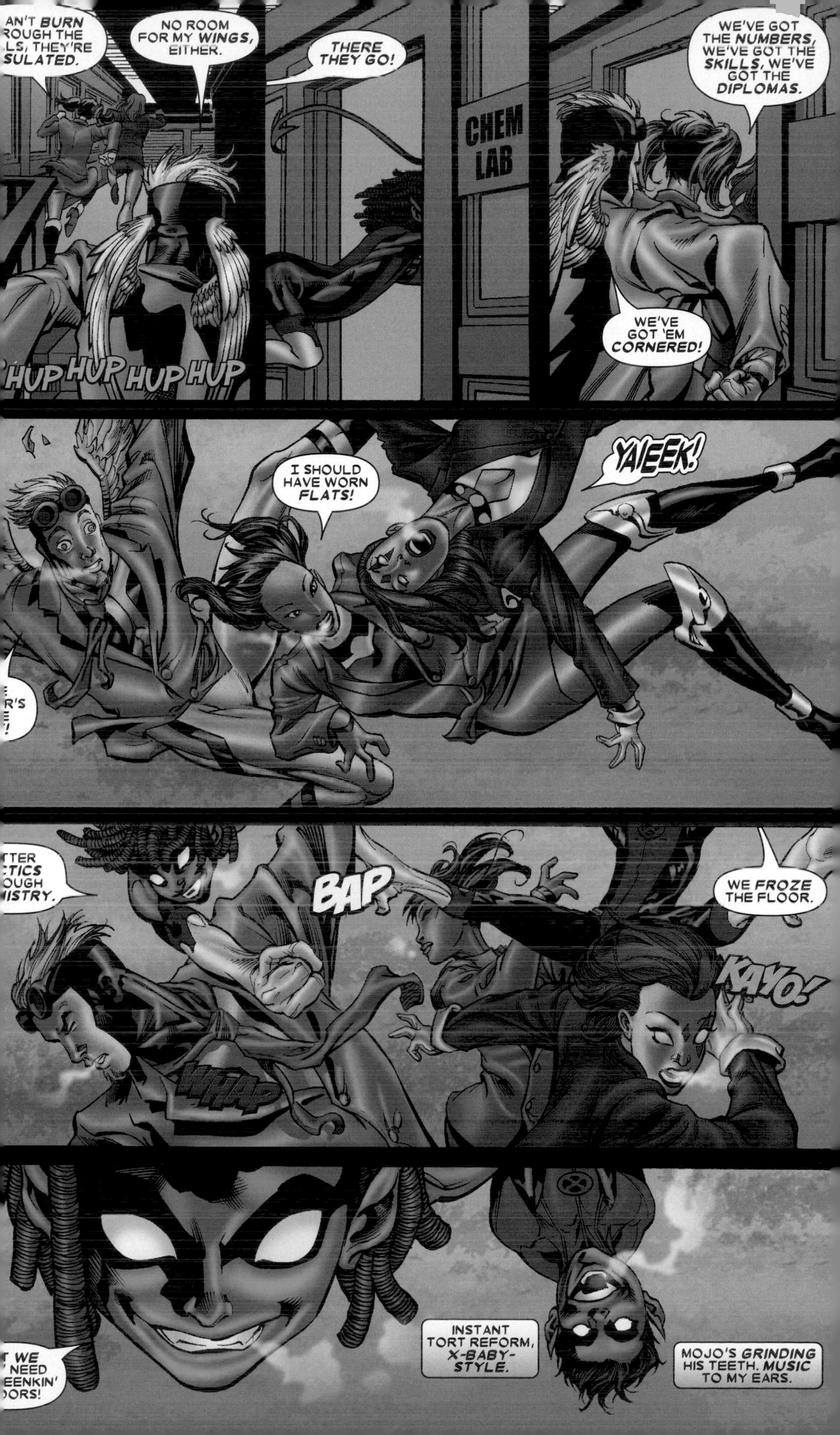
AN'T BURN
ROUGH THE
LS, THEY'RE
SULATED.
NO ROOM FOR MY WINGS, EITHER.
THERE THEY GO!
CHEM LAB
WE'VE GOT THE NUMBERS, WE'VE GOT THE SKILLS, WE'VE GOT THE DIPLOMAS.
WE'VE GOT 'EM CORNERED!
HUP HUP HUP HUP
YAIEEK!
I SHOULD HAVE WORN FLATS!
TTER
CTICS
OUGH
ISTRY.
BAP
WE FROZE THE FLOOR.
KAYO!
WHAP
T WE
NEED
EENKIN'
OORS!
INSTANT TORT REFORM, X-BABY-STYLE.
MOJO'S GRINDING HIS TEETH. MUSIC TO MY EARS.

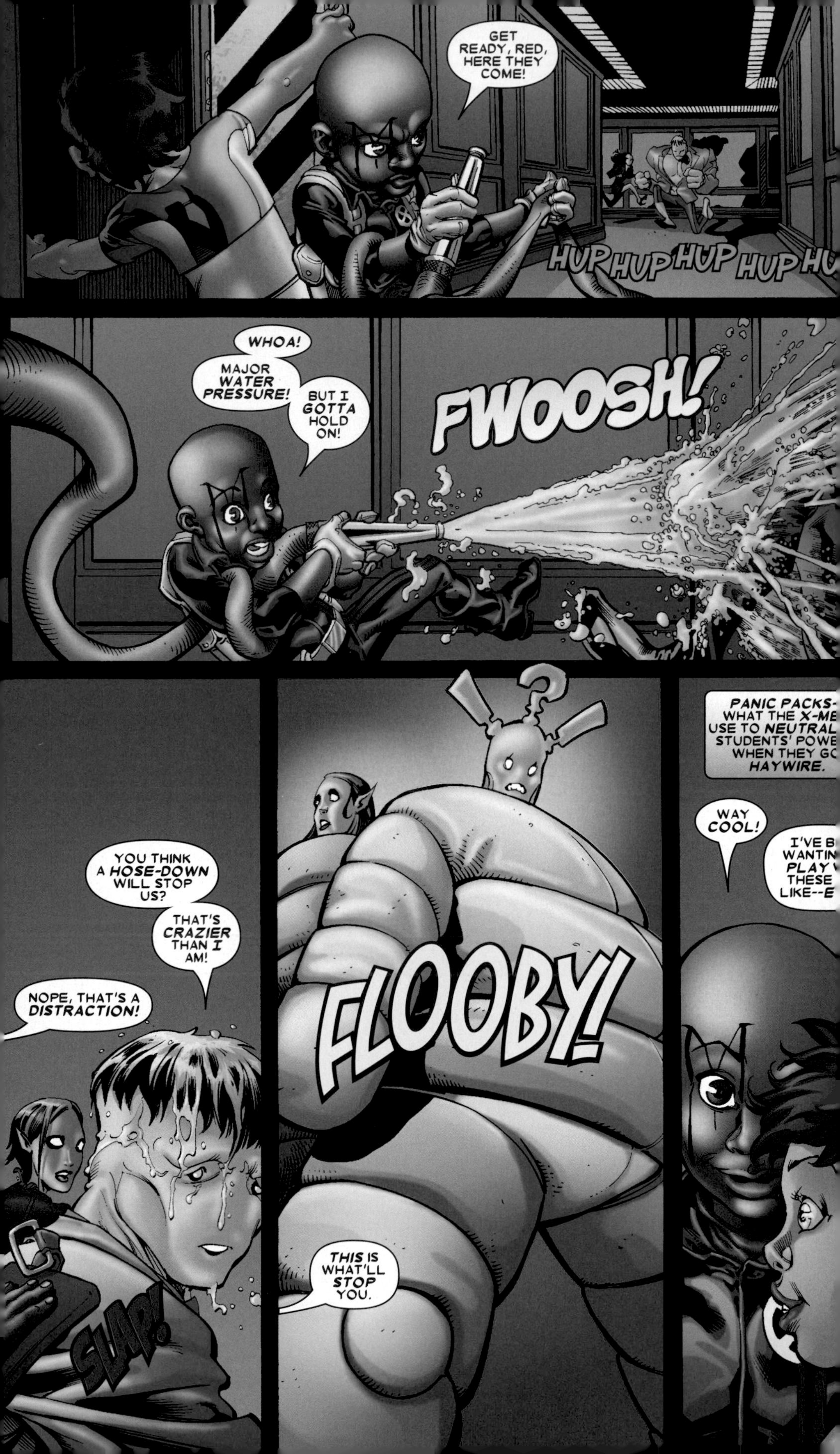

GET READY, RED, HERE THEY COME!
HUP HUP HUP HUP HU
WHOA!
MAJOR WATER PRESSURE!
BUT I GOTTA HOLD ON!
FWOOSH!
YOU THINK A HOSE-DOWN WILL STOP US?
THAT'S CRAZIER THAN I AM!
NOPE, THAT'S A DISTRACTION!
SLAP!
FLOOBY!
THIS IS WHAT'LL STOP YOU.
PANIC PACKS- WHAT THE X-ME USE TO NEUTRAL STUDENTS' POWE WHEN THEY GO HAYWIRE.
WAY COOL!
I'VE B WANTIN PLAY THESE LIKE--E

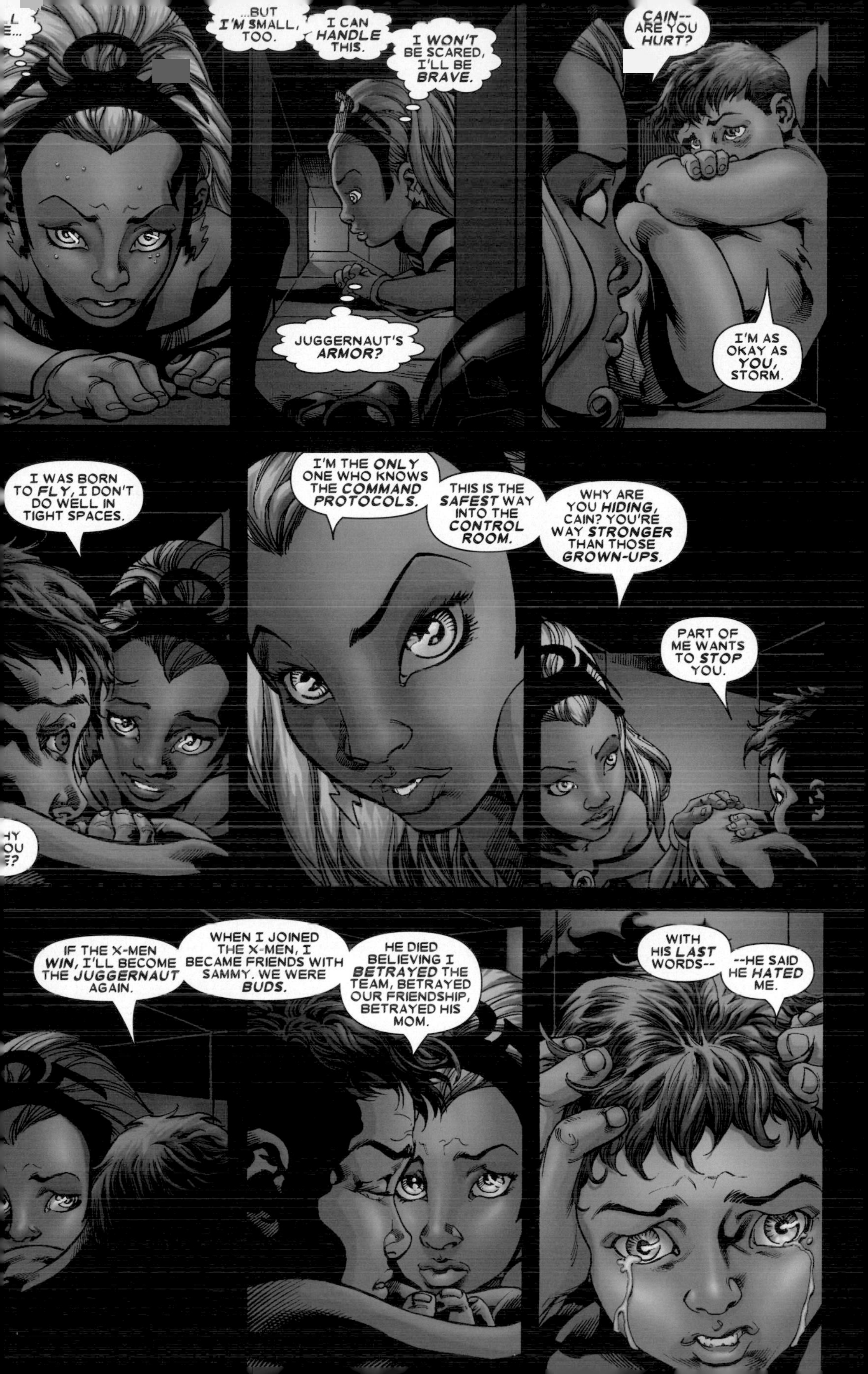
...BUT I'M SMALL, TOO.
I CAN HANDLE THIS.
I WON'T BE SCARED, I'LL BE BRAVE.
JUGGERNAUT'S ARMOR?
CAIN-- ARE YOU HURT?
I'M AS OKAY AS YOU, STORM.
I WAS BORN TO FLY, I DON'T DO WELL IN TIGHT SPACES.
I'M THE ONLY ONE WHO KNOWS THE COMMAND PROTOCOLS.
THIS IS THE SAFEST WAY INTO THE CONTROL ROOM.
WHY ARE YOU HIDING, CAIN? YOU'RE WAY STRONGER THAN THOSE GROWN-UPS.
PART OF ME WANTS TO STOP YOU.
IF THE X-MEN WIN, I'LL BECOME THE JUGGERNAUT AGAIN.
WHEN I JOINED THE X-MEN, I BECAME FRIENDS WITH SAMMY. WE WERE BUDS.
HE DIED BELIEVING I BETRAYED THE TEAM, BETRAYED OUR FRIENDSHIP, BETRAYED HIS MOM.
WITH HIS LAST WORDS--
--HE SAID HE HATED ME.

YOU *DIDN'T* BETRAY US, CAIN. I KNOW THE *STORY*.

IT WAS A *PRETEND* BETRAYAL, TO *SAVE* LIVES!

BUT MY *LIE* GOT SAMMY *KILLED*.

IT WASN'T YOUR FAULT!

HE'LL *NEVER* KNOW THAT!

SO WHAT D'YOU WANT TO DO?

CAN'T I JUST STAY A *KID*?

IF MY LIFE GETS A *DO-OVER*, MAYBE I CAN GET THINGS *RIGHT*?

SURE YOU CAN.

BUT IT'D BE *WRONG*.

FOR *US*, CAIN, THE *JOURNEY* MATTERS AS MUCH AS THE *DESTINATION*.

WE *ALL* WANT SECON CHANCES. BEIN *X-MEN* IS KIND HOW WE EAR THEM.

PART OF TH THE *BIG* PA MEANS ACCE RESPONSIB FOR WHAT V DONE.

THAT ISN'T *FAIR*.

SOMETIMES, NEITHER IS *LIFE*.

STAY *BEHIND*, CAIN. YOU'LL BE *SAFE* HERE.

LEAVE THE REST TO *ME*.

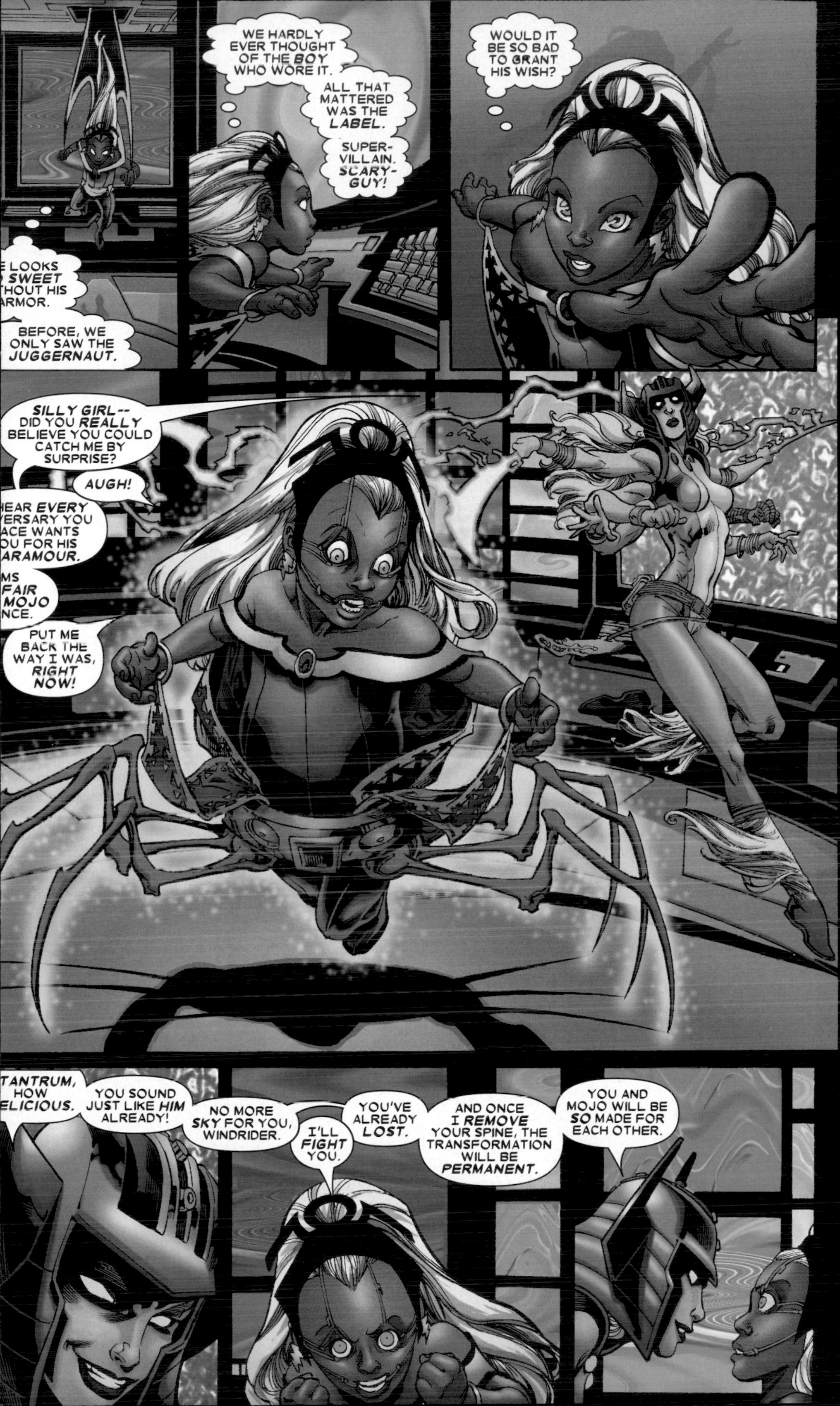

E LOOKS
O SWEET
THOUT HIS
ARMOR.
BEFORE, WE ONLY SAW THE JUGGERNAUT.
WE HARDLY EVER THOUGHT OF THE BOY WHO WORE IT.
ALL THAT MATTERED WAS THE LABEL.
SUPER-VILLAIN. SCARY-GUY!
WOULD IT BE SO BAD TO GRANT HIS WISH?
SILLY GIRL-- DID YOU REALLY BELIEVE YOU COULD CATCH ME BY SURPRISE?
AUGH!
HEAR EVERY
VERSARY YOU
ACE WANTS
OU FOR HIS
ARAMOUR.
MS
FAIR
MOJO
NCE.
PUT ME BACK THE WAY I WAS, RIGHT NOW!
TANTRUM, HOW
ELICIOUS.
YOU SOUND JUST LIKE HIM ALREADY!
NO MORE SKY FOR YOU, WINDRIDER.
I'LL FIGHT YOU.
YOU'VE ALREADY LOST.
AND ONCE I REMOVE YOUR SPINE, THE TRANSFORMATION WILL BE PERMANENT.
YOU AND MOJO WILL BE SO MADE FOR EACH OTHER.

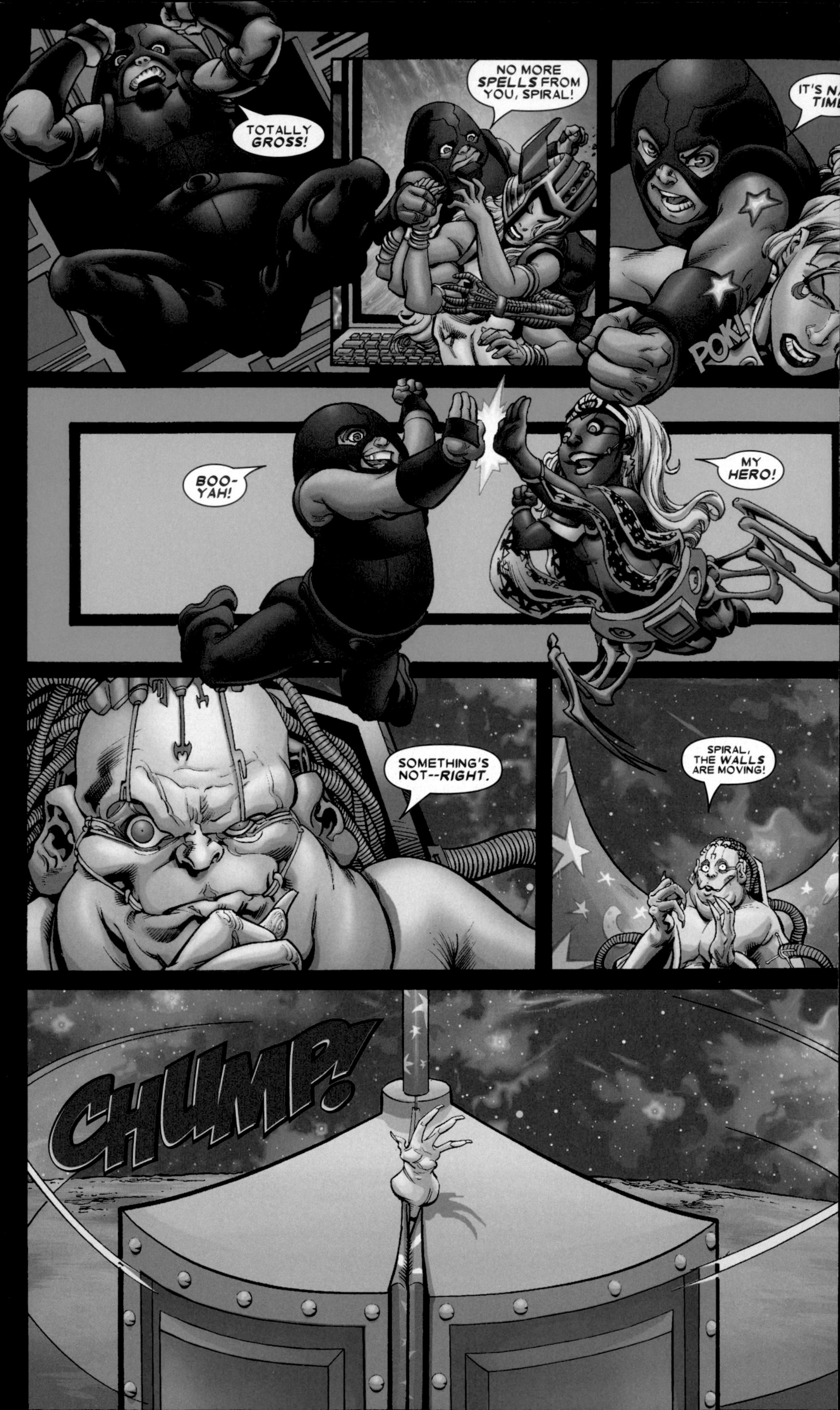
TOTALLY GROSS!
NO MORE SPELLS FROM YOU, SPIRAL!
IT'S NA TIME
POK!
BOO-YAH!
MY HERO!
SOMETHING'S NOT--RIGHT.
SPIRAL, THE WALLS ARE MOVING!
CHUMP!

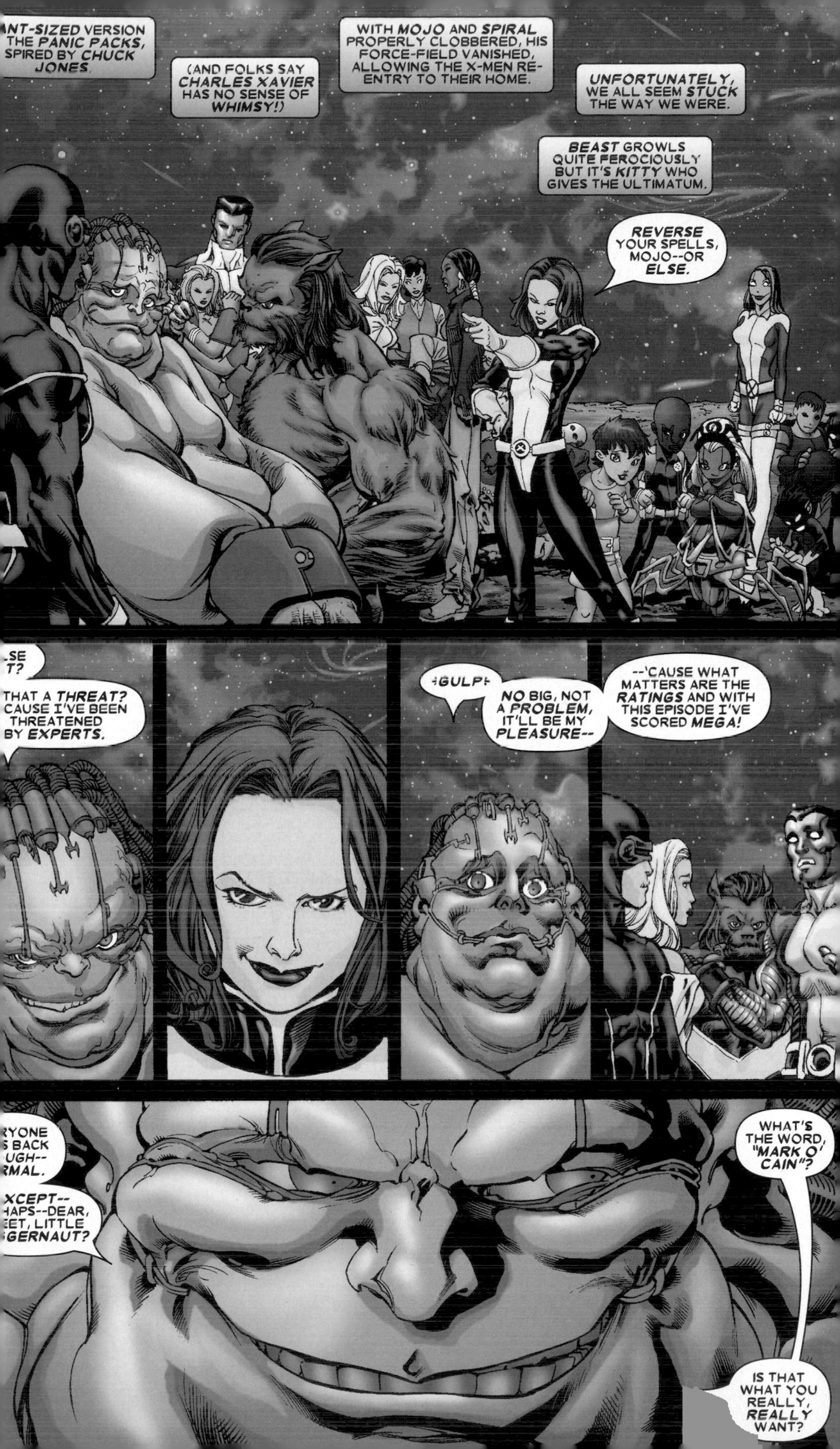

NT-SIZED VERSION THE PANIC PACKS, SPIRED BY CHUCK JONES.
(AND FOLKS SAY CHARLES XAVIER HAS NO SENSE OF WHIMSY!)
WITH MOJO AND SPIRAL PROPERLY CLOBBERED, HIS FORCE-FIELD VANISHED, ALLOWING THE X-MEN RE-ENTRY TO THEIR HOME.
UNFORTUNATELY, WE ALL SEEM STUCK THE WAY WE WERE.
BEAST GROWLS QUITE FEROCIOUSLY BUT IT'S KITTY WHO GIVES THE ULTIMATUM.
REVERSE YOUR SPELLS, MOJO--OR ELSE.
LSE T?
THAT A THREAT? CAUSE I'VE BEEN THREATENED BY EXPERTS.
-GULP-
NO BIG, NOT A PROBLEM, IT'LL BE MY PLEASURE--
--'CAUSE WHAT MATTERS ARE THE RATINGS AND WITH THIS EPISODE I'VE SCORED MEGA!
RYONE S BACK UGH-- RMAL.
XCEPT-- HAPS--DEAR, EET, LITTLE GERNAUT?
WHAT'S THE WORD, "MARK O' CAIN"?
IS THAT WHAT YOU REALLY, REALLY WANT?

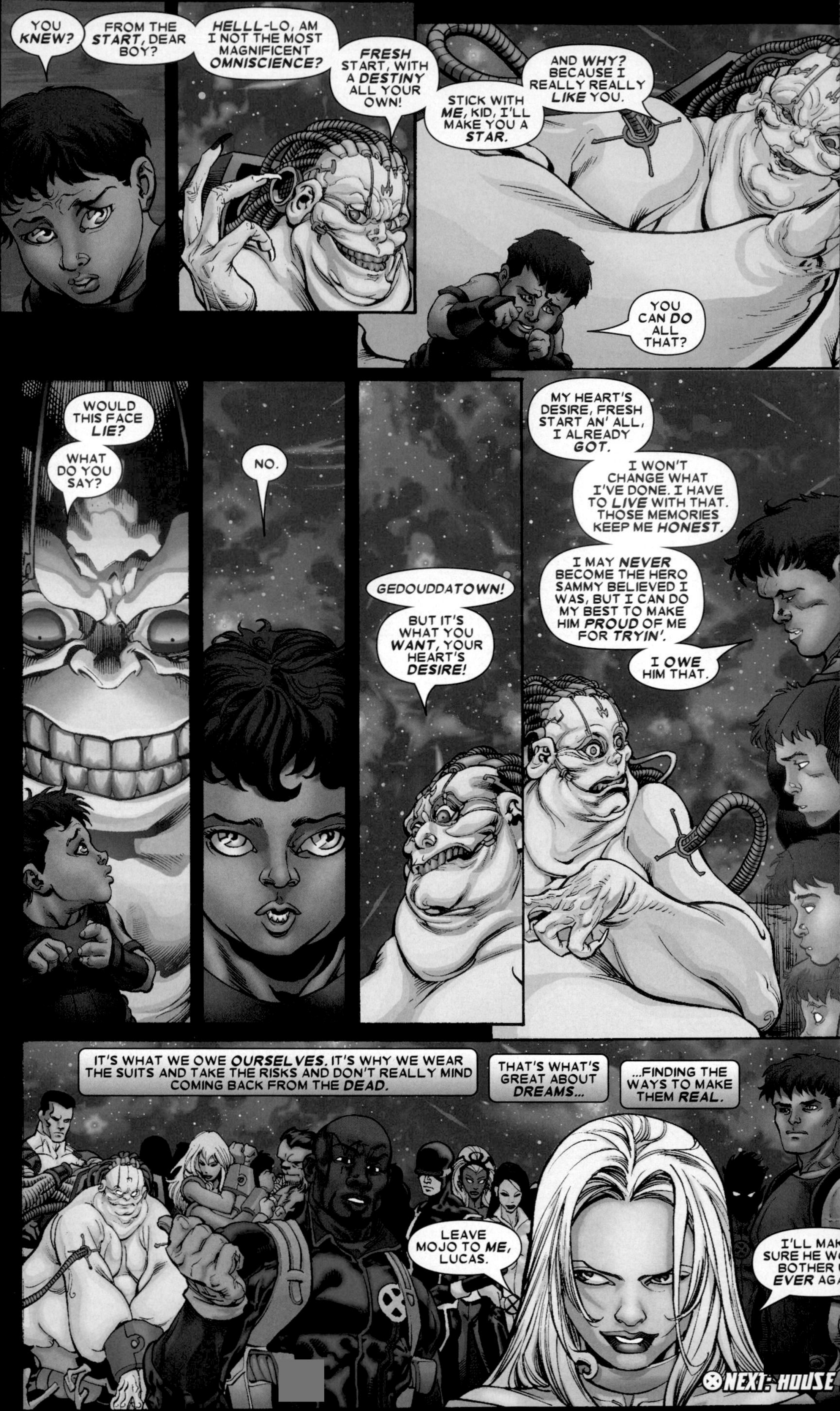

YOU KNEW?
FROM THE START, DEAR BOY?
HELLL-LO, AM I NOT THE MOST MAGNIFICENT OMNISCIENCE?
FRESH START, WITH A DESTINY ALL YOUR OWN!
STICK WITH ME, KID, I'LL MAKE YOU A STAR.
AND WHY? BECAUSE I REALLY REALLY LIKE YOU.
YOU CAN DO ALL THAT?
WOULD THIS FACE LIE?
WHAT DO YOU SAY?
NO.
GEDOUDDATOWN!
BUT IT'S WHAT YOU WANT, YOUR HEART'S DESIRE!
MY HEART'S DESIRE, FRESH START AN' ALL, I ALREADY GOT.
I WON'T CHANGE WHAT I'VE DONE. I HAVE TO LIVE WITH THAT. THOSE MEMORIES KEEP ME HONEST.
I MAY NEVER BECOME THE HERO SAMMY BELIEVED I WAS, BUT I CAN DO MY BEST TO MAKE HIM PROUD OF ME FOR TRYIN'.
I OWE HIM THAT.
IT'S WHAT WE OWE OURSELVES. IT'S WHY WE WEAR THE SUITS AND TAKE THE RISKS AND DON'T REALLY MIND COMING BACK FROM THE DEAD.
THAT'S WHAT'S GREAT ABOUT DREAMS...
...FINDING THE WAYS TO MAKE THEM REAL.
LEAVE MOJO TO ME, LUCAS.
I'LL MAK SURE HE WO BOTHER EVER AGA
NEXT: HOUSE

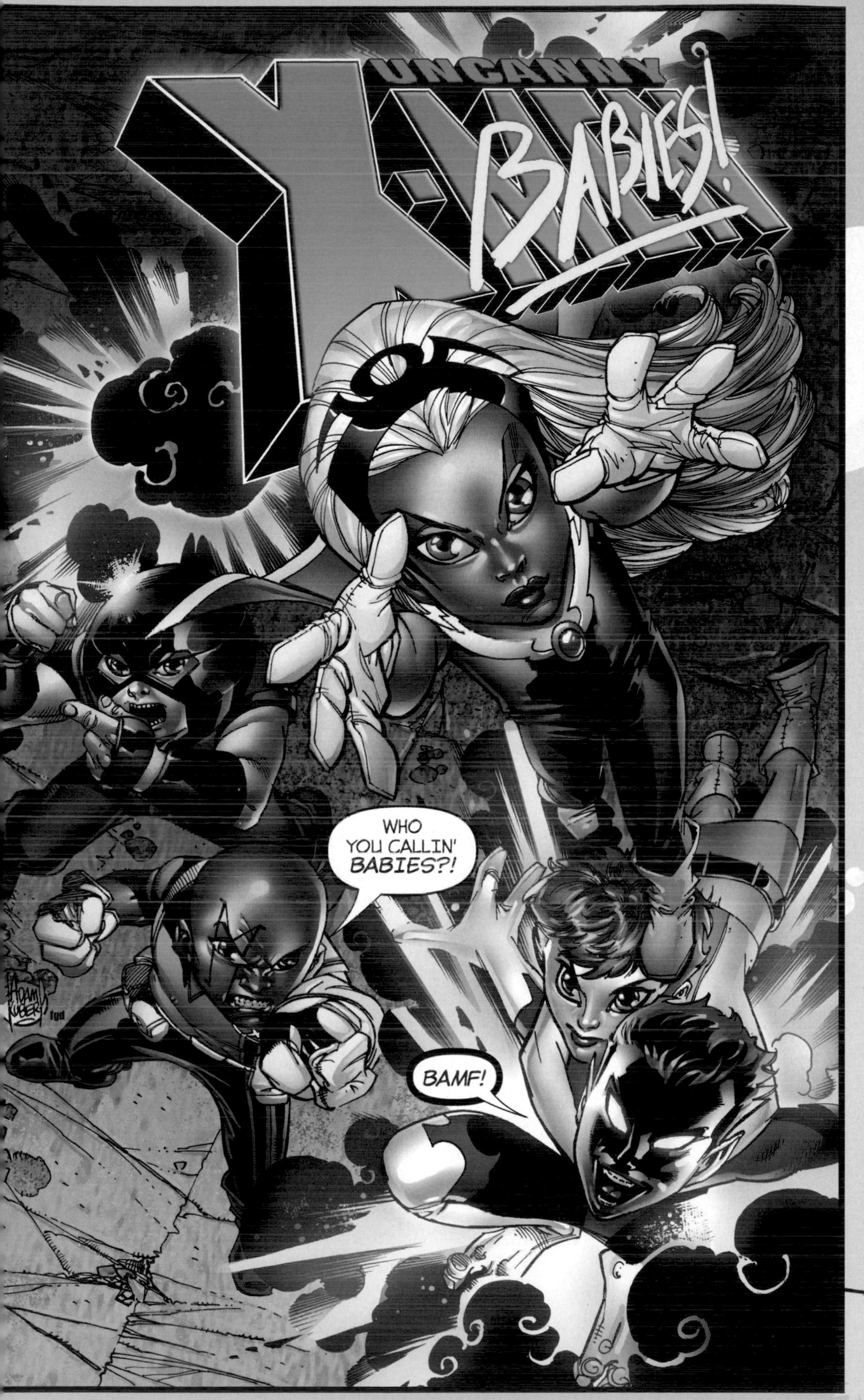
UNCANNY
X-MEN
BABIES!
WHO YOU CALLIN' BABIES?!
BAMF!
ADAM KUBERT
fgd

VARIANT COVER BY ADAM KUBERT & FRANK D'ARMATA

MARVEL GETS A RIBBING

THE SENSATIONAL SECRET ORIGIN OF "LI'L MARVELS"

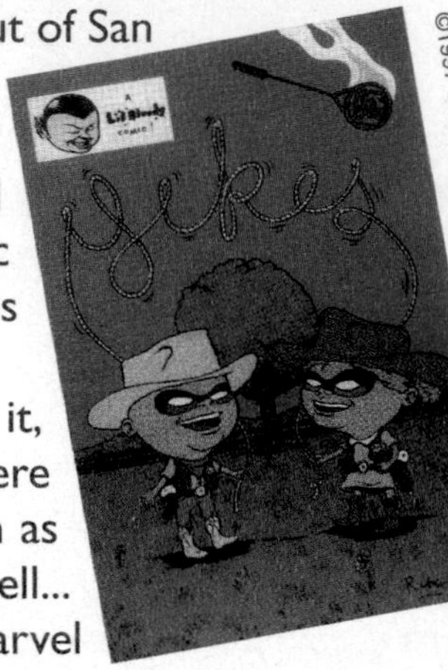

Okay, so there's this great cartoonist out of San Francisco who loves yellow and whose first Marvel Comic was an issue of JUNGLE ACTION. His name is Steve Weissman and he writes, draws, colors and letters a comic no one reads called YIKES (and sometimes TYKES).

And despite the fact that no one reads it, it's really very clever, and it suggests that there are truths regarding the origin of man, even as far back as Adam and Eve, that have been well... fabricated— especially in regards to the Marvel Universe itself. Shocking.

According to Steve, we've only seen the history we're supposed to know. As lovers of truth in all its forms, we got an idea (this is, of course, the House Of Ideas, duh). What if Steve, whom everyone calls Ribs, retold the history of the Marvel Universe? The real history. The true history. So that the record could show for all to bear witness.

The real reason the Invaders broke up!
How the Fantastic Four were really formed!
The true reason for the rivalry between Namor and the original Human Torch!

So, despite Steve's fervor to just eat mint chocolate chip ice cream 24 hours a day, and acting as if he were ignorant of his desire to draw only the Incredible Hulk and the Vulture, this issue he will begin telling the true history of the Marvel Universe— before the modern myth-makers mucked it up.

So prepare yourself for enlightenment.

And for you scoffers of truth, you naysayers of anything that would threaten the establishment, those out there unwilling to spit in the eye of the dragon, ask yourself this... Why would a guy named Ribs lie?

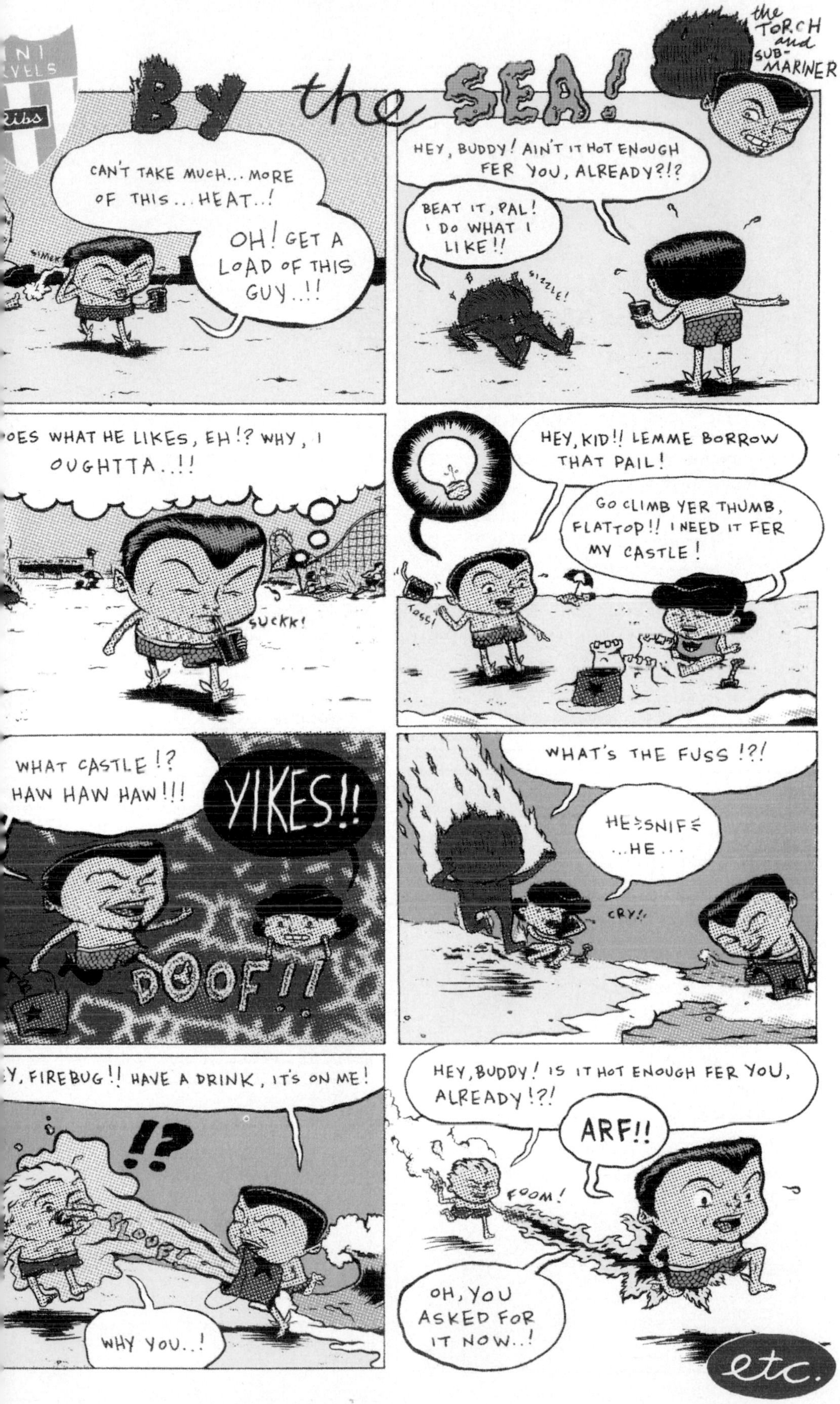
By the SEA!
the TORCH and SUB-MARINER!
CAN'T TAKE MUCH... MORE OF THIS... HEAT..!
OH! GET A LOAD OF THIS GUY..!!
HEY, BUDDY! AIN'T IT HOT ENOUGH FER YOU, ALREADY?!?
BEAT IT, PAL! I DO WHAT I LIKE!!
SIZZLE!
OES WHAT HE LIKES, EH!? WHY, I OUGHTTA..!!
SUCKK!
HEY, KID!! LEMME BORROW THAT PAIL!
GO CLIMB YER THUMB, FLATTOP!! I NEED IT FER MY CASTLE!
TOSS!
WHAT CASTLE!? HAW HAW HAW!!!
YIKES!!
DOOF!!
WHAT'S THE FUSS!?!
HE ≷SNIF≷ ...HE...
CRY!
Y, FIREBUG!! HAVE A DRINK, IT'S ON ME!
!?
PLOOF!
WHY YOU..!
HEY, BUDDY! IS IT HOT ENOUGH FER YOU, ALREADY!?!
ARF!!
FOOM!
OH, YOU ASKED FOR IT NOW..!
etc.

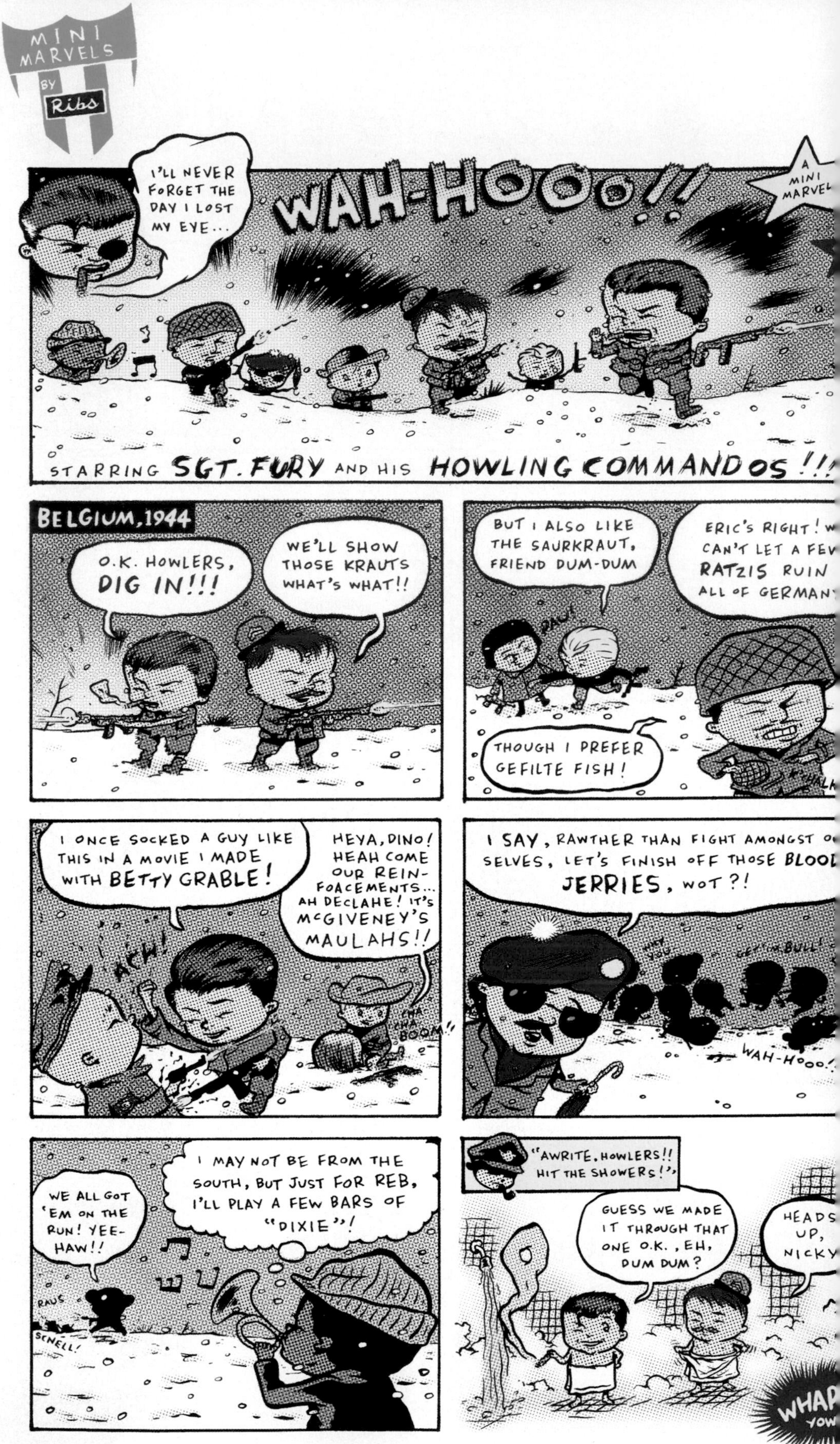

MINI MARVELS BY Ribs
I'LL NEVER FORGET THE DAY I LOST MY EYE...
WAH-HOOO!!
A MINI MARVEL
STARRING SGT. FURY AND HIS HOWLING COMMANDOS!!!
BELGIUM, 1944
O.K. HOWLERS, DIG IN!!!
WE'LL SHOW THOSE KRAUTS WHAT'S WHAT!!
BUT I ALSO LIKE THE SAURKRAUT, FRIEND DUM-DUM
ERIC'S RIGHT! W CAN'T LET A FEV RATZIS RUIN ALL OF GERMANY
THOUGH I PREFER GEFILTE FISH!
I ONCE SOCKED A GUY LIKE THIS IN A MOVIE I MADE WITH BETTY GRABLE!
ACH!
HEYA, DINO! HEAH COME OUR REIN-FOACEMENTS... AH DECLAHE! IT'S McGIVENEY'S MAULAHS!!
CHA CHA BOOM!
I SAY, RAWTHER THAN FIGHT AMONGST O SELVES, LET'S FINISH OFF THOSE BLOOD JERRIES, WOT?!
WAH-HOOO!
WE ALL GOT 'EM ON THE RUN! YEE-HAW!!
I MAY NOT BE FROM THE SOUTH, BUT JUST FOR REB, I'LL PLAY A FEW BARS OF "DIXIE"!
RAUS
SCHNELL!
"AWRITE, HOWLERS!! HIT THE SHOWERS!"
GUESS WE MADE IT THROUGH THAT ONE O.K., EH, DUM DUM?
HEADS UP, NICKY
WHAP

MARVEL VISION #26

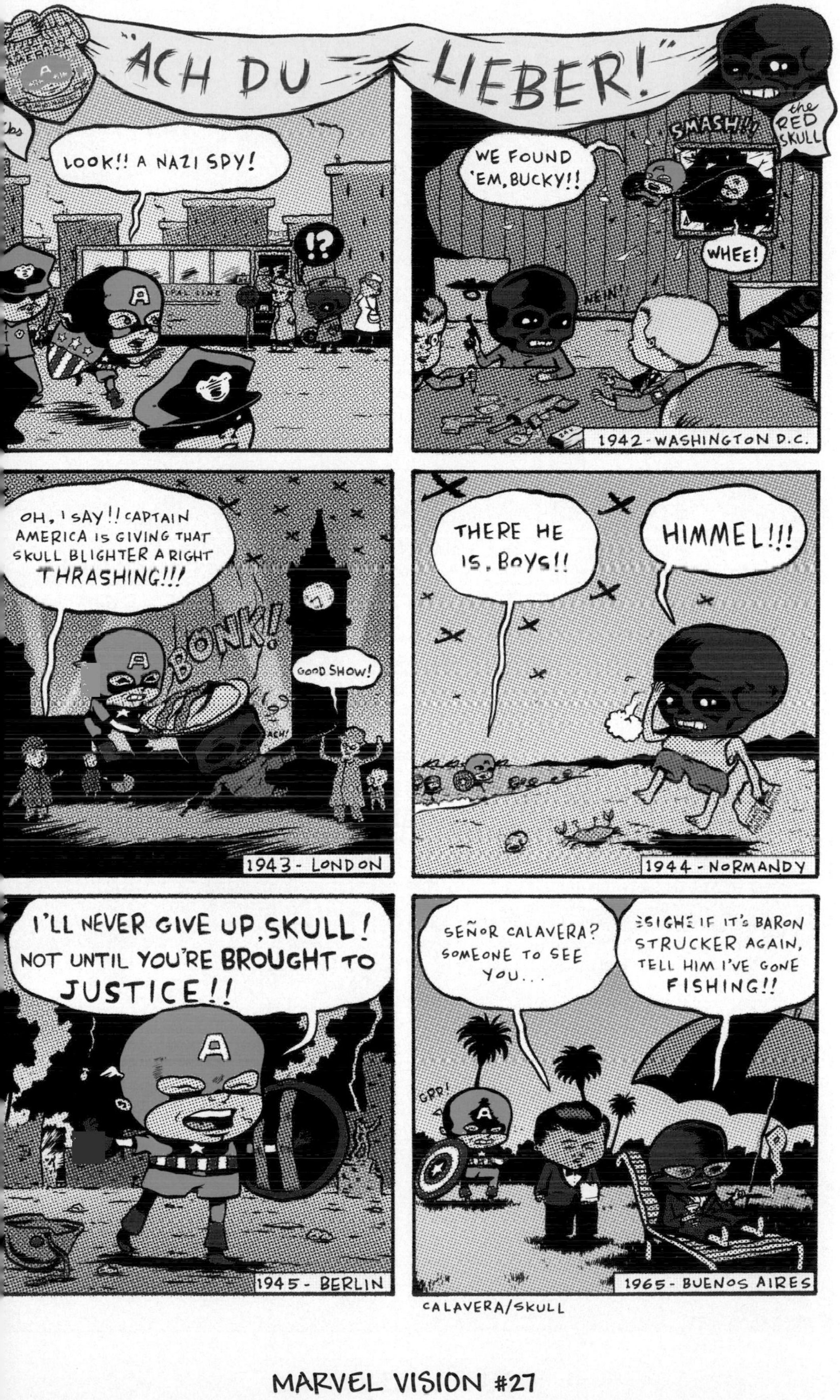

"ACH DU LIEBER!"
the RED SKULL
LOOK!! A NAZI SPY!
!?
WE FOUND 'EM, BUCKY!!
SMASH!!!
WHEE!
NEIN!
AMMO
1942 - WASHINGTON D.C.
OH, I SAY!! CAPTAIN AMERICA IS GIVING THAT SKULL BLIGHTER A RIGHT THRASHING!!!
BONK!
GOOD SHOW!
ACH!
1943 - LONDON
THERE HE IS, BOYS!!
HIMMEL!!!
1944 - NORMANDY
I'LL NEVER GIVE UP, SKULL! NOT UNTIL YOU'RE BROUGHT TO JUSTICE!!
1945 - BERLIN
SEÑOR CALAVERA? SOMEONE TO SEE YOU...
≡SIGH≡ IF IT'S BARON STRUCKER AGAIN, TELL HIM I'VE GONE FISHING!!
GRR!
1965 - BUENOS AIRES

CALAVERA/SKULL

MARVEL VISION #27

MINI MARVELS BY Ribs

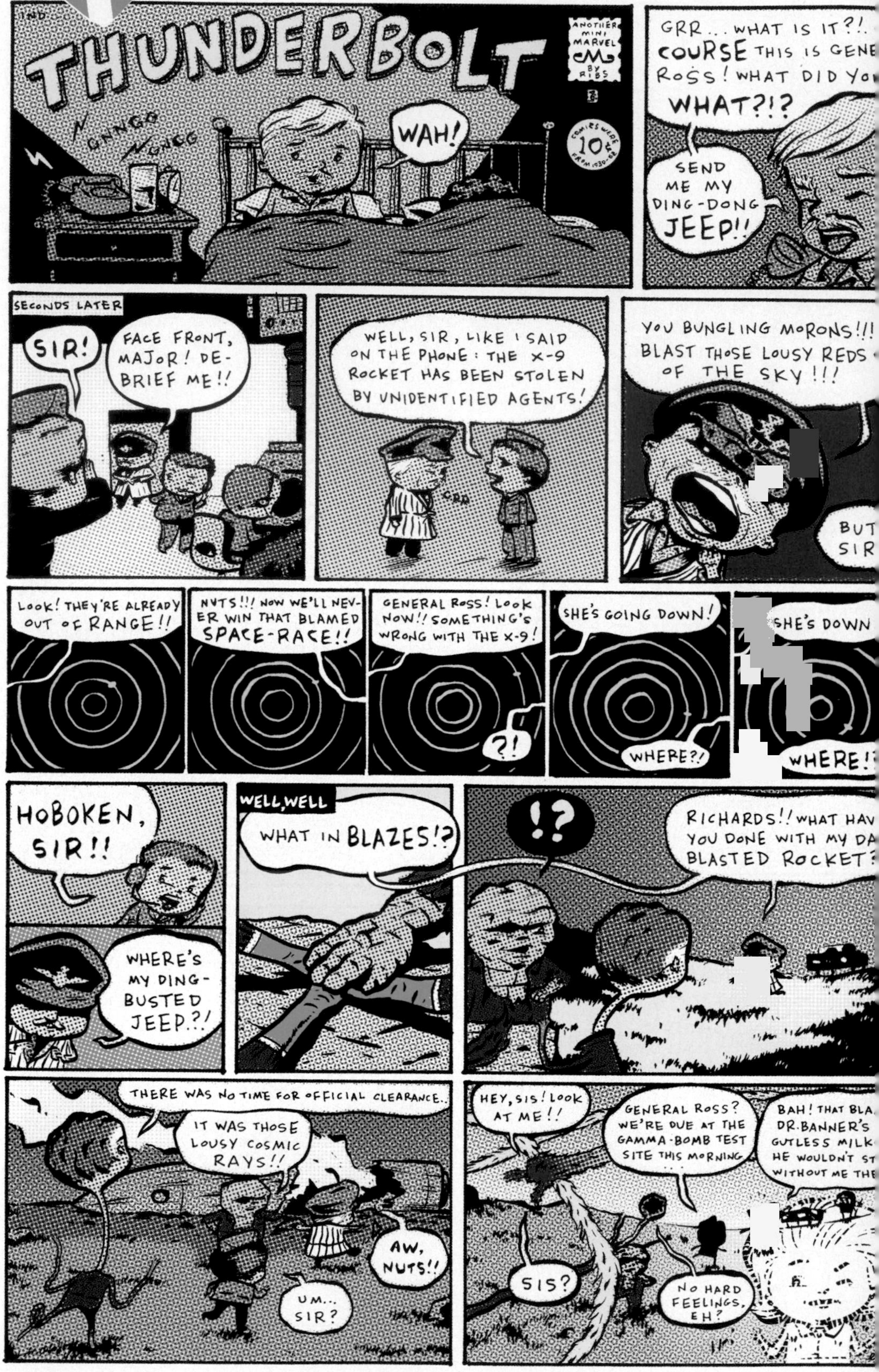

IND.
THUNDERBOLT
ANOTHER MINI MARVEL BY RIBS
COMICS WERE 10¢ FROM 1939-'62
GNNGG GNGG
WAH!
GRR... WHAT IS IT?!. COURSE THIS IS GENE ROSS! WHAT DID YO WHAT?!?
SEND ME MY DING-DONG JEEP!!
SECONDS LATER
SIR!
FACE FRONT, MAJOR! DE-BRIEF ME!!
WELL, SIR, LIKE I SAID ON THE PHONE: THE X-9 ROCKET HAS BEEN STOLEN BY UNIDENTIFIED AGENTS!
GRR
YOU BUNGLING MORONS!!! BLAST THOSE LOUSY REDS OF THE SKY!!!
BUT SIR
LOOK! THEY'RE ALREADY OUT OF RANGE!!
NUTS!!! NOW WE'LL NEVER WIN THAT BLAMED SPACE-RACE!!
GENERAL ROSS! LOOK NOW!! SOMETHING'S WRONG WITH THE X-9!
?!
SHE'S GOING DOWN!
WHERE?!
SHE'S DOWN
WHERE!
HOBOKEN, SIR!!
WHERE'S MY DING-BUSTED JEEP?!
WELL, WELL
WHAT IN BLAZES!?
!?
RICHARDS!! WHAT HAV YOU DONE WITH MY DA BLASTED ROCKET
THERE WAS NO TIME FOR OFFICIAL CLEARANCE..
IT WAS THOSE LOUSY COSMIC RAYS!!
AW, NUTS!!
UM... SIR?
HEY, SIS! LOOK AT ME!!
GENERAL ROSS? WE'RE DUE AT THE GAMMA-BOMB TEST SITE THIS MORNING...
BAH! THAT BLA DR. BANNER'S GUTLESS MILK HE WOULDN'T ST WITHOUT ME THE
SIS?
NO HARD FEELINGS, EH?

MARVEL VISION #28

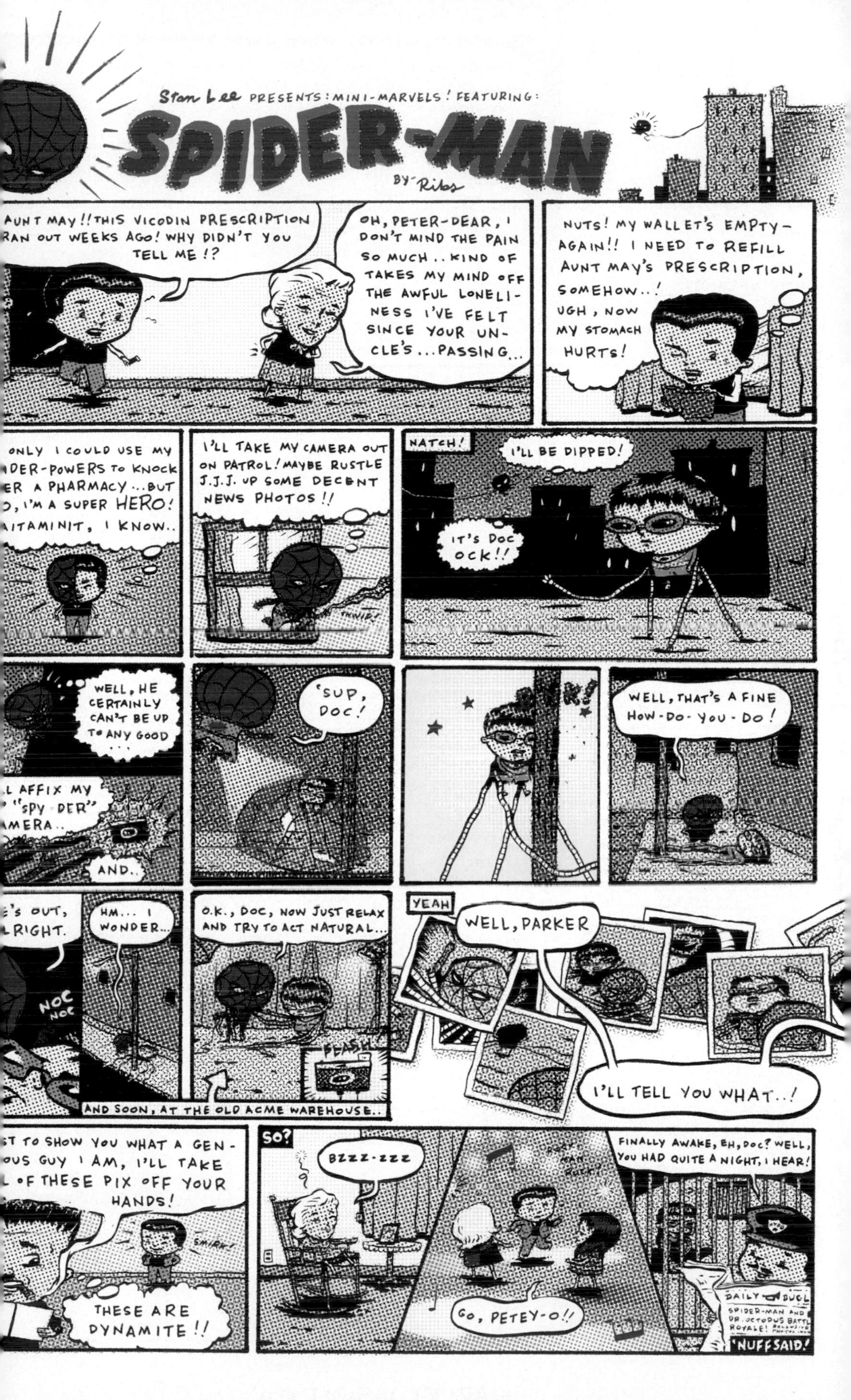
Stan Lee PRESENTS: MINI-MARVELS! FEATURING:
SPIDER-MAN
BY Ribs
AUNT MAY!! THIS VICODIN PRESCRIPTION RAN OUT WEEKS AGO! WHY DIDN'T YOU TELL ME!?
OH, PETER-DEAR, I DON'T MIND THE PAIN SO MUCH.. KIND OF TAKES MY MIND OFF THE AWFUL LONELI-NESS I'VE FELT SINCE YOUR UN-CLE'S...PASSING...
NUTS! MY WALLET'S EMPTY-AGAIN!! I NEED TO REFILL AUNT MAY'S PRESCRIPTION, SOMEHOW..! UGH, NOW MY STOMACH HURTS!
ONLY I COULD USE MY IDER-POWERS TO KNOCK ER A PHARMACY...BUT O, I'M A SUPER HERO! AITAMINIT, I KNOW..
I'LL TAKE MY CAMERA OUT ON PATROL! MAYBE RUSTLE J.J.J. UP SOME DECENT NEWS PHOTOS!!
THWIP!
NATCH!
I'LL BE DIPPED!
IT'S DOC OCK!!
WELL, HE CERTAINLY CAN'T BE UP TO ANY GOOD...
L AFFIX MY "SPY-DER" MERA..
AND..
'SUP, DOC!
WELL, THAT'S A FINE HOW-DO-YOU-DO!
'S OUT, RIGHT.
NOC NOC
HM... I WONDER...
O.K., DOC, NOW JUST RELAX AND TRY TO ACT NATURAL...
FLASH
AND SOON, AT THE OLD ACME WAREHOUSE..
YEAH
WELL, PARKER
I'LL TELL YOU WHAT..!
ST TO SHOW YOU WHAT A GEN-OUS GUY I AM, I'LL TAKE L OF THESE PIX OFF YOUR HANDS!
SMIRK
THESE ARE DYNAMITE!!
SO?
BZZZ-ZZZ
GO, PETEY-O!!
FINALLY AWAKE, EH, DOC? WELL, YOU HAD QUITE A NIGHT, I HEAR!
DAILY BUGL
SPIDER-MAN AND DR. OCTOPUS BATTLE ROYALE!
'NUFF SAID!

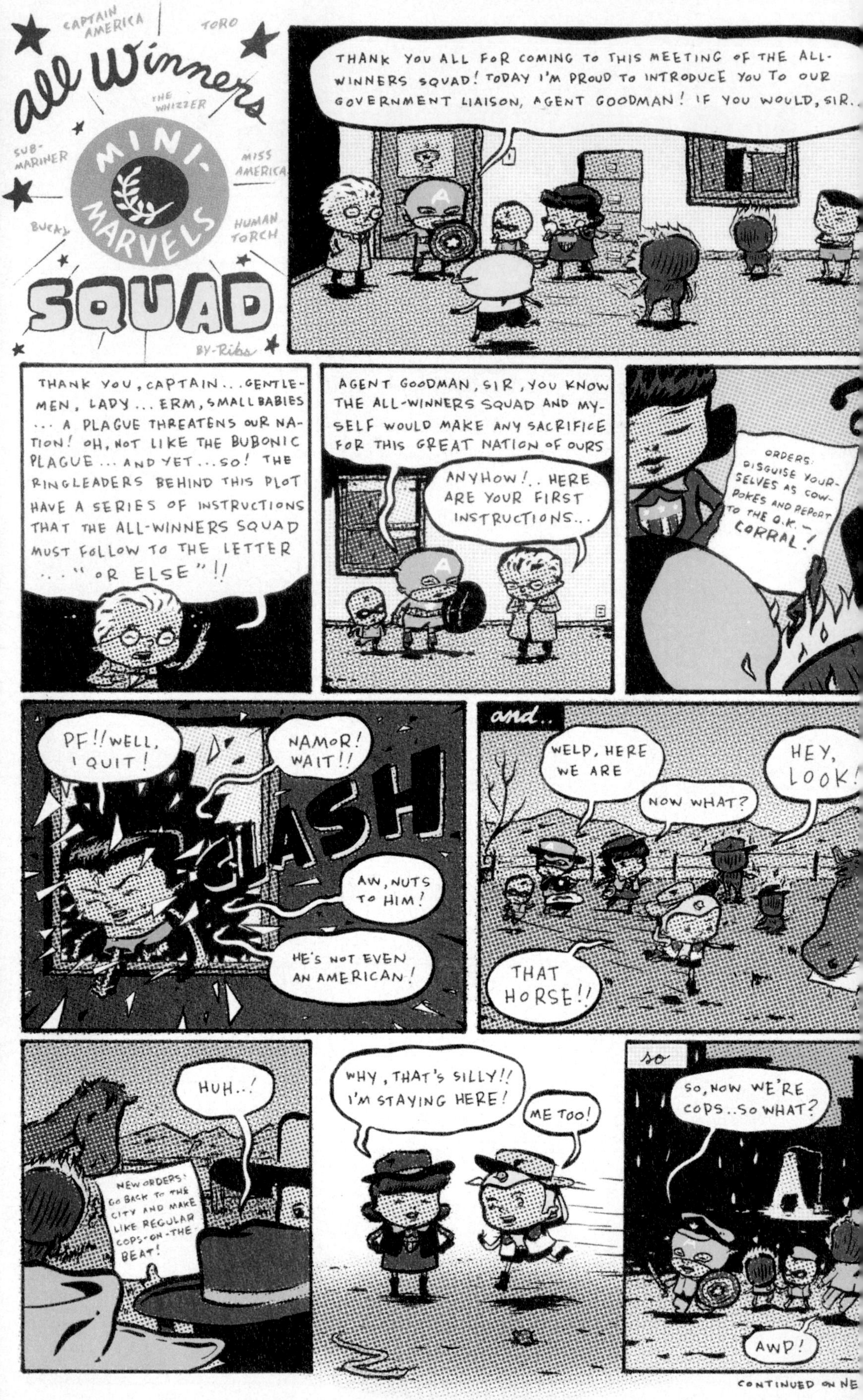
All Winners
MINI-MARVELS
SQUAD
CAPTAIN AMERICA
TORO
THE WHIZZER
SUB-MARINER
MISS AMERICA
BUCKY
HUMAN TORCH
BY-Riks
THANK YOU ALL FOR COMING TO THIS MEETING OF THE ALL-WINNERS SQUAD! TODAY I'M PROUD TO INTRODUCE YOU TO OUR GOVERNMENT LIAISON, AGENT GOODMAN! IF YOU WOULD, SIR..
THANK YOU, CAPTAIN...GENTLEMEN, LADY... ERM, SMALL BABIES... A PLAGUE THREATENS OUR NATION! OH, NOT LIKE THE BUBONIC PLAGUE... AND YET...SO! THE RINGLEADERS BEHIND THIS PLOT HAVE A SERIES OF INSTRUCTIONS THAT THE ALL-WINNERS SQUAD MUST FOLLOW TO THE LETTER ..."OR ELSE"!!
AGENT GOODMAN, SIR, YOU KNOW THE ALL-WINNERS SQUAD AND MYSELF WOULD MAKE ANY SACRIFICE FOR THIS GREAT NATION OF OURS
ANYHOW!.. HERE ARE YOUR FIRST INSTRUCTIONS...
ORDERS: DISGUISE YOURSELVES AS COW-POKES AND REPORT TO THE O.K. CORRAL!
PF!! WELL, I QUIT!
NAMOR! WAIT!!
CLASH
AW, NUTS TO HIM!
HE'S NOT EVEN AN AMERICAN!
and..
WELD, HERE WE ARE
NOW WHAT?
HEY, LOOK!
THAT HORSE!!
HUH..!
NEW ORDERS: GO BACK TO THE CITY AND MAKE LIKE REGULAR COPS-ON-THE-BEAT!
WHY, THAT'S SILLY!! I'M STAYING HERE!
ME TOO!
so
SO, NOW WE'RE COPS..SO WHAT?
AWP!

CONTINUED ON NE

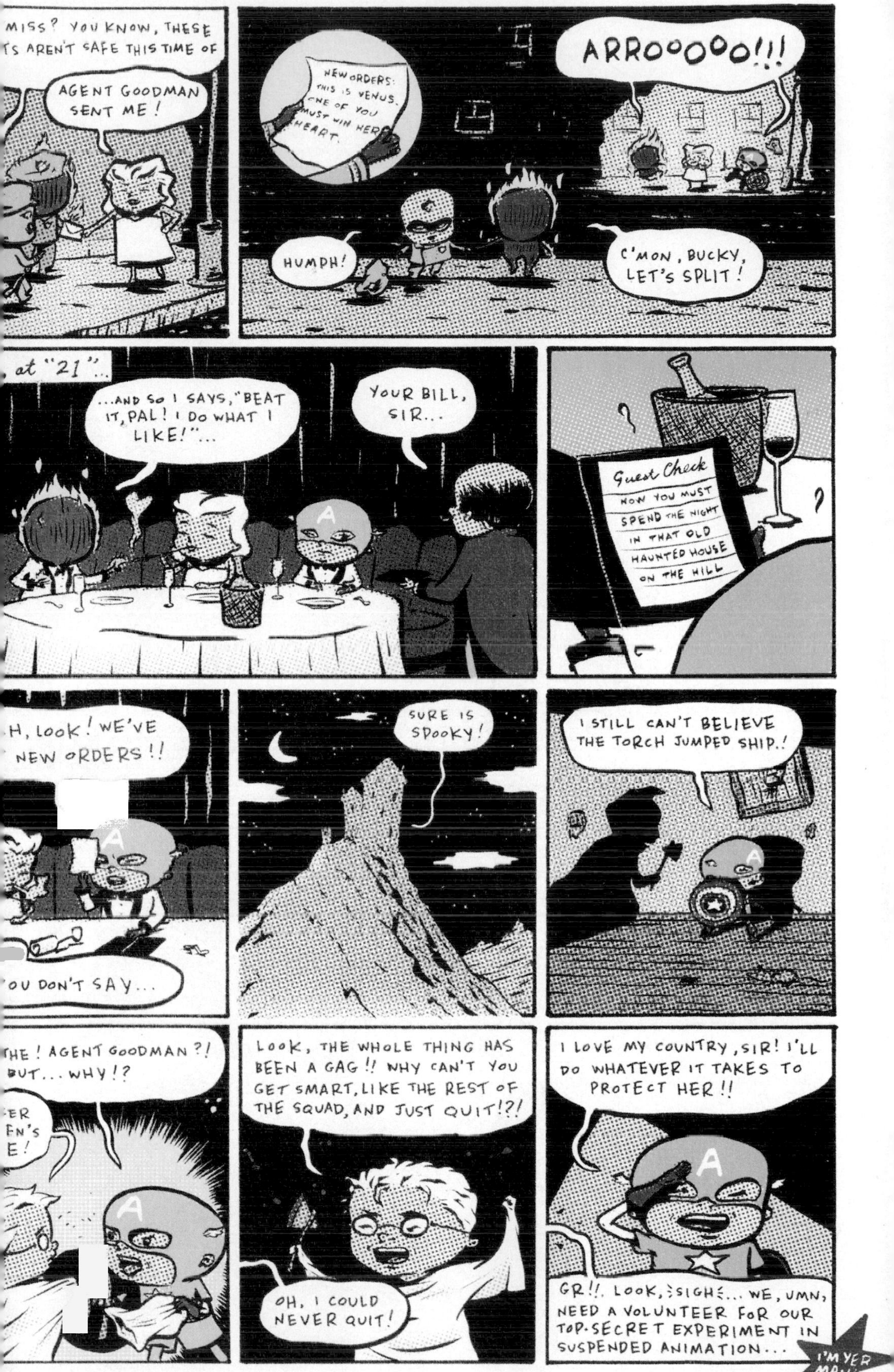
MISS? YOU KNOW, THESE
TS AREN'T SAFE THIS TIME OF
AGENT GOODMAN SENT ME!
NEW ORDERS: THIS IS VENUS. ONE OF YOU MUST WIN HER HEART.
HUMPH!
ARROOOOOO!!!
C'MON, BUCKY, LET'S SPLIT!
, at "21"...
...AND SO I SAYS, "BEAT IT, PAL! I DO WHAT I LIKE!"...
YOUR BILL, SIR...
Guest Check
NOW YOU MUST SPEND THE NIGHT IN THAT OLD HAUNTED HOUSE ON THE HILL
H, LOOK! WE'VE NEW ORDERS!!
OU DON'T SAY...
SURE IS SPOOKY!
I STILL CAN'T BELIEVE THE TORCH JUMPED SHIP.!
THE! AGENT GOODMAN?! BUT... WHY!?
ER EN'S E!
LOOK, THE WHOLE THING HAS BEEN A GAG!! WHY CAN'T YOU GET SMART, LIKE THE REST OF THE SQUAD, AND JUST QUIT!?!
OH, I COULD NEVER QUIT!
I LOVE MY COUNTRY, SIR! I'LL DO WHATEVER IT TAKES TO PROTECT HER!!
GR!!. LOOK, ≷SIGH≶... WE, UMN, NEED A VOLUNTEER FOR OUR TOP-SECRET EXPERIMENT IN SUSPENDED ANIMATION...
I'M YER MAN!

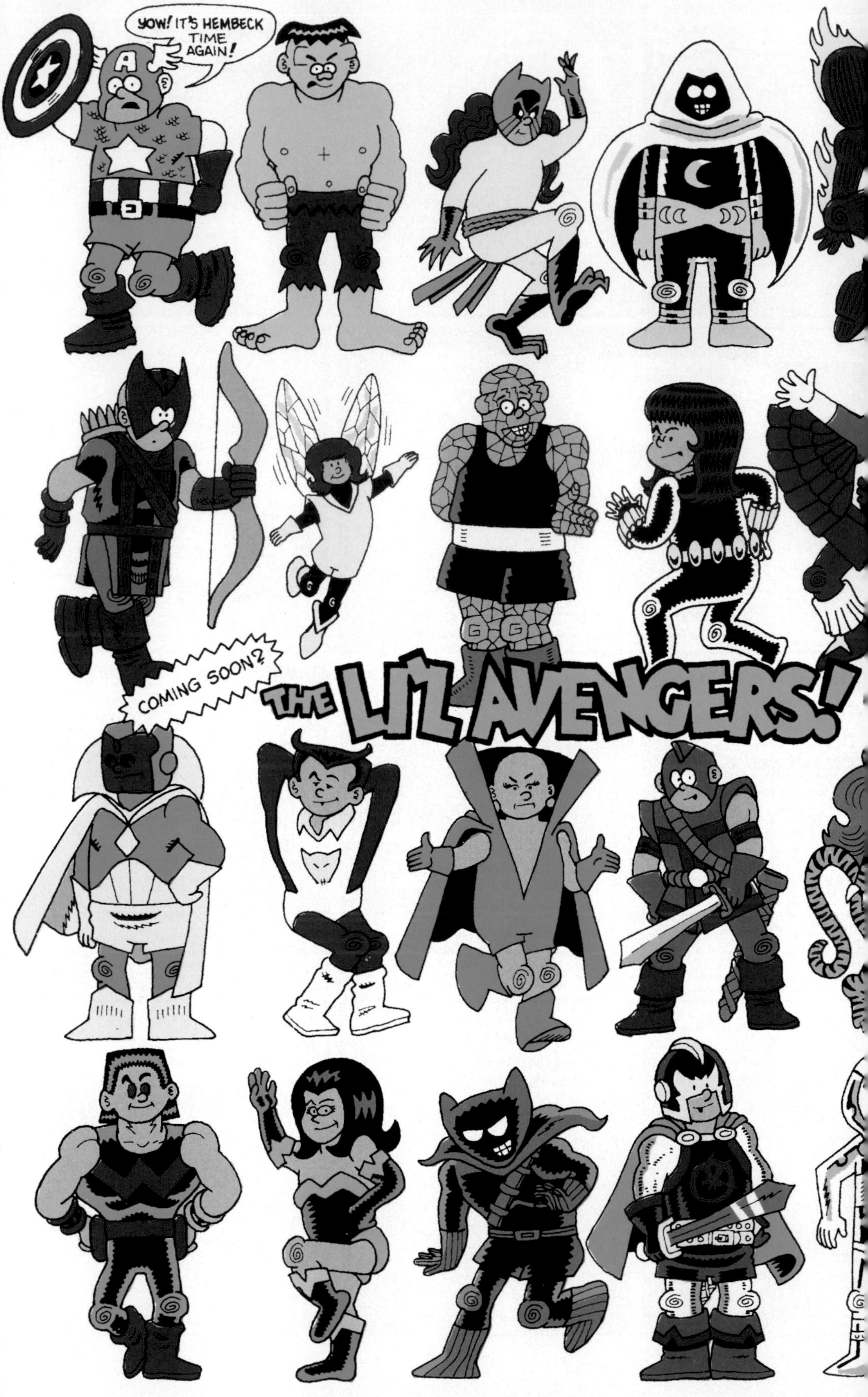
YOW! IT'S HEMBECK TIME AGAIN!
COMING SOON?
THE LI'L AVENGERS!

MARVEL AGE #93

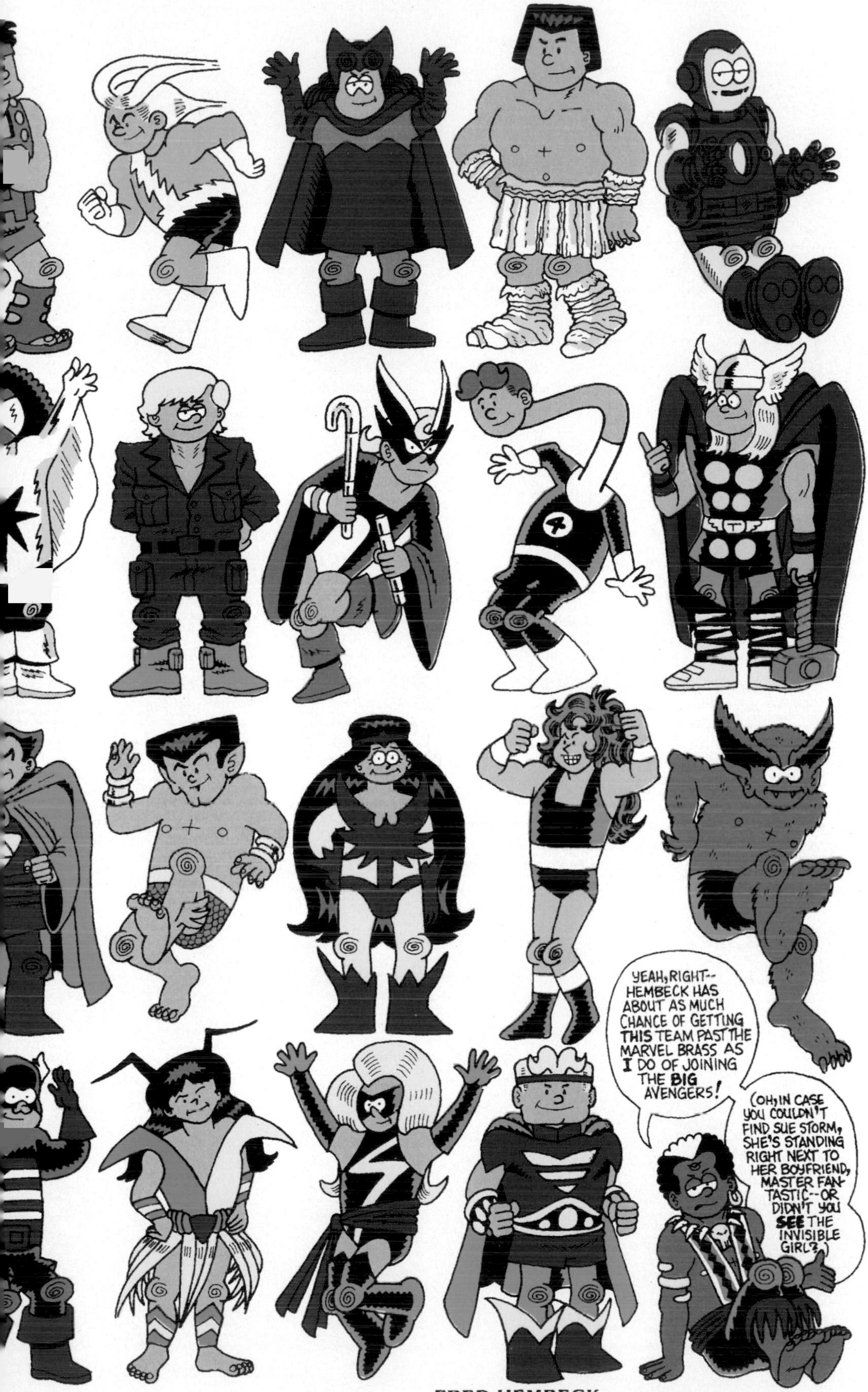

YEAH, RIGHT-- HEMBECK HAS ABOUT AS MUCH CHANCE OF GETTING THIS TEAM PAST THE MARVEL BRASS AS I DO OF JOINING THE BIG AVENGERS!
(OH, IN CASE YOU COULDN'T FIND SUE STORM, SHE'S STANDING RIGHT NEXT TO HER BOYFRIEND, MASTER FANTASTIC--OR DIDN'T YOU SEE THE INVISIBLE GIRL?)

FRED HEMBECK

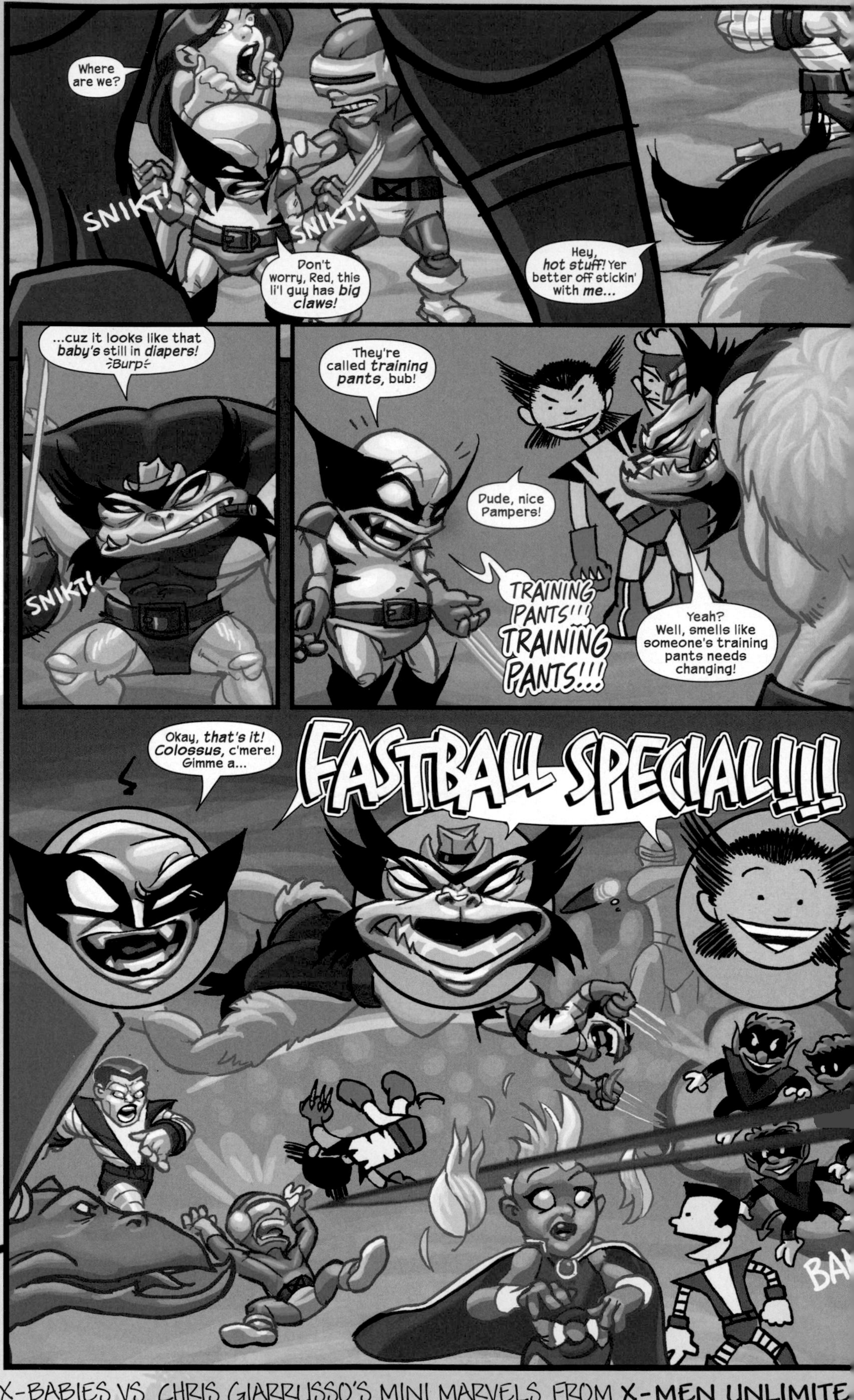
Where are we?
SNIKT!
SNIKT!
Don't worry, Red, this li'l guy has big claws!
Hey, hot stuff! Yer better off stickin' with me...
...cuz it looks like that baby's still in diapers! Burp
SNIKT!
They're called training pants, bub!
Dude, nice Pampers!
TRAINING PANTS!!! TRAINING PANTS!!!
Yeah? Well, smells like someone's training pants needs changing!
Okay, that's it! Colossus, c'mere! Gimme a...
FASTBALL SPECIAL!!!

X-BABIES VS. CHRIS GIARRUSSO'S MINI MARVELS, FROM **X-MEN UNLIMITE**

WRITER: KAARE ANDREWS • **ARTIST & COLORIST**: DAVE McCAIG • **LETTERER**: RA

GENTILE **ASSISTANT EDITOR**: MARK BEAZLEY • **EDITOR**: C.B. CEBULSKI

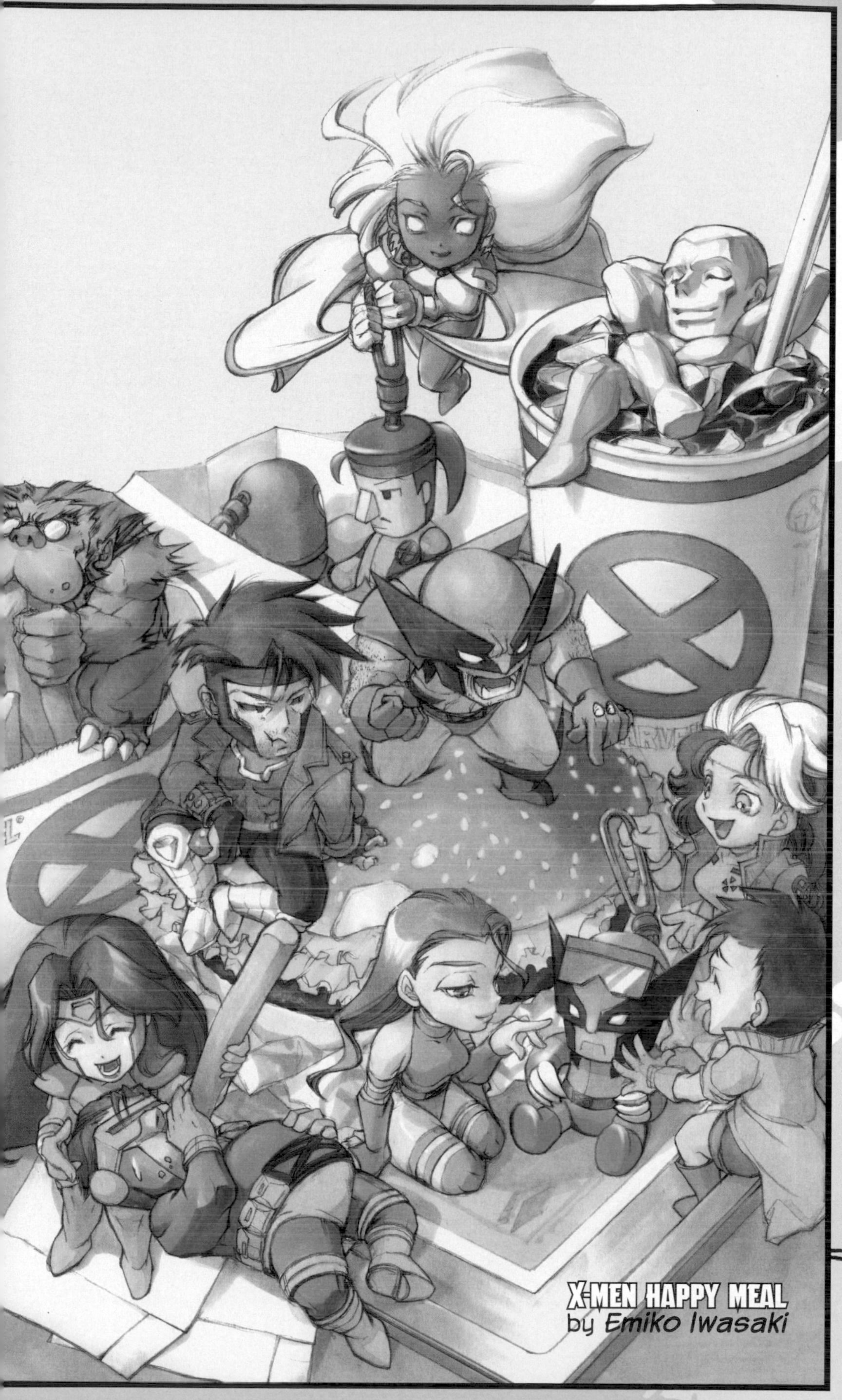
X-MEN HAPPY MEAL
by Emiko Iwasaki

X-MEN UNLIMITED #50 PINUP BY EMIKO IWASAKI

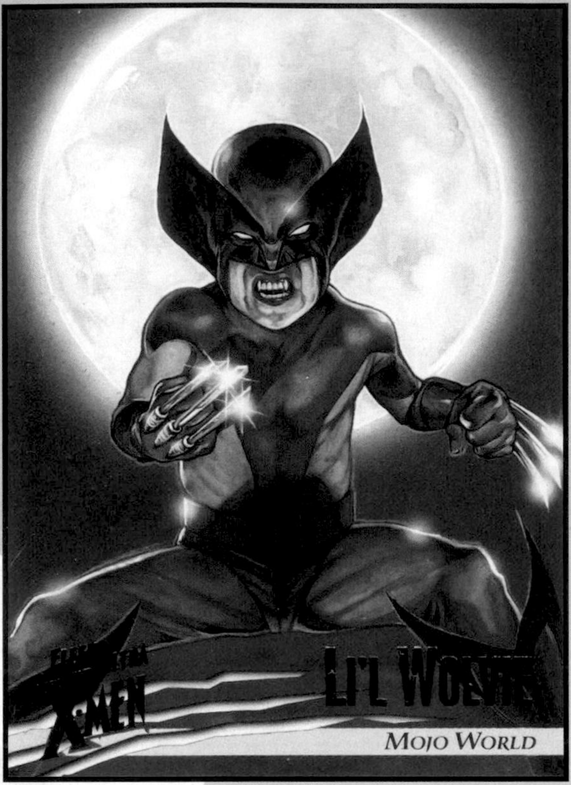
X-MEN
MOJO WORLD

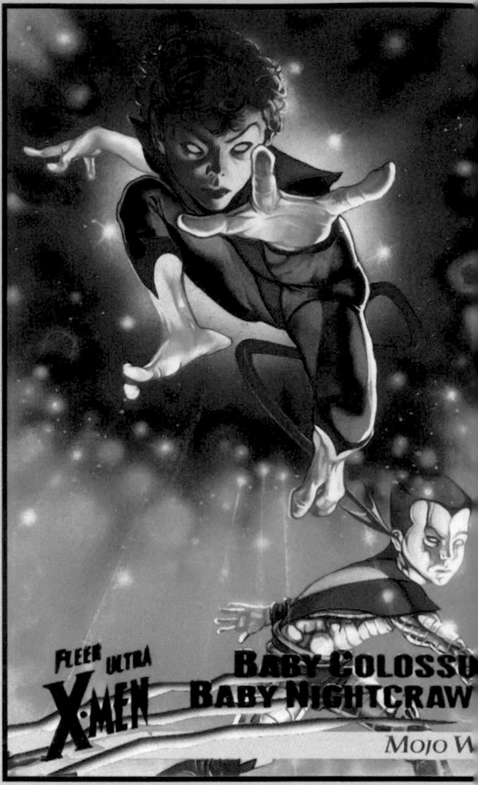
FLEER ULTRA
X-MEN
MOJO W

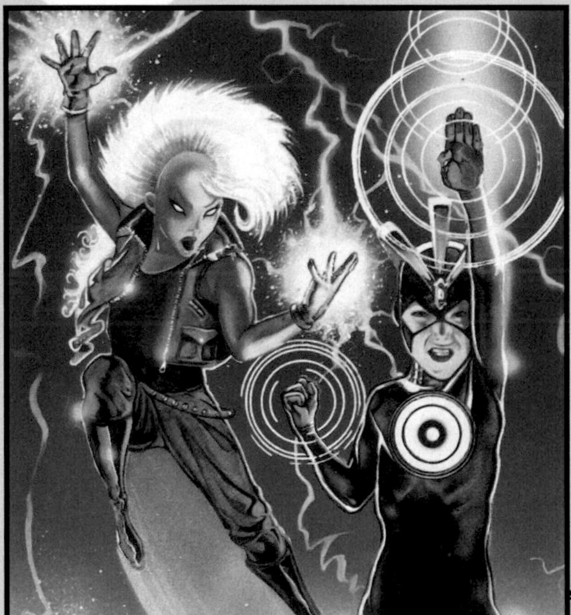
FLEER ULTRA
X-MEN
MOJO WORLD

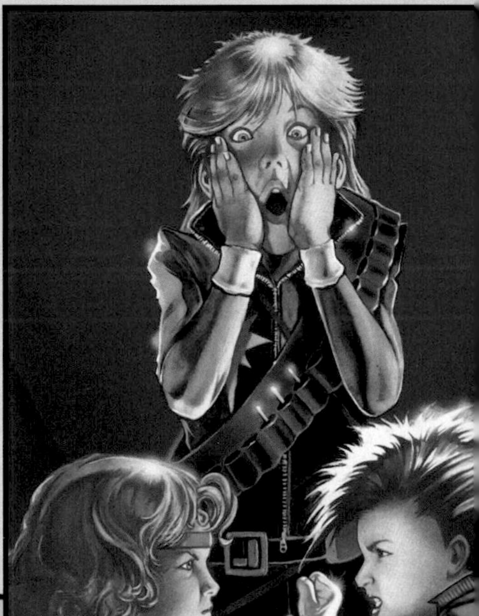
X-MEN
MOJO W

FLEER ULTRA X-MEN '96 TRADING-CARD ART BY TOM FLEMING

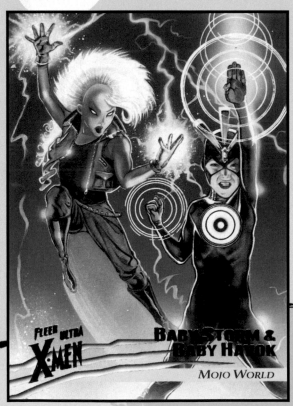

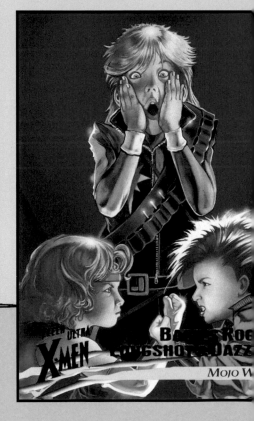

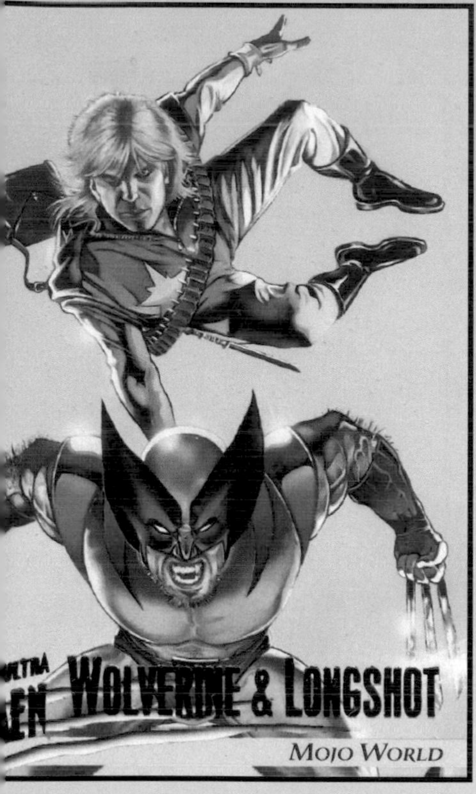
WOLVERINE & LONGSHOT
MOJO WORLD

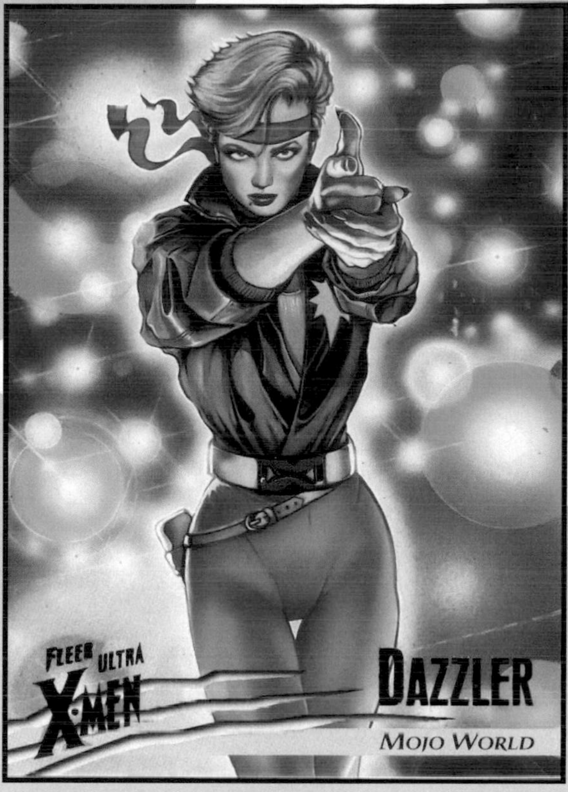
FLEER ULTRA
X-MEN
DAZZLER
MOJO WORLD

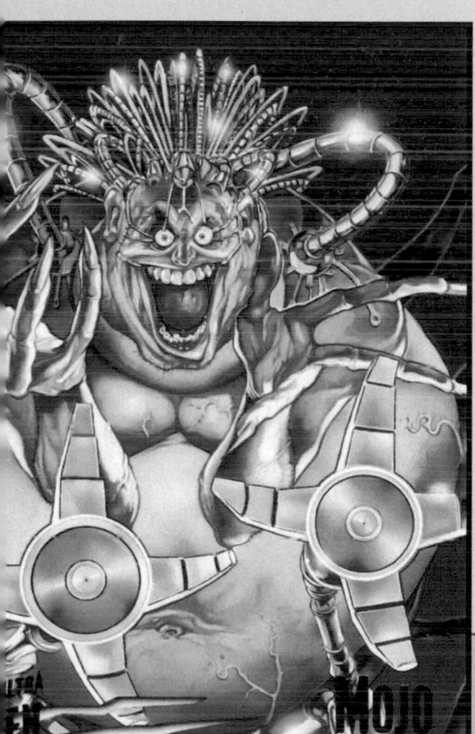
MOJO
MOJO WORLD

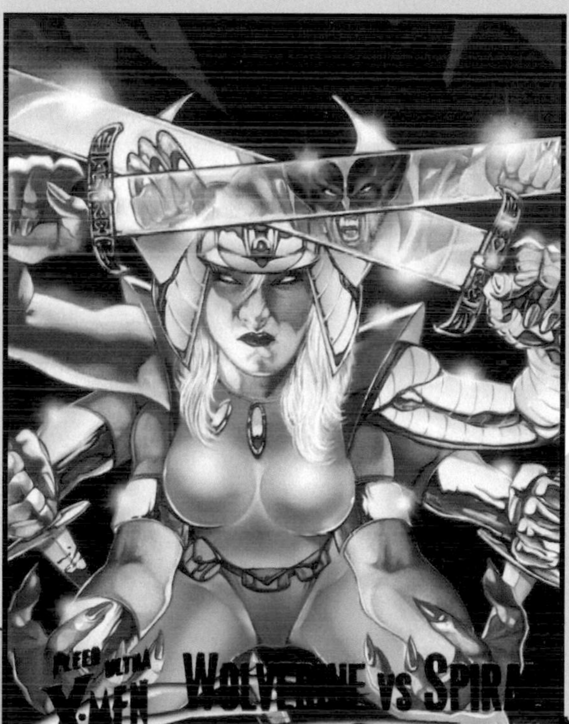
FLEER ULTRA
X-MEN
WOLVERINE vs SPIRA
MOJO WORLD

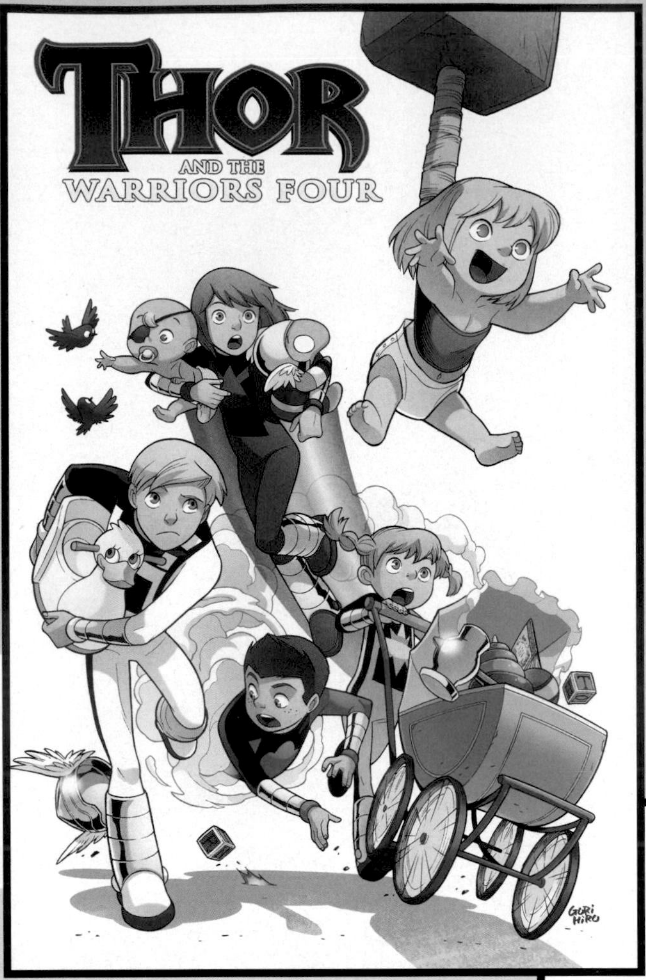
THOR
AND THE
WARRIORS FOUR
GURI HIRU

THOR AND THE WARRIO
FOUR #3 COVER BY GURI

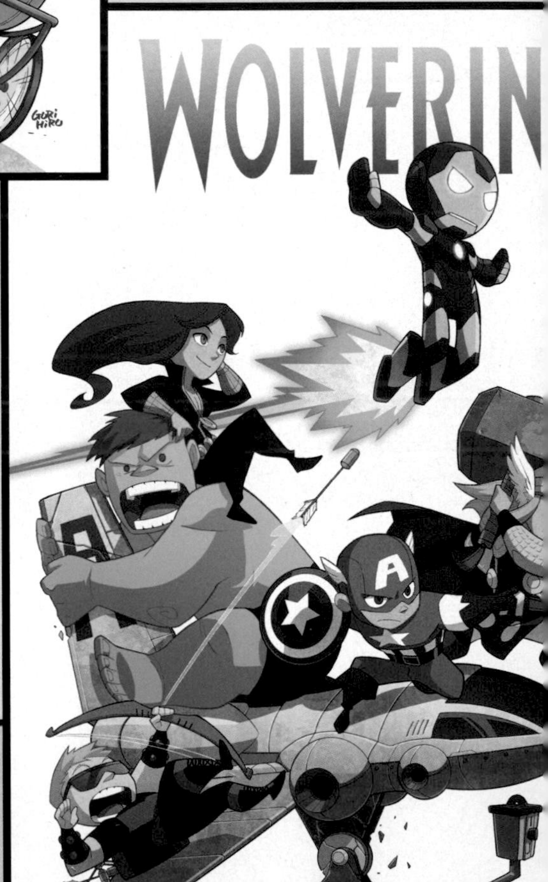
WOLVERIN

WOLVERINE #304 AVENGERS A
APPRECIATION VARIANT BY GURIH

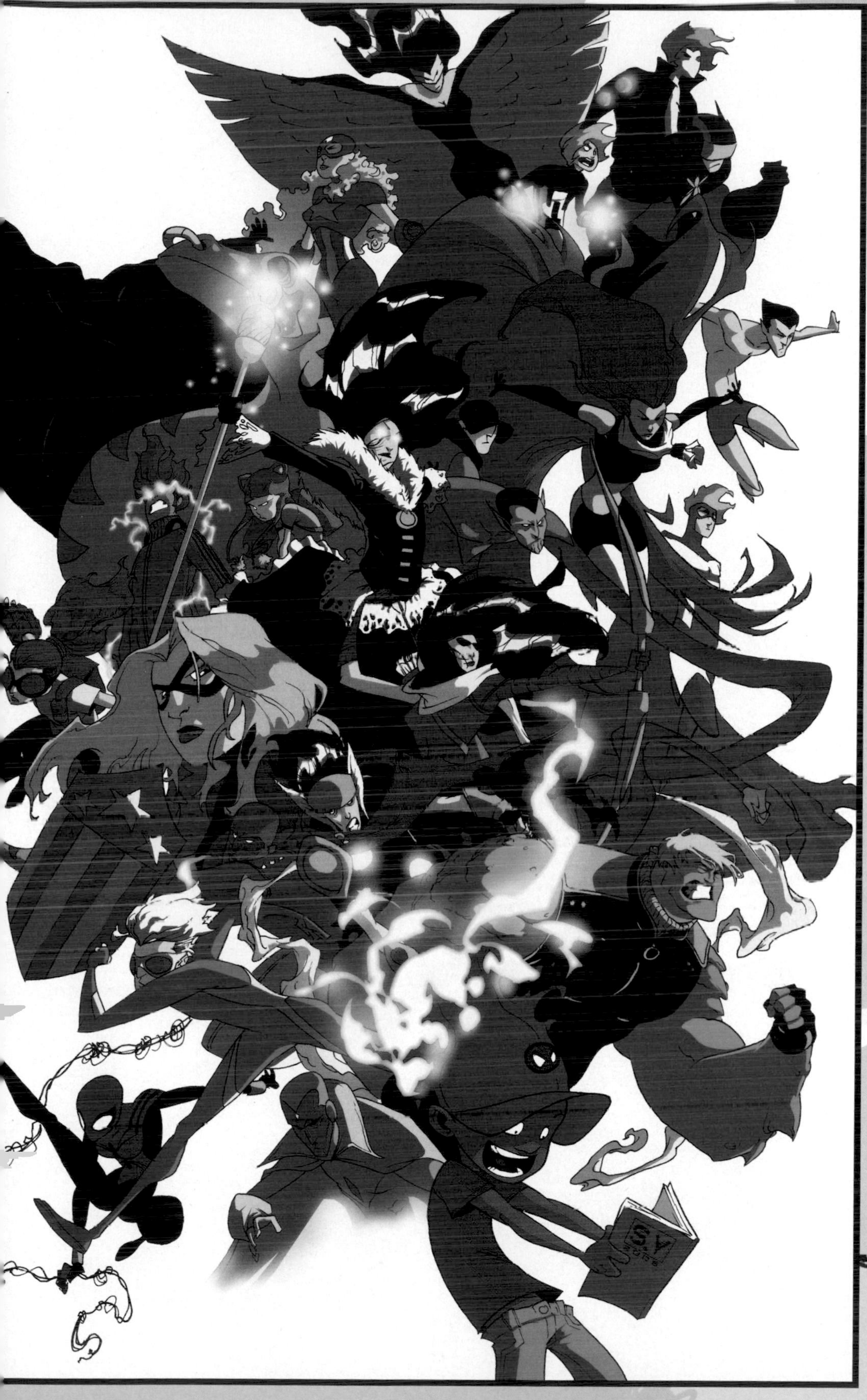

COVER FOR THE UNPUBLISHED **YOUNG MARVEL HANDBOOK**

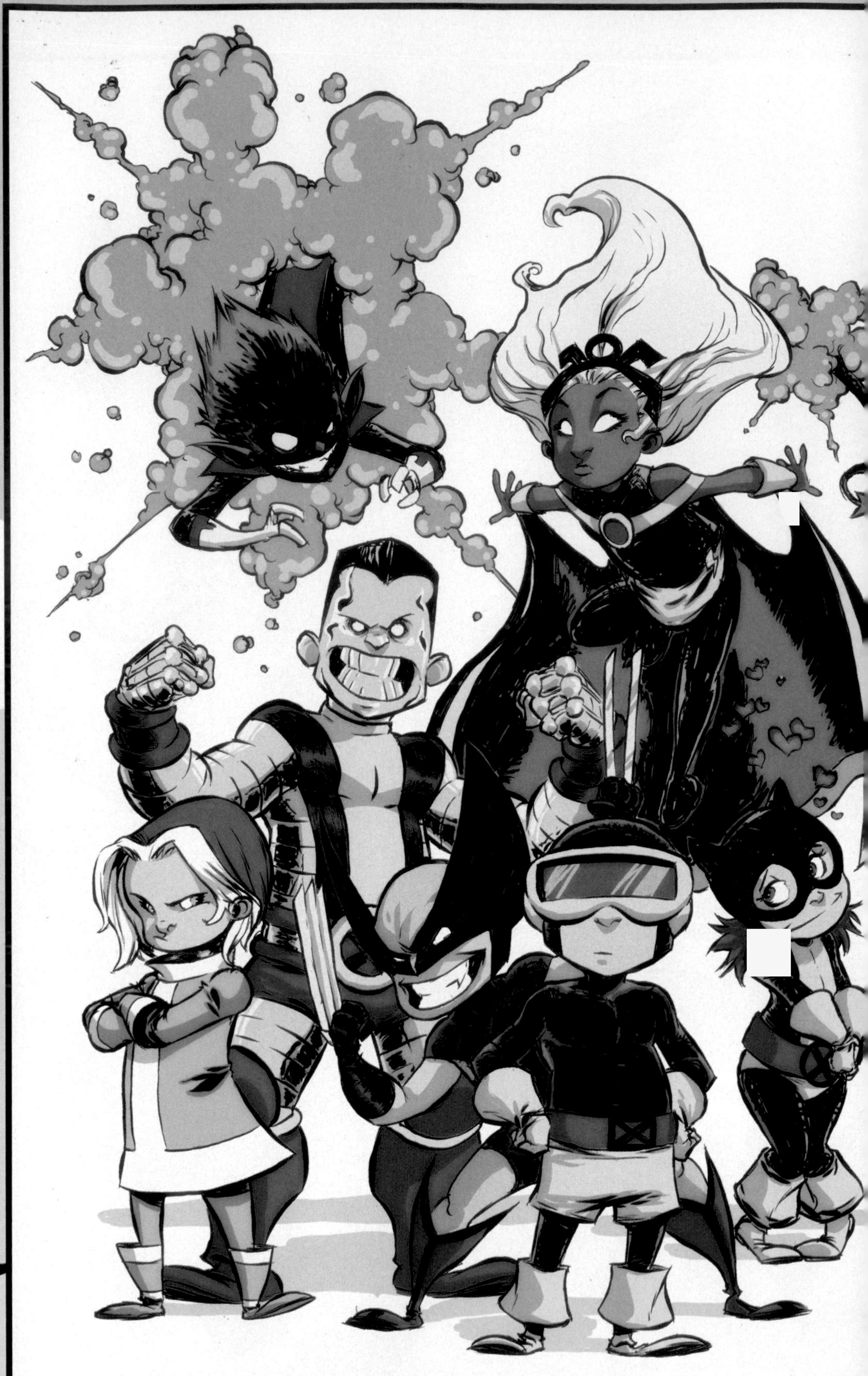

X-BABIES #1

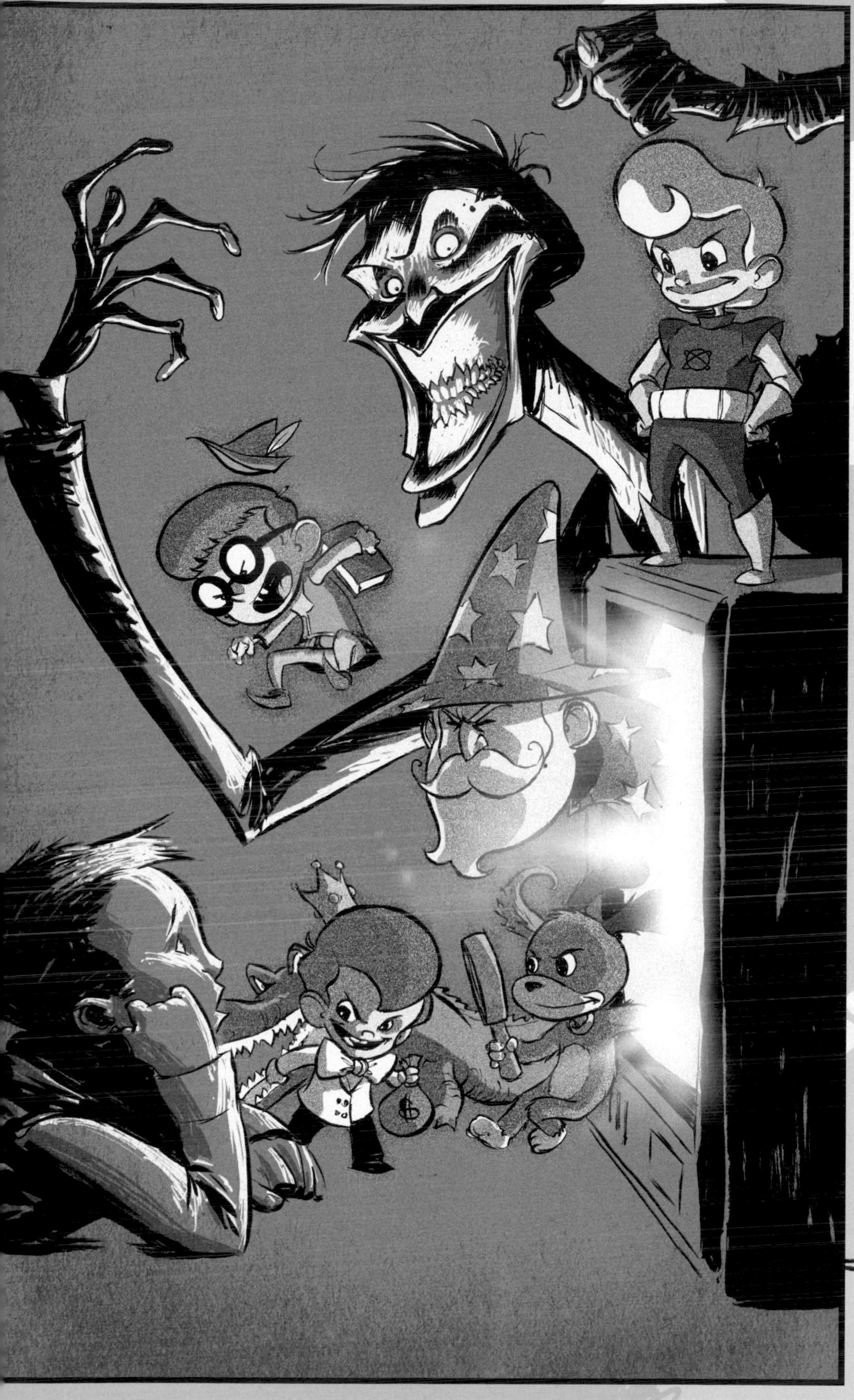

X-BABIES #2

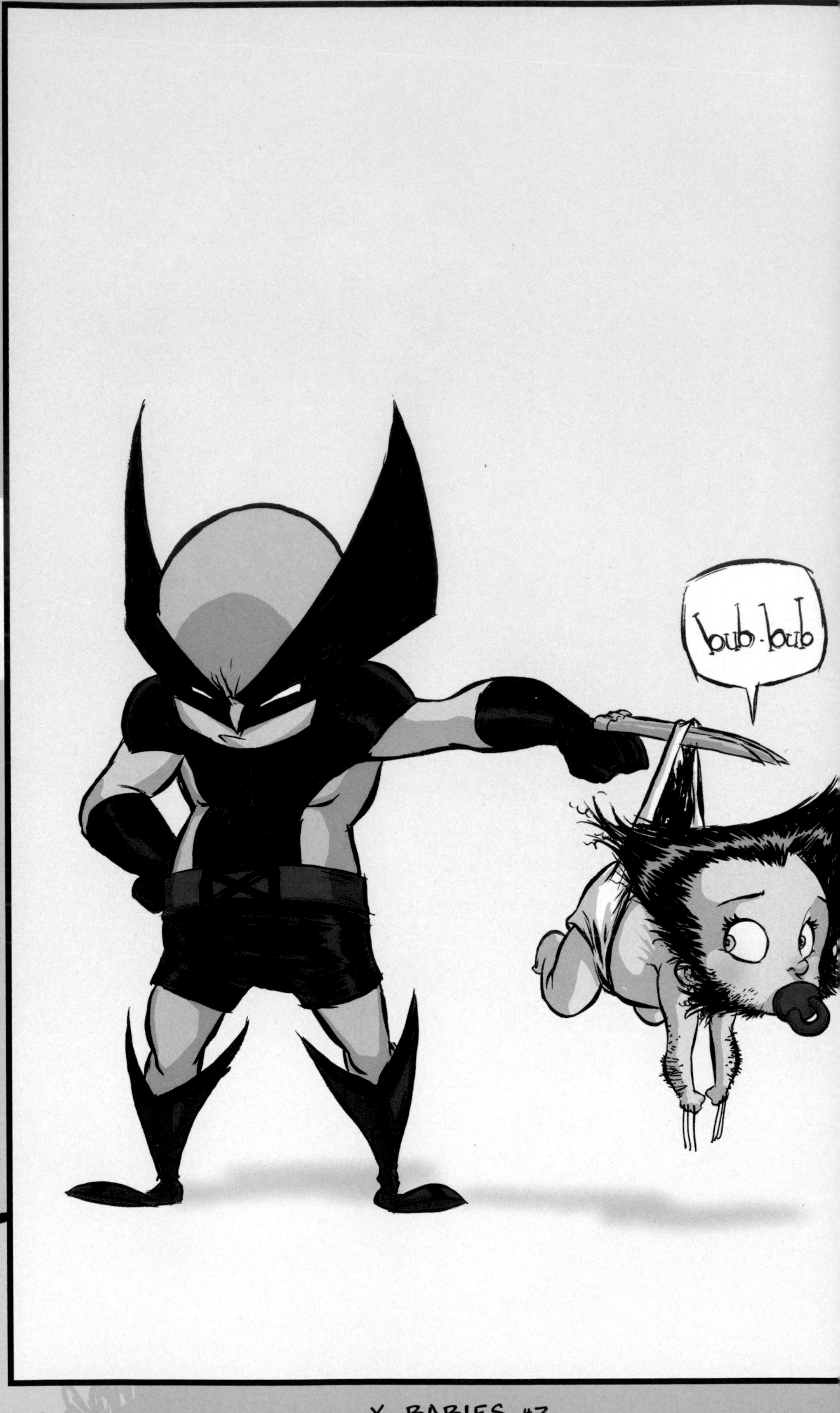
bub-bub

X-BABIES #3

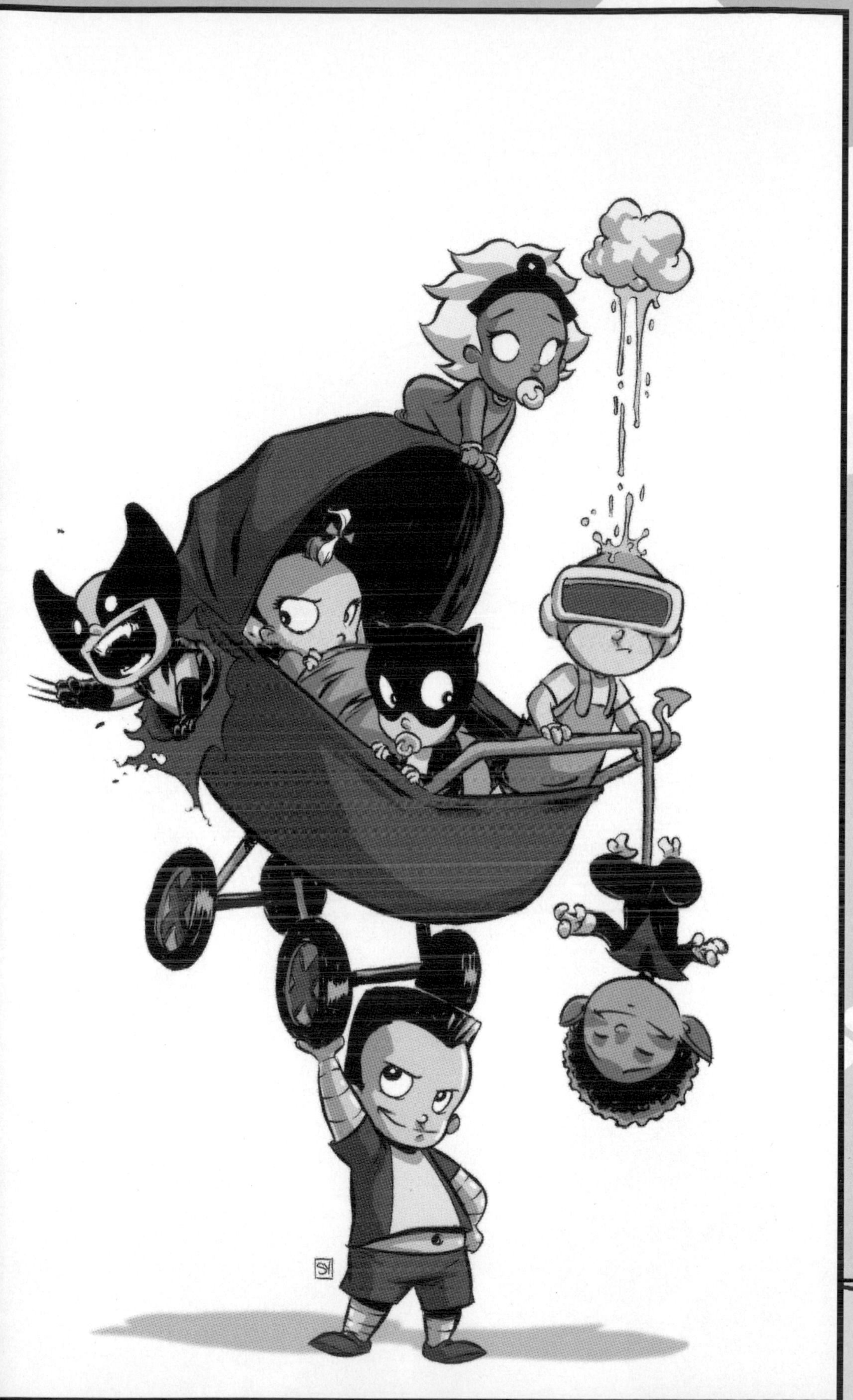

X-BABIES #4

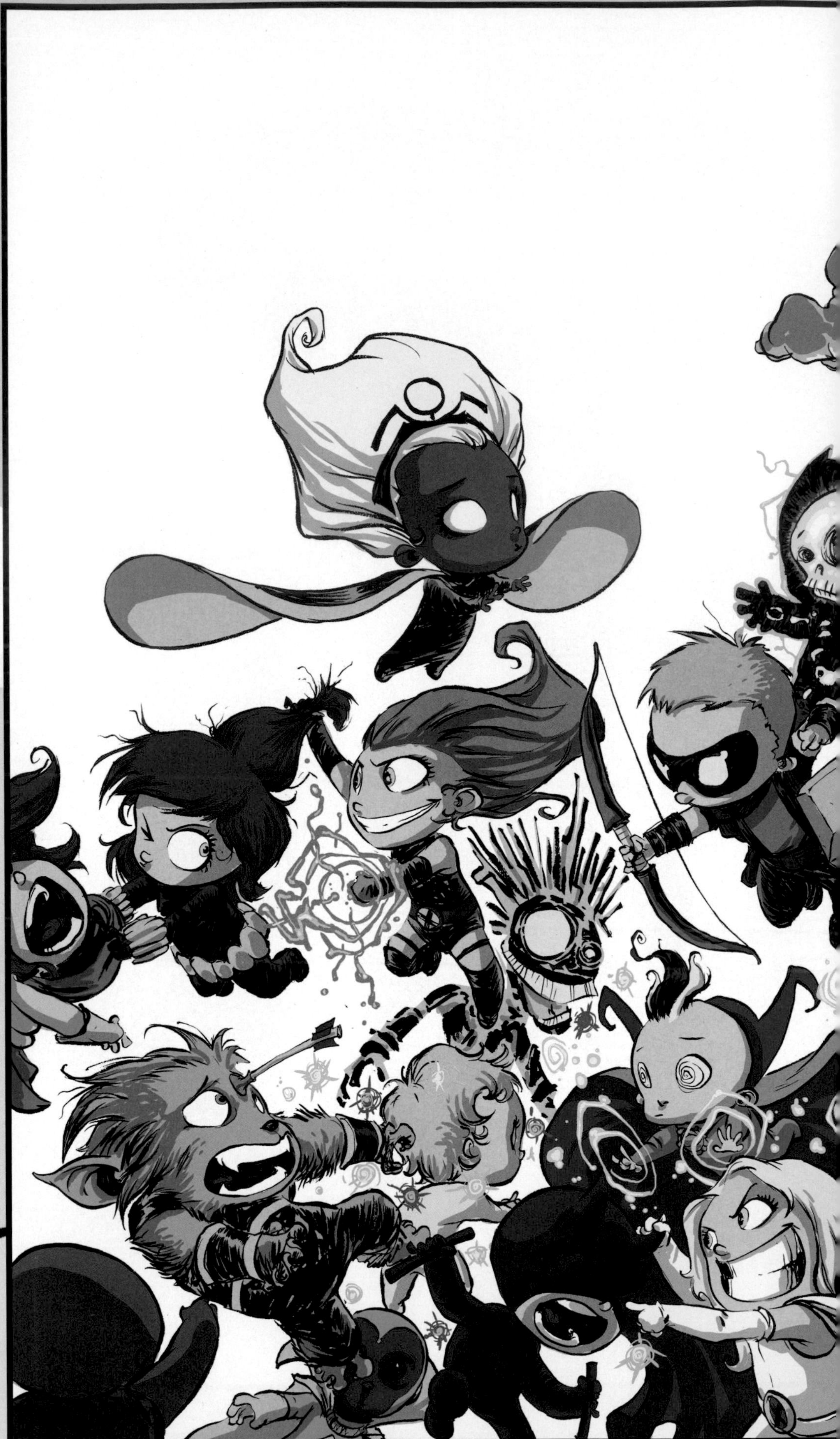

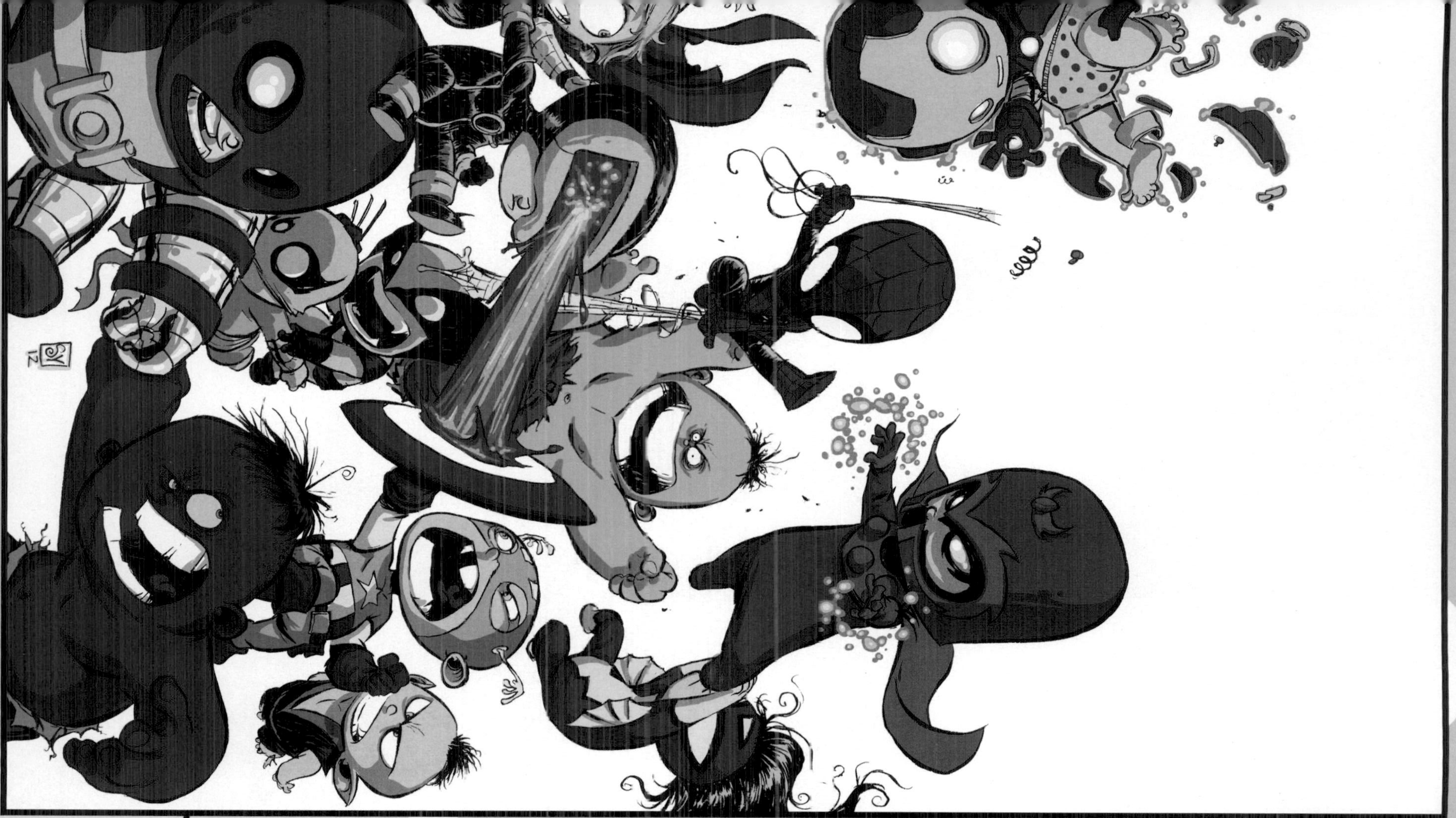

YOUNG MARVEL: LITTLE X-MEN, LITTLE AVENGERS, BIG TROUBLE TPB

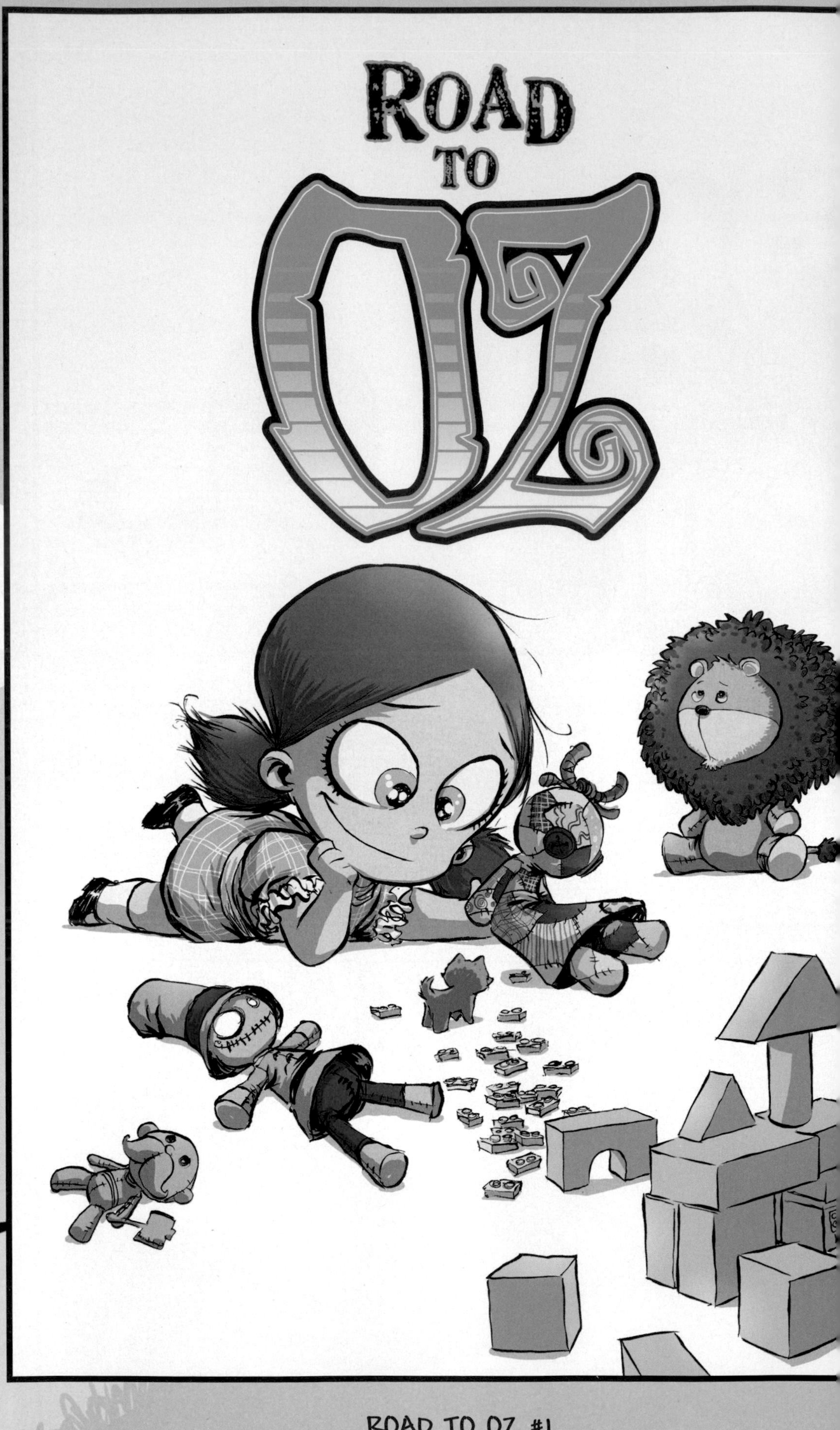
ROAD TO OZ

ROAD TO OZ #1

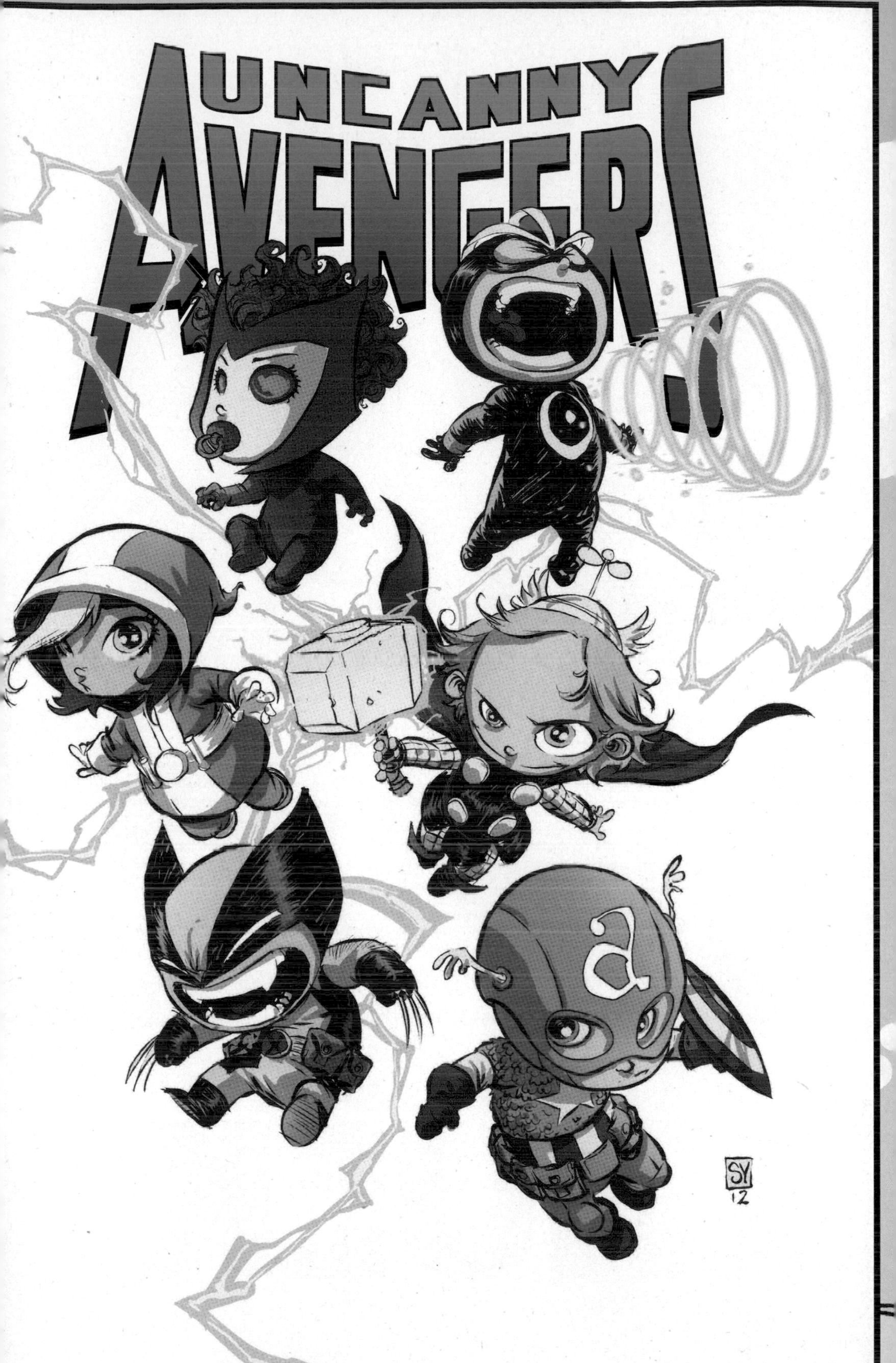
UNCANNY AVENGERS
SY
'12

UNCANNY AVENGERS #1

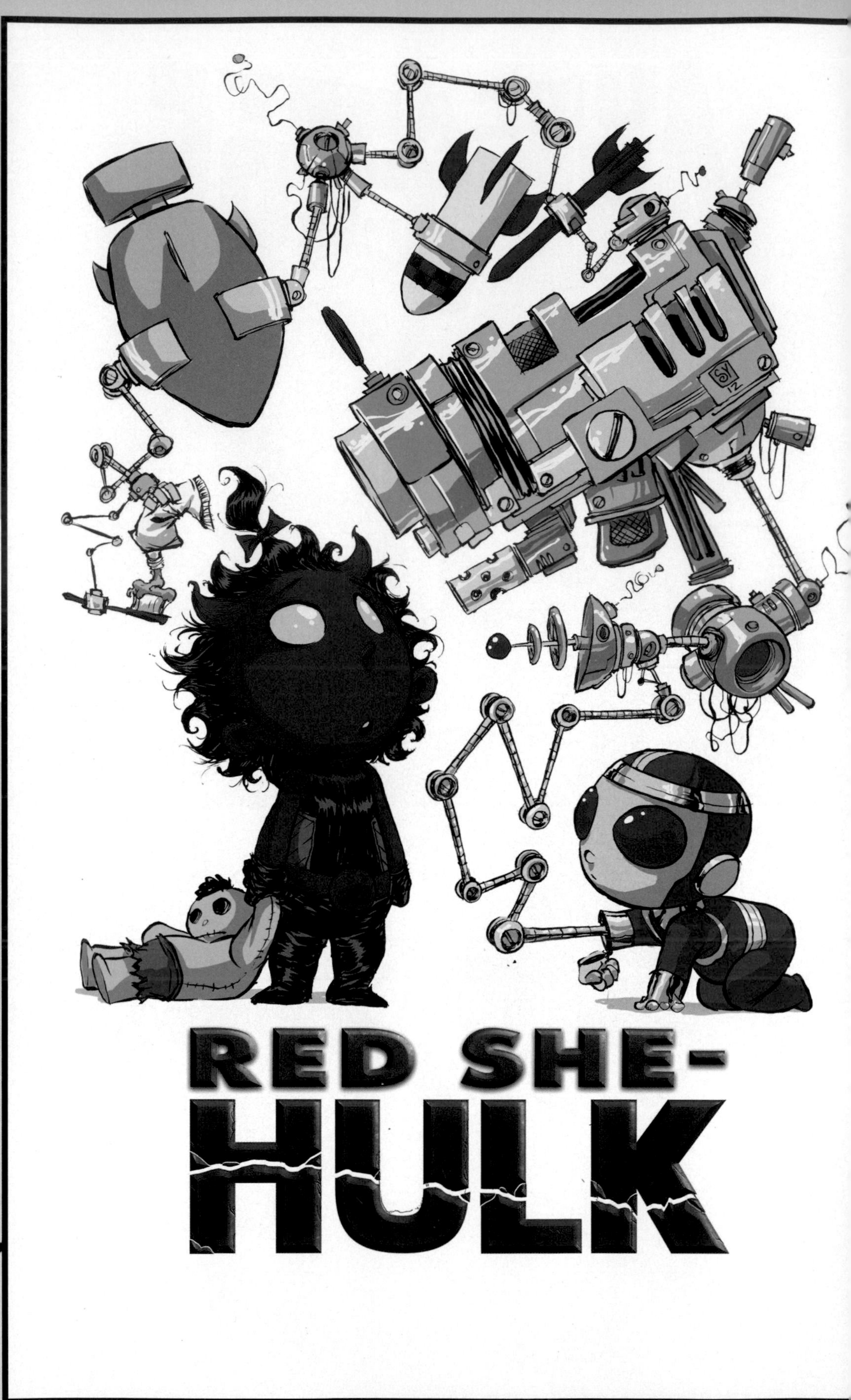
RED SHE-
HULK

RED SHE-HULK #58

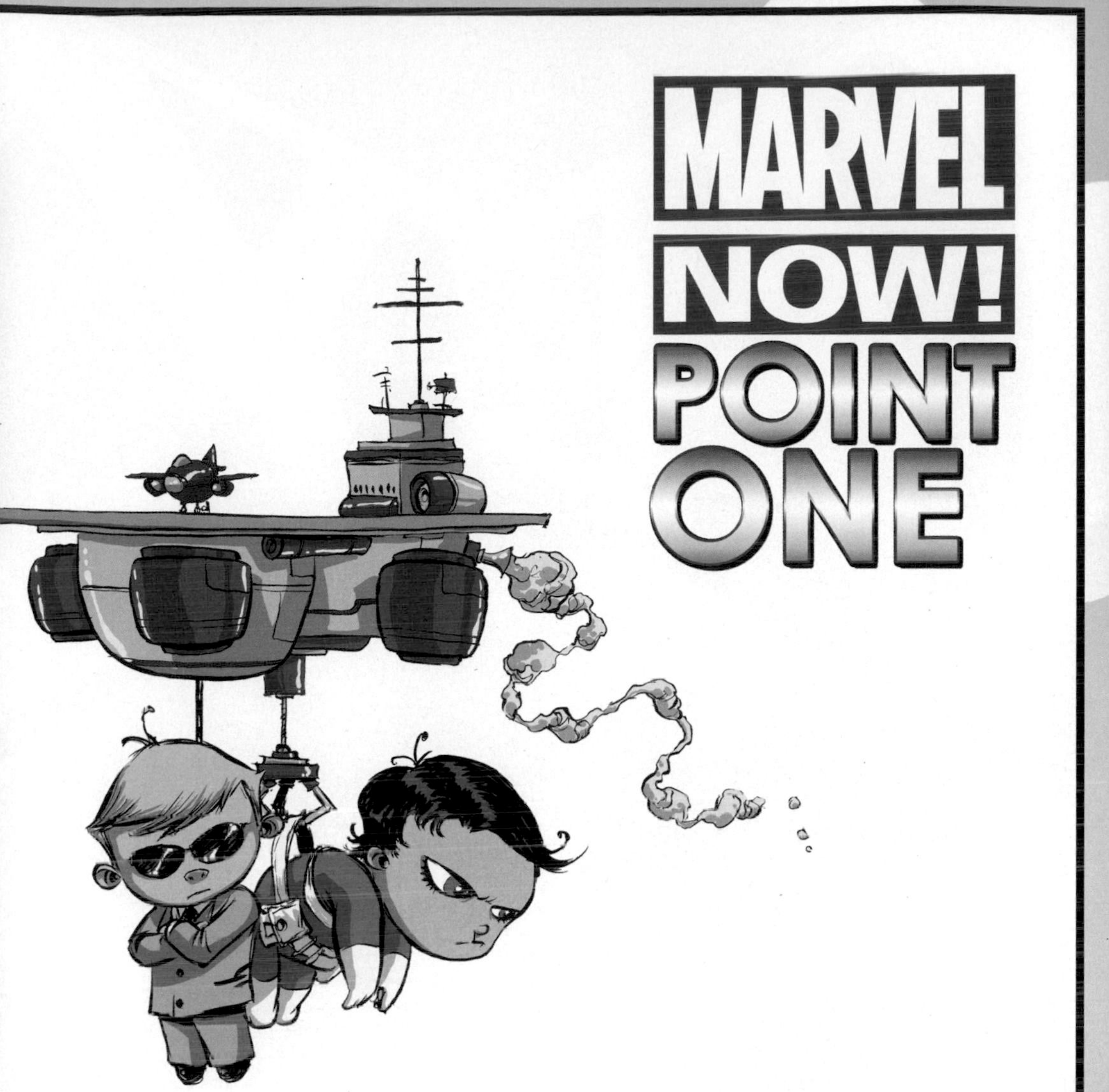
MARVEL
NOW!
POINT
ONE

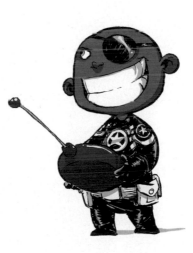

MARVEL NOW! POINT ONE #1

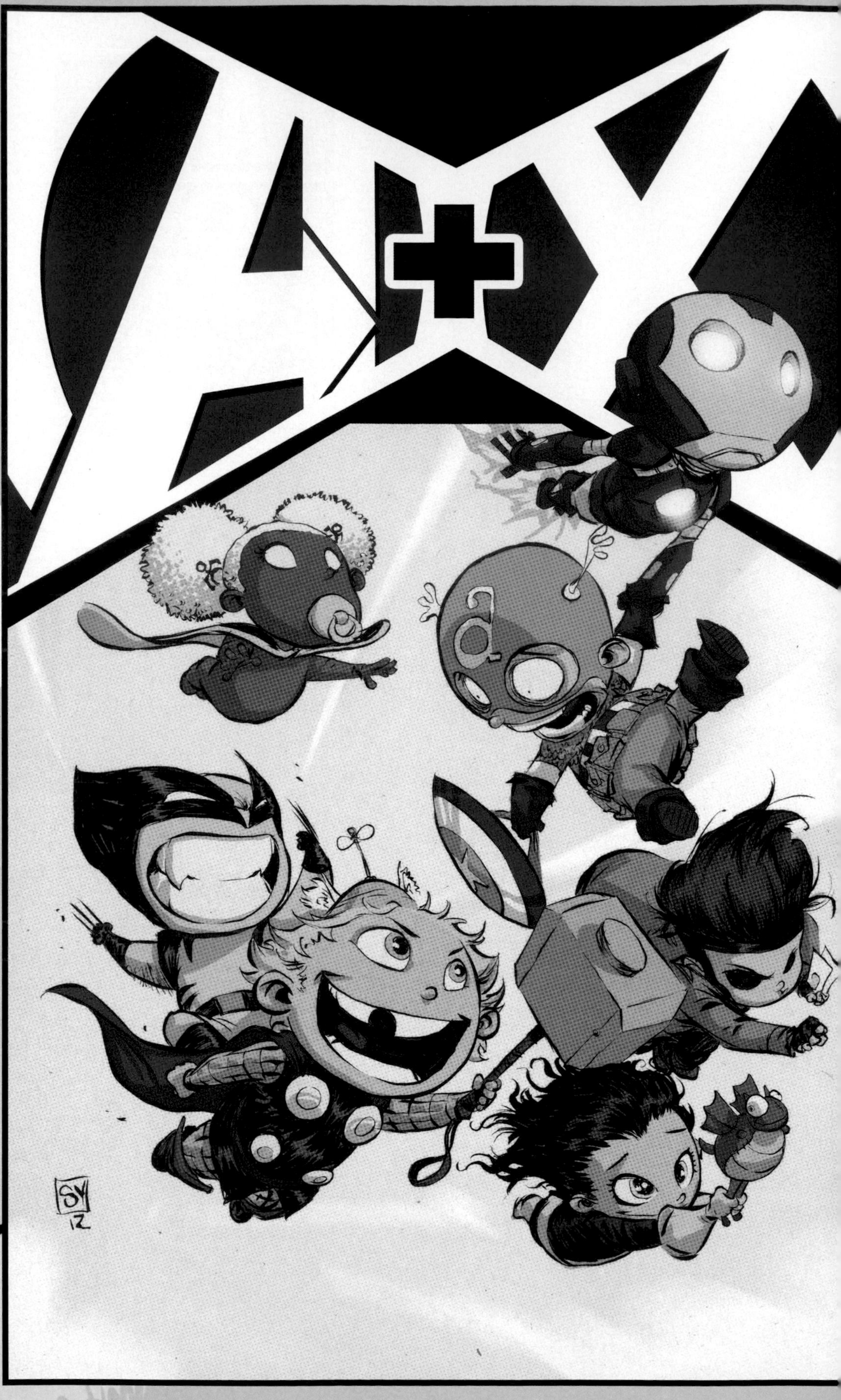
A+X
SY
12

A+X #1

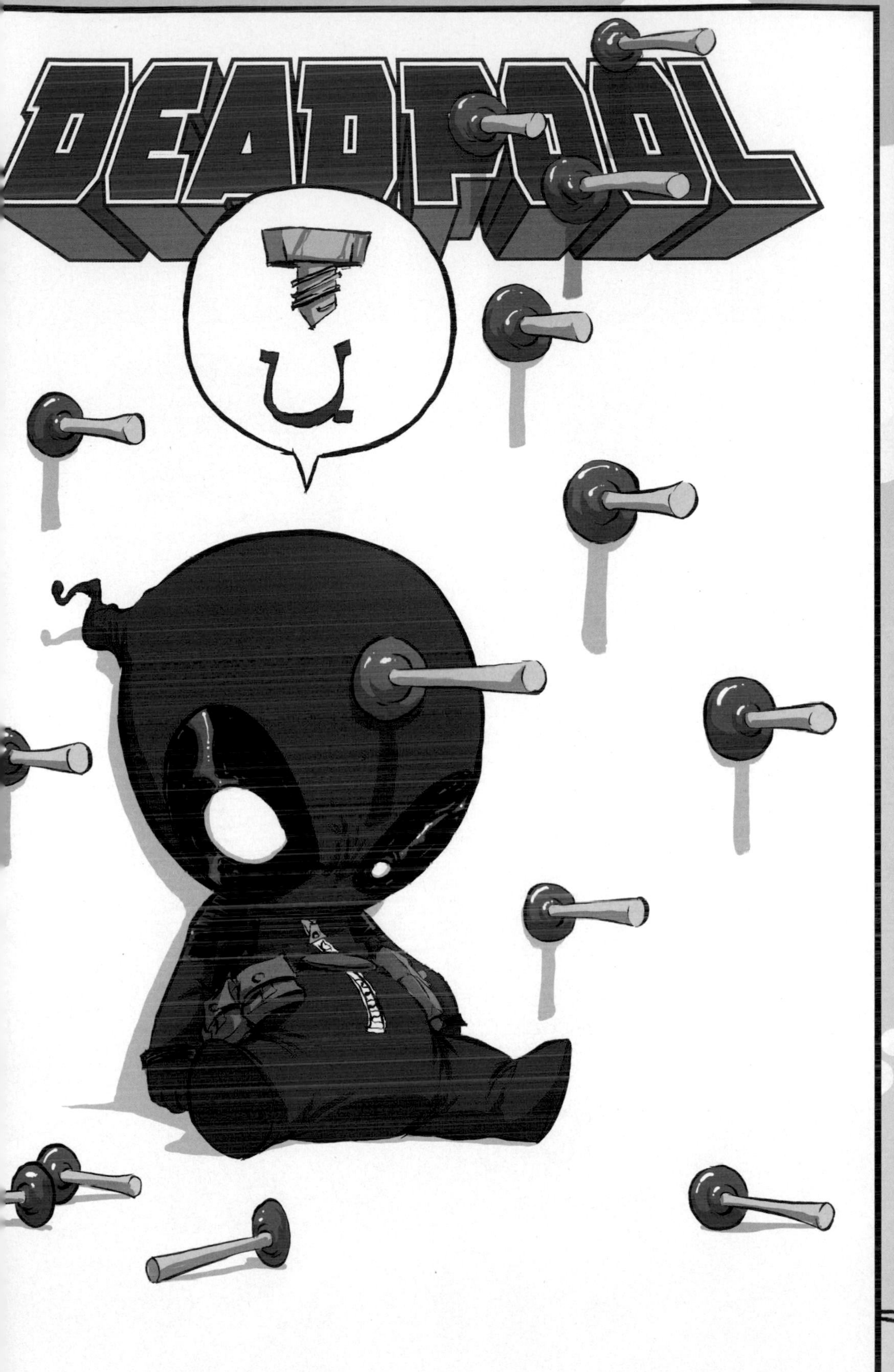
DEADPOOL
U

DEADPOOL #1

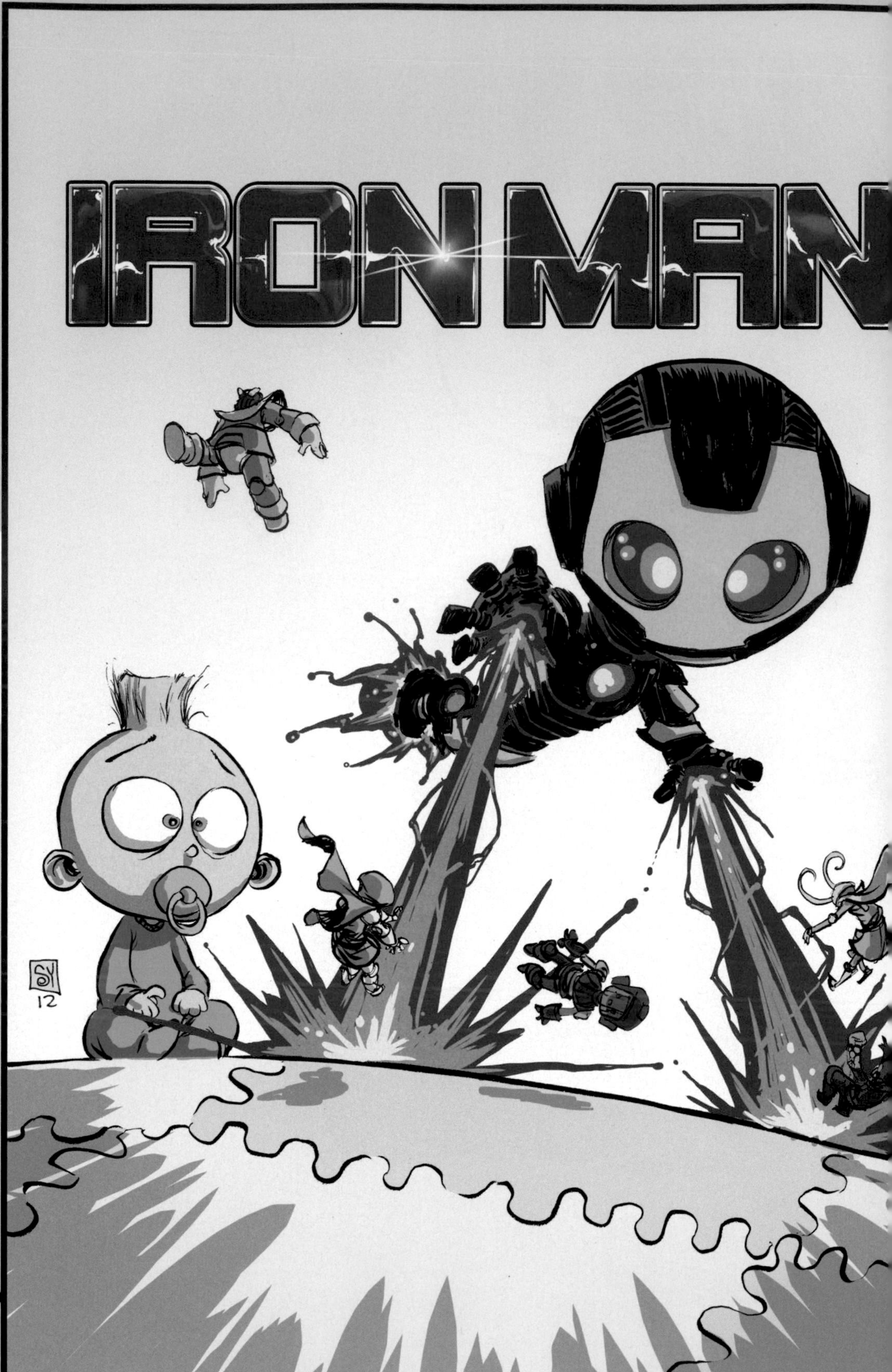
IRON MAN
SY
12

IRON MAN #1

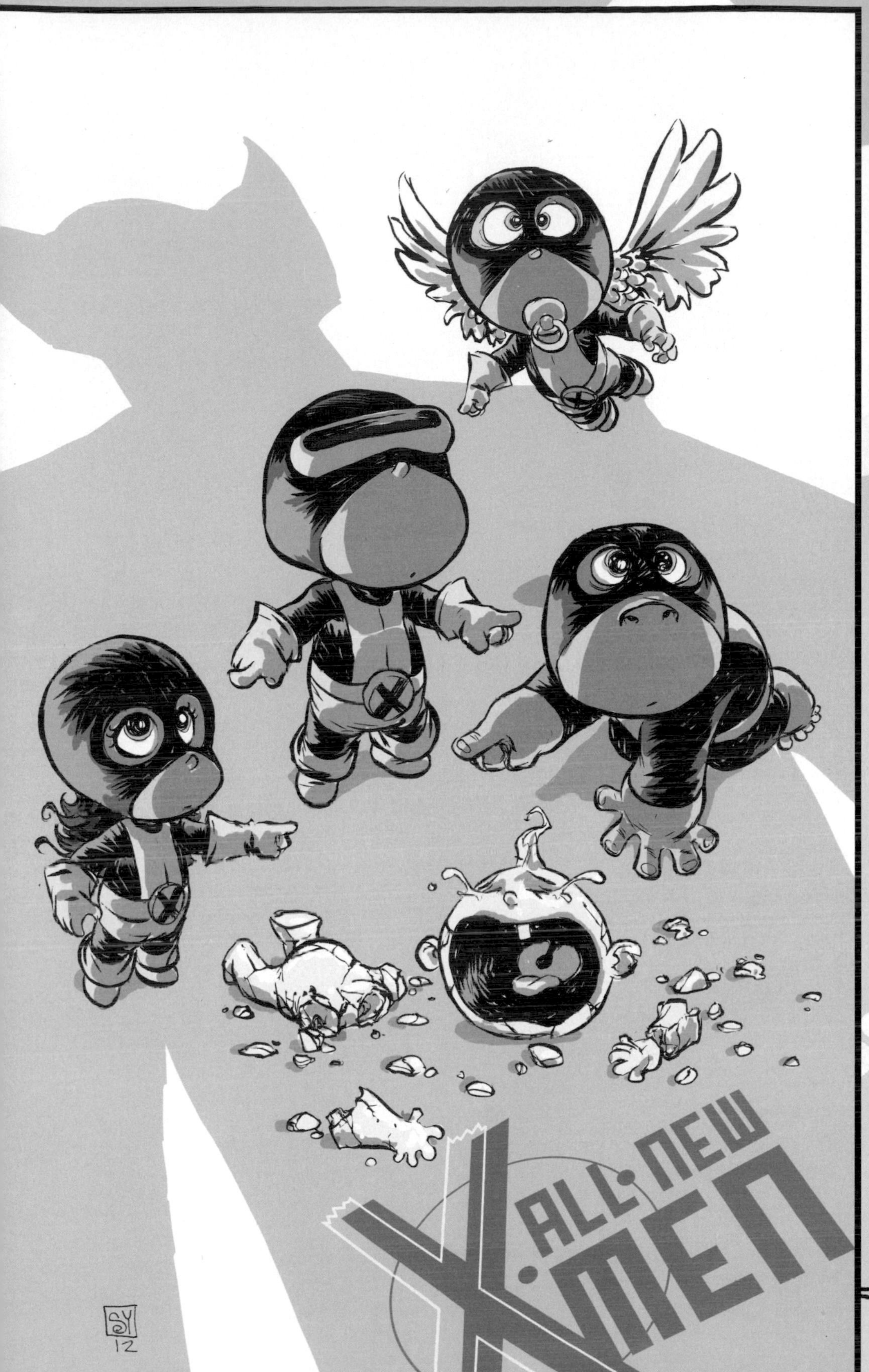

ALL-NEW
X-MEN
SY
12

ALL-NEW X-MEN #1

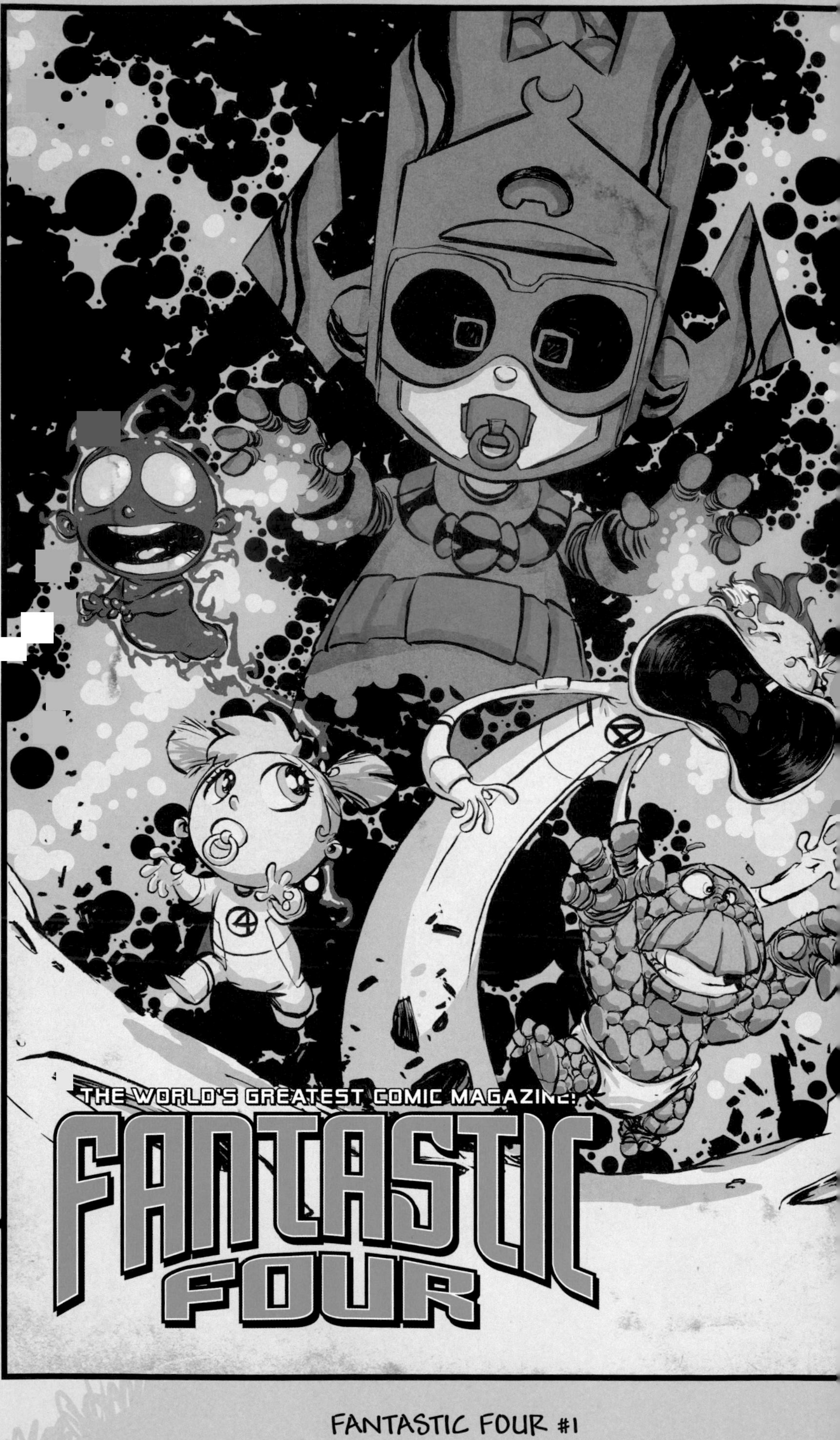
THE WORLD'S GREATEST COMIC MAGAZINE!
FANTASTIC
FOUR

FANTASTIC FOUR #1

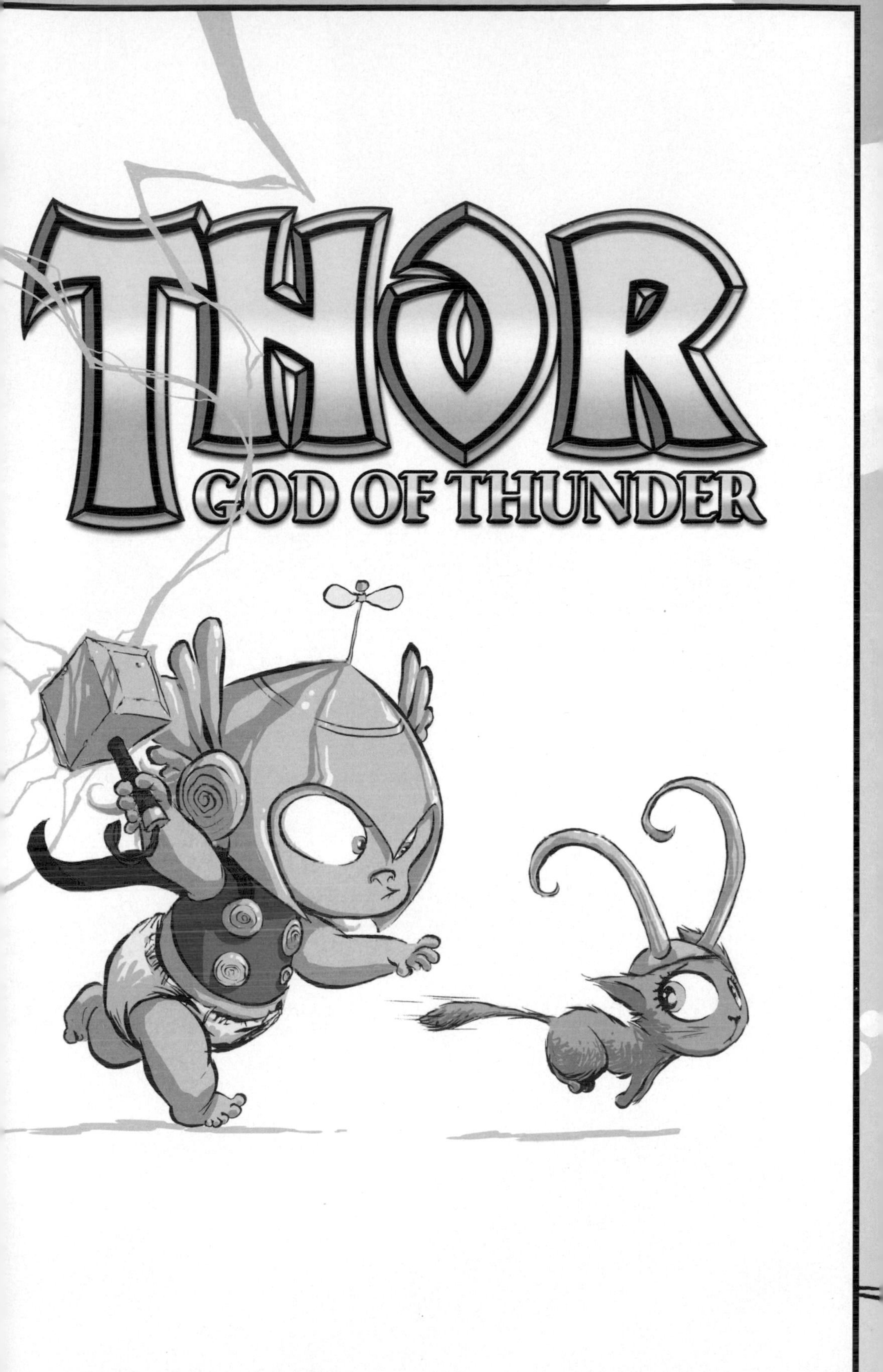
THOR
GOD OF THUNDER

THOR: GOD OF THUNDER #1

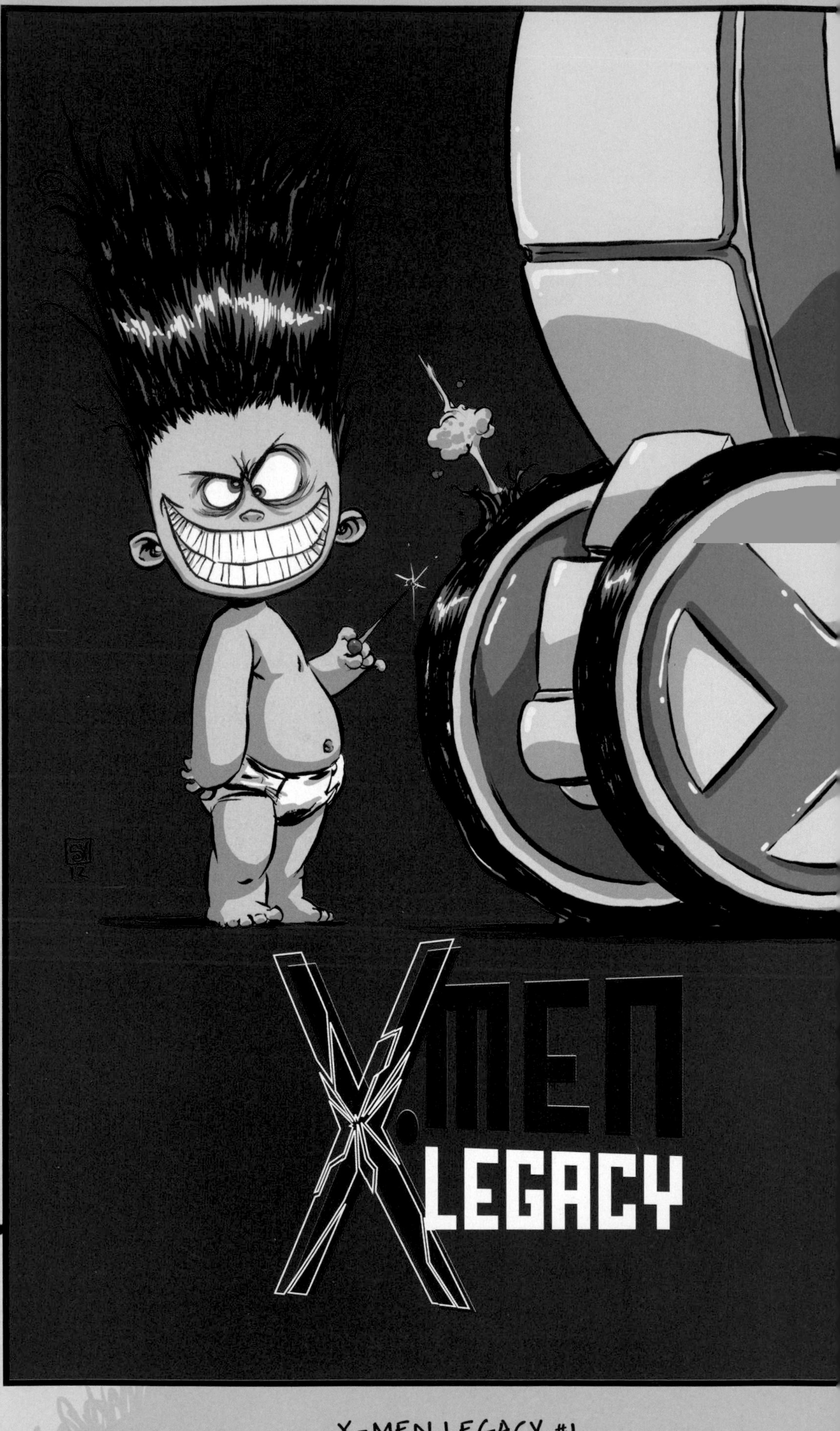
X-MEN
LEGACY

X-MEN LEGACY #1

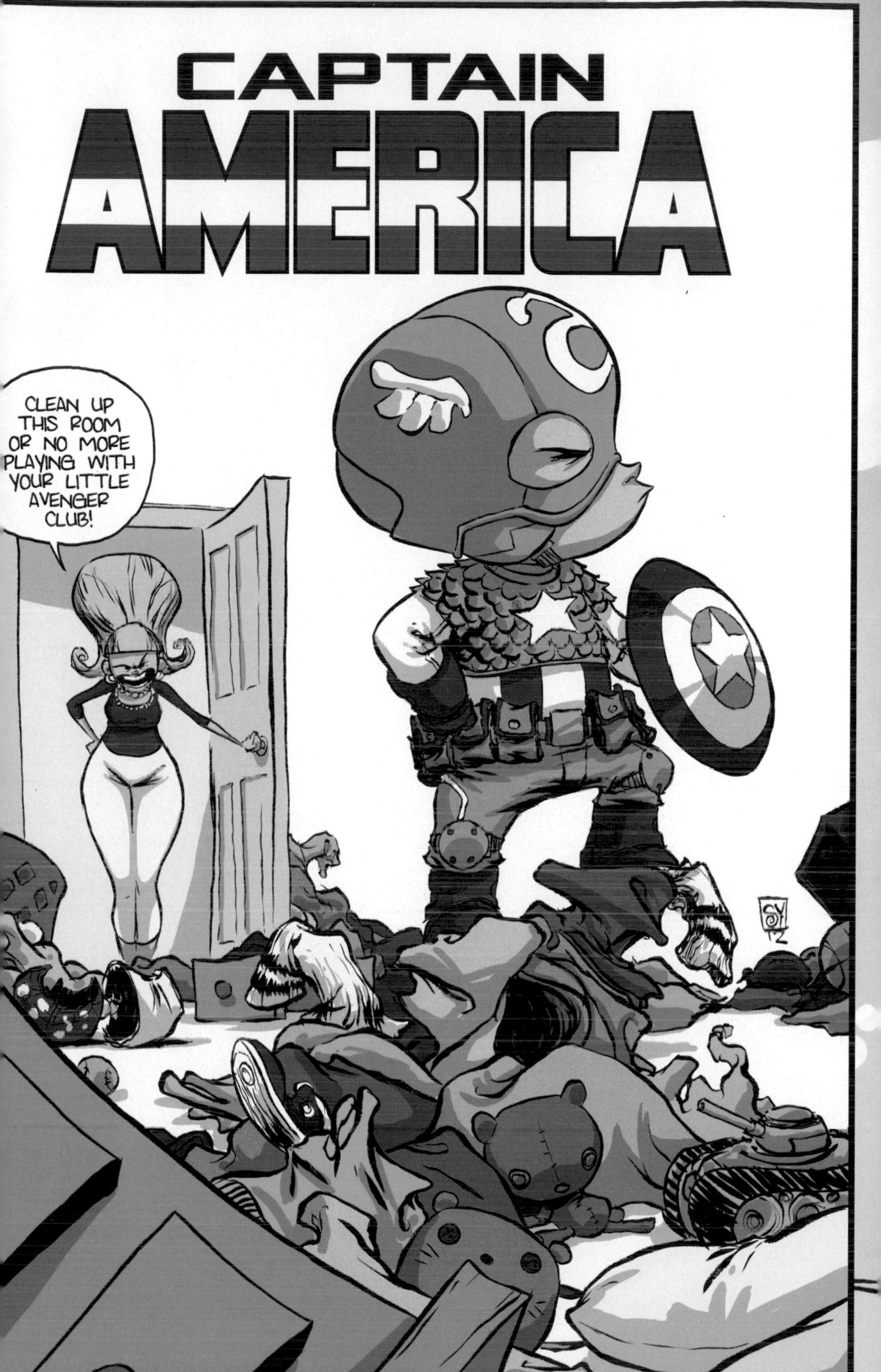
CAPTAIN AMERICA
CLEAN UP THIS ROOM OR NO MORE PLAYING WITH YOUR LITTLE AVENGER CLUB!
SY '12

CAPTAIN AMERICA #1

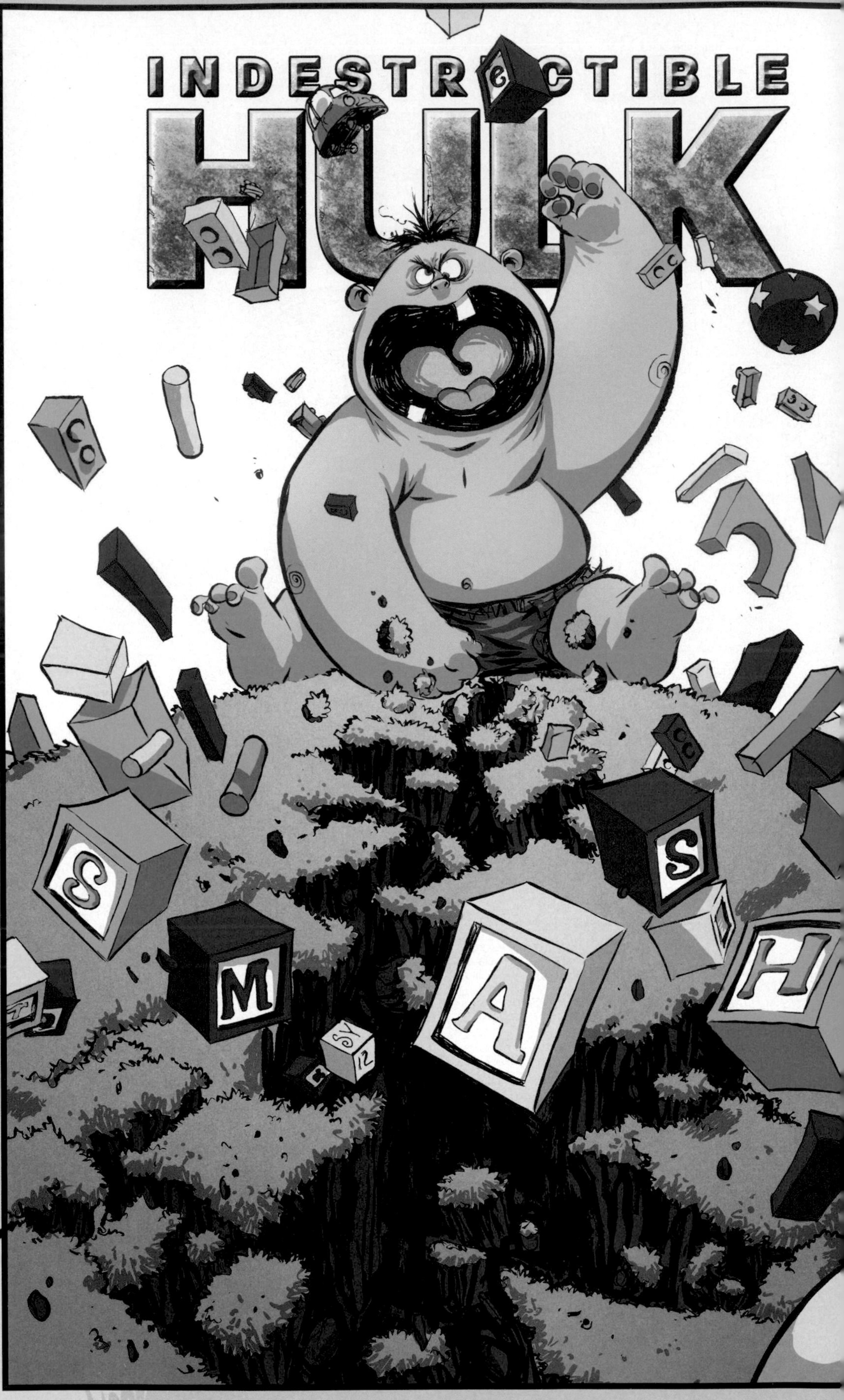
INDESTRUCTIBLE
HULK
S
M
A
S
H

INDESTRUCTIBLE HULK #1

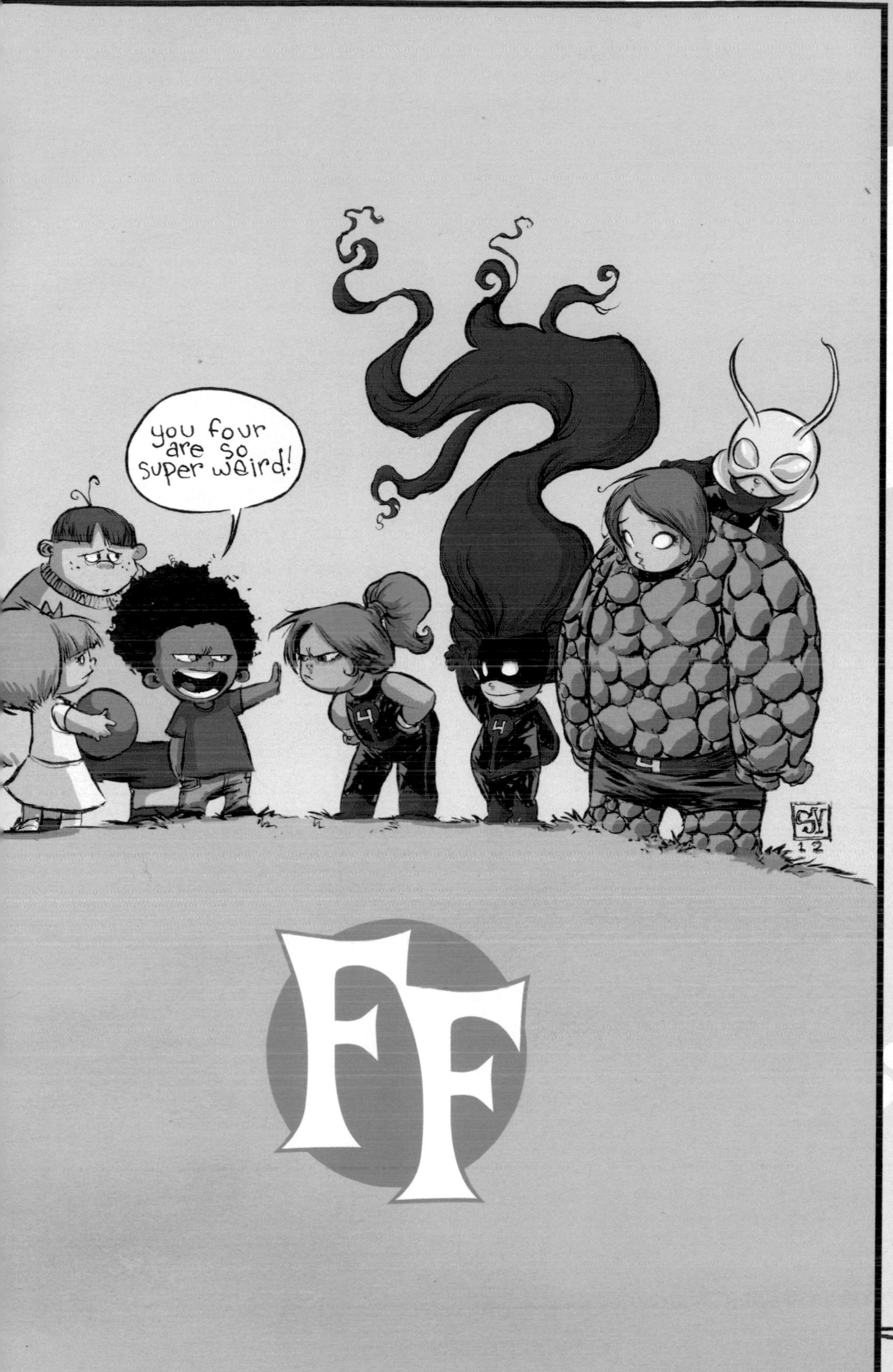
you four are so super weird!
FF

FF #1

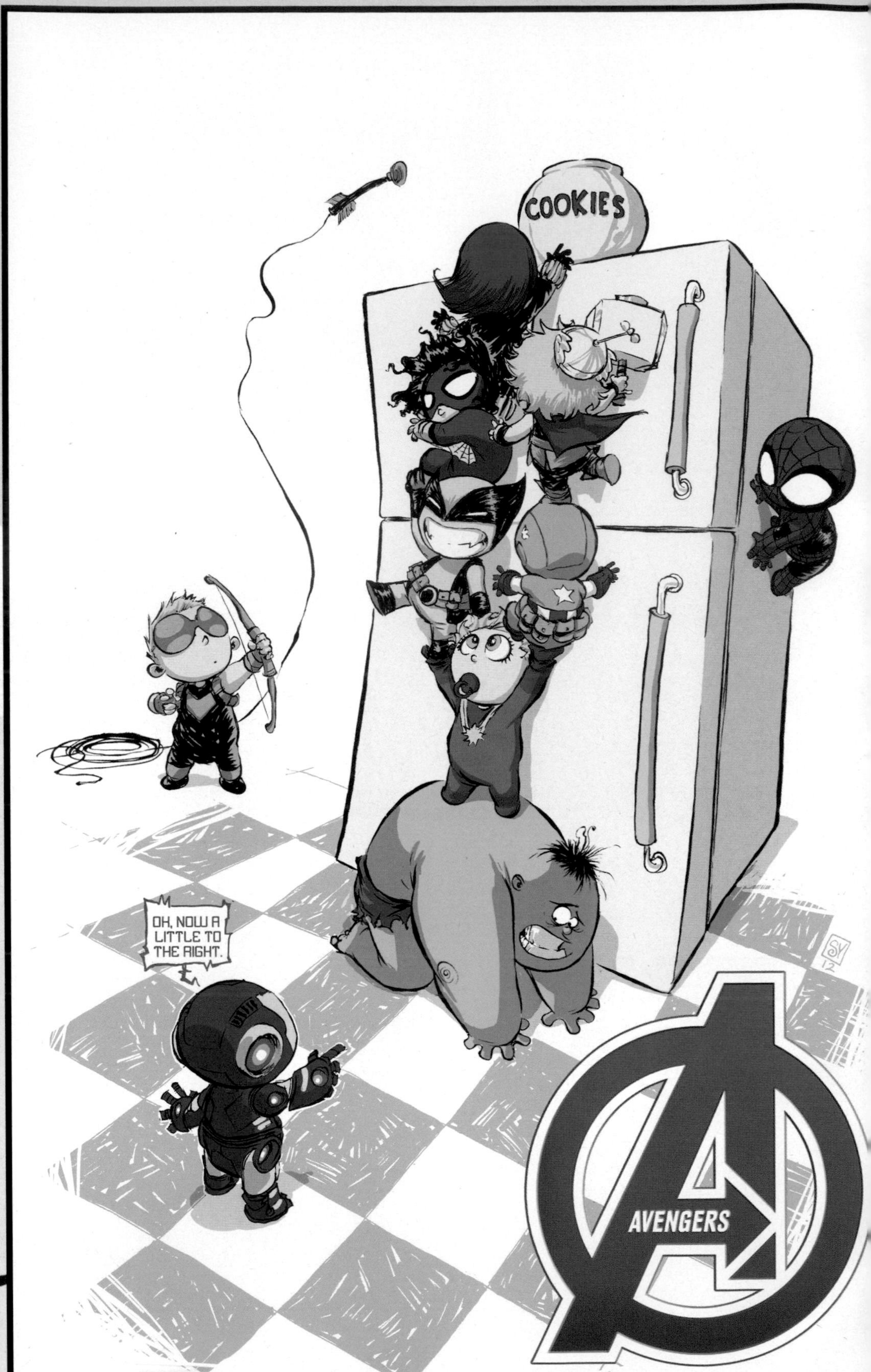
COOKIES
OH, NOW A LITTLE TO THE RIGHT.
SY 12
AVENGERS

AVENGERS #1

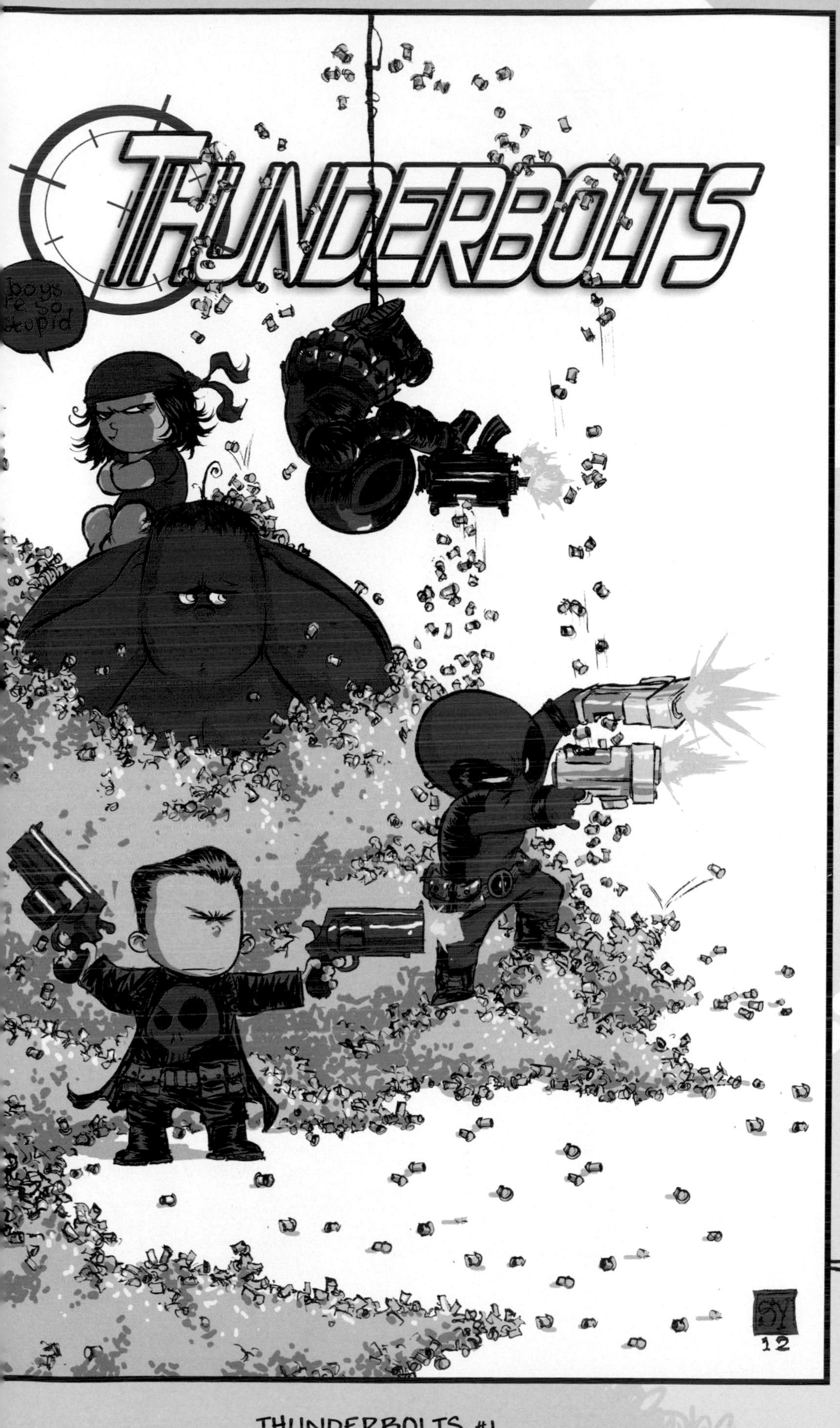
THUNDERBOLTS
boys re so stupid

THUNDERBOLTS #1

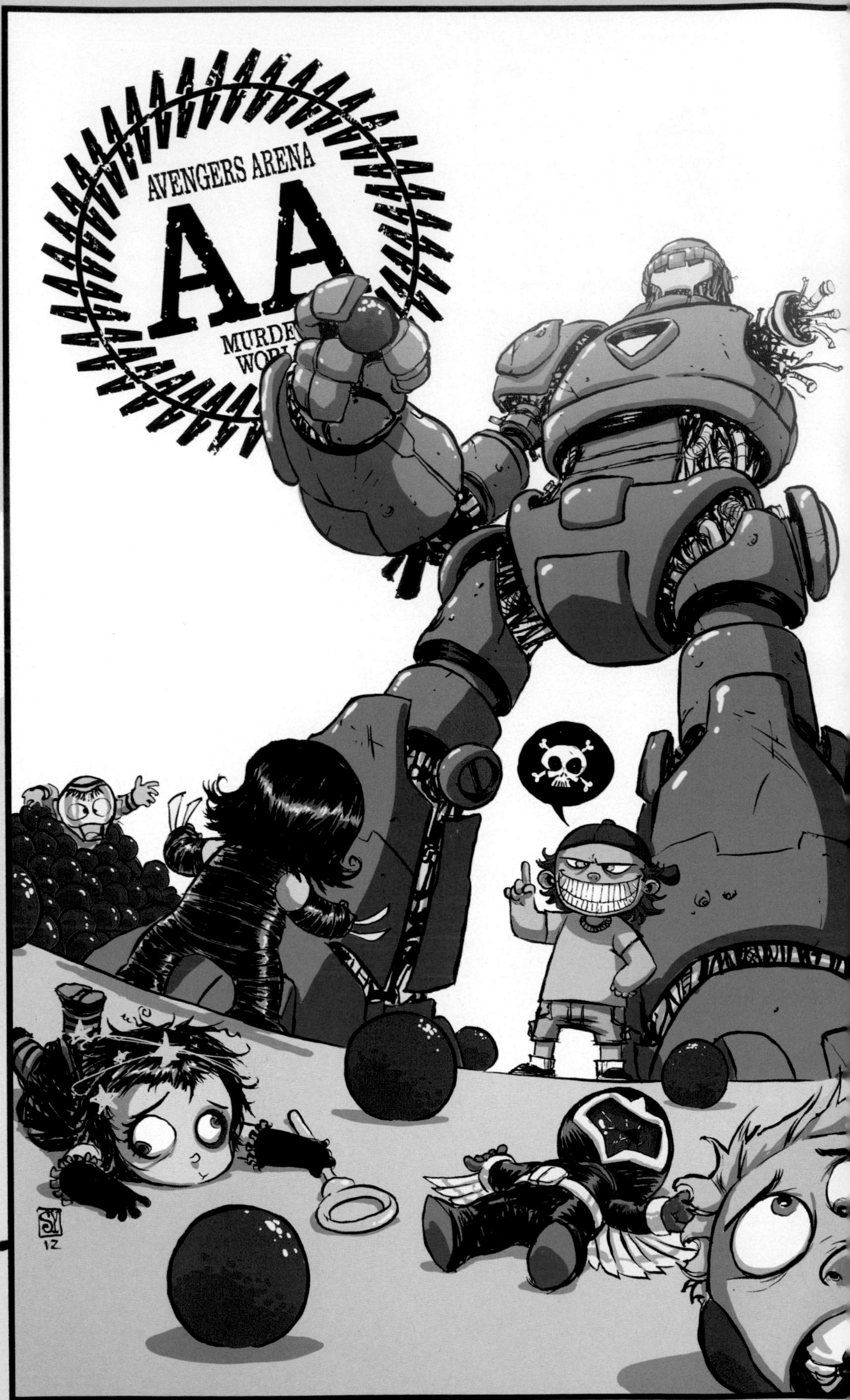
AVENGERS ARENA
AA
MURDE
WORL

AVENGERS ARENA #1

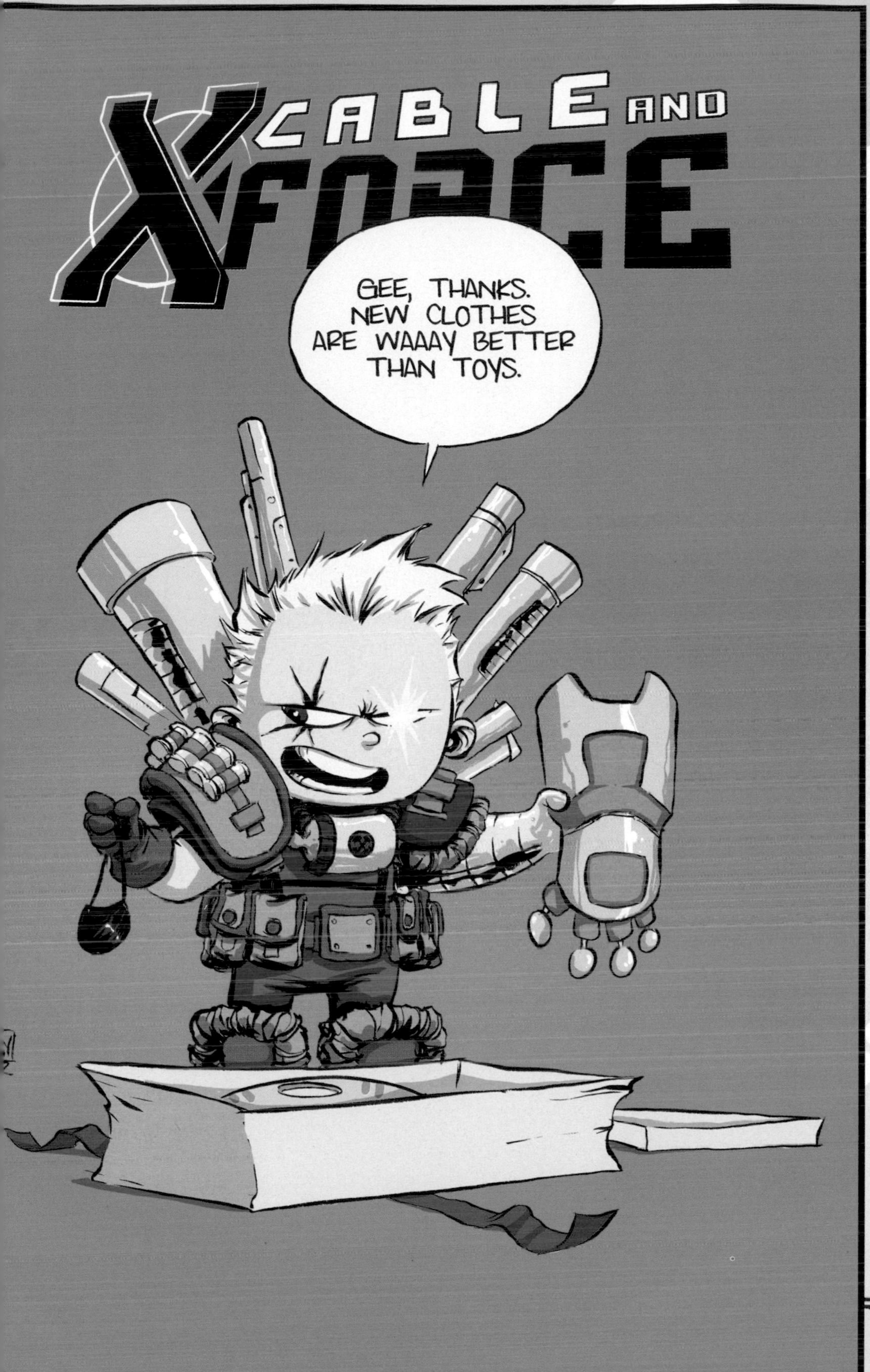
CABLE AND X-FORCE
GEE, THANKS. NEW CLOTHES ARE WAAAY BETTER THAN TOYS.

CABLE AND X-FORCE #1

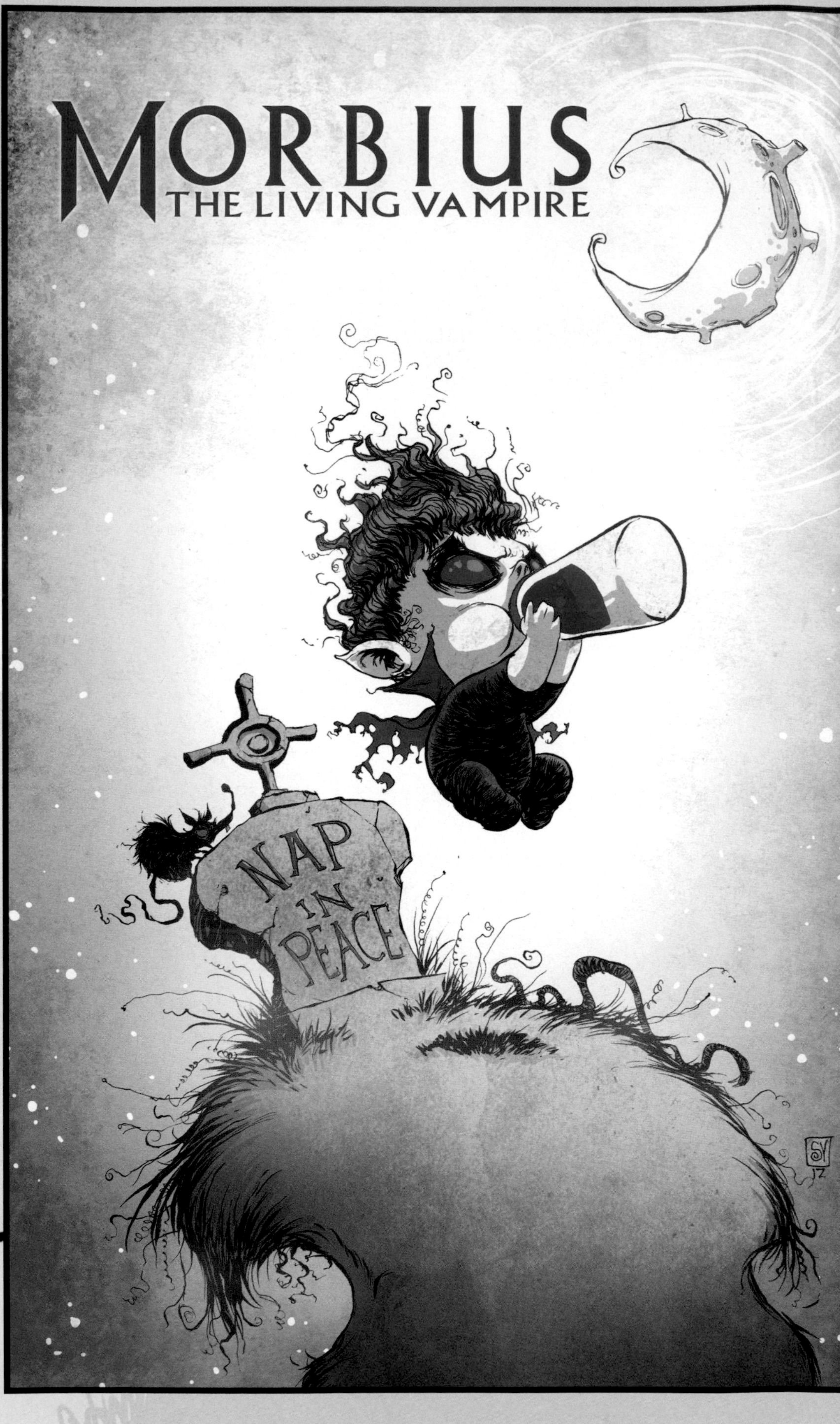
MORBIUS
THE LIVING VAMPIRE
NAP IN PEACE
SY 12

MORBIUS: THE LIVING VAMPIRE #1

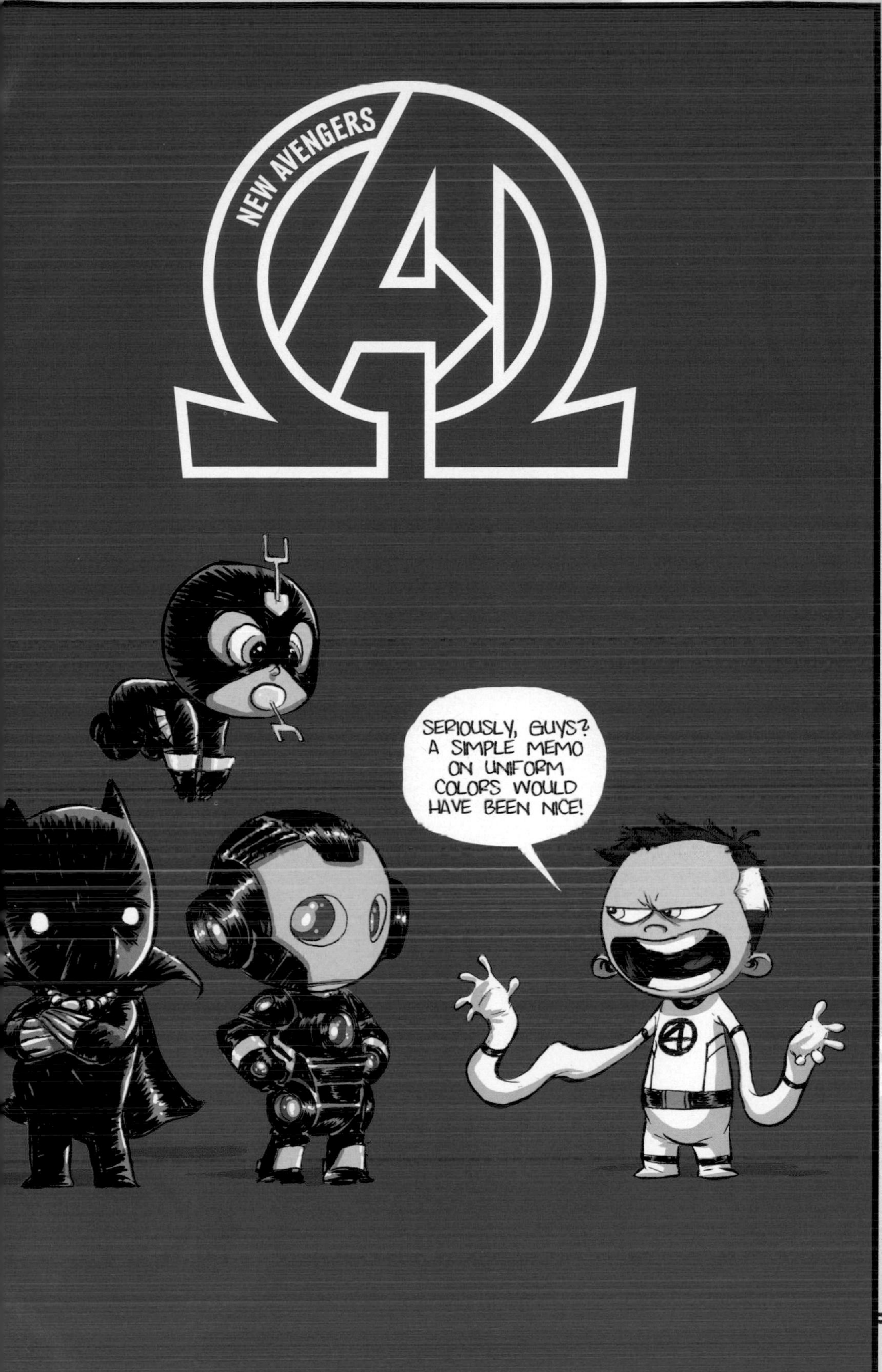
NEW AVENGERS
SERIOUSLY, GUYS? A SIMPLE MEMO ON UNIFORM COLORS WOULD HAVE BEEN NICE!

NEW AVENGERS #1

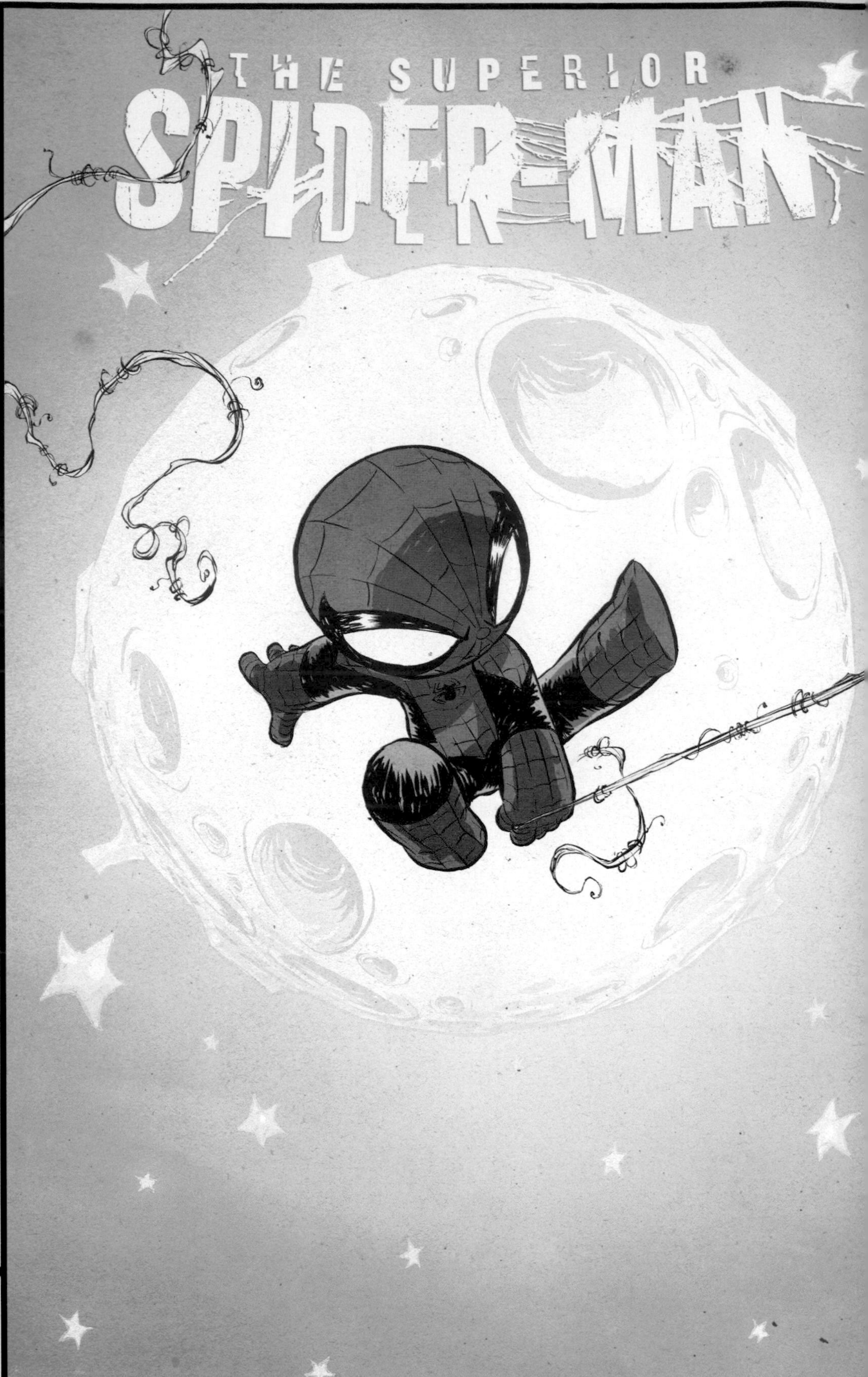
THE SUPERIOR
SPIDER-MAN

SUPERIOR SPIDER-MAN #1

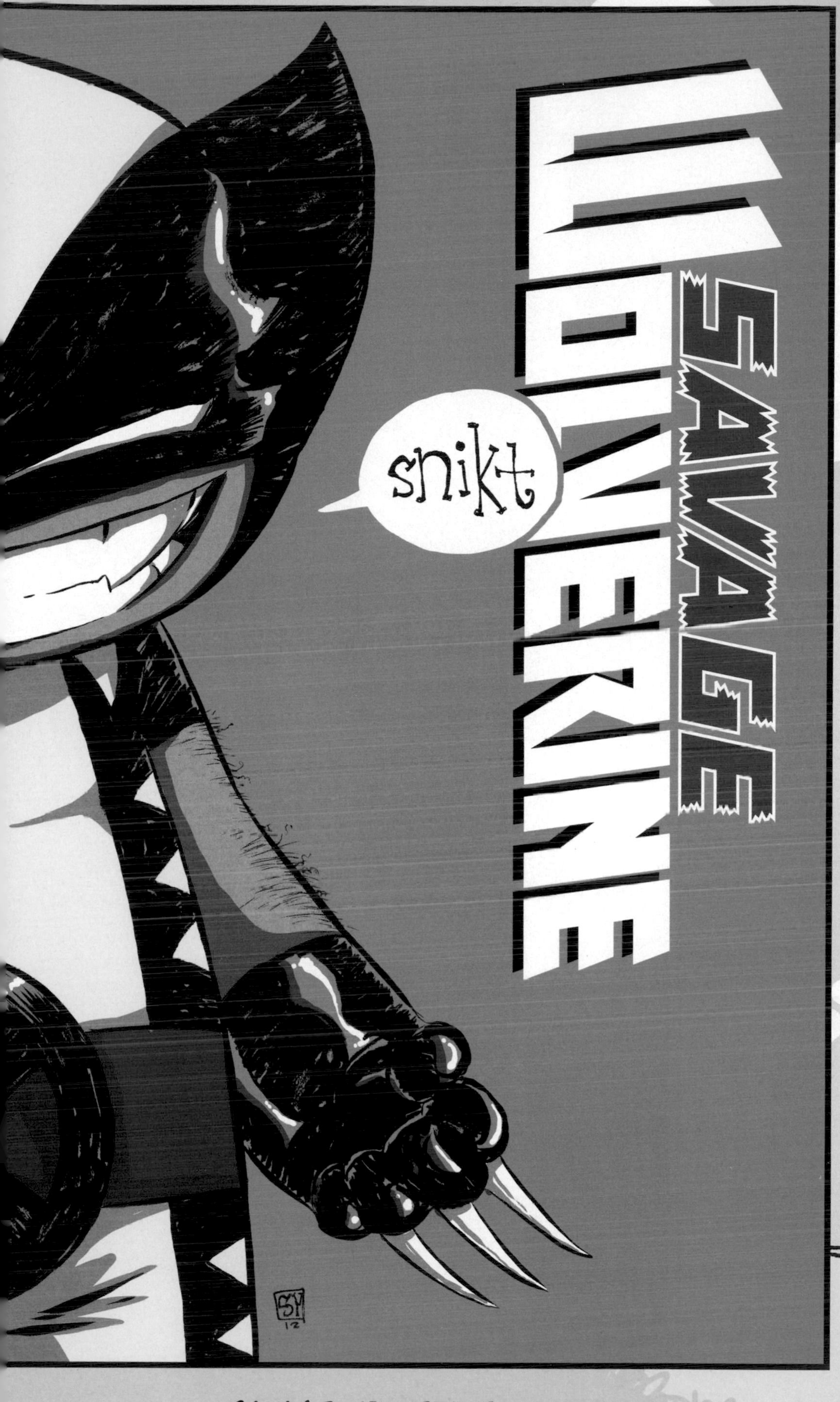
SAVAGE
WOLVERINE
snikt

SAVAGE WOLVERINE #1

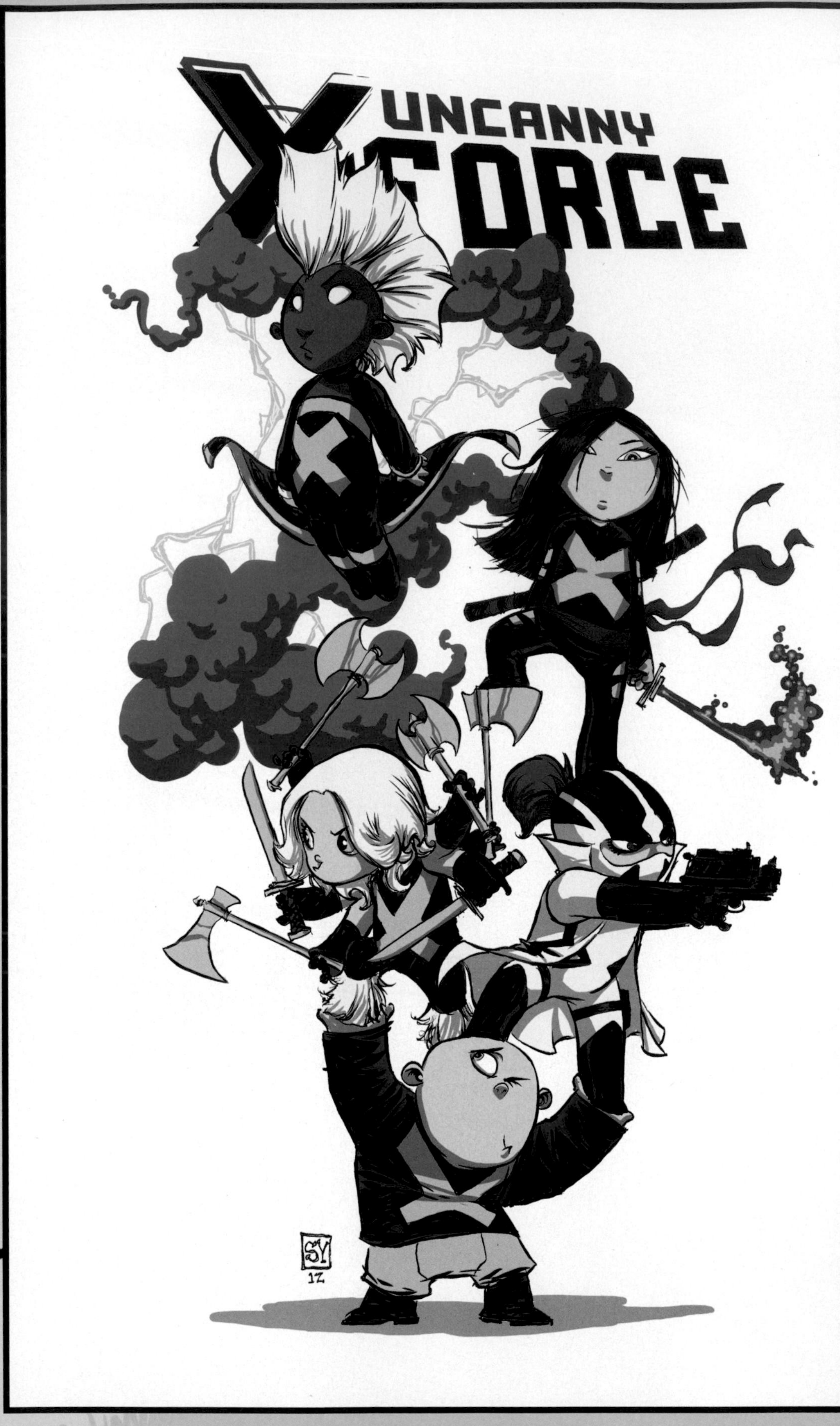
UNCANNY
X FORCE
SY
12

UNCANNY X-FORCE #1

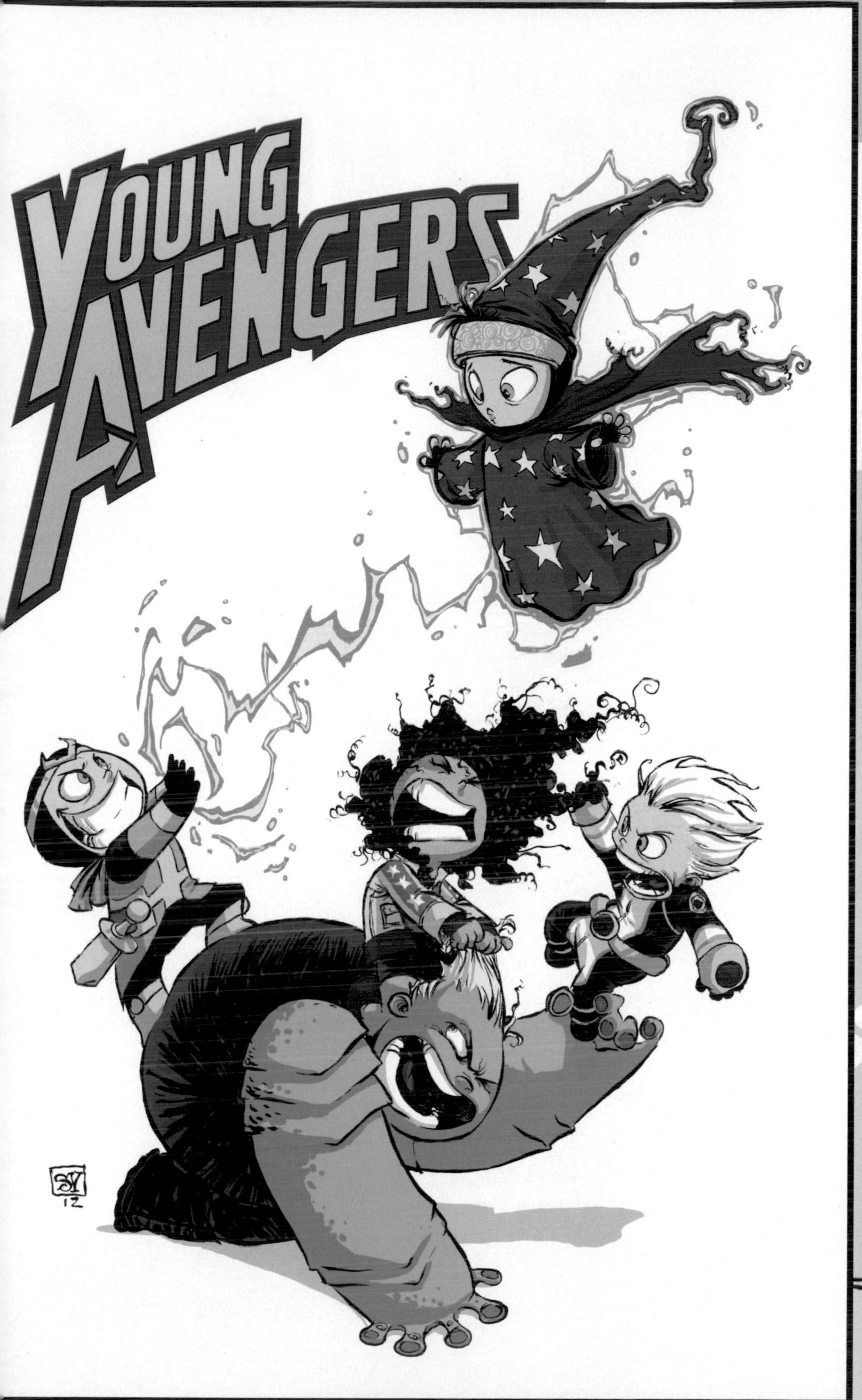
YOUNG AVENGERS

YOUNG AVENGERS #1

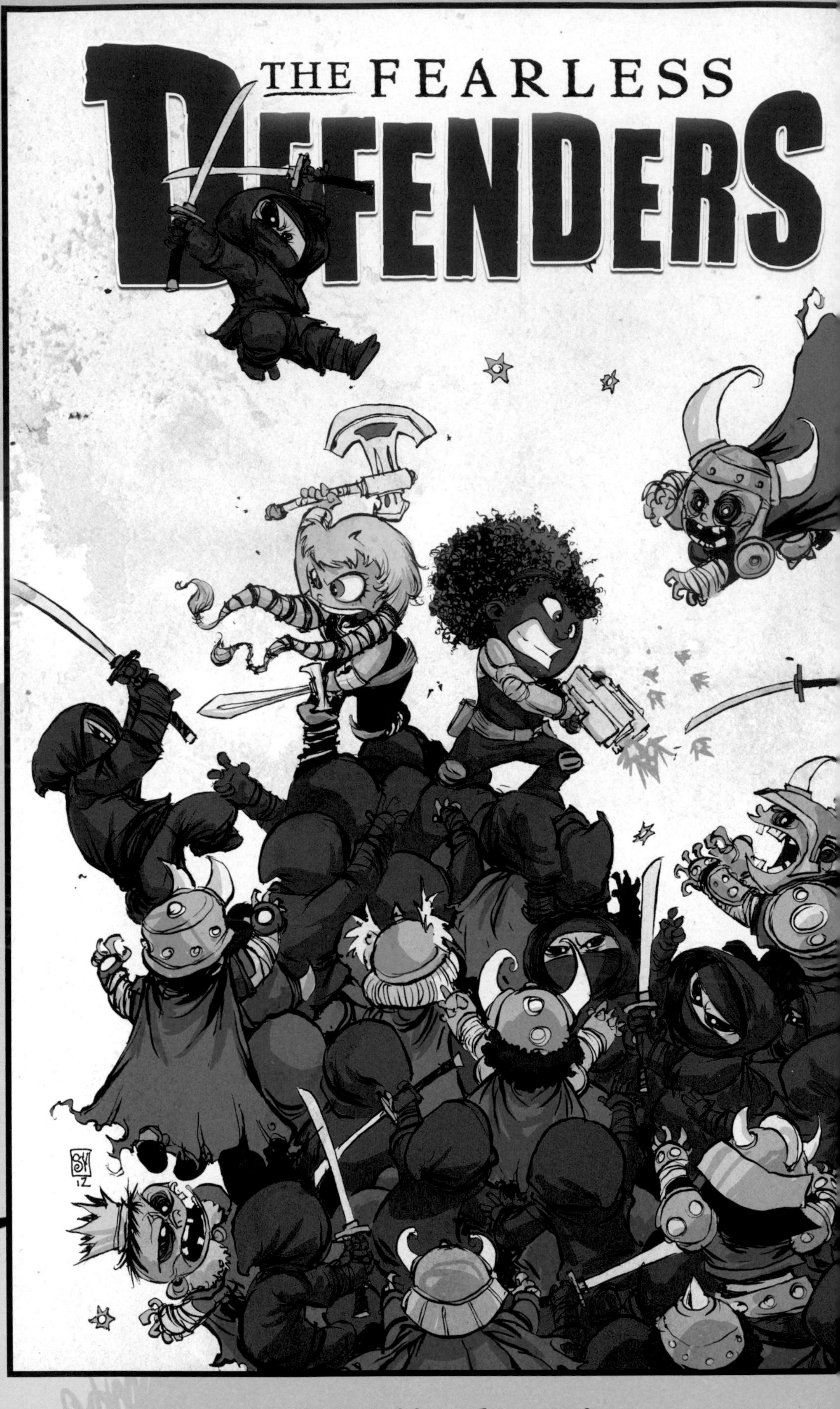
THE FEARLESS DEFENDERS
SY
'12

FEARLESS DEFENDERS #1

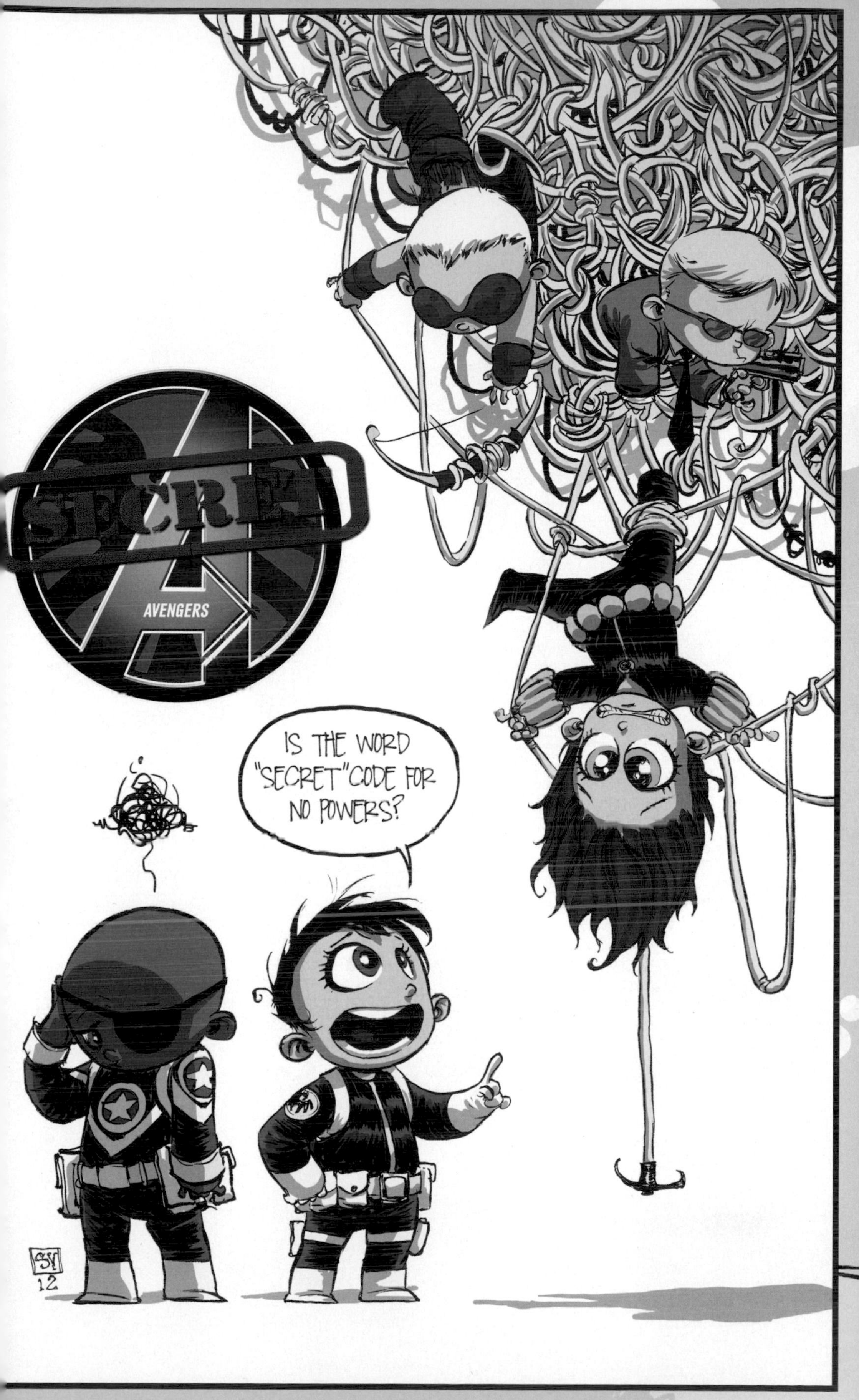
SECRET
AVENGERS
IS THE WORD "SECRET" CODE FOR NO POWERS?

SECRET AVENGERS #1

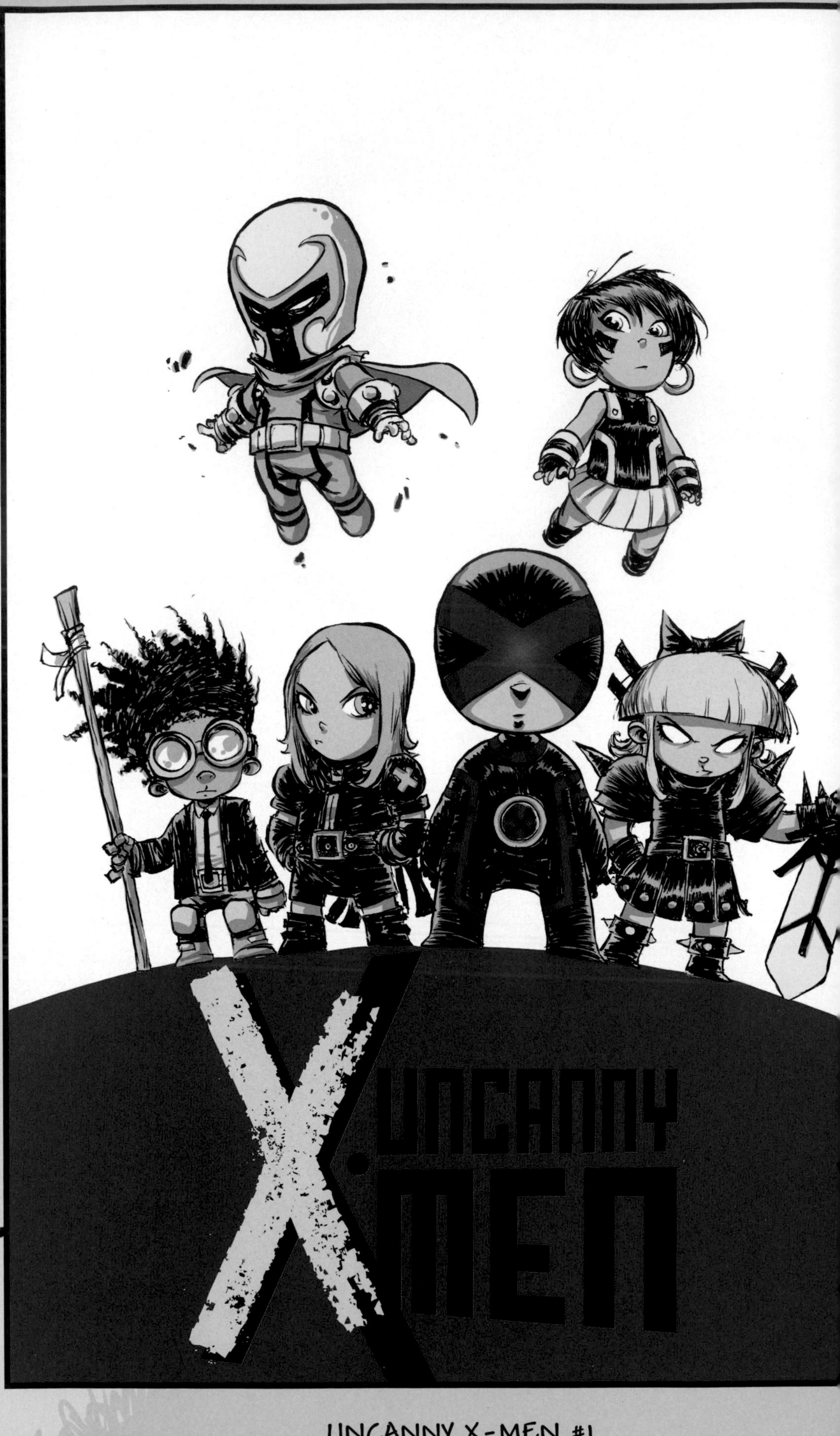
X
UNCANNY
MEN

UNCANNY X-MEN #1

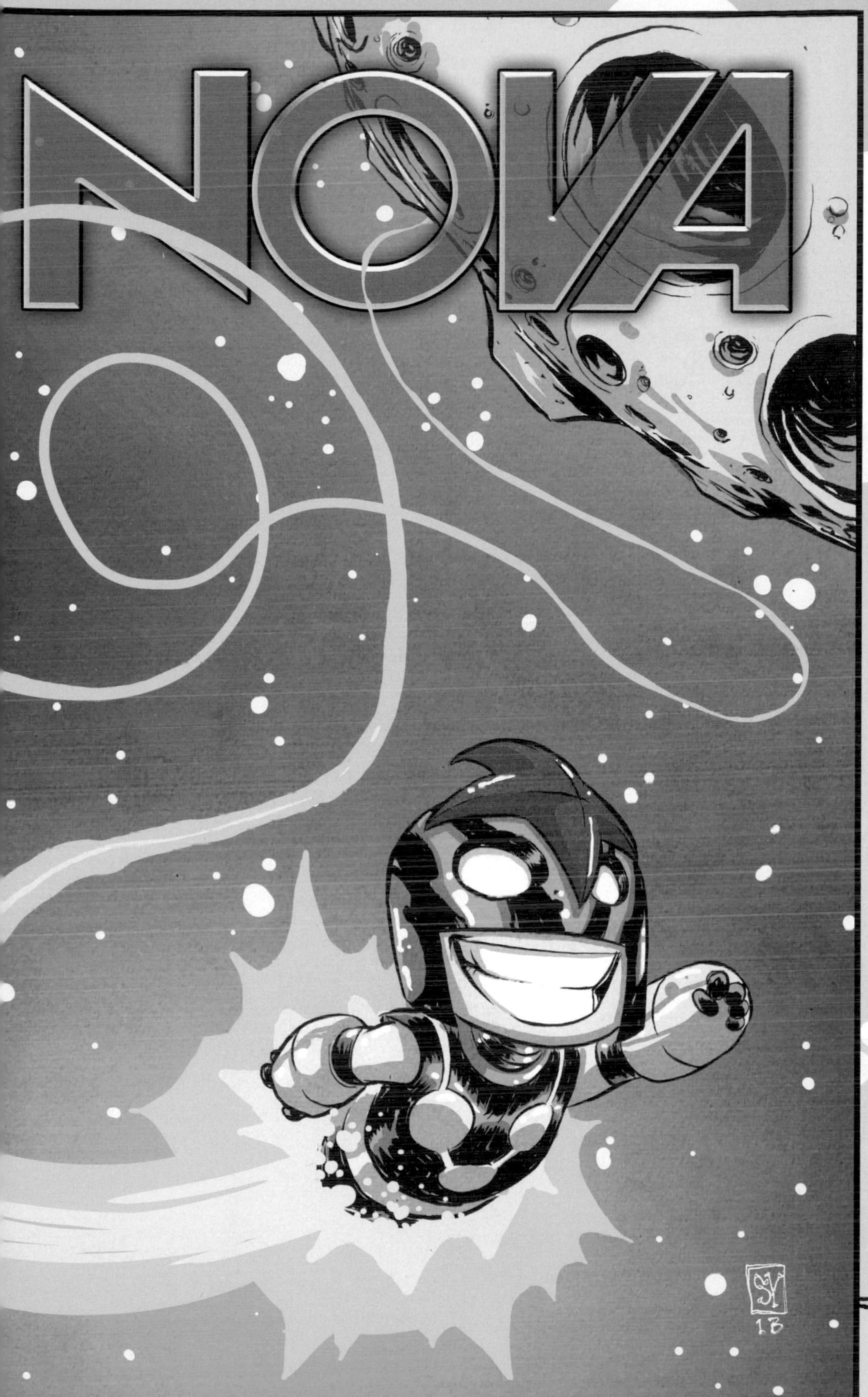
NOVA
SY 13

NOVA #1

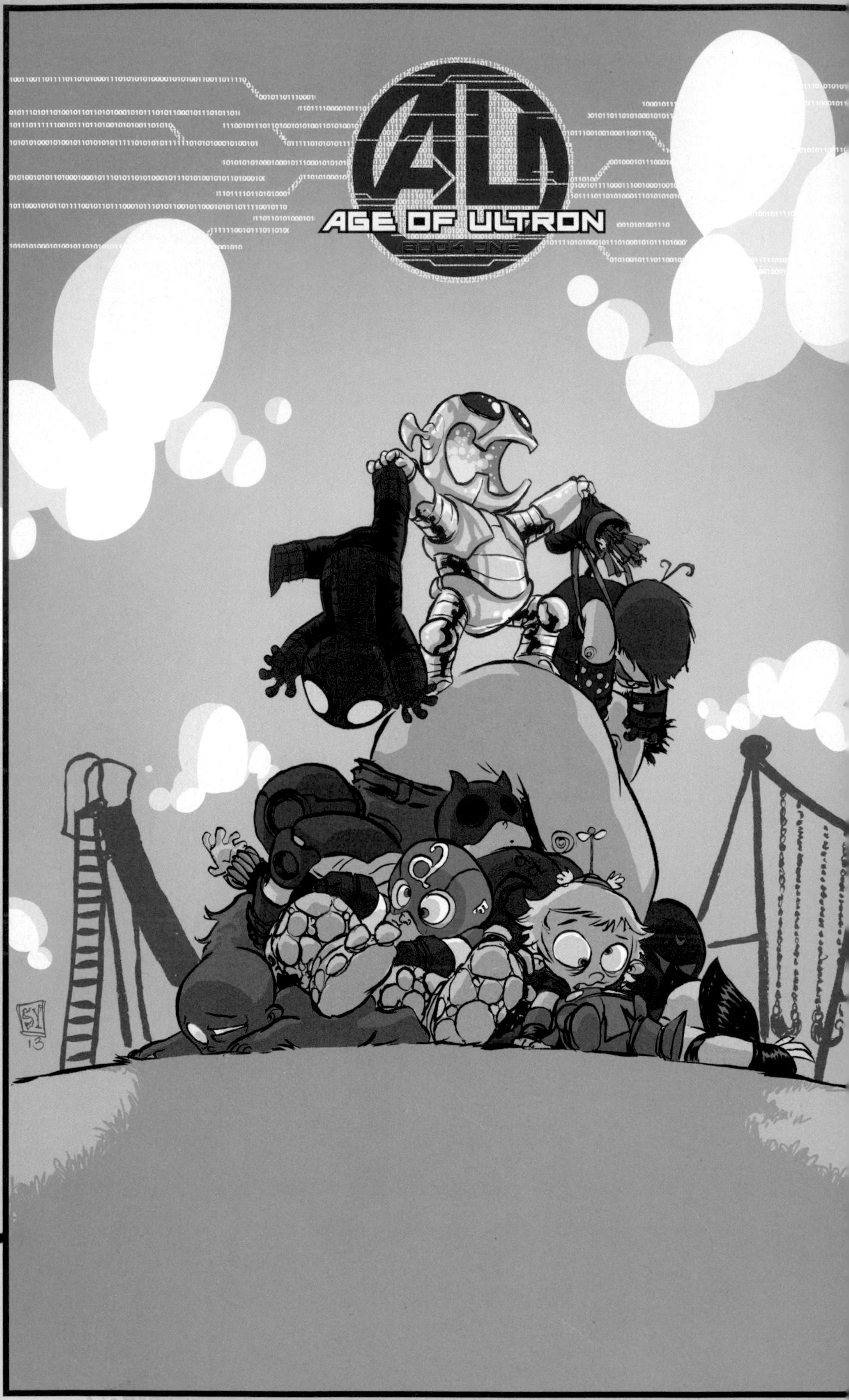
AGE OF ULTRON
BOOK ONE

AGE OF ULTRON #1

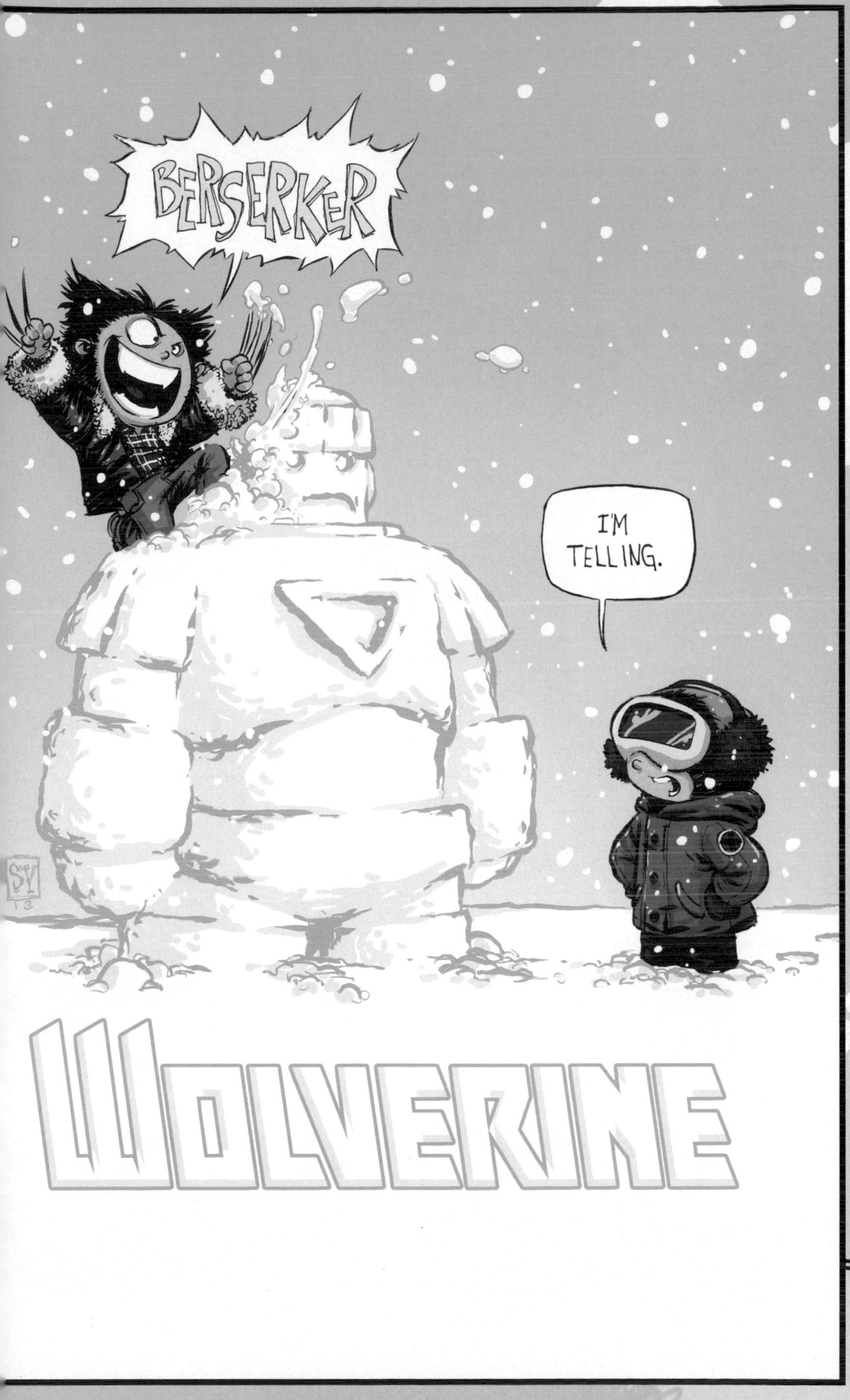
BERSERKER
I'M TELLING.
WOLVERINE

WOLVERINE #1

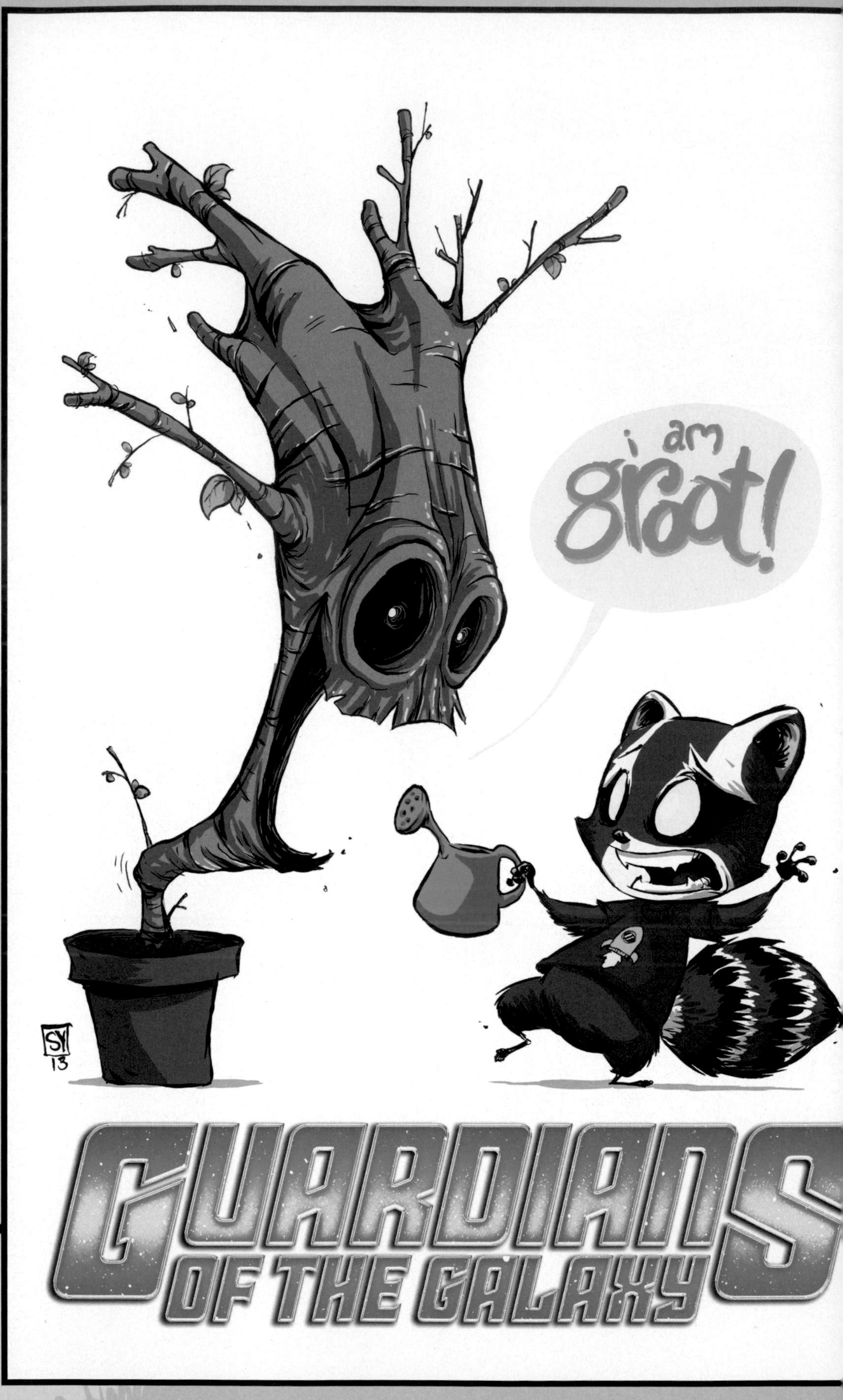
i am groot!
GUARDIANS OF THE GALAXY

GUARDIANS OF THE GALAXY #1

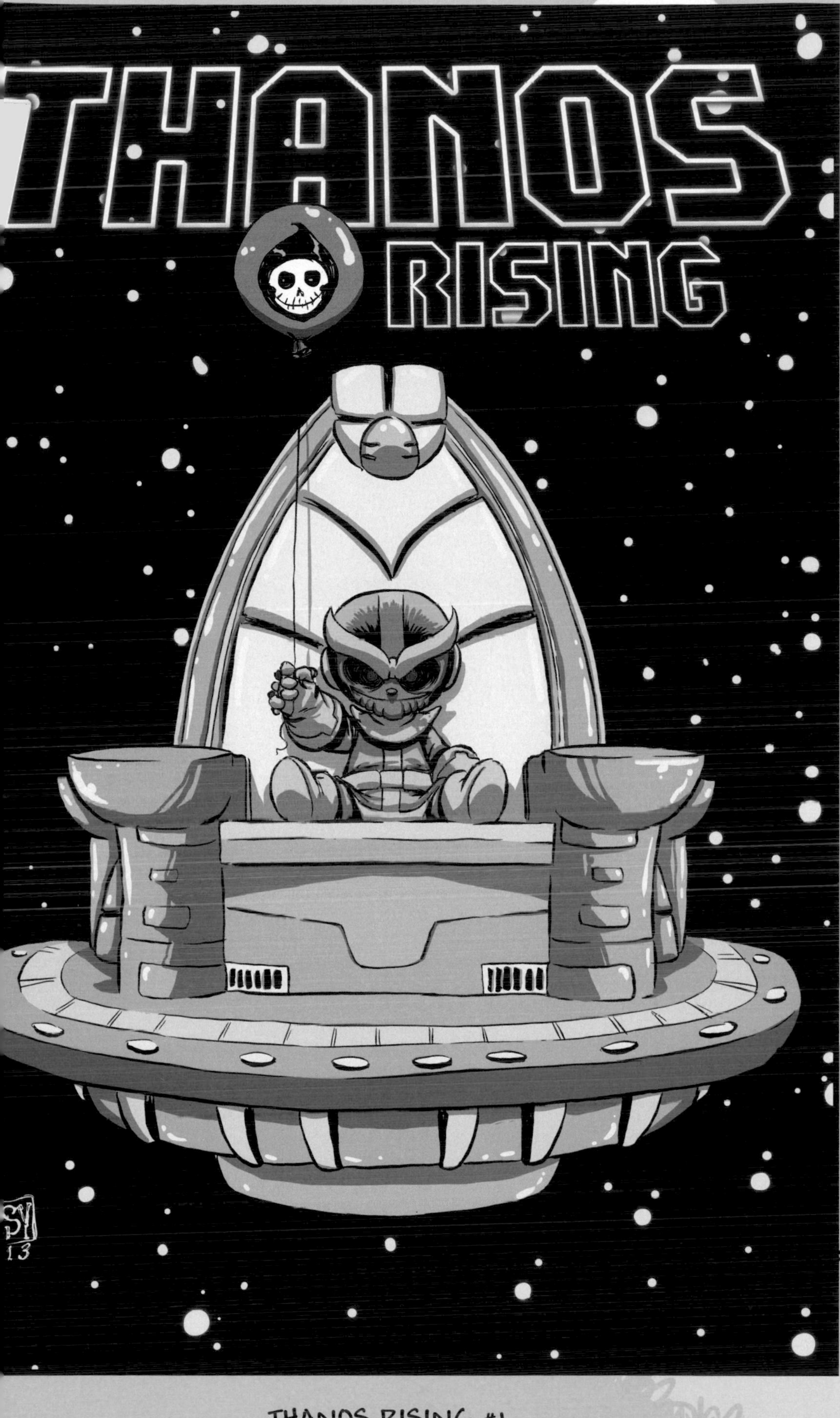
THANOS
RISING
SY 13

THANOS RISING #1

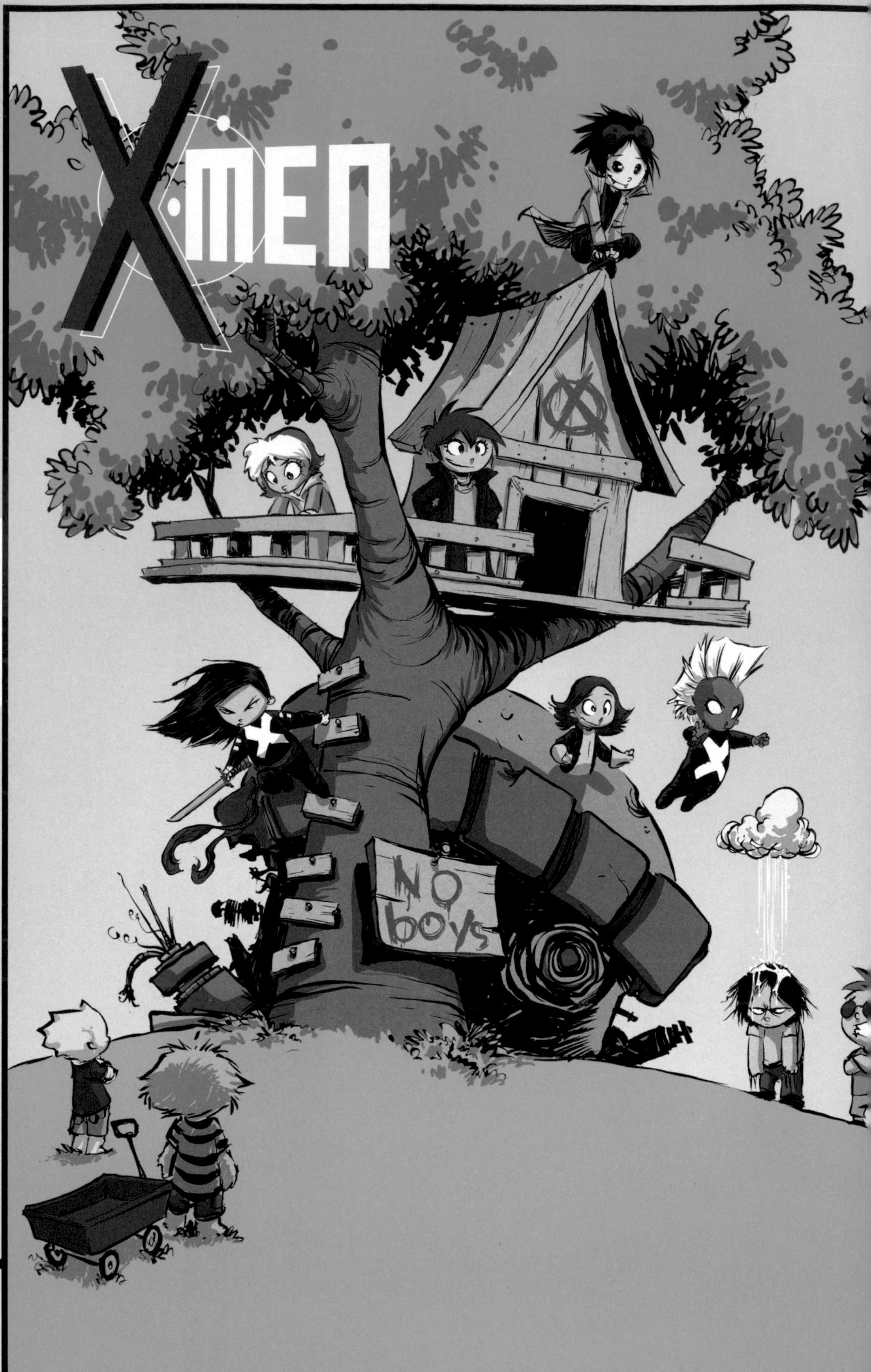
X-MEN
NO boys

X-MEN #1

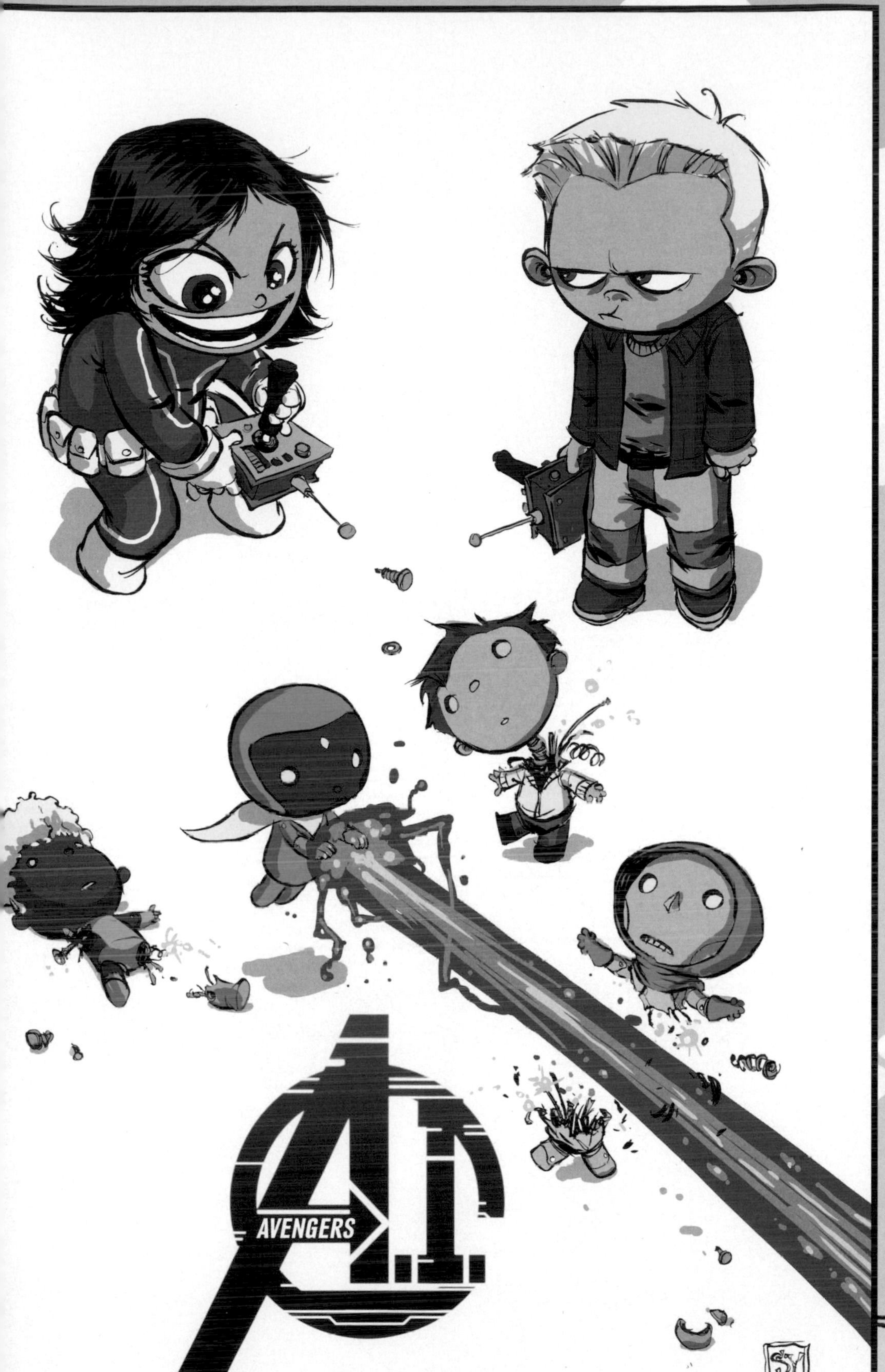
AVENGERS
A.I.
SY
13

AVENGERS A.I. #1

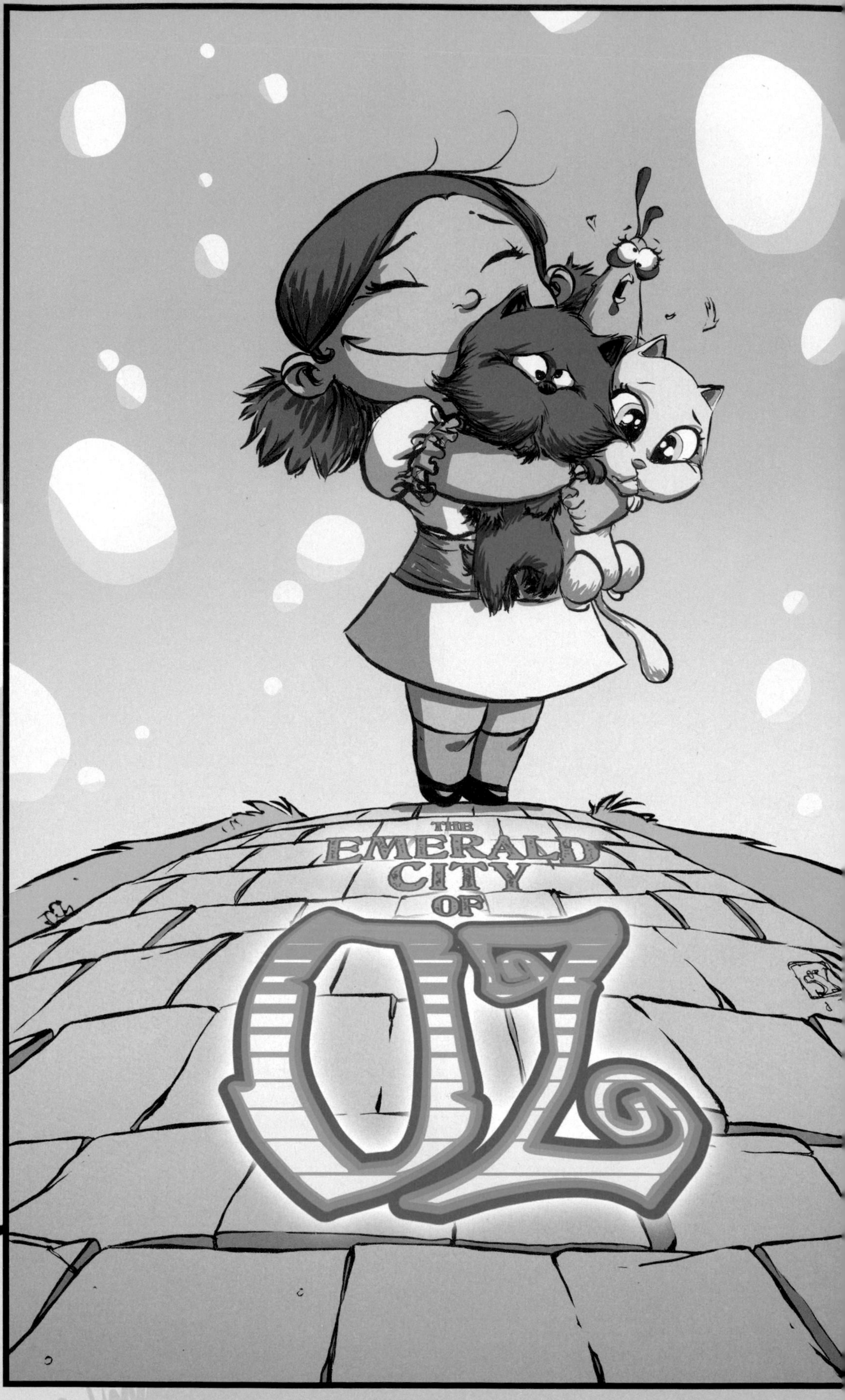
THE
EMERALD
CITY
OF
OZ
EMERALD CITY OF OZ #1

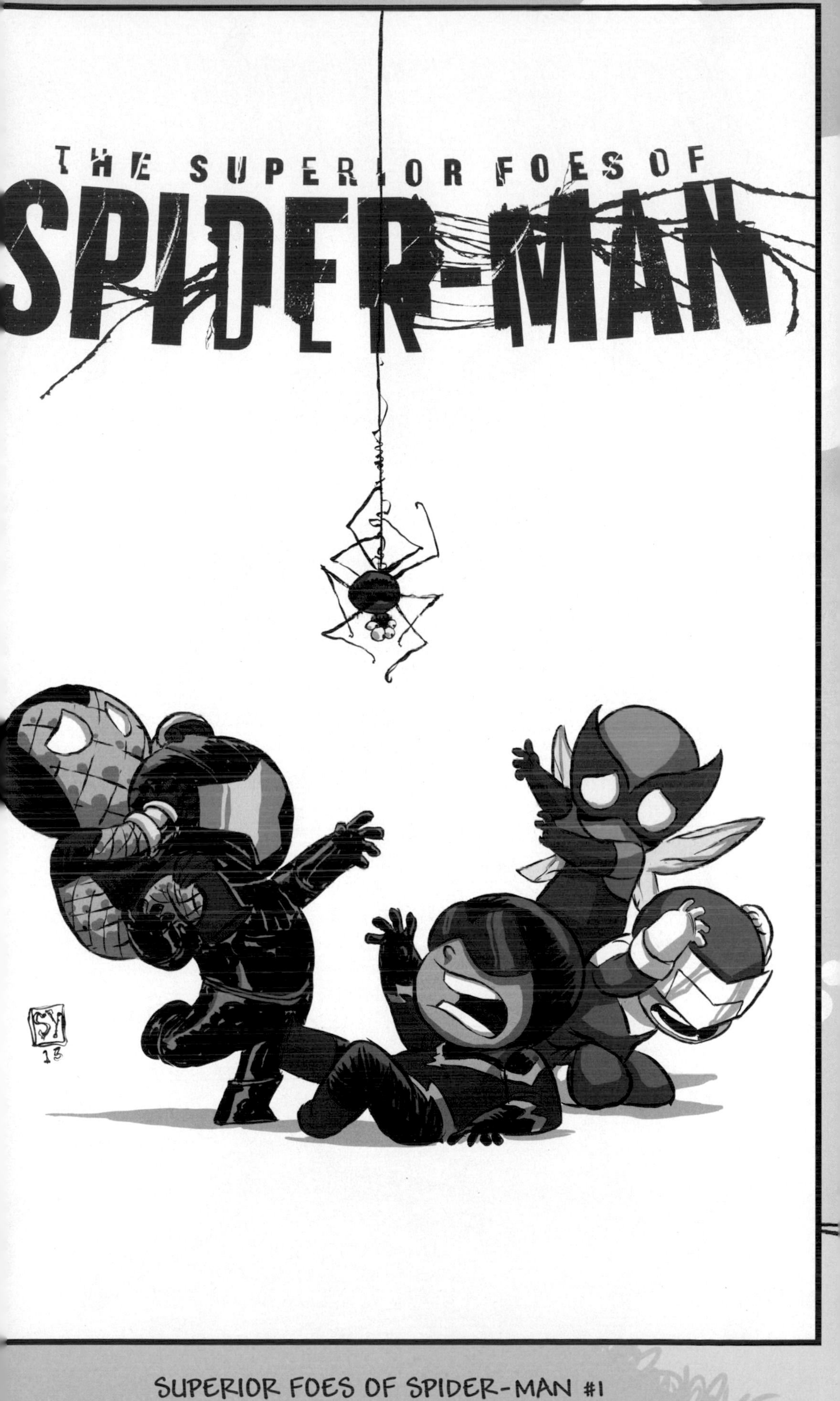
THE SUPERIOR FOES OF
SPIDER-MAN
SY
13

SUPERIOR FOES OF SPIDER-MAN #1

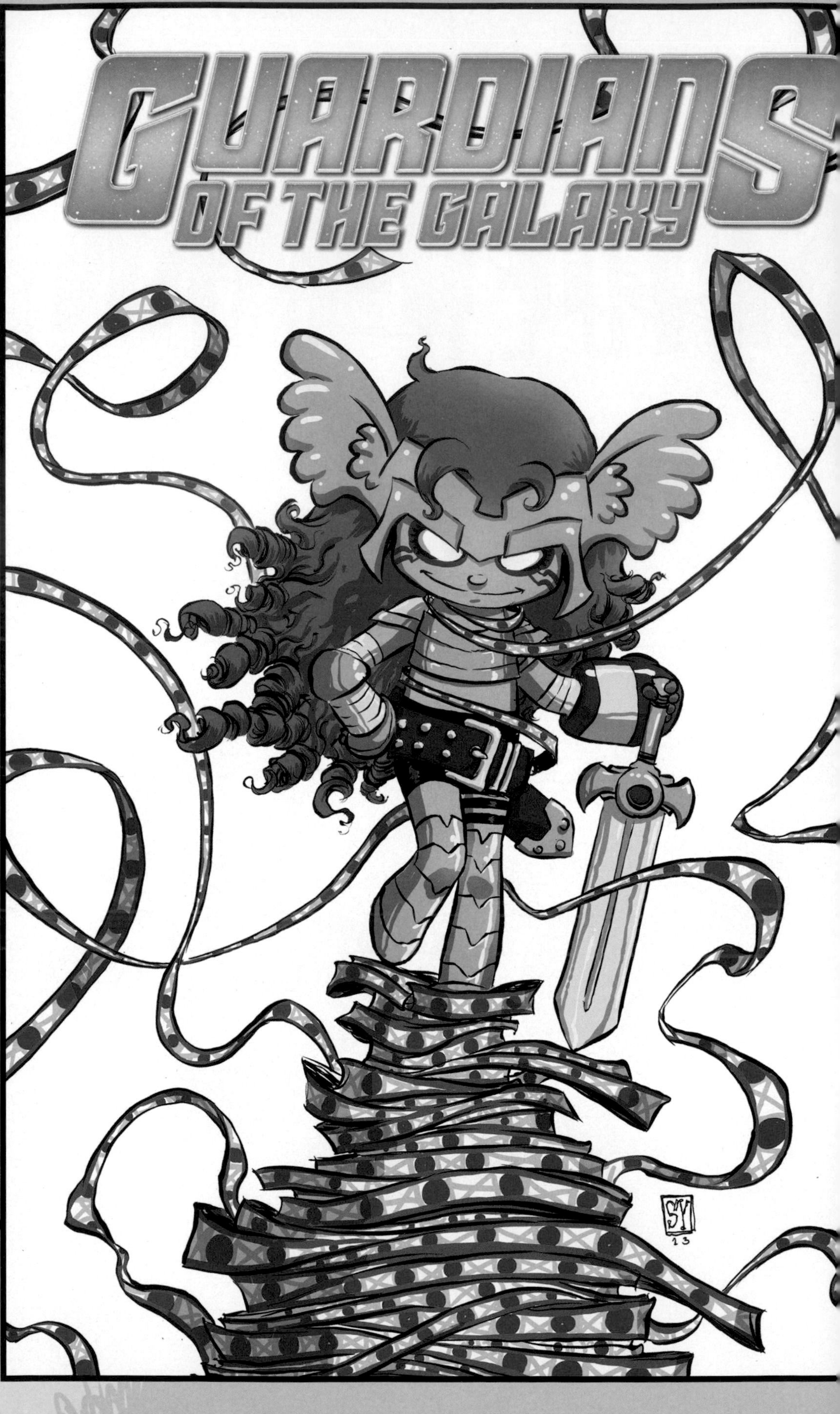
GUARDIANS OF THE GALAXY
SY
13

GUARDIANS OF THE GALAXY #5

A+X #1 COVER PROCESS

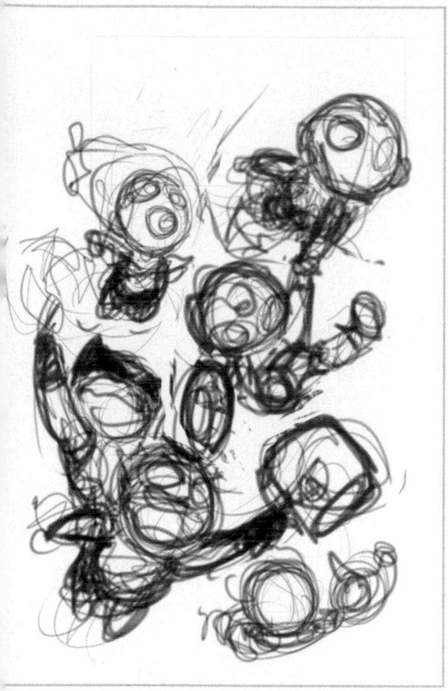

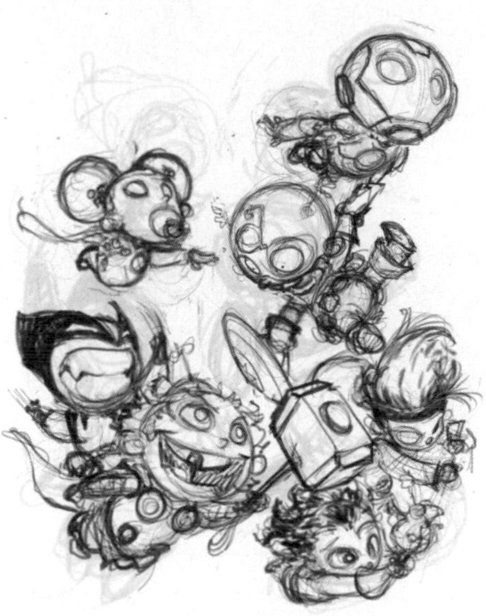

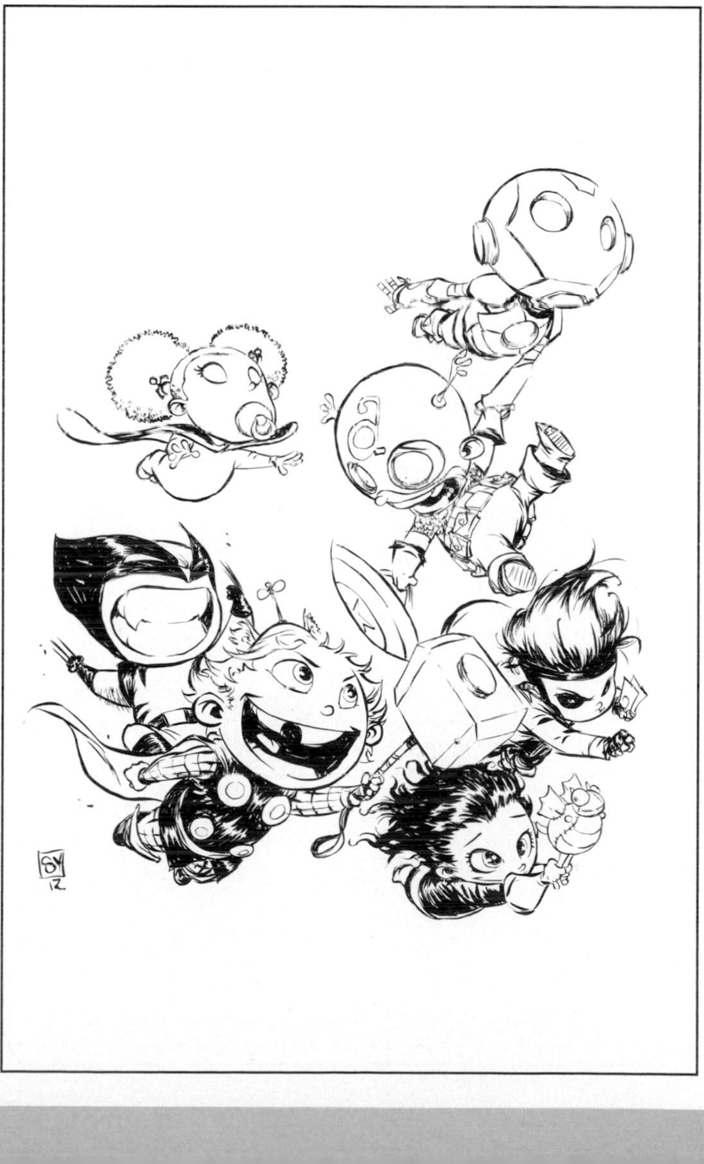

ALL-NEW X-MEN #1 COVER PROCESS

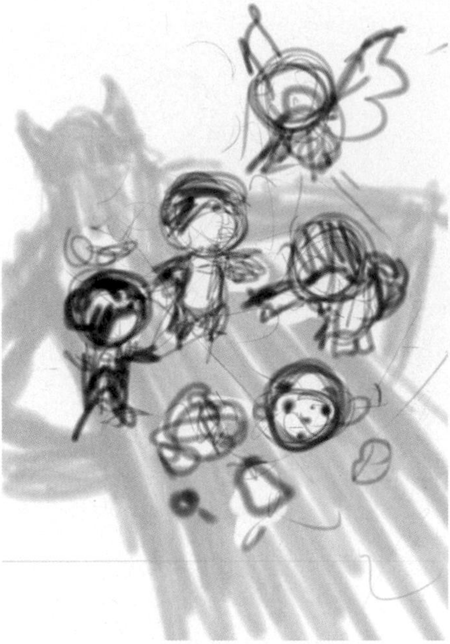

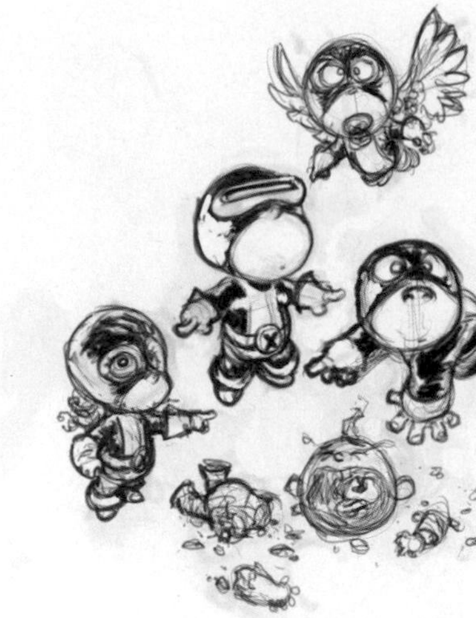

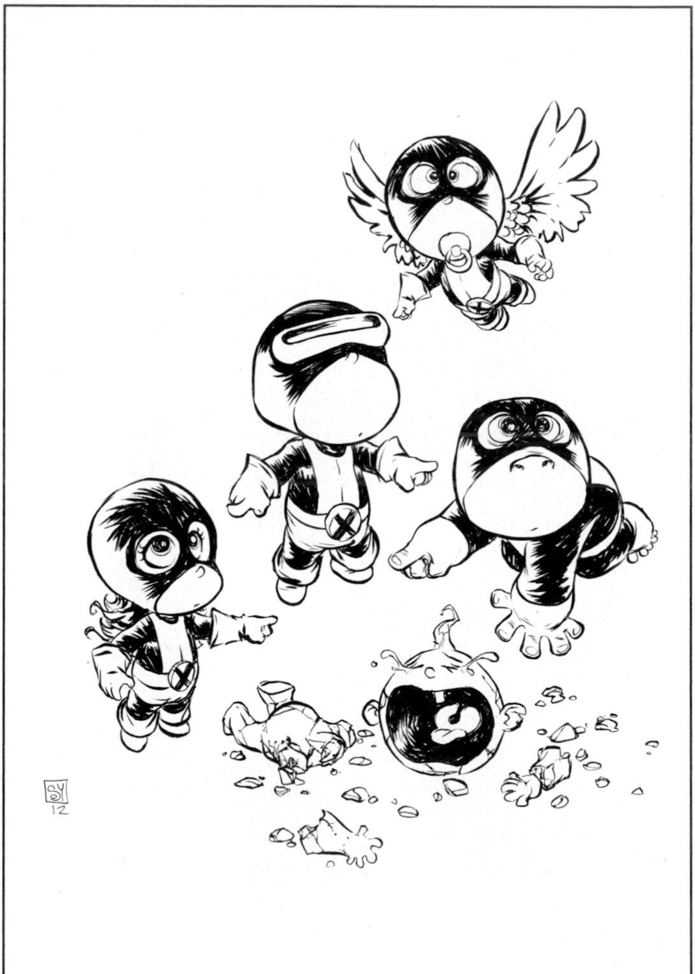

SUPERIOR SPIDER-MAN #1 COVER PROCESS

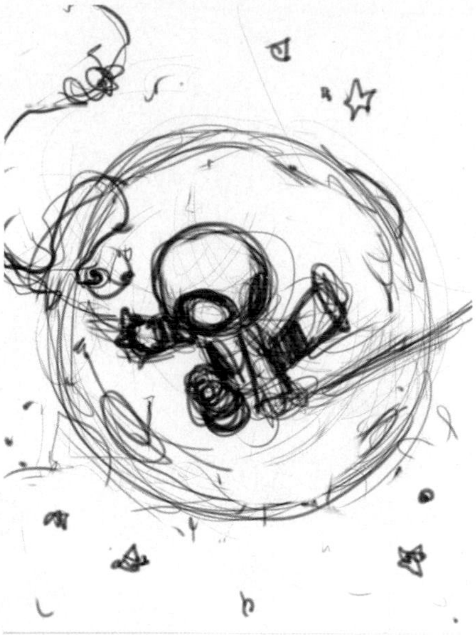

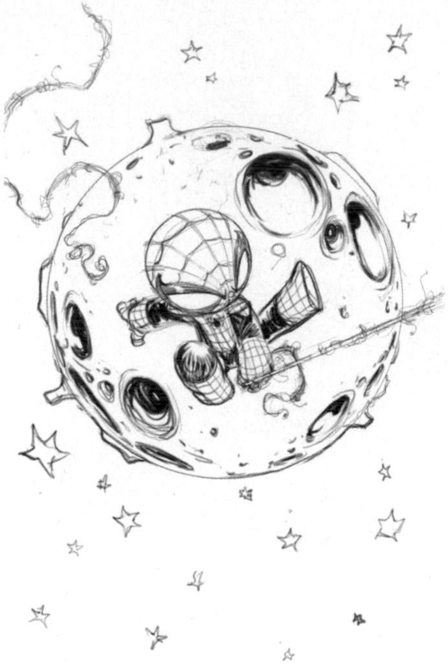

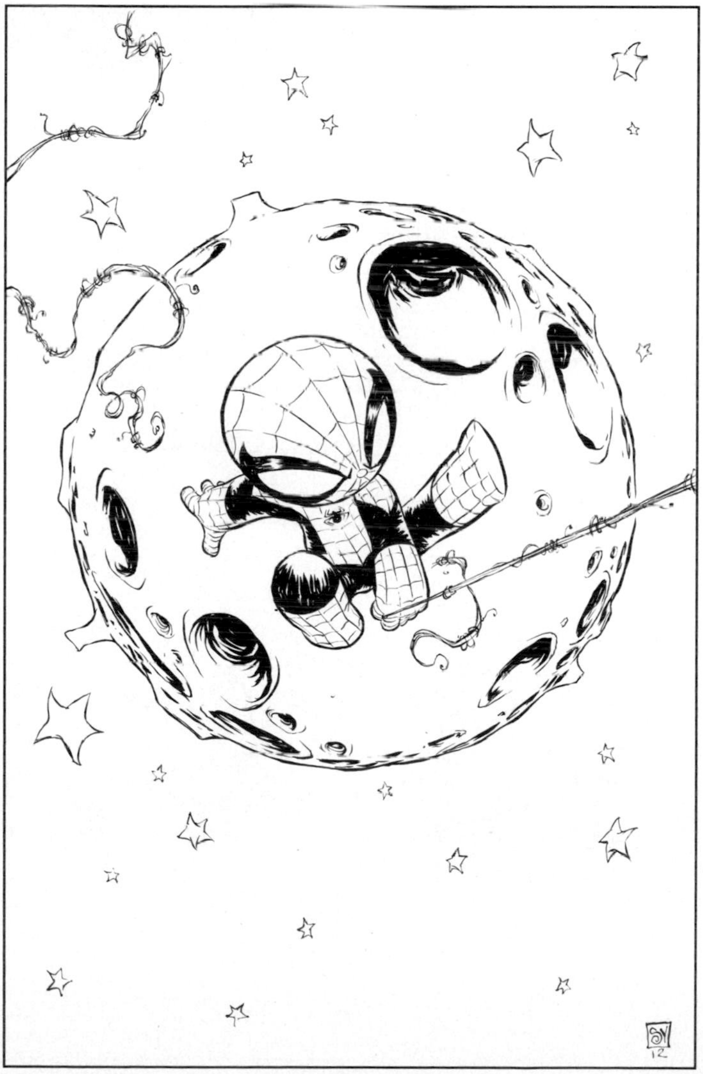

AVENGERS #1 COVER PROCESS

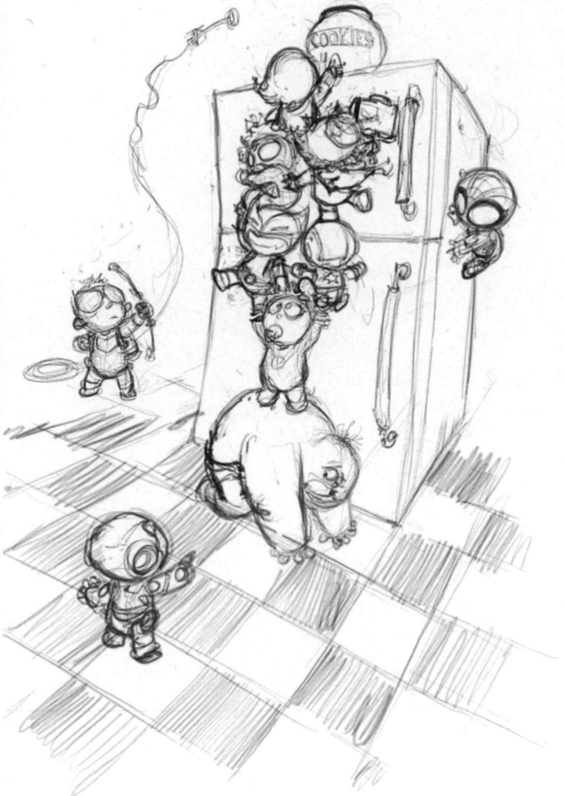
COOKIES

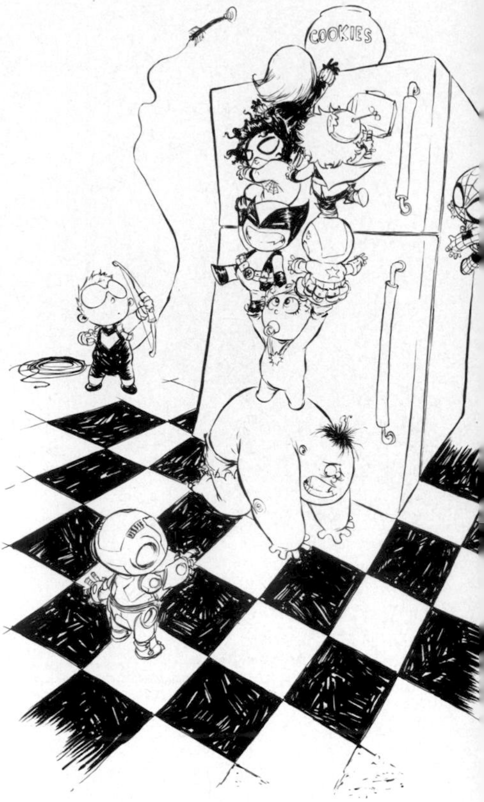
COOKIES

WOLVERINE #1 COVER PENCILS & INKS

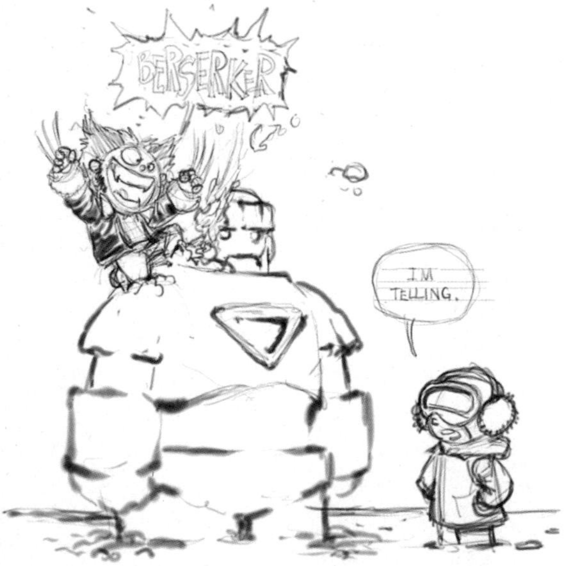
BERSERKER
IM TELLING.

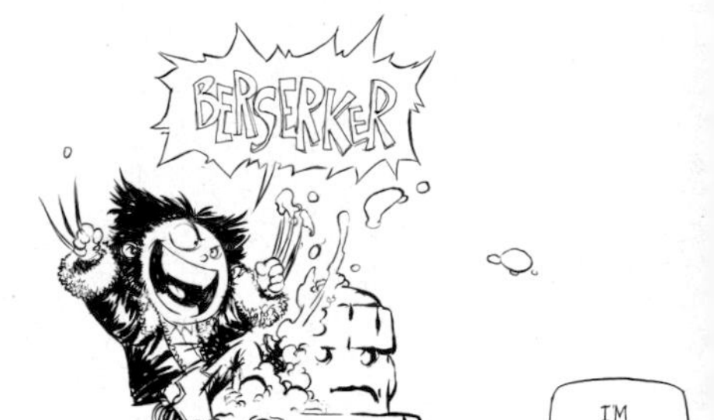
BERSERKER
IM TELLING.

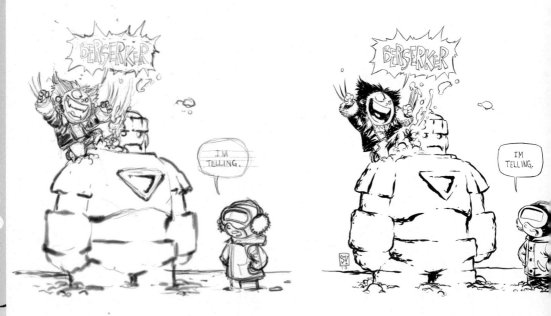

Collected Editions

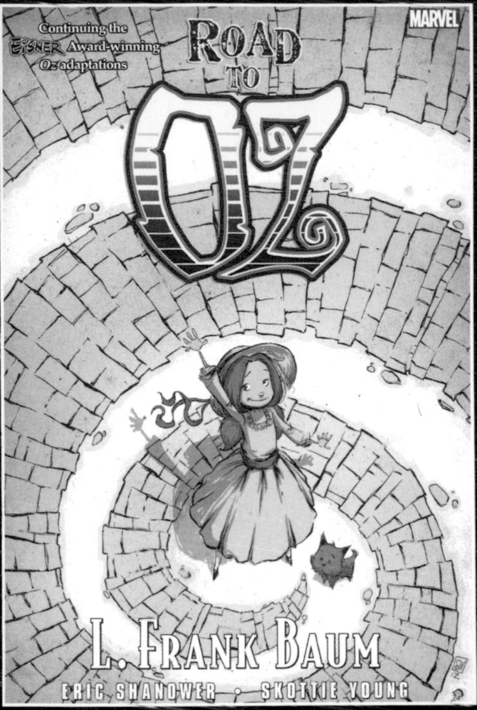

MARVEL
Continuing the Eisner Award-winning Oz adaptations
ROAD TO OZ
L. FRANK BAUM
ERIC SHANOWER • SKOTTIE YOUNG

Road to Oz

ISBN # 978-0-7851-9111-7

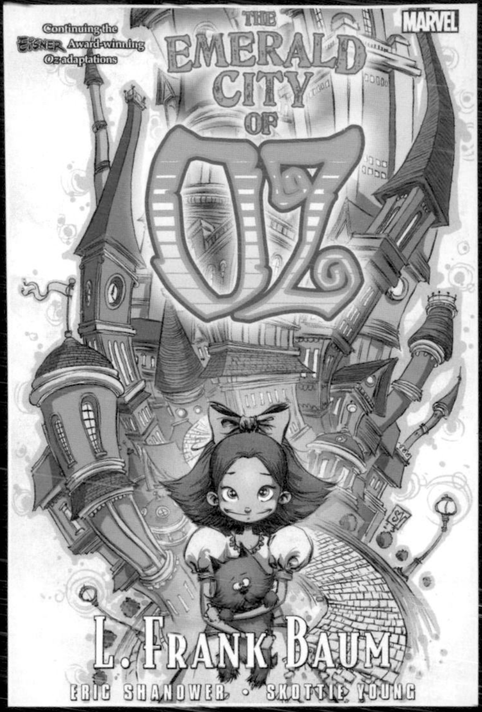

MARVEL
Continuing the Eisner Award-winning Oz adaptations
THE EMERALD CITY OF OZ
L. FRANK BAUM
ERIC SHANOWER • SKOTTIE YOUNG

Emerald City of Oz

ISBN # 978-0-7851-8389-1

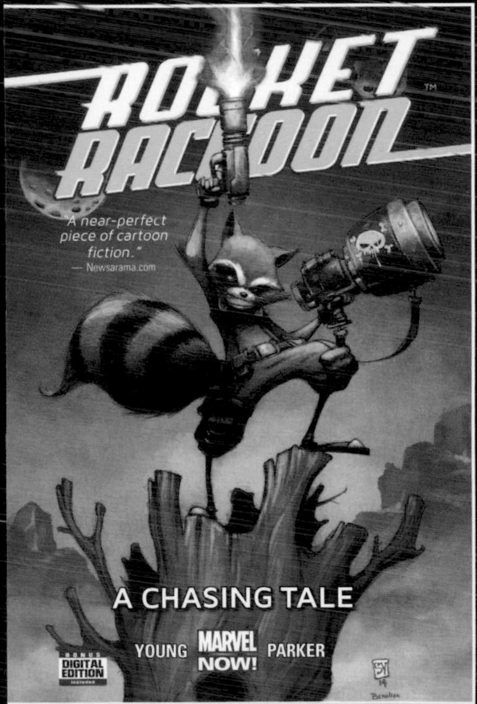

ROCKET RACCOON™
"A near-perfect piece of cartoon fiction." — Newsarama.com
A CHASING TALE
YOUNG
MARVEL NOW!
PARKER
BONUS DIGITAL EDITION included

Rocket Raccoon Vol. 1: A Chasing Tale Premiere Hardcover

ISBN # 978-0-7851-8388-4

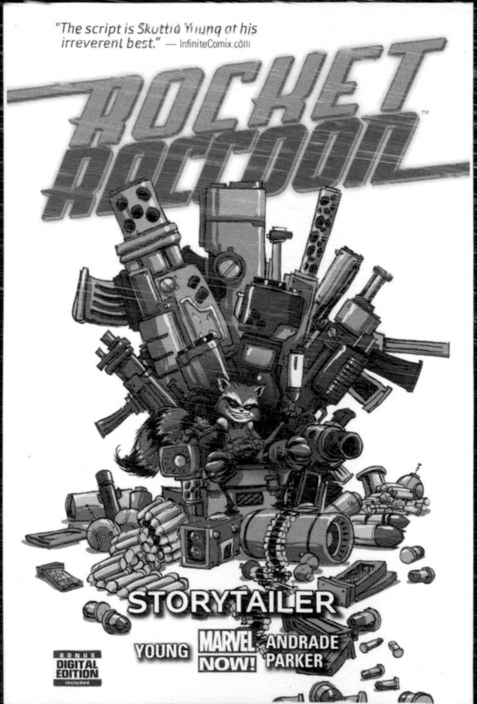

"The script is Skottie Young at his irreverent best." — InfiniteComix.com
ROCKET RACCOON™
STORYTAILER
YOUNG
MARVEL NOW!
ANDRADE PARKER
BONUS DIGITAL EDITION included

Rocket Raccoon Vol. 2: Storytailer Premiere Hardcover

ISBN # 978-0-7851-9390-6

THE **CHILDREN OF THE ATOM** MEET THE **MITEY 'VENGERS** IN THIS GIANT-SIZED COLLECTION OF PINT-SIZED SUPER HEROICS!

There's no pacifying Cyclops and Cap, who swap "ABC" for "AVX" as the playground becomes a battleground over cherished teddy bear! Then, when Mojo kidnaps Wolverine to star in his arena of death, it's Longshot, Dazzler and uncannily cute X-Babies to the rescue! And when these junior X-Men stand up to the Brotherhood of Mutant Bu in a murderous game show produced by Mojo and Arcade, will they be outdone by new kids on the block — or will one of their number dissolve back into the neoplasm from which they were formed?
Plus: a gallery of Skottie Young's ever-adorable Marvel NOW! variant covers!

Collecting *A-Babies vs. X-Babies* #1, *Wolverine* (1988) #102.5, *Pint-Sized X-Babies: Murderama*, *X-Babies Reborn* and *Uncanny X-Men* (1963) #461 — written by Skottie Young, Dan Slott, Ruben Diaz and Chris Claremont; and illustrated by Gurihiru, Mark Buckingham, J.J. Kirby, Tom Raney and Young.

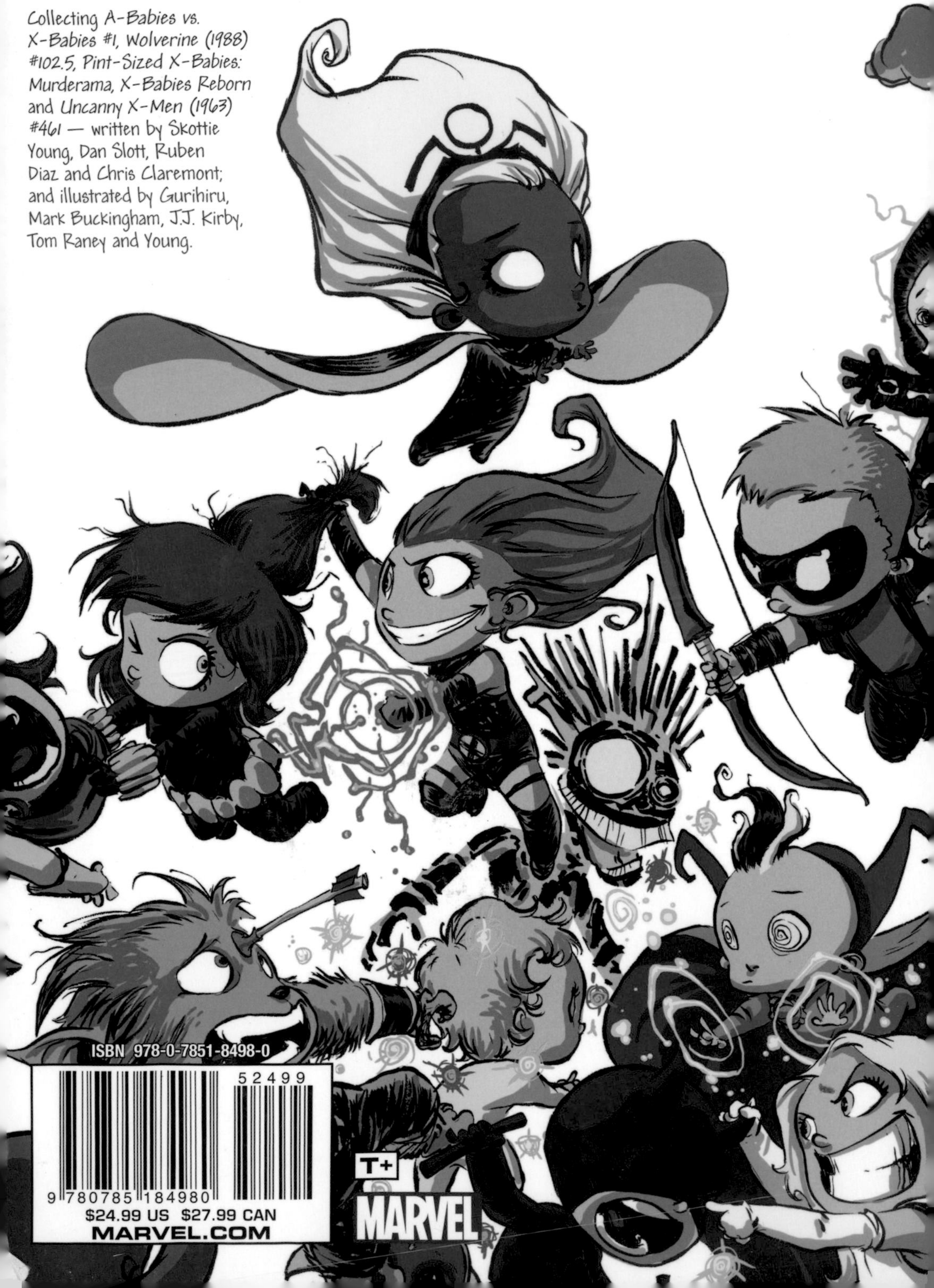

ISBN 978-0-7851-8498-0
52499
9 780785 184980
$24.99 US $27.99 CAN
MARVEL.COM

T+
MARVEL